LONDON LIVERY APPRENTICESHIP

Volume 39

TALLOW CHANDLERS' COMPANY 1633-1800

Abstracted and Indexed
by Cliff Webb

Published by the
Society of Genealogists Enterprises Ltd 2003

Published by
Society of Genealogists Enterprises Limited
14 Charterhouse Buildings
Goswell Road
London EC1M 7BA
Company Number 3899591
VAT Number 749 5602103

ISBN 1 903462 79 7

Society of Genealogists Enterprises Limited is a wholly owned subsidiary of Society of Genealogists, a registered charity, no. 233701

The Society gratefully acknowledge the financial contribution from the Tallow Pewterers Chandlers Company which enabled us to print this book.

British Library Cataloguing in Publication Data
A CIP Catalogue record for this book is available from the British Library

TALLOW CHANDLERS' COMPANY: APPRENTICES

TABLE OF CONTENTS

General Introduction to Series	v
Tallow Chandlers' Company Apprenticeships	vi
Index of Apprenticeships	1
Index of Masters	117
Index of Places	145
Index of Subjects	169

TALLOW CHANDLERS' APPRENTICESHIPS

GENERAL INTRODUCTION TO SERIES

The records of the Livery Companies of London are one of the greatest archival treasures of the world. Dating from the early medieval period to the present, they provide a mass of information for a variety of historians of innumerable subjects. For the family historian, they can provide an immense amount of genealogical and biographical details about their members.

A large proportion of these records are now deposited at the Guildhall Library, where they may be freely and conveniently consulted. Again, from the genealogical viewpoint, the two most important series of records tends to be those where people were apprenticed to a master, and those where individuals were admitted as freemen of the company in question.

In early records, persons who belonged to a given Livery Company would generally practise the trade to which that Company referred, but after about 1650, it became more and more common (until in some companies virtually universal) that members practiced another trade altogether. Searchers, therefore, even if they know the occupation of the subject of interest, may not be able to find the right Livery Company to search at all easily. By no means all those apprenticed went on to become freemen. Some died, some left their masters before their term expired and others while completing their apprenticeship simply never took up the freedom to which they were entitled. On the other hand, not all becoming free had been apprenticed. Sons of freemen (born when the father was free) were entitled to freedom 'by patrimony' and in most companies you could simply buy the freedom 'by redemption'. Freedom by redemption, indeed, became commoner and commoner during the latter part of the eighteenth century, and Livery Company records tend to become less interesting. For this reason it was decided that the priority should be to calendar apprenticeship records rather than freedom admissions.

This series is designed to provide family and other historians with the information provided by the records of apprenticeship of a number of the Livery Companies. Series have been selected from those companies whose apprenticeship records generally give good genealogical detail, principally, the name, parish and occupation of the apprentice's father. The records have been sorted into alphabetical order of apprentice, and supplemental indexes provided of masters, places and occupations. Generally, the work of abstraction will end about 1800, though generally abstraction will be to the end of a manuscript volume.

There are two alternate general sources for limited periods for London apprenticeships. Firstly, the original papers supporting a granting a freedom from apprenticeship survive in the Corporation of London Record Office from 1681. Though often very difficult to use - they were strung together through a hole in the middle - they are invaluable for companies whose records do not survive, or for which only undetailed records are extant. From 1710 until 1814, there was a duty on apprenticeship, and the records of this are preserved in the Public Record Office. Until about 1750, the father's name, parish and occupation are given, and there are a series of indexes for the period 1710 to 1774 at the Society of Genealogists. There were, however, a large number of exemptions under this act, and naturally as many people as possible sought this exemption, and so many apprenticeships which might be expected to be found in this index are not there. It is, again, however, an invaluable substitute, if partial, for lost records and as a general index and lucky dip.

The abstracts are generally limited to the name of the apprentice, his father's name, parish and occupation, the name of the master and the date of the indenture. If the father was stated to be dead, his name is marked with a dagger (†). If the record notes that he was subsequently turned over to another master, or, as is sometimes recorded, became free, died etc. this has also been noted. Details such as the street in which the master lived, the term of apprenticeship (usually seven years, but occasionally shorter or longer) and the premium paid have been omitted.

TALLOW CHANDLERS' APPRENTICESHIPS

Introduction to the Tallow Chandlers' Company Apprenticeships

The older records of this Company are deposited at the Guildhall Library.

The first register of apprentices (Guildhall Library Ms 6158/1 covering 1633-45) is only in roughly chronological order. Presumably the entries were made as they were registered at court, and the date of apprenticeship may therefore be some time before. Although there are only substantial numbers of entries from 1632, there is one isolated entry from 1629, presumably because of this factor. After the mid-1640s there are only occasional apprenticeship out of their correct chronological sequence.

The series continues with GL Ms 6158/2 containing apprenticeships 1662-85 which is damaged by what appears to be acidic damage to the paper in the middle of each page. It has invariably been possible to make good the name of the apprentice and master from the index at the back of the volume (which gives both these names) or from the Wardens' Accounts 1653-1701 (GL Ms 6152/3) which have been used (silently). The accounts also only give the bare names of the parties and the account year (as do earlier accounts from 1551). There are also two rough apprenticeship binding books (GL Ms 6159/1-2 covering 1686-1720 and 1720-82). These do contain full details and have been silently used to correct and add information. From late 1778 to 1782, indeed, GL Ms 6159/2 has been the primary source of information. However this lack of detail in some alternate sources means some information has been irretrievably lost. GL Ms 6161A contains presentation of apprentices 1674-85, bare names only, but exact dates which helped in a few cases.

After 1782, there is a full list of apprentices and masters in the Orphans' Duty book 1694-1867 (GL Ms 6160) in which, as usual, no details are given. The Court Minute Books (GL Ms 6153/12: 1747-79; GL Ms 6153/13: 1774-93 and GL Ms 6153/14: 1793-1821 give turnovers and also usually the name of the father of those apprentices admitted to the freedom. However, there is also in this period a rough Court Minute book (GL Ms 6154/4: 1782-98) which gives full details in almost all cases. A combination of these sources means that almost all details are available except for the period November 1798 to December 1799.

There are 6,104 apprenticeships recorded in this index. I am grateful for the permission of the Tallow Chandlers' Company and of the Corporation of London, Guildhall Library for their permission to publish this work.

Cliff Webb. October 2003

TALLOW CHANDLERS' APPRENTICES

Abbes John s Henry, Enfield, Mdx [? *in Ms* 'Hrt'], husbandman† to Thomas Pratt 28 Nov 1638
Abbott John s Timothy, Exeter, Dev, saddler to Elizabeth widow of Jonas Watts 4 Nov 1723
Abbott Thomas s John, North Kilworth, Lei, yeoman to Nicholas Beckett 13 Dec 1655
Abbott William s Henry, Enfield, Mdx, yeoman to John Noble 25 Feb 1633/4
Abdy Edward s Thomas, Stepney, Mdx, mariner† to Thomas Hill 30 Mar 1694
Ablett Mathew s Thomas, Doncaster, Yks, yeoman to Francis Kippinge 29 Sep 1632
Abnett John s Thomas, Audley, Sts, gentleman to John Acton 21 May 1638
Abrahams Thomas s Robert, Taunton, Som, woolcomber† to Thomas Ancketill 25 Sep 1689
Abram Thomas s Thomas, Bradley, ?† to Elizabeth widow of William Bateman 20 Jul 1668
Ace Chard s David, Winslow, Bkm, baker† to Richard Collier 7 Oct 1706
Ace otherwise East Charles s Charles to his father 3 Mar 1734/5
Achton Miles s William, Fenny Stratford, Hun, yeoman to Richard Makeham 25 Jul 1667
Acton William s Edward, 'Aldenham', Sal, baronet to Thomas Cleaver 15 Nov 1649
Adam Nathaniel s Nathaniel, citizen and glass-seller to John Greening 7 May 1694
Adams Ebenezer s Richard, citizen and merchant tailor to Edward Hitchcock 3 Oct 1700
Adams Nathaniel s William, Holborn, Mdx, tallow chandler† to William Mellor 3 Jul 1721
<turned over to Ann widow of Mark Mozant, citizen and joiner>
Adams Robert s Thomas, St Giles in the Fields, Mdx, grocer† to Elizabeth widow of John Hastings 25 Jul 1698
Adams Thomas s John to his father 16 May 1683
Adams Thomas s William, St Giles in the Fields, Mdx, waterman to Thomas West 30 Oct 1691
Adams Thomas s William, St Giles in the Fields, Mdx, waterman† to Thomas Dutton 21 Apr 1692
Adams Thomas s Richard, Cricklade, Wil, butcher to Jeremiah Ridge 6 May 1747 <17 Dec 1750 master† turned over with consent of Thomas Ridge, administrator to Robert Day>
Adams William s Thomas, Dunton, Bkm, yeoman† to John Adams 23 Jan 1664/5
Adams William s John, citizen and tallow chandler† to William Haydon 1 Oct 1698
Adcock John s William, Syston, Lei, yeoman to Francis Style 1 Jun 1724 <6 Mar 1726/7 turned over to Richard Washburn, citizen and bowyer>
Adcock William s John, Greenwich, Ken, yeoman to Nicholas Shepherd 25 Mar 1633
Adcocke Robert s Robert, Camberwell, Sry, farrier† to Thomas Hill 19 Sep 1688
Addames Richard s Henry, Cricklade, Wil, butcher to Jeremy Ridge 4 Mar 1739/40
Addams George s William, citizen and clothworker to John Davinport 1 Jul 1717
Addams John s Thomas, Dunton, Bkm, yeoman† to Samuel King 18 Dec 1657
Addams Joseph s Thomas, Ryton, Sal, yeoman to Edmund Barcock 29 Jun 1643
Addams Thomas s John, 'Crist', Gls† to George Pearce 25 Aug 1640
Addams William s William, citizen and brewer† to John Hill 29 Jul 1673
Addams William s William to his father 27 Apr 1654
Addenbrooke Josiah s John, Wednesbury, Sts, tanner to John Hastings 8 Feb 1693/4
Adderson George s Gabriel, Old Street, Mdx, labourer to Richard Worrell 8 Feb 1689/90
Addis Timothy s John, St John Horsleydown, Sry, mariner to Joshua Knight 5 Jan 1790
Adee John s John, citizen and fishmonger† to Richard Hodgkin 15 Oct 1689
Adison Thomas s Thomas, 'Goodland', Yks, yeoman to Robert Bruscop 25 Mar 1644
Ady Charles s John, Gracechurch Street, Lnd, haberdasher to William Littell 2 Feb 1796
Adye Francis s Francis, 'Shippin', Nth, yeoman to Michael Warren 3 Dec 1664
Agate Thomas s Thomas, Capel, Sry, butcher to Richard Holbert 3 Dec 1776
Ailwin William s James, Duncton, Ssx, yeoman to William Stephens 12 Mar 1646/7
Ainge Samuel s John, Lechlade, Gls, yeoman to Richard Sessions 4 Dec 1678
Ainsworth William s Edward, Dalbury, Dby, clerk† to Edward Walker 3 Oct 1698
Albon Henry s Henry, Blackman Street, Sry, victualler to Richard Rickwood 6 Jan 1795
Alcock Nathaniel s Nathaniel, Brentwood, Ess, victualler† to Edmund Milton 27 Mar 1671
Alcock Nathaniel s Mathew, St Giles Cripplegate, Lnd, brewer to Mathew Bullock 3 Aug 1681
Alcock Samuel s Thomas, Heaton Norris, Lan, draper to John Hulme 2 Oct 1710
Alcock Thomas s Thomas, Broad Hinton, Wil, clerk to John Saywell 5 Jan 1646/7
Alden Rudolph s Henry, Rickmansworth, Hrt, yeoman to Catherine widow of Richard Wilkinson 10 Feb 1663/4
Alden William s Henry, Rickmansworth, Hrt, yeoman to Richard Wilkinson 7 Dec 1658
Alderson Thomas s John, Chingford [? *in Ms* 'Chensford'], Ess, yeoman to John Webster 12 May 1634

TALLOW CHANDLERS' APPRENTICES

Alderson William s Simon, St Andrew Wardrobe, Lnd, labourer† to Thomas Gunston 12 Sep 1671
Aldrich John s William, Rumburgh, Sfk, gentleman to William Prince 31 Jan 1693/4
Aleworth Jonathan s Geoffrey, Lnd, gentleman† to Simon Dorrant 26 Apr 1689
Alexander Richard s Richard, Avebury [? *in Ms* 'Abery'], Wil, wheelwright† to William Alexander 3 May 1738
Alexander Samuel s Samuel, Worcester, Wor, coachmaker† to William Jefferys 10 Jul 1764 <3 May 1766 master† turned over with consent of Sarah Jeffers his widow and exec. to James Mitchell>
Alexander William s Richard, St Peter, Wil, maltster† to Isabel widow of Joseph Archer 1 Dec 1707 <4 Feb 1711/12 turned over to Daniel Hudson, citizen and founder>
Alkinton Robert s Robert, citizen and haberdasher to Francis Pittman 8 Nov 1650
Allalee James s Edward, Watford, Hrt, leatherdresser to John Davinport 3 May 1725
Allam William s William, St John Street, Mdx, innholder to Anthony Mosely 4 Oct 1654
Allavine Abraham s Paul, Gun Street, Liberty of the Tower, Lnd to Jacob Couppe 5 Apr 1725
Allcraft Edward s John, Sheering, Ess, yeoman to Andrew Thorowgood 26 Oct 1674
Allen Francis s Walter, Weston on the Green, Oxf, gentleman to William Mayne 7 Aug 1693
Allen James s Thomas to his father 6 May 1662
Allen John s John, 'Corby', Ham, yeoman† to Thomas Jarvis 4 Apr 1681
Allen John s Moses, Lambeth, Sry, husbandman to James Tetly 6 Sep 1708
Allen John s Thomas, Basted [Platt], Ken, tallow chandler† to Richard Ireland 10 Feb 1731/2
Allen John s Richard, citizen and clockmaker to Robert Wilkins 7 Mar 1738/9 <2 May 1739 turned over to Richard Allen, citizen and clockmaker>
Allen John s William, Husbands Street, Lnd, coal merchant to James Neale 5 Apr 1785
Allen Richard s William, Swinderby, Lin, yeoman† to Richard Worgan 15 Jul 1680
Allen Richard s Philip, citizen and haberdasher to John Smith 2 Jun 1687
Allen Robert s Robert, 'Tancombe', Oxf, yeoman to John Burbrough 29 Jan 1710/11
Allen Thomas s Thomas to his father 1 Jan 1655/6
Allen Thomas s Thomas, St Swithin Worcester, Wor, butcher to Richard Worgan 25 Sep 1672
Allen Thomas s Thomas, 'Scottsbitch', Lei, weaver to Edward Coles 26 Oct 1677
Allen Thomas s Robert, St Pancras, Mdx, yeoman† to Thomas Harris 20 Sep 1688
Allen Thomas s William to his father 26 Apr 1692
Allen Thomas s Thomas, Wellingborough, Nth, mason to William Allen 1 Dec 1758
Allen William s William, Stagsden, Bdf, victualler to John Sole 16 Apr 1657
Allen William s Thomas, Wellingborough, Nth, mason to Richard Darker 1 Dec 1729 <5 Dec 1735 turned over to Robert Hancock>
Allen William s Thomas, Wellingborough, Nth, mason to William Allen 12 Jan 1753
Allerton John s Joseph, St James Westminster, Mdx, cook to William Crowther 2 Nov 1719 <2 Oct 1721 turned over to Thomas Sutton>
Allett Henry s Henry, citizen and cordwainer† to Bartholomew Peele ? Mar 1668/9
Allett William s Henry, Enfield, Mdx, yeoman to John Noble 25 Feb 1633/4
Allett William s Thomas, Shuckburgh, War, gentleman to William Simonds 23 Aug 1634
Alley Francis s Thomas, Westminster, Mdx, gentleman† to Robert Udall 27 Jul 1670
Allin William s Thomas to his father ? May 1664
Allom Geal s Edward, Wokingham, Brk, baker to John Topott 1 Mar 1708/9 <6 Oct 1712 turned over to William Rood, citizen and draper>
Allsopp Charles s Edward, citizen and fishmonger† to John Bowden 16 Apr 1691
Allum William to William Limbery 3 Oct 1799 <4 Sep 1800 turned over to Marianne widow of William Limbery>
Allwinkle Robert s Robert to his father 4 Feb 1705/6
Alsop John s Rowland, Alfreton, Dby, butcher to William Thredder 18 Jan 1680/1
Alsop John s German, St Martin in the Fields, Mdx, butcher to William Collier 27 Mar 1682
Alston Thomas s John, Pavenham, Bdf, gentleman to John Caddy 3 Feb 1700/1
Ambrose Charles s Francis, Abingdon, Brk, maltster to William Gaunt 30 Jan 1682/3
Ambrose Ebenezer s Francis, Abingdon, Brk, yeoman to John Smith 20 Jul 1687
Amey Henry s Robert, Lnd, waterman to Robert Driver 18 Aug 1699
Ammon Daniel s Edward, St Alban Wood Street, Lnd, goldsmith to Edward Hooker 12 Jun 1649
Anchors James s Randolph, Clotton, Chs, yeoman† to Daniel Scott 20 Sep 1712
Ancketill Thomas s Francis, Taunton, Som, esquire to Peter Pickering 23 Nov 1677

TALLOW CHANDLERS' APPRENTICES

Anckle John s John to his father 13 Jul 1638
Anckle Thomas s Thomas to his father 13 Jul 1638
Ancktell John s Francis, Taunton Dale, Som, gentleman to Thomas Ancktell 2 Jun 1685
Anderson Charles s Charles, Guildford, Sry, bargeman to Thomas West 24 Sep 1717
Anderson Francis s Henry, Newcastle on Tyne, Nbl, merchant to Andrew Walker 31 Mar 1633
Anderson James George s Joseph, Bermondsey, Sry, shipwright to Thomas Hoskins 6 May 1794
Anderson John s James, St Benet Paul's Wharf, Lnd, brewer to William Reynolds 1 Jul 1700
Anderson John s Samuel, St Giles Cripplegate, Mdx, labourer to George Wane 5 Aug 1717
Anderson Samuel s Edward, St Stephen, Hrt, miller† to William Knight 7 Oct 1675
Anderson William s William, Dishforth, Yks, cordwainer† to John Church 6 Sep 1675
Anderstill Francis s John, 'Clatwin', Sal, yeoman to William Lee 10 Jul 1643
Andrew Henry s George, citizen and butcher to George Stretton 23 Jul 1645
Andrew James s Simon, Fulham, Mdx, cordwainer to William Pannett 4 Jun 1705
Andrew Samuel s Richard, Wooburn, Bkm, husbandman to Simon Dawson 8 Apr 1650
Andrewe William s William, Caldecote [? *in Ms* 'Carrecott'?], Hrt, yeoman to Robert Tiball 24 Jun 1633
Andrewes John s John, Barking, Ess, yeoman to Isaac Saffin 20 Apr 1664
Andrewes John s William, Desborough, Nth, yeoman to Robert Matthewes 14 Feb 1673/4
Andrewes William s John, Staines, Mdx, mealman to John Turner 5 Oct 1689
Andrewes William s Thomas, Farcett [? *in Ms* 'Thassett'], Hun, yeoman to William Collier 1 Jul 1700
Andrews Isaac s Abraham, West Ham, Ess, yeoman to Henry Cox 8 Feb 1643/4
Andrews James s James, St Giles Cripplegate, Lnd† to Thomas Kellner 28 Mar 1642
Andrews Mordecai s Mordecai, Artillery Lane, Liberty of the Tower, Lnd, minister† to Samuel Savage 20 Jul 1762
Andrews Richard s Mathew, citizen and dyer to Granado Chester 15 Sep 1702
Andrews Thomas s George, Kingsdon, Som, yeoman to John Back 3 Dec 1678
Andrews William s William to his father 2 Nov 1719
Andrews William s Thomas, Westminster, Mdx, yeoman to Joseph Tucker 1 Dec 1795
Angell Henry s Henry, Huntingdon, Hun, gentleman to William Wood 3 Oct 1662
Ann John s John, Highworth, Wil, chirurgeon to Thomas Harrison 7 Dec 1635 <bond from Thomas Brookes, citizen and shipwright>
Ansell John s Thomas, Tooting Graveney, Sry, blacksmith to William Massey 10 Aug 1680
Ansell Thomas s Thomas, Tooting Graveney, Sry, blacksmith to Robert Wyrill 2 Jul 1716
Ansell William s Thomas, Tooting Graveney, Sry, blacksmith to Robert Wyrill 13 Jan 1717/8
Ansley Abraham s Abraham, Alverstoke, Ham, mariner to Thomas Watts 31 Oct 1667
Appleton Thomas s John, West Rounton, Yks, yeoman to Samuel Fitch 13 Apr 1724
Appleyard John s Thomas, Brampton, Hun, gentleman† to Brian Ayliffe 26 Jun 1680
Appleyard Thomas s Thomas, Costessy, Nfk, gentleman to George Kitchinman 22 Sep and 22 Nov 1637
Apsley John s Thomas, citizen and clothworker to Thomas Obbison 2 Sep 1684
ap Thomas *see* Thomas Thomas
ap William *see* Thomas Thomas
Archer Arthur Frederick s George, Lambeth, Sry, gentleman to George Wild 7 Jan 1794
Archer John s John, Hainton, Lin, yeoman to William Gurney 1 Sep 1686
Archer Joseph s Thomas, Hertford, Hrt, yeoman to Nathaniel Winchester 19 Mar 1689/90
Archer Robert s Robert, Edmonton, Mdx, brewer† to Herbert Homan 8 Apr 1746
Archer William s Edward, Hoxton [Shoreditch], Mdx, surgeon to Thomas Kelke 18 Dec 1660
Arden Thomas s Thomas, citizen and innholder to William Goodman 6 May 1646
Ardinton Francis s Stephen, Henley, Oxf, yeoman to Thomas Rencher 13 May 1689
Arewater Thomas s Thomas, Waltham Abbey, Ess, yeoman to Samuel Dare 20 Dec 1749
Argent Samuel s Peter, Whitechapel, Mdx, joiner to Christopher Leake 14 Jan 1657/8
Argins John s Emery, St Margaret Westminster, Mdx, carpenter to Thomas Cole, snr. 10 Jun 1695
Arkesden Thomas s Thomas, Apsley, Bdf, minister to Henry Pauncefoote 30 May 1655
Armestrong Richard s Jeremiah, St James Westminster, Mdx, clothier to John Hankins 1 Dec 1686
Armiger James s John, citizen and founder† to Nathaniel Winchester 5 Jun 1694
Armitage John s Thomas, Deptford, Ken, gentleman to Joshua Knight 6 May 1794

TALLOW CHANDLERS' APPRENTICES

Armitage Samuel s William, Mortlake, Sry, victualler to William Mellor 11 Aug 1722 <turned over to William Pope, citizen and broderer; 7 Sep 1724 to Thomas Woolhead; 7 Aug 1727 by Catherine widow of Thomas Woolhead to Thomas Nash>
Armstrong Joseph s James, Henley, Oxf, tallow chandler to Joseph Boord 3 Apr 1798
Arnell Thomas s Thomas, Godmanchester, Hun, yeoman to Thomas Harrison 11 May 1657
Arnold Jeremiah s Joseph, Walton, Yks, roper† to Thomas Nettleton 24 Apr 1646
Arnold Mathew s Robert, Flecknoe, War, farmer to Samuel Osborn 3 Mar 1734/5
Arnold Ralph s William, Beddington, Sry, yeoman to Francis Tegg 19 Aug 1655
Arnold Robert s John, St Martin in the Fields, Mdx, victualler to Elizabeth widow of Francis Rakestraw 1 May 1721
Arnold Thomas s John, Somerford, Wil, weaver to Mary widow of William Allen 6 Dec 1725 <3 Jun 1728 mistress† turned over by Peter Mellin, exec. to John Baldwin, citizen and feltmaker>
Arnoux James s Claudius, Holborn, Mdx, clerk to Herbert Homan 2 Sep 1752
Arpwood Stephen s Henry, Bermondsey, Sry, brewer† to William Russell 28 Nov 1754
Arundell Charles s Samuel, Northolt, Mdx, yeoman to Thomas Harris 4 Nov 1695
Arundell Henry s Samuel, Northolt, Mdx, yeoman to Edward Strowde 20 Mar 1689/90
Arundell John s Francis, Effingham, Sry, yeoman† to Edward Stroude 7 May 1679
Arundell Thomas s Samuel, Northolt, Mdx, yeoman to Thomas Kender 10 Dec 1685
Ascough Josiah s John to his father 2 May 1677
Ash John s Nathaniel, Saltby, Lei, clerk† to James Green 4 Jun 1694
Ash Richard s Richard, St Giles Cripplegate, Mdx, blacksmith to Giles Cooke 8 Dec 1718
Ashbee William s William, Gawcott, Bkm, labourer to Henry Wyne 25 Jun 1668
Ashbey James s James, citizen and baker to William Chater 16 Jun 1698
Ashburner John s Francis, Gleaston, Lan, yeoman to Thomas Ashburner 22 Jun 1671
Ashburner Thomas s Francis, citizen and merchant tailor to Daniel Clarebutt 6 Aug 1657
Ashby Edward s Edward, Clapham, Sry, farmer to Edward Clarke 19 Jul 1769 <5 Feb 1771 turned over to John Mason, citizen and carpenter>
Ashcroft Edward s John, Streatham, Sry, gentleman† to Daniel Wane 9 Dec 1697
Ashley Eleazar s Thomas, citizen and merchant tailor to William Badham 28 Aug 1677
Ashton Richard s Thomas, Stevington, Bdf, yeoman to William Williams 1 Oct 1722
Ashworth John s Robert, 'Lower Wake', Yks, carrier† to John Fisher 11 Mar 1683/4
Ashworth William s John, Bromley, Ken, locksmith to John Garmeson 18 Aug 1686
Askew John s John, near Ipswich, Sfk, clothier to Humphrey Hill 23 Jan 1651/2
Askew John s Thomas, citizen and distiller† to William Thatcher 3 Feb 1685/6
Askew Robert s Thomas, citizen and distiller† to Peter Pickering 31 Jul 1688
Assely Edward s Henry, Geddington, Nth, yeoman to Richard Walker 20 May 1634
Aston Thomas s Robert, Burford, Oxf, innholder to John Meridale 2 Jun 1679
Atchison James s William, Holborn, Mdx, yeoman to Samuel Snape 21 Jan 1762
Atherton Humphrey s Humphrey, Bledlow, Bkm, gentleman to Henry Langley 17 Feb 1657/8
Atkins Edward s Edward, Stepney, Mdx, labourer to Hugh Miller 9 Jan 1709/10
Atkins John s John, Deptford, Ken, cordwainer to Francis Dawson 5 Apr 1796
Atkinson John s Henry, Lnd, yeoman to Thomas Ford 19 Mar 1632/3
Atkinson John s Edward, Plaistow, Ess, farmer to Joseph Taylor 7 Jan 1783
Atkinson Samuel s William, citizen and vintner to John Maxfeild 3 May 1664
Atkinson Samuel s Joshua, Stepney, Mdx, weaver to Edward Copeland 5 Apr 1714
Atkinson Thomas s Richard, Newington, Sry, gardener† to William Surman 10 Jun 1686
Atlee John s George, Tandridge, Sry, yeoman to Thomas Barrett 12 Aug 1635
Attfield Thomas s Thomas, Nightingale Lane, Mdx, blockmaker to Isaac Phillips 2 Jan 1787
Atwood Harman s King, Sanderstead, Sry, clerk to Nicholas Charlton 11 Dec 1658
Atwood John s John, Clapham, Sry, gardener to Richard Towne 3 Apr 1710
Atwood Thomas s John, Wandsworth, Sry, carpenter to Samuel King 7 Dec 1681
Aubrey Thomas s William, Norfolk Street, Mint, Southwark, Sry, tallow chandler to Thomas Merriman 7 Mar 1780
Ausiter Robert s Robert, Hayes, Mdx, esquire† to Nathaniel Porter 25 Jun 1684
Austin Edward s Jacob, Leverton [Hungerford], Brk, carpenter to William King 4 Jul 1698 <turned over to Frances widow of Thomas Clare; 9 May 1704 to William King>
Austin George s John, St Martin in the Fields, Mdx, turner† to Robert Munden 10 Sep 1705

TALLOW CHANDLERS' APPRENTICES

Austin Thomas s Samuel, Bermondsey, Sry, gentleman to George Searle 5 Aug 1783
Austrey Thomas s Thomas, St James Westminster, Mdx, tallow chandler† to Thomas Obbinson 1 Sep 1707
Austry Thomas s James, citizen and merchant tailor to William Powell 11 Jan 1680/1
Avenell Henry s Philip, Rudgwick, Ssx, carpenter to John Richbell 30 Apr 1635
Avenell Richard s Philip, Rudgwick, Ssx, carpenter to John Heyward 18 May 1633
Averitt Elizabeth d William, Fulham, Mdx, brickmaker† to William Howes 22 Mar 1679/80
Avery William s Oliver, Newbury, Brk, draper† to Francis Houghton 4 Sep 1673
Awdley Richard s Francis, Hitchin, Hrt, maltster to John Bryan 24 Jul 1654
Axe John s James, Rochester, Ken, clerk† to Edward Worgan 5 Aug 1723
Aycrigg John s James, Salisbury, Wil, smith to Samuel Berry 12 Aug 1674
Ayden John s Thomas, Twywell, Nth, yeoman to Thomas Higgins 18 Mar 1679/80
Ayers Adam s Ralph, Wing, Bkm, gardener to Richard Ayers 11 Dec 1691
Ayliff John s John to his father 4 Dec 1704
Ayliffe Brian s Joseph, Milson, Sal, clerk to Edward Barker 19 Aug 1652
Ayliffe John s Joseph, Overton, Ham, clerk to Brian Ayliffe 1 Aug 1668
Ayliffe Robert s Brian to his father 12 Sep 1689
Aylwin Thomas s Alexander, Stepney, Mdx, mariner† to Richard Walker 15 Sep 1709
Ayre John s William, Watford, Hrt, chirurgeon† to William Ingram 20 Apr 1689
Ayres Cornelius s Christopher, Ely, Cam, victualler† to Francis Buggey 21 Mar 1669/70
Ayres Edmund s Edward, Mixbury, Oxf† to Rebecca widow of Richard Barnard 3 Oct 1664
Ayres Richard s Ralph, Wing, Bkm, gardener to Thomas Dowdswell 8 Jul 1684
Ayres Thomas s Thomas, St Martin in the Fields, Mdx, yeoman to William Gurney 29 Jul 1682
Ayres William s William, Southrop, Gls, farrier† to William Minchin 9 Feb 1657/8
Ayres William s Valentine, Norton, Nth, yeoman to John Rumball 18 Dec 1658

Babbs Charles s William, St James Westminster, wheelwright† to Edward Mortimer 7 May 1716
Baber Noah s Noah, Walham Green, Mdx, baker to Robert Fitz 7 May 1782
Bach William s John, Tamworth, War, husbandman to John Richbell 20 Jun 1638
Bachelor Thomas s Thomas, Pershore, Wor, clerk to Robert New 15 Oct 1647
Back Thomas s Thomas, Hinxhill, Ken, gentleman to Samuel Bellchambers 9 Jul 1674
Backhouse Richard s Edward, Drayton, Mdx, yeoman to John Tyson 21 Aug 1660
Baddam William s William, citizen and clothworker† to Robert Hicks 8 Feb 1644/5
Baddely Ann d Henry, Islington, Mdx, yeoman to Thomas Smith 14 Jun 1672
Baddy Benjamin s Benjamin, Clapham, Sry, watchmaker to Edward Clarke (of Stangate, Sry, boat builder) 7 Jun 1769
Badger Daniel s Nicholas, Dulwich, Sry, yeoman to George Laman 19 Aug 1661
Badger Richard s Francis, Dulwich, Sry, husbandman to Thomas Hatton 10 Mar 1653/4
Badham William s William, Leominster, Hef, yeoman to Philip Peirson 1 Aug 1664
Badily Radcliff s John, Kingswinford, Sts, gentleman to William Alexander 2 Mar 1729/30
Badnage Thomas s William, Leominster, Hef, husbandman to Richard Williamson 23 Apr 1638
Bagbey John s Thomas, Hackney, Mdx, cordwainer to Silvester Cordy 13 Nov 1651
Bagbie Henry s Thomas, Hackney, Mdx, cordwainer to Silvester Cordy 3 Jul 1655
Bagge Thomas s Mathew, Cow Honeybourne, Gls, yeoman† to Mathew Bagge 14 Jul 1638
Baggs Giles s Giles, citizen and fishmonger† to Edward Marshall 27 Apr 1654
Baggue James s James, Whitechapel, Mdx, glass maker to Samuel Smith 4 Mar 1705/6
Baglie Edmund s Edward, Shrewsbury, Sal, tallow chandler to Richard Wooding 20 Apr 1682
Bague James s James to his father 13 Jul 1737
Bailey John s Jeremiah, St Katherine Creechurch, Lnd, poulterer† to Richard Tirrell 22 May 1699
Bailey John s Thomas, St James Westminster, Mdx, cooper to John Gould Smith 5 Apr 1758
Bailey William s John, Lyneham, Oxf, yeoman to Thomas Kelke 14 Apr 1646
Bailie Robert s John, Shrivenham, Brk, yeoman to Richard Parrott 20 Aug 1661
Bailie William s William, Holbeach, Lin, husbandman to William Bateman 12 Apr 1682
Baily Whittman s Mathew, Hampstead, Mdx, labourer to Joseph Lane 6 Apr 1737
Bainbridge Thomas s Richard, Wilburton, Cam, clerk to William Bowyer 10 Jul 1668
Baines Thomas s William, Rainham, Ess, yeoman to William Heather 20 Oct 1711
Baker Benjamin s John, Groombridge [Withyham], Ssx, esquire† to Peter Pickering 2 Feb 1659/60
Baker Charles Bowles s Thomas, Cobham, Ken, shopkeeper to Richard Ireland 6 May 1740

Baker Edmund s Mathew, Uxbridge, Mdx, yeoman to Richard Wilkinson 27 Aug 1647
Baker Edmund s Mathew, Uxbridge, Mdx, felmonger† to John Childe, jnr. 11 Nov 1713
Baker George s William, Newark, Ntt, draper to James Powell 14 Jul 1652
Baker Henry s Henry, Holy Trinity Minories, Lnd, broad weaver to Timothy Hooke 11 Jan 1685/6
Baker James s Richard, Uxbridge, Mdx, tanner† to William Prime 8 Apr 1686
Baker John s Nicholas, 'Kingswood', Wil, clothier to William Osmond 2 Feb 1646/7
Baker John s Richard, Chipstead, Sry, husbandman to John Brookes 28 Sep 1661
Baker John s Samuel, Knightsbridge, Mdx, tallow chandler† to John Childe 13 Sep 1692
Baker Joseph s Joseph, Etwall, Dby, husbandman to John Harrison 24 Jun 1693
Baker Joshua s David, St Andrew Hertford, Hrt, gardener to Joseph Pett 12 Aug 1690
Baker Robert s Edward, Lewes, Ssx, yeoman to John Browne 4 Dec 1655
Baker Roger s John, Wrington, Som, barber chirurgeon† to William Leach 16 Mar 1674/5
Baker Samuel s Samuel, Hemel Hempstead, Hrt, mercer to John Hooker 22 Mar 1664/5
Baker Samuel s John, citizen and merchant tailor to Randolph Watson 4 Apr 1698
Baker William s William, citizen and clothworker to John Anckle 13 Apr 1636
Baker William s Peter, Fowey, Con, merchant† to Ralph Peirson 17 Mar 1676/7
Baldry Thomas s John, Framlingham?, Sfk, yeoman to John Jeanes 27 May 1669
Baldwin Isaac s Thomas, Lnd, vintner to William Parker 1 Jul 1734
Baldwin James s Sackfield, Loose, Ken, turner to William Massey 28 Jun 1681
Baldwin James s John, Framilode [Fretherne], Gls, miller to Nathaniel Owen 5 Jul 1764
Baldwin Joshua s Henry, St Saviour Southwark, Sry, ropemaker to John Wynn 11 Mar 1686/7
Baldwyn Jasper s Jasper, citizen and woodmonger† to John Phelps 30 Aug 1649
Balenger Thomas s Walter, Iver, Bkm, yeoman to Robert Udall 3 Dec 1651
Balfour Bartholomew s William, Thames Ditton, Sry, esquire† to Thomas Biggs 4 Oct 1732
Balis William s William, Marsh Gibbon, Bkm, yeoman to John Bowden 22 May 1694
Ball William s William, Lichfield, Sts, ? to Robert Butcher 19 Mar 1669/70
Ballard John s ?...d, 'Hunnybull', ?Gls to Robert Mathewes 30 Mar 1675
Ballard Richard s Richard, citizen and frameworkknitter to John Knowles 2 Aug 1697
Ballard Robert s John, Hatfield Broad Oak, Ess, gentleman to Thomas Giver 2 Jul 1662
Ballatt Susanna d John, St Andrew Holborn, Lnd to Moses Scotton 1 Jun 1724
Balston John s Robert, Islip, Nth, yeoman to James Holworthie 17 Jul 1657
Bampton William s William, Aylesbury, Bkm, yeoman to Joseph Tokefeild 26 Dec 1676
Bandy Edward s William, Stepney, Mdx, yeoman to Henry Burton 23 May 1673
Banister Richard s John, Farnham, Sry, innholder to Joseph Pett 27 Mar 1683
Banister William s Richard, Churchdown, Gls, gentleman to John Wilse 6 Dec 1650
Banks Thomas s Thomas, Paddington, Mdx, yeoman to William Tomkins 12 Nov 1722
<15 Feb 1727/8 turned over to Thomas Stephenson, citizen and draper>
Bannister Francis s John, Parke Hill, Lan to Roger Urmestone 18 Jul 1662
Bannister George s John, Ruislip, Mdx, gentleman to Richard Redding 22 Sep 1641
Bannister William s William, Whalley, Lan, husbandman to Henry Burnley 1 Jul 1664
Bantocke John s Walter, Bookham, Sry, yeoman to William Spencer 2 Feb 1635/6
Barber Francis s Thomas to his father 21 Sep 1749
Barber James s Joseph, Strand, Mdx, victualler to Francis Robins 7 May 1733
Barber Jeremiah s John, Ipswich, Sfk, cordwainer to Richard Warde 28 Nov 1672
Barber Thomas s John, Killinghall, Yks, yeoman to Joseph Burton 14 Apr 1669
Barber Thomas s Francis, Salisbury, Wil, cutler to William Mayne 29 May 1716
Barber Thomas s Thomas to his father 10 Feb 1747/8
Barcock Edmund s Edmund to his father 1660
Barcock Mathew s ..., Weston, Hun, yeoman to Richard Reynolds 29 Sep 1633
Bardwell Robert s Edward, Holborn, Mdx, coachman† to Phineas Patershall 13 May 1755
Barker Ambrose s William, Oaksey?, Wil† to Leonard Turner 12 Mar 1643/4
Barker Arthur s Arthur, Dunham, Chs, clothworker to William Miller 21 Apr 1670
Barker John s John, St Sepulchre, Mdx, porter to William Ritte 3 Jun 1641
Barker John s John, Swaton, Lin, plumber† to Thomas Barker 7 Dec 1667
Barker Oswald s Thomas, Halton, Lan, yeoman† to Daniel Man 1 Aug 1651
Barker Robert s William, 'Legginton', Dby, husbandman to John Wilcock 7 Jan 1652/3
Barker William s Nathaniel, Stoke Talmage, Oxf, clerk to Philip Pearson 6 Mar 1648/9
Barksdale Thomas s Edward, Newbury, Brk, clothier to Thomas Haines 2 Dec 1686

TALLOW CHANDLERS' APPRENTICES

Barlee Richard s William to his father 2 Oct 1738
Barling Edward s Walter, St Mary, Ken, clerk to John Ragdale 7 Jun 1661
Barlow Edward s Robert, Fifield, Wil, yeoman to Richard Whitcher 8 Mar 1655/6
Barlow George s George, Smisby, Dby, farmer to Joseph Barlow 20 Jun 1769
Barlow Henry s Joseph, Newington, Sry to his father 6 Feb 1798
Barlow John s Joseph, Bermondsey, Sry, carpenter to Joseph Barlow 27 Dec 1758
Barlow Joseph s Joseph, Bermondsey, Sry, carpenter to Mathew Thompson 28 May 1751
Barlowe Thomas s Robert, St Martin in the Fields, Mdx, clothsmith† to William Eyre 29 Dec 1681
Barnard John s Francis, Shenley, Hrt, yeoman to Oliver Hill 7 Jan 1642/3
Barnard Thomas s Robert, Winchester, Ham, gardener to Humphrey Hill 17 Mar 1645/6
Barnerd Richard s Richard, citizen and salter to John Bigg 1 May 1635
Barnes Arkinstall s Edward, Lambeth, Sry, grazier† to James Tetley 6 May 1723
Barnes Francis s Francis, St Clement Danes, Mdx, labourer† to Thomas West 2 Dec 1700
Barnes James s John, St Giles Cripplegate, Lnd, weaver to John Blackmore 1 Dec 1707
<1 May 1710 turned over to Jeremy Bentham, citizen and scrivener>
Barnes John s Humphrey, St Martin in the Fields, Mdx, farrier to John Parker 2 Apr 1690
Barnes Richard s John, Northampton, Nth, innkeeper to William Gaunt 5 Jul 1660
Barnes Stephen s John, Chichester, Ssx, gentleman to William Blomefeild 6 Mar 1709/10
Barnes William s John, citizen and cooper to John Meridale 11 Jul 1681
Barnes William s John, St Giles in the Fields, Mdx, yeoman to Thomas Baynard 5 Dec 1683
Barnett Robert s William, Stepney, Mdx, butcher to William Noss 3 Aug 1713 <18 Nov 1717 turned over to John Fisher, citizen and cutler>
Barnsley John s William, citizen and draper† to Edward King 25 Nov 1653
Barnwell William s Lionel, Huntingdon, Hun, tailor to George Staines 26 Jun 1680
Barnwell William s William, Burbage, Lei, yeoman† to Noel Whiteing 17 Nov 1698
Barrabee Richard s Richard, Grove, Bkm, farmer to Peter Leigh 7 Aug 1732
Barrat John s Samuel, citizen and salter† to William Mayne 27 Feb 1688/9
Barrett George s John, Dunstew, Oxf, farmer to Adrian Roberts 1 May 1727
Barrett Richard s Richard, citizen and joiner to Thomas Williams 23 Nov 1726
Barrett Thomas s William, citizen and bricklayer to Thomas Spencer 27 May 1671
Barrett Thomas s Thomas, Old Street Square, Mdx, banker† to William Lucas 2 May 1726
Barrett Thomas s William, citizen and tallow chandler† to Eleanor widow of William Barrett 6 Aug 1745
Barrett William s Thomas, citizen and broderer† to Robert Bly 3 May 1714
Barrett William s James, Brentford, Mdx, bricklayer to Margaret widow of James Scott 4 Sep 1727
Barrett William s William, citizen and tallow chandler† to Thomas Barrett 2 Mar 1758
Barringer Henry s Mathew, Harrow, Mdx, harnessmaker to William Cock 18 Dec 1668
Barrington Valentine s Thomas, Bumpstead, Ess, gentleman to Nathaniel Ragdale 13 Jan 1687/8
Barrodell Samuel s Thomas, Farndon, Nth, clerk to William Clarke 15 Jun 1647
Bartholomew Humphrey s Leonard, Little Peckham, Ken, gentleman to John Thompson 8 May 1717
Bartholomew William s Walter, Chaddleworth, Brk, tailor to Thomas Cooper 18 Jun 1640
Bartholomew William s Edward, St Giles in the Fields, gentleman to Anthony Chestroe 3 Jan 1697/8
Bartlett John s John, Burrough Green, Cam, yeoman† to William Couzens 5 Feb 1672/3
Bartlett Stackford s Robert, Twickenham, Mdx, gardener to Hannah widow of John Meadowes 1 May 1665
Bartlett Thomas s John, Horsham, Ssx, gentleman† to Robert Fluellin 18 May 1671
Barton George s George, Hawkeswell [Coleshill], War, yeoman to Joseph Watts 23 Dec 1671
Barton Henry s Henry, Bradford, Wil, yeoman to Christopher Robotham 17 Jul 1633
Barton John s Thomas, Brigstock, Nth, gentleman to Jeremiah Broadgate 27 Jul 1686
Barton Jonathan s David, St Saviour Southwark, Sry, pinmaker to Henry Batten, snr. 5 Oct 1719
Barton Robert Dodge s Samuel, Stockport, Chs, farmer to Samuel Barton 5 Nov 1793 <2 May 1797 turned over to Richard Davies>
Barton Thomas s John, Chester, Chs, silk weaver to Frances widow of Thomas Wigg 29 Mar 1707
Barwell Mathew s Edward, Drayton, Lei, yeoman to Joseph Coggs 15 Jun 1671
Barwell Richard s Richard, Drayton, Lei, yeoman to Mathew Barwell 12 Jun 1679
Barwell Thomas s Thomas, Medbourne, Lei, husbandman† to Mathew Barwell 23 Sep 1690
Barwell Thomas s Mathew to his father 5 Mar 1704/5
Barwell William s William, Great Easton, Lei, tallow chandler to Mathew Barwell 3 Nov 1701

Barwiss Francis s William, 'Nuddleskew', Cul, gentleman to Richard Backhouse 24 Dec 1679
Baseley Samuel s William, Smeeton Westerby, Lei, yeoman to James Byard 24 Oct 1668
Basie Catherine d George, Hackney, Mdx, cordwainer to Robert Butcher 1 Aug 1654
Bass Thomas s Mathew, Olney, Bkm, labourer to John Gill 8 Dec 1712
Bassett John s John, St Giles in the Fields, Mdx, tailor† to Richard Ayers 11 Dec 1691
Bassill Jonathan s Samuel, Harpenden, Hrt, yeoman† to John Carter 13 Jan 1717/8
Batcock Nicholas s Richard, Stepney, Mdx, mariner to Thomas Edrop 5 Mar 1710/11
Bateman John s Thomas, Holborn, Mdx, gentleman† to John Merrick 21 Jul 1673
Bateman William s George, Eggborough, Yks, yeoman to John Milton 21 Nov 1634
Bates Edward s Edward, St Botolph Bishopsgate, wiredrawer† to Benjamin Kendall 4 Nov 1717
Bates James s James, Reading, Brk, clothworker to Joseph Slowe 3 May 1661
Bates Robert s Robert, citizen and tinplateworker to Samuel Woodfield 3 Apr 1721
Bates William s John, Tamworth, War, husbandman to John Richbell 19 Jul 1638
Bather Owen to John Briscoe 1661/2
Batten Alice d Ralph, St Saviour Southwark, Sry, waterman to Henry Batten 13 Nov 1684
Batten Edward s Simon, Appleton, Brk, husbandman to John Mathew 2 Nov 1639
Batten Henry s Rudolph, St Saviour Southwark, water carrier to Edward Masters 13 Feb 1665/6
Batten Henry s Henry to his father 21 Oct 1689
Batten John s Henry to his father 30 Apr 1706
Batty James s Edward, Aldermanbury, Lnd, mercer† to William Reading 9 Apr 1658
Baugh John s Richard, Tibberton, Wor, gentleman to William Finney 26 May 1666
Baugh Stephen s Richard, Tibberton, Wor, gentleman† to John Baugh 2 Dec 1673
Bavin John s Bartholomew, Shirburn, Oxf, yeoman to Thomas Rowles 5 Jan 1712/3
Baxter Edward s Edward, Whetstone, Mdx, gentleman† to Roger Price, jnr. 30 Jan 1637/8
Baxter Simon s Simon, Thorpe Arnold, Lei, gentleman to William Palmer 25 Nov 1645
Bayle Richard s Richard, citizen and feltmaker† to John Wynn 14 Jul 1698
Bayley John s John, Woolwich, Ken, tallow chandler to John Randall 7 Jul 1789
Bayley Joseph s John, Woolwich, Ken, tallow chandler to John Randall 2 Jul 1793
Bayley Thomas s Thomas, Hampstead, Mdx, yeoman to Francis Robins 5 Mar 1721/2
Bayly Francis s Francis, St Giles in the Fields, Mdx, baker† to John Palmer 28 Sep 1674
Bayly Francis s Edward, All Saints, Nth, silversmith to Thomas Higgins 12 Nov 1705
Baynard Thomas s Richard, Marston, Nth, yeoman† to John Kettle 23 Feb 1668/9
Baynes Roger s John, citizen and cook to Josiah Ragdale 26 Sep 1681
Baynham Edward s Edward, Brackley, Nth, yeoman to John Watts 29 May 1699
Bayton Leonard s William, Holborn, Mdx† to John Toms 28 Jun 1641
Bayzand John s Richard, Hinton, Gls, farmer to John Chenney 7 Aug 1737
Bayzand Joseph s Joseph, Ashton under Hill, Gls, yeoman to Robert Dove 6 Mar 1703/4
Bazlee William s William, Daventry, Nth, yeoman† to Jonas Watts 5 Feb 1710/11
Beacham John s Thomas, Hadley, Mdx, husbandman to Nicholas Farrant 18 Nov 1658
Beachfield Arthur s John, Eldersfield, Wor, gentleman† to John Darcey 2 Jul 1692
Beale John s John, 'Fafield', Hef, yeoman to John Ford 11 May 1683
Beale John s John to his father 5 Mar 1715/6
Beale Mathew s Mathew, Southwark, Sry, feltmaker to Thomas Jekell 16 Dec 1634
Beale Richard s John, Maidstone, Ken, gentleman† to Richard Towne 15 Jul 1695
Beamont Joseph s Henry, Flitton, Bdf, yeoman to Francis Warner 12 Apr 1654
Beamont William s Henry, Shenley, Hrt, yeoman to John Harris 29 Sep 1632
Beamont William s Thomas, Barrowby, Lin, yeoman to John Yarling 11 Sep 1655
Bean Stephen s Richard, Lnd, cook† to James Brent 3 Aug 1713
Beane Maurice s Maurice, St Margaret Westminster, confectioner to Jeremiah Ridge 4 Nov 1717
Beard Richard s Henry, Spoonbed, Painswick, Gls, gentleman to William Webb 2 Nov 1664
Beard Robert s Richard, Frimley, Sry, gentleman to Thomas Lawrence 12 Aug 1653
Beard Thomas s Nathaniel, Leonard Stanley, Gls, clothier to William Hoare 30 Apr 1766
Bearden Thomas s Henry, Hurst, Hun, yeoman† to John Harrison 29 Sep 1670
Beardoe Charles s John, Teddington, Mdx, gentleman† to Daniel Scutt 27 Sep 1679
Beaten James s Isaac, Stepney, Mdx, weaver† to Isaac Beaten 7 Apr 1707
Beaton Isaac s Isaac, Stepney, Mdx, weaver to William Smaldridge 7 Mar 1699/1700
Beauchampe William s John, Cosgrave, Nth, yeoman† to Thomas Harrison 20 Apr 1664
Beaumont Edward s Edward, Biggleswade, Bdf, maltster to William Collyer 3 Jun 1728

Beaumont John s John, St James Westminster, Mdx, victualler to John Ayscough 6 Sep 1692
Beaumont John s William, citizen and coachmaker to Frances widow of Thomas Wigg 1 Mar 1713/4
Beck John s William, Sandwich, Ken, tallow chandler† to James Waggoner 8 Jan 1662/3
Beck Robert s Thomas, citizen and draper to Nathaniel Messenger 3 Sep 1690
Becke Thomas s Thomas, Westminster, Mdx, brewer† to Bartholomew Paris 25 May 1637
Beckett George s John, Rode, Chs, miller to Jasper Geery 17 Jan 1690/1
Beckett Jarvis s Richard, Westerdale, Yks† to Nicholas Beckett 12 Apr 1649
Beckett Nicholas s Richard, Whisperdales, Yks, yeoman to Edmund Barcocke 28 Oct 1637
Beckett Richard s Richard, Westerdale, Yks† to Nicholas Beckett 12 Apr 1649
Beckman John s John, citizen and stationer† to John Jones 10 Jul 1711
Beckwith Thomas s John, Rivenhall, Ess, yeoman to Henry Hawkes 1 Nov 1655
Beddwell Richard s William, Stanton Harcourt, Oxf, yeoman to Ann widow of Stephen Hake 10 Mar 1639/40
Bedford John s James, Lambeth, Sry, cordwainer to John Johnson 5 Aug 1734
Bedle Thomas s Thomas, East Grinstead, Ssx, mercer to John Bodle 30 Apr 1674
Bedwell John s Nathaniel, Cirencester, Gls, yeoman to Samuel Bedwell 5 Sep 1680
Bedwell John s Samuel, St Margaret Westminster, Mdx, mealman to Samuel Bedwell 8 Jan 1693/4
Bedwell Samuel s Maurice, Swansea, Gla, clerk† to Samuel Bedwell 2 May 1665
Bedwell William s Richard, citizen and tallow chandler to Richard Bedwell 30 Oct 1671
Beesly Edward s John, citizen and haberdasher to Richard Kirby 4 Apr 1715
Beirton William s John, Stone, Bkm, labourer to Henry Soames 20 Dec 1775
Belchamber John s William, Reading, Brk, tanner to Samuel Belchamber 17 Oct 1648
Belchamber John s Samuel to his father 5 Dec 1677
Belchamber John s John, Cliddesden, Ham, yeoman to Robert Uppington 28 Nov 1683
Belchamber Samuel s William, Reading, Brk, tanner to Simon Greenehill 26 Mar 1635
Belchamber Samuel s William, Reading, Brk, tanner to Samuel Belchamber 13 Mar 1655/6
Belchamber William s John, Havant, Ham, clerk to Samuel Belchamber 29 Mar 1653
Bell George s Joseph, St George Southwark, Sry, tallow chandler to Thomas Gregory 6 Aug 1776
Bell Henry s William, St Martin in the Fields, Mdx, tailor to Thomas Day 15 Mar 1680/1
Bell James s Moses, citizen and stationer† to Michael Hale 13 Oct 1663
Bell Michael s Michael, St Giles in the Fields, Mdx, labourer to Nathaniel Chandler 1 Dec 1742 <30 May 1746 turned over with consent of James Bwye, an exec. to John Lambert, citizen and cooper>
Bellamy Robert s Henry, Evesham, Wor, yeoman to Martin Gardener 5 Dec 1633
Bellenie Joseph s Robert, citizen and tallow chandler to Richard Carter 6 Nov 1721 <1 Jul 1723 turned over to Addington Turner>
Bellenie Robert s Robert, Stepney, Mdx, dyer to Thomas Johnson 4 Nov 1728
Bellis George s John, Edmonton, Mdx, yeoman to Thomas Chewter 3 Feb 1706/7
Bellis Nathaniel s George, citizen and tallow chandler† to Mary widow of George Bellis 3 May 1738
Belson Edmund s Edmund, citizen and tallow chandler† to James Packit 17 Oct 1691
Benbrose William s Thomas, Burton by Lincoln, Lin, yeoman† to Thomas Pratt 30 Jun 1636
Benham Mathew s Thomas, Shabbington, Bkm, yeoman to James Church 2 May 1673
Bennett Henry s Samuel, citizen and cooper to Nathaniel Chandler 6 Aug 1711
Bennett John s Robert, Tower of London, gentleman to Mathew Woodward 4 Apr 1751
Bennett Richard Busshire s Richard, Whitechapel, Mdx, mariner† to William Alexander 5 Jan 1735/6 <9 Jun 1736 turned over to Robert Bringhurst, citizen and founder>
Bennett Thomas s Thomas, citizen and tallow chandler† to Mary widow of Thomas Bennett 5 Sep 1715
Bennitt Nicholas s Nicholas, Bermondsey, Sry, leatherseller† to William Nelson 29 Oct 1656
Bennitt Peter s William, Wellsborough [Sibson], Lei, yeoman to Thomas Rosse 13 Jan 1652/3
Bennitt Thomas s Thomas, Shaftesbury, Dor, yeoman to William Cranwell 29 Jun 1681
Benson Charles s George, Shoreditch, Mdx, looking glass maker† to Daniel Dale 9 Jun 1687
Benson John s John, citizen and weaver to Henry Hawkes 20 Apr 1686
Benson John s Joseph, St Saviour Southwark, Sry, butcher to Henry Ventrice 6 Jul 1724
Benson Joseph s Henry, St Olave Southwark, Sry, butcher to Charles Godwin 29 Dec 1687
Benson Joseph s Charles to his father 1 Jun 1719
Benson Peter s Peter, Harrogate, Yks, yeoman to Henry Burton 7 Jun 1675
Benson Richard s Richard, St Giles Cripplegate, Lnd, shoemaker to Charles Goodman 30 Jun 1654

Bentfeild Henry s Edward, Wokingham, Brk, husbandman to David Morris 21 Oct 1654
Bentham Samuel s Samuel, citizen and merchant tailor† to Richard Webster 13 Apr 1724
Bentley Francis s Fulk, Wick, Wor, yeoman to Henry Bullock 26 Dec 1639
Bentley Samuel s William, Leicester, Lei, mercer† to Jacob Horton 22 Jan 1696/7
Bentley Saul s Saul, Wick, Wor† to Robert Bedall 26 May 1642
Bentley William s William, Wandsworth, Sry, yeoman to John Rudson 26 Feb 1637/8
Bentley William s John, St Mary Woolchurch Haw, Lnd, butcher† to Sarah widow of Nathaniel Bellis 8 Aug 1766 <6 Sep 1771 turned over to Joseph Meyers>
Benwell Samuel s Samuel, citizen and innholder to Robert Ayliffe 6 Oct 1709
Benwell Thomas s William, Henley, Oxf, mealman† to Joseph Taylor 23 Aug 1769
Benyon Benjamin s Robert, citizen and apothecary to Richard Joyce ? Mar 1670/1
Berd Francis s John, Harrow, Mdx, yeoman† to Henry Hill 2 Jun 1675
Bernard William s William, citizen and merchant tailor to John Harbert 7 Mar 1682/3
Berrey John s John, Felmersham, Bdf, yeoman to William Gurney 8 Dec 1685
Berridge Charles s William, Deptford, Ken, tallow chandler to John Berridge 6 Oct 1778
Berridge John s William, St Marylebone, Mdx, tallow chandler to Richard Savage 6 Mar 1769
Berry Henry s Thomas, Wandsworth, Sry, cooper to Robert Kerby 7 Jan 1722/3
Berry John s Edmund, Bedford, Bdf, yeoman to Thomas Paine 3 Sep 1633
Berry Samuel s Edward, Henlow, Bdf, yeoman to John Berry 23 Jun 1652
Bett Giles s Edward, Southam, War, yeoman to Arden Makepeace 1 May 1641
Bett James s George, Etton, Nth, yeoman† to Joseph Woollhead 5 Feb 1689/90
Betts Ivo s Ivo, Harold Wood, Ess, yeoman† to William Gurney 17 Jul 1675
Bettsworth Peter s Thomas, Fyning, Rogate, Ssx, esquire to James Potenger 26 Oct 1673
Beverstock Thomas s Thomas, Chatham, Ken, caulker to John Freeman 4 Mar 1722/3
Bew Timothy s John, North Heath, Brk, farmer† to Francis Leech 16 Aug 1750
Bexhill Samuel s John, Warblington, Ham, gentleman to John Langrish 25 Feb 1667/8
Bexhill Samuel s Thomas, Havant, Ham, tanner to Samuel Bexhill 30 Mar 1681
Bibbey William s John, Manchester, Lan, weaver† to Nicholas Hawatt 15 Mar 1675/6
Bickerstaffe Thomas s Thomas, citizen and skinner† to William Gaunt 3 Oct 1698 <20 Jan 1701/2 turned over to John Stainsby, citizen and cooper>
Bickerton Andrew s Anthony, Tenbury, Wor, yeoman† to Thomas Cox 4 Mar 1656/7
Bickford Benjamin s Oakes, St Giles in the Fields, Mdx, locksmith to William Wateridge 9 Nov 1727 <6 Dec 1731 turned over to James Marter>
Biddall Samuel s Martin, Oxford, Oxf, tallow chandler to Edward Tibbey 7 Sep 1646
Bidden Joseph s Henry, Wallingford, Brk, fuller to Richard Holdsworth 31 Oct 1640
Biddle Richard s Richard, citizen and plumber† to John Johnson 7 Mar 1719/20
Biggs William s Peter, Walton on Thames, Sry, farmer† to Benjamin Crakenthorpe 4 May 1742
Biggs William s Joseph, citizen and frameworkknitter to Lancelot Vibart 3 Apr 1744
Bigland Ralph s Richard, Ratcliffe, Mdx, tallow chandler to Edward Olive 9 Nov 1727
Bigland Ralph s Richard, Ratcliffe, Mdx, tallow chandler† to Edward Olive 1 Apr 1728
Bignell Digory s John, Basingstoke, Ham, tailor to Humphrey Hill 1 Jun 1647
Bignell William s William, citizen and plumber† to Philip Pickering 2 Mar 1723/4
Bignold Isaac s Henry, Deptford, Ken, shipwright† to John Berridge 9 Oct 1776 <8 Feb 1780 turned over to William White, citizen and merchant tailor>
Billing Francis s Martin, Ravensthorpe, Nth, clerk to Joseph Watts 2 Apr 1656
Billing Nathaniel s William, Enfield, Mdx, yeoman to John Noble 22 Jan 1637/8
Billing Richard s Richard, Fulham, Mdx, yeoman to Arthur Barker 4 Dec 1678
Billingay William s Henry, Islington, Mdx, innholder to Samuel Osborn 6 Jun 1726 <6 Aug 1729 master† turned over by his widow Elizabeth to Nathaniel Edwards, citizen and butcher>
Billingsley John s Nicholas, Blakeney, Gls to John Veland 17 Mar 1678/9
Billingsley Margaret d Thomas, Bristol, Som, gentleman† to John Tewer 31 Jul 1660
Billopp Francis s Thomas, Deptford, Ken, mariner to John Watts 6 Dec 1725
Bincks William s ?, Bennington, Hrt, yeoman to Ellen Dubber ? Jan 1667/8
Birch Henry s Henry, Winwick, Lan, stonecutter to Susanna widow of Henry Cooper 30 May 1666
Birch John s Nicholas, Hungerford, Brk, brewer to William Buckler 12 Jan 1653/4
Birchmore Thomas s Henry, Aldenham, Hrt, yeoman to Edward Harris 26 Dec 1666
Bird George s Roger, Andover, Ham, innholder to Joseph Callcott 8 Jan 1710/11 <17 Jun 1714 turned over to Thomas Woolhead, jnr.>

Bird George s William, Greenwich, Ken, tallow chandler to Thomas Barber 8 Jan 1754
Bird George Martin s George, Greenwich, Ken to his father 2 Nov 1784
Bird John s Henry, Bradford, Wor, yeoman to Samuel Denny 26 Apr 1687
Bird John s John, Holborn, Mdx, labourer to George Smith 8 Dec 1749
Bird Josias s Richard, citizen and carpenter† to Simon Dawson 23 Apr 1646
<bond from William Bird, citizen and white baker>
Bird Robert s John, citizen and grocer to Joseph Woolhead 24 Jul 1682
Bird Robert s John, Holborn, Mdx, porter to Benjamin Kendall 7 Oct 1717
Bird Thomas s Richard, Kings Stanley, Gls, carpenter to George Bird 1 Oct 1770
Bird William s Anthony, Field [Leigh], Sts, gentleman to William Bird 26 Jun 1663
Bird William s Richard, Everton, Nth, yeoman to John Carter 7 Dec 1702
Bird William Turner s William, Greenwich, Ken, tallow chandler to Francis Barber 8 Dec 1761
Birkby William s Samuel, Highgate, Mdx, butcher to Henry Stent 5 Oct 1784
Birkhead Francis s Francis, Gamston, Ntt, clerk to William Bowyer 23 Sep 1662
Birt Thomas s John, Shepton Mallet, Som, clothier to Samuel Bexhill 13 Jan 1682/3
Biscoe Thomas s John, St Thomas Southwark, Sry, clerk to Jane widow of Robert More 1 May 1650
Bishop Benjamin s Nathaniel, Lambeth, Sry, cooper to Thomas Searle 6 Jun 1771 <23 Sep 1773
turned over to Francis Barrell Searle>
Bishop Richard s Richard, Rugby, War, maltster to William Payne 22 Sep 1687
Bishop Robert s Robert, Lnd, biscuit baker† to Ralph Peirson 5 Sep 1687
Bishop Thomas s Thomas, Oxford, Oxf, gentleman† to Richard Yates 5 May 1701
Bishopp John s Ephraim, Kingston, Sry, mercer† to John Jeanes 21 Feb 1670/1
Bishopp Richard s Richard, Boddington, Gls, yeoman to Richard Parrott 6 Jul 1652
Bishopp Samuel s Richard, Boddington, Gls, gentleman† to Thomas Cox 12 May 1657
Bishopp William s William, Bermondsey, Sry, yeoman to William Bateman 7 Jan 1655/6
Bissill Jeremiah s John, Charterhouse, Lnd, gentleman to Mathew Barwell 19 Aug 1686
Blackman Anthony s Thomas, Stratfield Saye, Brk, yeoman to Anthony Philp 19 Nov 1640
Blackmore John s William, Stratford le Bow, Mdx, wheelwright to William Badham 14 May 1696
Blackwell John s John, Chedworth, Gls, yeoman to Thomas Wall 26 Jan 1633/4
Blagrave Alexander s Charles, St James Clerkenwell, Mdx, doctor in physic† to Nathaniel Ragdale
22 May 1695
Blake John s Richard, Didcot, Brk, yeoman to John Goode 27 May 1669
Blake John s John, Shaftesbury, Dor, mason† to William Couzens 15 May 1672
Blake John s Charles, citizen and lorimer to James Bague 7 Mar 1714/5
Bland David s John, Deptford, Ken, carpenter to John Compton 25 Feb 1745/6
Bland David s David, Rosemary Lane [St Botolph Aldgate], Mdx to his father 4 Jul 1780
Bland John s David, Rosemary Lane [St Botolph Aldgate], Mdx to his father 2 Mar 1784
Blandford Joseph s Thomas, Marden, Wil, yeoman to Joseph Tovey 2 Mar 1723/4
Blanker Thomas s Peter, Ely, Cam, yeoman to Martha Harbert, sp. 1 Jun 1719
Blatt James s Edmund, Barking, Ess, gentleman to Michael Warren 1 Oct 1662
Blea Alexander s Alexander, St Margaret Westminster, Mdx, victualler to Elizabeth widow of
Francis Rakestraw 4 May 1719
Bleake Tobias s Bartholomew, Wapping, Mdx, smith† to George Kitchinman 3 Nov 1633
Bleming Robert s Robert, St James Clerkenwell, Mdx, coachman† to John Watson 9 Feb 1680/1
Blessard William s John, Read [Whalley], Lan, cabinet maker to John Greenwood 8 Jun 1767
Bletsoe James s Edward, Irchester, Nth, yeoman† to Edmund Belson 14 Jan 1681/2
Blew Edward s True, Brickhill, Bkm [? *in Ms* 'Mdx'], innholder to Thomas Higgins 9 Feb 1707/8
Bligh David s David, St Martin le Grand, Lnd, oilman to John Bryan 5 Jan 1790
Bliset John s John, Henley, Oxf, yeoman to John Jackson 5 Sep 1643
Bliss James s James, Reading, Brk, butcher† to John Harding 6 May 1723
Bliss John s Thomas, Wick, Gls, yeoman† to Ann widow of Richard Bliss 28 Apr 1687
Bliss Jonathan s Thomas, Painswick, Gls, yeoman to John Bliss 6 Jul 1696
Blith William s Francis, Coventry, War, gentleman to John Hunt 27 Apr 1682
Blizard John s John, citizen and armorer to Thomas Peirson 2 Apr 1679
Blizzard John s John, Bermondsey, Sry, mariner† to Joseph Tovey 7 Apr 1712
Blocke Bernard s Edward, Hadley, Mdx, husbandman to Robert Asplin 17 Oct 1637
Blomefeild William s Francis, Attleborough, Nfk, draper to John Eyre 3 Sep 1697

Blower Joseph s Joseph, Sudbury, Sfk [? *in Ms no county*], woolcomber† to Samuel Blower 2 Mar 1784
Blower Robert s Richard, citizen and mercer to Thomas Higgins 6 Jul 1724
Blower Samuel s John, St Sepulchre, Mdx, tallow chandler to Charles Dare 16 Sep 1773
Blucke Thomas s Peter, Isleworth, Mdx, gentleman to Thomas Smith 6 May 1723
Bly Robert s John, citizen and brewer† to Randolph Watson 29 Nov 1686
Bly William s John, Sydenham, Oxf, clerk to Thomas Bennett 9 Jan 1709/10
Boak Isaac s Isaac, Southwark, Sry, shoemaker† to Thomas Payne 14 May 1752 <9 May 1754 turned over to Henry Soames>
Boble James s James, Midhurst, Ssx, yeoman to Henry Cowper 28 Aug 1662
Boddeley John s John, Spitalfields, Mdx, weaver to Samuel Savage 1 Mar 1737/8
Boddington John s Walter, Turvey, Bdf, husbandman† to Joseph Clifton 17 May 1652
Boddy James s John, St Gregory, Lnd, copper plate printer to Job Orton 25 Mar 1762
Bodely James s George, Kelmarsh, Nth, yeoman to John Monck 17 Apr 1634
Bodington William s George, Turvey, Bdf, husbandman to George Partridge 1 Feb 1731/2
Bodkin William to Sarah Downes 7 Feb 1799
Bodle John s Thomas, East Grinstead, Ssx, yeoman to William Nelson 9 Sep 1664
Bodman John s Humphrey, Rotherhithe, Sry, glazier to William Hutchins 17 Jul 1723
Bolden Benjamin s John, Wimborne, Dor, clerk† to William Cranwell 21 May 1685
Bolton John s John, citizen and founder† to Thomas Woolhead 5 Mar 1710/11
Bolton William s Cuthbert, Kirkham, Lan, yeoman to John Noble 31 Aug 1647
Bolton William s William, Ipsley, War, yeoman to Anthony Moseley 1 Mar 1650/1
Bond Andrew, St Stephen Walbrook, Lnd to Thomas Hopkins 8 May 1693
Bond Elias s William, Wareham, Dor, gentleman† to Nicholas Gold 19 Oct 1685
Bond John s William, Ilton, Som, shoemaker to Thomas Parker 15 Oct 1639
Bond William s Edward, Foxcott, Ham, yeoman† to Robert Southwood 2 Dec 1674
Bones Samuel s John, Toppesfield, Ess, husbandman to William Thompson 27 May 1678
Bonnaby Richard s Richard, Portsmouth, Ham, tailor to Christopher Somner 1 Aug 1682
Bonner Thomas s William, Henley, Oxf, maltster to Thomas Page 15 Jul 1658
Bonnick Robert s Robert, Harrow, Mdx, yeoman† to Robert Apsley 16 May 1650
Bonsey Samuel s Samuel, Hillingdon, Mdx, yeoman to Samuel Walker 24 Jan 1634/5
Boone Roger s William, citizen and clothworker to George Stretton 28 Jul 1654 <bond from Margaret Rainsford and Thomas Tueson, vintner>
Boorer Thomas s Henry, Warnham, Ssx, gentleman to Richard Thorneton 24 Apr 1673
Booth Barron s John, Lnd, stocking logger to John Wilford 26 Sep 1726
Booth George s George, Barnsley, Yks to Henry Wine 23 Jan 1666/7
Booth Joseph s Joseph, citizen and grocer to Daniel Kirton 18 Mar 1684/5
Booth Thomas s William, St Andrew Holborn, Lnd, gentleman to Hugh Evans 16 Apr 1663
Boothby John s Richard, Markfield, Lei, gentleman to Lawrence Carter 6 Feb 1692/3
Bord Thomas s Samuel, Batcombe, Som, stocking maker to Edward Fitz 6 Oct 1736
Boreman Thomas s Thomas, St Saviour Southwark, Sry, sawyer† to Joseph Massey 26 Jan 1679/80
Borne Thomas s Edmund, Epsom, Sry, yeoman to Henry Collett 4 Mar 1644/5
Borraston Thomas s Thomas, Hampstead, Mdx, gentleman to George Shelley 6 Aug 1705
Bosely Thomas s Thomas, White Waltham, Brk, husbandman† to Robert Voucher 21 Jan 1690/1
Bossingham Richard s Thomas, St Martin in the Fields, Mdx, baker† to John Hankinson 10 Jul 1687
Boswell William s William, Lambeth, Sry, mason to Andrew Myers 7 Aug 1781
Boteler Richard s James, Ware, Hrt, bargeman to George Scott 3 Jan 1652/3
Bottom John s John, Little Paxton, Hun, yeoman† to John Wilse 12 Aug 1661
Bottsford Edward s Daniel, Holborn, Mdx, carpenter† to Benjamin Munn 3 Jul 1688
Boughton George s Leneve, St Margaret Westminster, Mdx, clerk to Philip Pickering 3 Aug 1719
Boult Charles s John, Westminster, Mdx, gentleman to William Gurney 20 Apr 1676
Boulton John s Edward, All Hallows Barking, Lnd, carpenter to Henry Pullen 1 Jul 1728
Boulton Thomas s George, East Smithfield [Wapping], Mdx, painter to William Butler 4 May 1641
Bounsey Robert s Edward, Littleton, Mdx, yeoman to William Gunston 10 Aug 1641
Bourne William s Clowes, Holy Trinity Minories, perukemaker to Andrew Jordaine 6 Aug 1761
Bovingdon William s William, Beaconsfield, Bkm, yeoman† to Mathew Woodward 23 Mar 1701/2
Bow William s James, Burton, Wes, yeoman to Daniel Man 7 Aug 1656
Bowden John s George, Twyford, Bkm, shepherd to William Wickins 20 Dec 1666

Bowden John s Richard, Twyford, Bkm, husbandman† to John Bowden 12 Feb 1705/6 <10 Nov 1709 master† turned over by Robert Pratt now husband of Lydia Pratt, widow and exec. of John to Samuel Parsons, citizen and leatherseller>
Bowder Francis s Peter, Lamburne [?Brk or Ess]† to William Grove 25 Aug 1673
Bowen Benjamin s Henry, Llanelli, Gla, gentleman† to William Miller 4 Aug 1668
Bowers Thomas s Samuel, Hanwell, Oxf, yeoman to Thomas Obbinson 5 Mar 1700/1 <4 Aug 1703 turned over to John Obbinson; 2 Oct 1704 to George Gerrard, citizen and salter>
Bowes Samuel s Thomas, citizen and turner to Daniel Scott 14 Oct 1702
Bowles Richard s John, citizen and ...† to John Harrison 26 Apr 1692
Bowles Stevens s Thomas, citizen and joiner to Samuel Savage 14 Mar 1743/4
Bowles William s Valentine, 'Deane', Ken, grocer to Edward Parsons 14 May 1689
Bowman James s Isaac, St Katherine by the Tower, Mdx, brewer to Thomas Snape 18 Aug 1634
Bowman John s William, Stanstead Abbots, Hrt, yeoman to John Yarling 24 Jul 1656
Bowry Thomas s Thomas, Horton, Bkm, yeoman to Thomas Gerrard 1 Feb 1702/3 <20 Nov 1705 turned over to John Argins>
Bowtell Josiah s Abraham, Burton, War, clerk† to Joseph Muston 20 Nov 1645
Bowyer John s Thomas, Kidderminster, Wor, weaver to Robert Gunsun 5 Apr 1655
Bowyer Samuel s John, Whitechapel, Mdx, cordwainer to John Harding 2 Apr 1717 <11 Apr 1720 turned over to John Bourne, citizen and weaver>
Bowyer William s William to his father 28 Jul 1635
Boyse Thomas s Thomas, Bewdley, Wor, cooper† to Thomas Nicholls 14 Oct 1641
Bradbridge Joseph s Joseph, Reading, Brk, brewer to Richard Clements 4 Jun 1689
Bradford John s John, Yarmouth, Nfk, gentleman to Richard Tyler 3 Jan 1797
Bradgate Jeremiah s Richard, Kirkby Lonsdale, Wes, tailor to Daniel Mann 22 Jun 1664
Bradley Francis s Henry, Nunnington, Yks, yeoman† to John Sims 3 Feb 1674/5
Bradley Francis s Thomas, Wombwell, Yks, yeoman to Robert Bradley 1 Jul 1647
Bradley Robert s Henry, citizen and blacksmith to Samuel Woodfeild 6 Dec 1714 <5 May 1718 turned over to Benjamin Anderton, citizen and blacksmith; 2 Mar 1718/9 to Ferdinand Ladbrooke>
Bradley William s Mathew, Enfield, Mdx, yeoman to John Noble 19 Mar 1637/8
Bradney Jane d Edward, Coventry, War, draper to William Mayne 13 Oct 1692
Bradshaw John s John, Alford, Lin, clerk† to John Twell 4 May 1681
Bradshawe Robert s Robert, Newark, Ntt, husbandman† to Silvester Cordey 2 Apr 1639
Bradshawe Thomas s Peter, citizen and merchant tailor† to Richard Glyd 7 Nov 1638 <bond from Edward Bradshawe, Grays Inn, Mdx, esquire>
Bradstreet Richard s Richard, citizen and pewterer† to Francis Gigner 5 Dec 1743
Bradwin William s William, Watford, Hrt, ironmonger† to Thomas Obbinson 7 Jul 1712 <turned over to Daniel Collier, citizen and fishmonger>
Braffett Joseph s Benjamin, St Clement Danes, Mdx, saddler to William Long 5 Sep 1771
Brandling John s Richard, Kingston, Sry, carpenter to Thomas Hopkins 2 Aug 1703
Brandon Gilbert s ?, citizen and vintner† to John Maxfeild 24 Jun 1668
Brapple Joseph s Joseph, Shad Thames, Sry, mariner to Edward Butcher 7 Dec 1724
Brasier Samuel s Thomas, Ingatestone, Ess, innholder to George Evans 8 Nov 1666
Brasse Lawrence s Lawrence, Great Grimsby, Lin, grocer† to Thomas Obbinson 1 Sep 1718 <turned over to William Hayden, citizen and blacksmith>
Brathwaite James s James to his father 3 Mar 1700/1
Brathwaite James s James, citizen and tallow chandler† to John Harrison 8 Jun 1705 <turned over to Daniel Collier, citizen and fishmonger>
Braventon Mathew s Mathew, Reading, Brk, innholder† to William Cogan 28 Feb 1743/4
Bray Edward s Edward, citizen and weaver to Thomas Obbinson 16 Apr 1713 <turned over to Thomas Higgins, citizen and leatherseller>
Bray Francis s Francis, citizen and brewer to Richard Hodgson 17 Mar 1657/8
Brecknell Thomas Aynsworth to Cleophas Comber 4 Dec 1798
Breed Charles s John, College Hill, Lnd, porter to William Williams 1 Jun 1730
Breind Thomas s Nicholas, South Marston, Wil, gentleman to Marmaduke Doleman 19 Nov 1639
Brenand Thomas s Richard, Chelsea, Mdx, distiller to Thomas Wilson 2 Apr 1705
Brent James s Philip, Covent Garden, Mdx, woollen draper† to William Cranwell 12 Jun 1704
Brent Robert s Robert, Braintree, Ess, gentleman to Robert Clay 27 Aug 1696

Brereton Ralph s Roger, Newcastle under Lyne, Sts, esquire to William Perkins 22 Nov 1647
Bretherton Mathew s John, Winwick, Lan, gentleman to Henry Cowper 9 Jun 1659
Brett Arthur s WNm citizen and merchant tailor† to Elizabeth widow of John Hastings 1 Jul 1706
Brett Thomas s Richard, Sawbridgeworth, Hrt, carpenter to Robert Collins 6 Dec 1774
Brett William s William, Ingatestone, Ess, mercer† to George Evans 3 Feb 1662/3
Brewin Robert s Richard, 'Winston', Lei, yeoman to Richard Darker 5 Dec 1720
Brewis William s John, Claycoton, Nth, yeoman to John Warman 20 Dec 1697
Brickley Barbara d Roger, Newcastle on Tyne, Nbl, maltster† to John Coates 11 May 1686
Bricklowe Charles s John, Ewell, Sry, husbandman† to Richard Thornton 15 Nov 1684
Bricknell Thomas s William, Headington, Oxf, yeoman to Mathew Woodward 8 Dec 1708
Bridges Richard s Acton, St James Westminster, Mdx, gentleman to Lancelot Vibart 7 Sep 1730
Bridges Rowland s John, citizen and baker† to Henry Pullen 4 Jan 1719/20
Bridgis Henry s John, St Martin, Mdx, victualler to John Ayscough 4 Mar 1699/1700
Bridgman Patrick s John, Higham Ferrers, Nth, baker to John Blackmore 19 Jul 1709
Brigdale James s Edward, Shrewsbury, Sal, tallow chandler† to William Leach 23 May 1671
Briggs Francis s Francis, Rotherhithe, Sry, mariner† to Lewis Driver 3 Nov 1712
Briggs George to George Goodwin 4 Dec 1798
Briggs Thomas s Thomas, citizen and stationer to Clifford William Phillips 6 Aug 1723
Bright John s John, Melton Mowbray, Lei, smith to Robert Day 3 May 1751
Brimsmed Henry s Samuel, citizen and apothecary† to Nathaniel Eeles 28 Nov 1672
Bringhurst John s Robert, citizen and founder to Robert Combes 5 Jan 1735/6 <9 Jun 1736 turned over to Robert Bringhurst, citizen and founder>
Bringus Saunder s John, citizen and weaver† to Joseph Pett 3 Nov 1701
Briscoe Francis s Abel, Watford, Hrt, tanner to John Burgess 16 Jun 1684
Briscow Henry s Henry, St Olave Southwark, Sry, pack thread spinner† to Francis Barrell Searle 24 Oct 1757 <10 Sep 1761 turned over to Thomas Searle>
Brise Samuel s Samuel, Ratcliffe [Stepney], Mdx, mariner† to Matthias Wheatley 6 Sep 1725
Bristo Henry s Henry, Fulham, Mdx, yeoman† to Samuel Wilkin 16 Jun 1653
Bristo John s John, Cricklade, Wil, yeoman† to John Rumball 7 Jul 1664
Britain Richard ts Richard, Chelsea, Mdx, bricklayer† o Nathaniel Mathews 4 Oct 1791
Britton Thomas s Christopher, Bermondsey, Sry, carpenter† to Aurelius Hodson 7 Jul 1773
Brittridge Richard s William, Kensington, Mdx, yeoman to William Parrett 27 Feb 1704/5
Broadbanck Thomas s Richard, Hertford, Hrt, innholder† to William Gurney 21 Jun 1680
Broadgate Benjamin s Richard, Keswick, Wes, tailor† to Jeremiah Broadgate 22 Nov 1676
Broadhurst Samuel s ..., St John Horsleydown, Sry, shipwright to James Titley 5 Sep 1739
Broadley Charles s William, Hatfield, Yks, yeoman to Thomas Dodswell 22 Nov 1676
Broadway Edward s Edward, Winchcombe, Gls, apothecary† to Thomas Higgins 8 Jun 1705 <turned over to William Gason, citizen and blacksmith>
Broadway Giles s Edmund, Winchcombe, Gls, gentleman to Robert Haden 9 Dec 1696
Brock Thomas s Thomas, Baldon, Oxf, yeoman† to Humphrey Atherton 3 Jul 1665
Brock William s William, citizen and brewer† to Benjamin Free 1 Apr 1717
Brockelsby Edward s Edward, Kirkby, Lin, gentleman to Thomas Kearne 29 Sep 1634
Brograve Augustine s Thomas, Dunham, Nfk, gentleman† to Peter Chysshire 4 Apr 1706
Brograve Thomas s Thomas, Dunham, Nfk, gentleman† to Peter Chesshyre 3 Jul 1707 <24 Jun 1709 turned over to Edward Bee, citizen and painter stainer>
Broksby Obadiah s John, Leicester, Lei, mercer to William Mayne 20 Sep 1690
Bromhall John s John, 'Witchwall Bank', Chs, gentleman† to Peter Pickering 1 Mar 1670/1
Bromley James s James, Balterley, Chs, gentleman to Samuel Wright 2 Dec 1723
Bromsall John s Thomas to his father 1 Feb 1696/7
Bromsall Thomas s Thomas, citizen and cutler to William Gurney 14 Jul 1687
Bromsall Thomas s Thomas to his father 1 Oct 1722
Bromsgrave Arthur s William, 'Horne', Wor, gentleman to Robert Mathewes 8 Apr 1662
Bromwich Thomas s Thomas, Hillmorton, War, gentleman to Mary widow of Thomas Rencher 6 Jun 1709
Bromwich William s Thomas, Hillmorton, War, gentleman to William Mayne 5 Feb 1699/1700 <27 Nov 1702 turned over to Mary widow of Thomas Rencher>
Brond John s Samuel, Dedham, Ess, clothier† to Michael Warren 3 Aug 1671
Brooke Henry s Henry, Collier's End [Standon], Hrt, gentleman to William Hayden 19 May 1687

Brooke William s William, citizen and merchant tailor to Anthony Brooke 18 Dec 1646
Brooker Edward s Robert, 'Brockson', Ken, yeoman to Jeremy Lenton 2 Jul 1640
Brookes Benjamin s ..., Oundle, Nth, yeoman† to William Egerton 6 Nov 1710
Brookes Christopher s Samuel, citizen and goldsmith† to William Miller 4 Sep 1678
Brookes Edmund s Robert, Heckmondwike, Wry, clothier to John Webster 29 Sep 1629
Brookes Henry s Henry, North Mimms, Hrt, gentleman to Robert Brisco 13 May 1641
Brookes John s John, Holborn, Mdx, cordwainer† to John Harrison 21 Jun 1666
Brooks Edward s Thomas, Churchill, Oxf, farmer to Richard Savage 29 Nov 1764
Brooks Richard s Richard, Artillery Lane, Mdx, shoemaker to Henry Stent 6 May 1788
Brooks Turpin Griffith s Nicholas, Ratcliffe, Mdx, waterman to Jonas Lawrence 4 Oct 1748
Broome Richard s Benjamin, citizen and weaver† to John Ricketts 1 Oct 1722
Broster Jabez s Jabez, Ross, Hef, saddler† to Mary widow of William Allen 3 May 1725
<1 Jul 1728 turned over by Peter Mellin, exec. to John Shipman, citizen and feltmaker>
Broughton Leonard s Jeremiah, Seawell [Blakesley], Nth, yeoman to Thomas Ford 29 Aug 1633
Broughton Robert s ..., St Botolph Aldersgate, Lnd, carpenter to James Miller .. Apr 1662
Broughton Samuel s Samuel, Oundle, Nth, weaver to Ellen widow of John Keywood 5 Feb 1704/5
Broughton William s William, Holborn, Mdx, yeoman to Charles Crosier 4 Jul 1715
Brown Daniel s John, Nailstone [? *in Ms* 'Knavestone'], Lei, grazier to James Jenner 3 Jun 1777
Brown Edward s Richard, North Mimms, Hrt, baconman to William Tenter 3 Aug 1713
Brown Francis s John, St Thomas Southwark, Sry, carpenter to George Harlow 11 Jul 1775
Brown Samuel s George, Stepney, Mdx, ropemaker to William Tally 1 Feb 1730/1
Brown Thomas s Thomas, Hollowell, Nth, farmer† to William Lucas 7 Jun 1736
Brown William s Benjamin, St Sepulchre, Lnd, carman to George Harlow 2 Sep 1777
Browne Daniel s George, citizen and joiner† to John Bradstreete 13 Jul 1636
Browne Daniel s John, Painswick, Gls, yeoman to Thomas Hatton 7 Feb 1643/4
Browne Daniel s Thomas, Earith, Hun, waterman to William Bateman 21 Feb 1647/8
Browne Erasmus s Alexander, Westminster, Mdx, cordwainer to Henry Bullock 28 Jul 1650
Browne John s John, Longdon, Sts, husbandman to Thomas Harrison 4 Sep 1641
Browne John s Ralph, St Andrew Holborn, Lnd, white baker to William Knight 2 Aug 1644
Browne John s Richard, Uxbridge, Mdx, cordwainer to Samuel Hamond 5 Nov 1674
Browne John s Benjamin, Winwick, Hun, husbandman to James Teale 24 May 1692
Browne John s Francis, Kingston, Sry, husbandman to Thomas West 7 Mar 1697/8
Browne Philip s Ralph, Holborn, Mdx, baker† to William Knight 4 Jan 1642/3
Browne Robert s Thomas, Holborn, Mdx, gentleman to William Ayres 30 Sep 1668
Browne Samuel s Samuel, St Martin in the Fields, Mdx, gentleman† to John Ferne 2 Dec 1670
Browne Samuel s Devereux, Winstone, Gls, husbandman to John Harrison 21 Jun 1693
Browne Thomas s John, 'Sarfield', Hrt to Thomas Anckle 24 Jun 1633
Browne Thomas s Thomas, citizen and leatherseller to William Dwight 29 Sep 1633
Browne Thomas s George, Windermere, Wes, husbandman to Charles Goodman 1 May 1663
Browne William s John, Astbury, Chs, yeoman to John Gainsford 9 Jan 1638/9
Browne William s John, Basing, Ham, gentleman to William Massey 13 Jul 1664
Browne William s Robert, Penn, Bkm, yeoman† to William Alden 2 Dec 1670
Brownesmith Benjamin s William, Lnd, clerk† to Anthony Philpe 23 Nov 1648
Browning John s John, Chiswell Street, Mdx, brewer† to Thomas Underwood 7 Jul 1778
Brumley Robert s Edward, Lambeth, Sry, shoemaker to Thomas Searle 5 Aug 1723
Brummedge James s Thomas, Brilley, Hef, yeoman† to John Rowland 21 Jun 1666
Brushfeild Thomas s William, East Norton, Lei, grazier to Henry Hill 15 Aug 1681
Bryan John s Thomas, Yelvertoft, Nth, tallow chandler to William Hulls 3 Jan 1684/5
Bryan John s John, St Faith, Lnd, grocer to ... Scollough 8 Jan 1767
Bryan John s John, Newgate Street, Lnd to his father 1 Jan 1793 <4 Aug 1795 turned over
to Philip Thompson, citizen and butcher>
Brymer John to John Russel 5 Apr 1785
Brynton John s Richard, Worcester, Wor, dyer† to Nicholas Beckitt 13 Nov 1656
<bond from Edward Browning, Cambridge, Cam, gentleman>
Buck Mary d John, Hampton, Mdx, clothworker to Grace Clare 5 Mar 1732/3
Buck Thomas s Leonard, Chatham, Ken, mariner to Jonas Watts 7 Jun 1714 <4 Mar 1714/5
turned over to William Robinson, citizen and merchant tailor>
Buckby Thomas s Thomas, Maidwell, Nth, yeoman to James Wood 2 Jan 1655/6

Bucken Isaac s Abraham, Bethnal Green, Mdx, weaver to Edward Furness 2 Feb 1741/2
Buckingham Thomas s Richard, Ratcliffe, Mdx, blockmaker to Joseph Petty 1 Mar 1735/6
Buckland Thomas s James, citizen and draper to Thomas Brushfield 10 Mar 1690/1
Buckler Nicholas s Thomas, Dorchester, Dor, tailor† to William Hewett 25 Jul 1648
Buckler William s Thomas, 'Wilconin', Dor† to Thomas Lawrence 12 Mar 1641/2
Buckley Nicholas s John, Newdigate, Sry, gentleman to William Steeres 17 Mar 1667/8
Buckstone George s Thomas, Burton Dassett, War, husbandman to Thomas Hatton 6 Jul 1641
Budd George s George, citizen and salter to John Mathew 1 Sep 1651
Budd William s William, Stony Stratford, Bkm [? *in Ms* 'Nth'], gentleman to Henry Wine 6 Sep 1659
Bugby John s John, Arthingworth, Nth, yeoman to John Ascough 13 Jul 1680
Buggie Francis s Francis, Gawcott, Bkm, blacksmith to Henry Wine 1 Jun 1657
Bull alias Leech John s Thomas, St Botolph Bishopsgate, Lnd, soap boiler to Daniel Clarebutt 14 Oct 1646
Bull John s William, citizen and poulterer to Richard Barnard 13 Jul 1654
Bull John s John, Little Waldingfield, Sfk, clothier to Richard Warde 19 Aug 1670
Bull John s John, citizen and merchant tailor to Edward Palmer 1 Aug 1677
Bull Nicholas s John, Bishops Sutton, Ham, yeoman to John Hooker 11 Sep 1656
Bull Richard s Richard, citizen and tallow chandler to John Bryan 16 May 1661
Bull Richard s William, citizen and haberdasher† to Thomas Williams 10 Sep 1722
Bull Robert s Robert, St Clement Danes, Mdx, coachman† to Richard Parker 27 Feb 1768 <5 Jul 1771 turned over to William Cragg, citizen and butcher>
Bullimore James s William, Oakham, Rut, mercer† to John Child 17 Oct 1676
Bulwer Edward s Edward, Scoulton, Nfk, clerk to Thomas Ross 26 Jun 1650
Buncher Thomas s John, Paulerspury, Nth, yeoman† to Francis Burton 7 Nov 1638
Bunker Charles s George, Garsington, Oxf, labourer to John Radburne 5 Dec 1692
Bunn Francis s Henry, St James Clerkenwell, Mdx, butcher† to Christopher James 29 Sep 1681
Bunny Richard to Charles Dare 6 Jun 1799 <turned over to William Homan>
Burbidge Nathaniel s Thomas, Barking, Ess, yeoman† to Richard Haddon 4 May 1654
Burbidge Richard s Christopher, Byfield, Nth, labourer to James Coates 4 Sep 1753
Burbidge Robert s John, Queniborough, Lei, yeoman† to Brian Ayliffe 23 Mar 1671/2
Burborough John s John, Wicken, Nth, tallow chandler† to William Gurney 1 Jul 1684
Burbridge Christopher s Christopher, Byfield, Nth, labourer to James Coates 2 Jul 1760
Burbridge Denis s Denis, Husbands Bosworth, Lei, yeoman to Walter Wilford 15 May 1668
Burbrough John s John to his father 5 Sep 1715
Burch John s John, Abbots Bromley, Sts, yeoman to Silvester Card 14 Apr 1641
Burchard John s Nathaniel to his father 8 Apr 1746
Burd William s William, Pebworth, Gls, yeoman to William Butler 1 Jul 1635
Burdett Thomas s Edward, Willimoteswyke, Nbl, gentleman† to John Tewer 18 Dec 1660
Burdett Thomas s James, Seven Dials, Mdx, watchmaker to Henry Soames 2 Dec 1777
Burditt Thomas s John, Hackney, Mdx, labourer† to George Wightman 2 Aug 1708
Burge Thomas s William, Cricklade, Wil, yeoman† to Thomas Obbinson 13 Jun 1677
Burges Elizeus s Elizeus, Northfleet, Ken, clerk to Robert Marchant 1 Oct 1647
Burgess Robert s Robert, Lambourne, Ess, farmer to Elizabeth widow of Francis Leach 25 Feb 1769
Burgis Anthony s Elizeus, Southfleet, Ken, clerk to Robert Marshall 10 Oct 1654
Burgis Edward s Edward, Cheshunt, Hrt, yeoman to John Burgis 19 Nov 1655
Burgis John s John, Watford, Hrt, grocer to Samuel Belchamber 24 Jun 1653
Burgis Richard s William, Tur Langton, Lei, yeoman to Thomas Cose 7 Aug 1656
Burgis John s Thomas, 'Godsport', Alverstoke, Ham, blacksmith to Robert Driver 8 Aug 1687
Burkett Charles s William, Westminster, Mdx, labourer to Edward Clarke 27 Jul 1756
Burmbie Richard s Thomas, Wyton, Hun, yeoman to Edward Barker 25 Feb 1647/8
Burnell John s Richard, Aldeby, Nfk, gentleman to William Greenupp 4 Jan 1649/50
Burniston Jonathan s Robert, citizen and glover to John Woodward 11 Apr 1715 <8 Dec 1718 turned over to Edward Rose, citizen and haberdasher>
Burnley Henry s Nicholas, Burnley, Lan, mercer† to Thomas Hatton 1 Apr 1639
Burnley William s William, Ratcliffe, Mdx, mealman to Jonas Watts 7 Sep 1719
Burrard John s John, citizen and apothecary† to Richard Dale 3 Nov 1718
Burrell John s Richard, Gainford, Dur, butcher to William Collier 7 Jul 1712

Burrell Walter s ?, Cuckfield, Ssx, ? to Peter Pickering ? 1670
Burrett Simon s John, St Giles in the Fields, Mdx, yeoman to William May 10 Dec 1694
Burron John s Arthur, Warrington, Lan, gentleman† to Peter Pickering 27 Apr 1685
Burrow Francis s John, Sherborne, Dor, tailor to Thomas Burrow 3 Apr 1693
Burrow Thomas s John, Sherborne, Dor, tailor to Joseph Rydout 25 Jun 1678
Bursill Richard s George, Brentford, Mdx, butcher to Richard Savage 6 Jul 1779
Burton George s Henry, Kensington, Mdx, carpenter to Francis Robins 7 Jun 1743 <2 Oct 1744 turned over to Thomasine widow of John Williams>
Burton Henry s William, Killinghall, Yks, yeoman to Peter Prince 2 Dec 1656
Burton Henry s Henry to his father 11 Jan 1683/4
Burton Isaac s Isaac, Long Lane, Southwark, Sry, farmer to William Long 7 Aug 1787
Burton John s Christopher, Stewkley, Bkm, yeoman† to Samuel Bedwell 21 May 1674
Burton John s Samuel, Thurnham, Ken, gentleman to Peter Cheshire 25 Jul 1699
Burton Joseph s William, Killinghall, Yks, yeoman† to Peter Prince 8 Jan 1660/1
Burton Nathaniel s John, Winceby, Lin, gentleman† to Anthony Palmer 7 Jun 1659
Burton William s John, Thame, Oxf, labourer† to Robert Boucher 14 Feb 1703/4
Bury Samuel s Samuel, Stanford on Teme, Wor, miller to Mary widow of George Bellis 2 Oct 1765 <3 Apr 1769 turned over to Mary Bellis, exec. of same>
Bush Daniel s Benjamin, Barking, Ess to John Davenport 3 Oct 1715
Bush Henry s Henry, Hawkwell, Ess, yeoman† to William Hedgeland 1 Nov 1771 <4 Feb 1774 turned over to James Hull Pye, citizen and fishmonger>
Bush James s John, 'Chacehurst', Hrt, woolcomber† to William Heather 6 Nov 1721
Bush John s George, citizen and brewer to Thomas Davies 13 Aug 1650
Bush John s James, Greenwich, Ken, maltster to Jonas Watts 5 Sep 1715 <7 Nov 1720 turned over to Richard Walker>
Bush John s John, Giltspur Street, St Sepulchre, Lnd, planemaker to his father 5 Mar 1771
Bushell Benjamin s Joseph, St Martin in the Fields, Mdx, tailor to William Gurney 24 Feb 1682/3
Bushell Samuel s Joseph, St Martin in the Fields, Mdx, slopseller to Jeremiah Broadgate 9 Oct 1685
Bushnell John s John, Lnd, orange merchant to Mary widow of Vincent Peach 4 Apr 1749
Buskin John s Thomas, Bedford, Bdf, labourer to Robert Cooke 23 Sep 1689
Butcher Edward s John, Astrop [King's Sutton], Nth, yeoman to Daniel Dale 4 Aug 1712 <2 Aug 1714 master† turned over by Thomas Hedges, exec. to Richard Pountney>
Butcher Humphrey s John, Great Horwood, Bkm, yeoman to John Bavin 7 May 1664
Butcher John s Richard, Wolvercote, Oxf, husbandman to Ellen widow of Thomas Noble 29 Jul 1647
Butcher Richard s Richard, Wolvercote, Oxf, husbandman† to Robert Butcher 21 Oct 1656
Butcher Robert s Richard, Wolvercote, Oxf, husbandman to Ellen Noble, widow 5 Dec 1645
Butcher Robert s Robert to his father 1 May 1676
Butcher Robert s Robert, Hoxne, Sfk, gentleman† to Hugh Lake 8 Nov 1750
Butler George s William, Aston, Brk, gardener to Henry Soames 3 Jul 1781
Butler Thomas s Thomas, Leigh, Ken, yeoman to George Bellis 3 Jul 1721
Butler Thomas s Thomas, St Giles, Mdx, bricklayer to George Harlow 6 May 1774
Butler William s Richard, Birlingham, Wor, yeoman to Thomas Harrison 2 Sep 1635
Butler William s William to his father 22 Nov 1659
Butler William s John, Southwark, Sry, weaver to Edward Clarke 10 May 1749
Butt John s Henry, citizen and tallow chandler† to John Warman 4 Apr 1709
Butterfeild Richard s Richard, Chesham, Bkm, husbandman to Richard Wilkinson 10 Jan 1648/9
Butterfeild Thomas s Ralph, citizen and tallow chandler to Thomas Vaughan 22 Nov 1660
Butterfield John s William, Barking, Ess, butcher to Robert Lloyd 11 Jul 1775
Butterwick Samuel s Thomas, Yarm, Yks, felmonger to Samuel Fitch 1 Jun 1713
Butterworth Isaac s Bartholomew, Bethnal Green, Mdx, perukemaker to Jacob Butterworth 4 Feb 1783 <2 Aug 1785 turned over to John Fearon>
Butterworth Jacob s Bartholomew, Bethnal Green, Mdx, perukemaker to John Mansell 21 Jan 1774
Buttler Hugh s Hugh, St Saviour Southwark, Sry, clerk to Robert Wilcocks 1 May 1644
Button John s Ralph, Wilton, Wil, clothier† to Samuel Phillips 7 Oct 1742
Button Richard s John, St ? in the Fields, Mdx, tallow chandler to Robert Mathewes 21 Oct 1668
Butts John s John, Shoreditch, Mdx, plasterer to William Fowler 1 Sep 1747 <11 Oct 1748 turned over to Thomas Whitton>

TALLOW CHANDLERS' APPRENTICES

Byard Bartholomew s Samuel, citizen and baker to Nathaniel Winchester 31 Jan 1686/7
Byard Ezekiel s Humphrey, Birmingham, War, blacksmith to Thomas Chambers 9 Dec 1679
Byard James s Bartholomew, Mowsley, Lei, yeoman to Nicholas Beckitt 7 Oct 1657
Bye Thomas s Thomas, Chelsea, Mdx, butcher† to Edmund Hall 20 Oct 1685
Byron James s William, citizen and gunmaker to John Clarke 13 Jan 1706/7

Caddy William s William, Rougholme [Muncaster], Cul, yeoman to John Caddy 3 Mar 1700/1
Cadell Bartholomew s Mathew, Brackley, Nth, yeoman to James Harding 15 Jul 1651
Calcot Joseph s Oliver, Thame, Oxf, butcher† to William Mayne 13 Sep 1687
Calcott Thomas s John, Dinton, Bkm, butcher to William Mayne 2 Dec 1696
Calcott William s Oliver, Thame, Oxf, butcher† to William Mayne 22 Apr 1685
Calladine Thomas s Thomas, Lenton, Ntt, basketmaker† to Edmund Hunt 27 Dec 1669
Callant John s Silas, Maidstone, Ken, gentleman to David Heywood 29 Mar 1683
Callant Robert s Robert, Lnd, merchant† to David Heywood 3 Oct 1709
Callaway Richard s Charles, Knightsbridge, Mdx, innholder† to Joseph Wedgebrough 5 Mar 1721/2
Calvert John Davies s James, Shadwell, Mdx, shipwright to Joseph Barlow 22 Mar 1774
<5 Aug 1777 turned over to Anthony Stoakes Wormull, citizen and saddler>
Cambrook James s Thomas, Walthamstow, Ess, shoemaker to Richard Collins 7 Jan 1775
Camp James s William, Cheshunt, Hrt, tanner† to Thomas Broadbank 16 Aug 1711
Camp Stephen s James, Barkway, Hrt, collarmaker to Francis Leech 15 Aug 1764
Campe George s George, Knebworth, Hrt, yeoman to John Gast 15 Mar 1643/4
Camper Burford s Edmund, Shadwell, Mdx, victualler to Thomas Cave 20 Dec 1763
Campion John s Robert, St Luke Old Street, Mdx, victualler to Richard Wiggins 7 Nov 1775
Campion Robert s William, Stoke, Nth, yeoman to Thomas Stiles 29 Sep 1633
Cannell John s John to his father 23 May 1692
Cannell Samuel s Edward, Brampton, Nth, yeoman† to John Cannell 14 Jun 1671
Cannon Josiah s Erasmus, Dunmow, Ess, tanner to James Westall 3 May 1743
Cantrell Thomas s John, St Gregory, Lnd, baker to Richard Dale 1 Dec 1707
Capell Abraham s Garrett, East Smithfield, Mdx, distiller to George Laman 6 Aug 1651
Capell Frank s Robert, St George Hanover Square, Mdx, gentleman† to James Westall 7 Mar 1748/9
Caper James s James, Westhoughton [Deane], Lan, brickmaker to George Staines 9 Nov 1669
Capett Thomas s Thomas, Pilsgate [Barnack], Nth, gentleman to Thomas Stone 23 Apr 1658
Caplinn Charles s William, St Margaret Westminster, Mdx, carpenter to William James 3 May 1745
Capon Simon s Richard, citizen and blacksmith† to Thomas Taylor 6 Sep 1678
Cappe Edward s Humphrey, Saldon [Mursley], Bkm, yeoman to Andrew George 14 Dec 1637
Carew George s Thomas, Haccombe, Dev, esquire to Nicholas Charlton 17 Jun 1654
Carey Anthony s John, West Wellow, Wil, husbandman to Silvester Cordey 18 Apr 1638
Carlton Erasmus s William, Dullingham, Cam, yeoman to Thomas Hibens 4 Mar 1643/4
Carlton Robert s Robert, Retford, Ntt, tanner† to Mathew Woodward 9 Dec 1695
Carpenter Charles s Robert, Marlborough, Wil, tobacconist† to Thomas Woollhead 10 May 1690
Carpenter Edmund s William, citizen and currier to Robert Matthewes 7 Jun 1686
Carpenter George s George, Bermondsey, Sry, trotterman to John Gilgrest 2 Dec 1717
Carpenter John s Richard, Dilwyn, Hef, yeoman to Edward Boyce 14 Feb 1637/8
Carpenter Samuel s John, St Martin in the Fields, Mdx, bodicemaker to Richard Cooper 3 Oct 1670
Carr George s William, Jevington, Ssx, clerk to John Child 12 Jun 1684
Carre George s John, Hampstead, Mdx, baker† to John Burges 6 Dec 1637
Carrington Pilley s James, Guisborough, Yks, gentleman† to Thomas Steevens 31 May 1681
Carrique Charles s Thomas, Lnd, merchant† to Edward Pendlebury 24 Mar 1680/1
Carroll Joseph s Thomas, Bermondsey, Sry, victualler to John Hills 2 Aug 1738
Carroll Nathaniel s Joseph, St John Horsleydown, Sry to his father 1 Jan 1770
Carryer Richard s Richard, Wincanton, Som, diamond cutter to John Tovey 14 Sep 1758
<4 Jun 1764 turned over to Joseph Hunt, citizen and clothworker>
Carter Charles s Francis, citizen and clothworker to Lancelot Vibert 6 Aug 1711
Carter Durban s George, Brill, Bkm, gentleman† to Henry Durban 7 Apr 1701
Carter Felix s Felix, Cowley, Mdx, yeoman† to Edward Tibbey 22 Mar 1647/8
Carter Henry s Henry, Upper Clatford, Ham, wheelwright to Robert Southwood 2 Dec 1674
Carter James s Walter, St Martin in the Fields, Mdx, blacksmith† to Lawrence Carter 10 Jan 1708/9

Carter James s John, Lnd, gentleman to Joseph Booth 1 Apr 1725 <21 May 1728 turned over to Samuel Higgs, citizen and baker>
Carter John s William, Moreton in the Marsh, Gls, innkeeper to Samuel Wilkin 14 Jun 1649
Carter John s John, Hexton, Hrt, yeoman to Josias Hobbs 9 May 1651
Carter John s Richard, Wallingford, Brk, innholder to Petley Wyborne 30 Apr 1663
Carter John s William, St Clement Danes, Mdx, yeoman† to Randolph Watson 1 Apr 1695
Carter John s John, citizen and tallow chandler† to Eleanor widow of John Carter 5 Feb 1721/2
Carter John s John, Stone, Bkm, yeoman to Henry Soames 3 Oct 1780
Carter Joseph s Henry, Richmond, Sry, gentleman to Humphrey King 19 Jun 1671
Carter Joseph s William, Soho, Mdx, joiner† to Joseph Lasinby 6 Mar 1711/12 <turned over to Bartholomew Bonner, citizen and merchant tailor>
Carter Lawrence s Lawrence, Harborough, Lei, yeoman to Thomas Pitman 29 Dec 1634
Carter Lawrence s Walter, Stanford, Brk, yeoman to Henry Wyne 3 Jul 1672
Carter Richard s Richard, Whitechapel, Mdx, cordwainer to Thomas Broadbanck 4 Jun 1705
Carter Samuel s Thomas, citizen and grocer† to Thomas Nash 1 Apr 1734
Carter Samuel s Theodore, Stratford, Ess, tallow chandler to William Shepherd 7 Apr 1789
Carter Thomas s Richard, St Giles in the Fields, Mdx to Herbert Homan 16 Feb 1767
Carter William s John, Wootton, Oxf, farrier to Henry Wine 25 Aug 1662
Carter Woolstone s Robert, St Saviour Southwark, Sry, butcher to Andrew Godwin 7 Jun 1687
Cartwright Edmund s Thomas, Bishops Cleeve, Gls, husbandman to Thomas Allen 7 Mar 1647/8
Carvell John s John, citizen and longbowstringmaker† to Samuel Withers 8 Aug 1698
Carvell Joseph s John, Spratton, Nth, butcher to John Tovey 10 Dec 1741
Case Thomas s George, Royston, Hrt, vintner to Edward Leman 24 Jun 1693
Casebert Joseph s Joseph, Stowe, Bkm, brewer† to Jasper Baldwin 18 May 1660
Casswell George s Robert, Brentford, Mdx, vintner† to Thomas Kendar 29 Jul 1680
Caswell Wheat John s John, St Giles, Mdx, surgeon† to Joseph Dorrell 2 Nov 1742
Catchpole William s Gabriel, Ipswich, Sfk, gentleman to Ralph Humfreys 9 Jul 1647
Cater Henry s Roger, Melksham, Wil, clothworker to Thomas Stephenson 18 May 1692
Cater John s John, 'Easmell', War, yeoman to John Smarte 17 Oct 1638
Catkett Nicholas *see* Nicholas Katkett
Caudell Robert s Robert, Bury St Edmunds, Sfk, cordwainer to John Garland 15 Feb 1680/1
Caunt William s William, Thorpe Arnold, Lei, weaver to Daniel Giles 20 Apr 1640
Cave Benjamin s Philip, Banbury, Oxf, brazier to John Meadowes 9 Oct 1662
Cave Newell s William, Normanton, Lin, yeoman† to Daniel Wayne 13 Dec 1705
Cave William s Thomas, Headington, Oxf, yeoman to John White 1 Jun 1702
Cawne Thomas s Robert, Tamworth, War, tallow chandler to Nathaniel Messenger 6 Oct 1693
Caygill Richard s Richard, citizen and farrier to Thomas Hopkins 5 Mar 1721/2 <1 Nov 1725 master† turned over by Thomas, son and exec. to widow Noble, citizen and haberdasher>
Caysell Mathew s John, Orleton, Hef, husbandman† to Robert Munden 22 Jul 1690
Celbe Nicholas s John, All Hallows London Wall, Lnd, porter† to Ralph Humfrey 27 Oct 1642
Ceney Randolph s Edward, Warfield, Brk, clerk to Robert Asplin 17 Oct 1637
Chace Joseph s Richard, St Martin in the Fields, Mdx, salter to James Horton 11 Apr 1682
Chadsey Henry s William, Whitechapel, Mdx, victualler to Samuel Redmire 3 Mar 1736/7
Chadsey John s John, Upper Thames Street, Lnd, chandler to Job Orton 3 Aug 1790 <7 Jun 1796 turned over to Ann Orton>
Chadwell Lamb s John, Cookham, Brk, flower dresser to Peter Greening 4 May 1734
Chaire Henry s Thomas, Lnd, brewer to Roger Kinser 24 Jun 1633
Challener Francis s Francis, Knowle, Sts, gentleman to Samuel Wheeler 1 Dec 1691
Challoner John s William, Stratford on Avon, War, gentleman to William Chesshyre 1 Jul 1713 <17 Feb 1715/6 turned over to Ebenezer Ibbotson>
Challoner Ninian s Walter, St Clement Danes, Mdx, tailor to William Jeanes 7 Apr 1701
Chambers Edward s John, citizen and currier to Thomas Browne 17 Dec 1645
Chambers James s John to his father 7 Nov 1754
Chambers John s Thomas, citizen and tallow chandler† to Thomas Chambers 30 Jan 1667/8
Chambers John s James, Holborn, Mdx, coachman† to John Davenport 7 Jun 1731
Chambers Joseph s Joseph, citizen and shipwright to William Prince 8 May 1699
Chambers Thomas s Thomas to his father 24 Jan 1688/9
Chambers William s Arthur, Pershore, Wor, husbandman† to Thomas Hatton 8 May 1662

Champion Richard s Stephen, citizen and clothworker to Samuel Withers 5 Jul 1692

Champion Stephen s Stephen, citizen and clothworker to Samuel Withers 7 Sep 1687

Champion William s Henry, Bolney [Harpsden], Oxf, farmer to Richard Kirby 6 Oct 1741

Champney John s John, Rotherhithe, Sry, mariner† to Thomas Hawes 7 Apr 1707

Chandler Benjamin s Kenelm, Tewkesbury, Gls, grazier to Thomas Harris 29 Oct 1664

Chandler Benjamin s Nathaniel to his father 1 Jul 1706

Chandler John s John, St Mary Magdalen Southwark, Sry, gardener† to Robert Butcher 12 Sep 1659

Chandler Nathaniel s Kellam, Tewkesbury, Gls, butcher† to Samuel Peirce 11 May 1660

Chandler Richard s Richard, St Martin le Grand, Lnd, chandler to Robert Williams 17 Jul 1647

Chandler Samuel s Samuel, Dundee, Sco, merchant to Thomas Spencer 28 Sep 1670

Channing Robert s John, citizen and apothecary to John Child, jnr. 3 Jul 1721

Chanye William s Thomas, Luton, Bdf, attorney† to Richard Ayres 6 Mar 1698/9

Chapman John s Thomas, Wilmington, Ssx, yeoman to Richard Hill 25 May 1676

Chapman John s John, Belbroughton, Wor, grocer to Charles Dare 5 Jun 1792

Chapman Joseph s James, St Martin Vintry, Lnd, chaff cutter to Charles Brood 5 Apr 1765

Chapman Joseph s Joseph, Shoreditch, Mdx, tallow chandler† to Saunderson Turner Sturtevant 8 Feb 1792

Chapman Richard s Richard, St Sepulchre, Mdx, bricklayer to Ferdinand Ladbrooke 8 Dec 1747 <3 Oct 1749 turned over to William Hoare>

Chapman Thomas s Ralph, Stortford, Ess, yeoman to Thomas Spencer 6 Mar 1675/6

Chapman William s Francis, Prittlewell, Ess [? *in Ms* 'Yks'], potter? to Thomas Hilliard 23 Feb 1682/3

Chapman William s Richard, Petworth, Ssx, farrier to William Hodman 24 Feb 1637/8

Chappell Richard s John, Burcott, Bkm, yeoman to John Ayscough 27 Nov 1679

Chappell William s James, Mansfield, Ntt, husbandman to Thomas Haies 19 May 1670

Chappell William s Jonathan, citizen and cordwainer to John Ascough 29 Sep 1682

Chappman Hodges s William, citizen and barber chirurgeon to Samuel Isted 29 Mar 1673

Chare John s John, citizen and haberdasher to John Lowke 27 Apr 1677

Chare William s James, citizen and butcher† to James Waggoner 27 Sep 1664

Charles Timothy s John, citizen and draper to William Cranwell 19 Aug 1671

Charleton Nicholas s Nicholas, Chilwell, Ntt, gentleman to Roger Price 25 Oct 1639

Charley Joseph s John, Coventry, War, innholder to James Horton 9 Oct 1677

Charlton George s George, Lambeth, Sry, lathmaker to Mary widow of William Hunt 27 Nov 1699

Charlton Nicholas s Nicholas, Chilwell, Ntt, gentleman to Roger Price 25 Oct 1640

Charme Richard s Humphrey, citizen and stationer† to John Shakemaple 24 Nov 1669

Chase Robert s William, Lnd, gentleman† to James Powell 12 Jun 1647

Chater Henry s Samuel, Barston, War, blacksmith to William Chater 3 Aug 1719

Chater William s John, Shuckborough, War, yeoman to William Bagley 24 Nov 1679

Chatfield Jeremiah s John, citizen and tallow chandler† to James Mitchell 3 Jun 1756 <4 Jul 1759 turned over to George Hines, citizen and draper>

Chatfield John s John, Chichester, Ssx, tailor to William Heather 5 Dec 1715

Chatfield Joseph s Joseph, citizen and tallow chandler† to Mary Chatfield 6 Sep 1748

Chatt John s Henry, Edenbridge, Ken to Henry Cox 20 Oct 1642

Chatwin William s William, Swanscombe, Ken, chandler to Thomas Hasted 27 Aug 1655

Chauncey Thomas s Alexander, West Malling, Ken, gentleman to Petley Wybourne 28 Apr 1649

Chaundler Giles s Thomas, Battersea, Sry, tanner to John Meddowes 28 Feb 1649/50

Chaveney Joseph s Peter, Quorndon, Lei, gentleman to Benjamin Brownesmith 24 Feb 1668/9

Cheany John s Thomas, Lnd, lighterman to Thomas Thatcher 7 Mar 1725/6 <6 Apr 1730 turned over to James Prince>

Checkley Thomas s Edward, Gretton, Nth, yeoman to Thomas Parker 20 Dec 1650

Checkley William s William, St Giles in the Fields, tallow chandler to Thomas Smith 7 Dec 1730

Cheeseman Richard s John, Goudhurst, Ken, bricklayer to Christopher Proudlove 24 Jan 1683/4

Cheeseman William s Robert, Tonbridge, Ken, husbandman to Thomas Hopkins 5 Feb 1699/1700

Cheney Thomas s Thomas to John Briscoe 2 Aug 1662

Chesheir Peter s Thomas, Halton, Chs, gentleman to Peter Pickering 16 May 1681

Chesheire Samuel s Thomas, Halton, Chs, gentleman to William Thatcher 5 Jun 1672

Cheshire William s Robert, Rostherne, Chs, clerk to Peter Cheshire 8 May 1695

Chester Granado s Granado, citizen and grocer to Mathew Woodward 10 Jan 1687/8

Chesterman Joseph s John, Chippenham, Wil, yeoman† to Philip Hall 17 Mar 1725/6
Chestroe Anthony s Daniel, Cheltenham, Gls, yeoman† to John Higgs 10 May 1679
Chestroe William s Anthony to his father 22 Aug 1710
Chew Edward s William, Billington, Lan, yeoman to Gabriel Benyon 13 Oct 1635
Chewter John s Thomas, Windlesham, Sry, yeoman to Richard Brice 30 Jan 1632/3
Chewter John s John, Edmonton, Mdx, weaver to Thomas Chewter 7 Jun 1703
Chewter Thomas s Nathaniel, citizen and clothworker to John Chewter 3 Oct 1673
Cheyney Thomas s George, citizen and mercer† to John Prick 31 May 1654
Cheyney William s William, Abingdon, Brk, gentleman to Francis Robins 6 Sep 1725
Chichley Mark s Alexander, Stepney, Mdx, yeoman to Richard Thornton 2 May 1681
Child Daniel s Robert, Heddington, Wil, yeoman to William Pheasant 22 May 1658
Child John s Thomas, Acton, Mdx, yeoman† to Richard Joyce 3 Apr 1660
Child John s John, Newport Pagnell, Bkm, laceman† to William Threader 22 Jul 1691
Child Matthias s Matthias, citizen and dyer† to Edward Burgis 3 Feb 1679/80
Child Samuel s John to his father 3 Apr 1727
Chilley Joseph s John, Heathfield, Ssx, yeoman to Andrew Walker 5 Mar 1644/5
Chinn Thomas s Thomas, Shapwick, Som, yeoman† to William Jenkins 24 Aug 1637
Chinnall John s Thomas, West Ham, Ess, yeoman to Edward Radcliff 3 Oct 1672
Chittock William s Valentine, Old Pye Street, Westminster, chandler to Stephen Flindall 3 Oct 1780
Choice John s Sampson, Oakham, Rut, clerk to Bartholomew Wimberley 5 Mar 1699/1700
Chretien John George s Peter, Bacon Street, Bethnal Green, Mdx to Jacob Butterworth 6 Nov 1792
Christopher Edward s Richard, Newtown, Ham, currier† to John Parker 22 Nov 1698
Christopher Ralph s Thomas, Fisherton Anger, Wil, cooper to Robert Udell 24 Aug 1641
Church Arthur s Thomas, Saxelby, Lei, yeoman to Daniel Clarebutt 29 May 1658
Church James s Daniel, Great Bromley, Ess, yeoman to Henry Hawkes 17 Jun 1650
Church John s Thomas, Sileby, Lei, yeoman to Joseph Sibley 3 Jul 1655
Church John s John, Witney, Oxf, husbandman† to Robert Butcher 3 Jun 1665
Church Richard s George, Overton, Wil to Gabriel Binion 11 Apr 1648
Church Thomas s Thomas, Sileby, Lei to John Church 23 Jul 1663
Claggett Mathew s Thomas, Grove Green, Maidstone, gentleman to Phineas Patershall 13 Nov 1765
Clapcott John s Henry, Winterbourne Abbas, Dor, gentleman to Nicholas Gould 5 Jun 1666
Clapham James to John Frisbee Waites 7 Mar 1799
Clapham John s John, St John, Hrt, yeoman to Joseph Pett 25 Jun 1680
Clare George s George, Newton Burgoland [Swepstone], Lei, yeoman to John Goode 6 Sep 1647
Clare John s Leonard, Great Easton, Lei, yeoman to Mathew Barwell 8 Mar 1682/3
Clare Joseph s George (snr.), Newton Burgoland, Lei, yeoman† to George Clare, jnr. 15 Oct 1657
Clare Samuel s Thomas, 'Beadle', Wor, yeoman to Richard Patterson 28 Jul 1644
Clarebutt Daniel s Mark, Sandwich, Ken, yeoman to Richard Hell 7 Sep 1634
Clarebutt John s Mark, Lambeth, Sry, gardener† to William Tucker 5 Jul 1659
Claridge Richard s Joseph, Warwick, War, cordwainer to Samuel Wheeler 3 Nov 1701
Clark Henry s Francis, Market Harborough, Lei, innholder to William Pannett 6 Jul 1691
Clark John s Humphrey, 'Chester Over', War, yeoman to William Treddar 18 Oct 1684
Clark John s John, Coverley Fields, Whitechapel, Mdx, weaver to Richard Markhall 7 Oct 1740 <6 May 1746 turned over to Mark Trinder, citizen and joiner>
Clark Richard s Richard, Kensington, Mdx, yeoman to John Pattinson 26 Mar 1761
Clark Thomas s Thomas to his father 6 Jul 1730
Clark William s Ambrose, Waltham Holy Cross, Ess, yeoman to George Cooke 30 Apr 1635
Clarke Abraham s Samuel, St Saviour Southwark, Sry, gentleman† to ... Goodman 3 May 1636
Clarke Benjamin s John, Little Baldon [Marsh Baldon], Oxf, yeoman† to Frances widow of Thomas Claro 3 May 1703 <9 May 1704 turned over to William King; 4 Mar 1705/6 to Edward Tomkins, citizen and cutler>
Clarke Charles s Thomas, Barnet, Mdx, butcher to Joseph Wedgbrough 3 May 1725
Clarke Daniel s Richard, Oadby, Lei† to Mary widow of William Minchin 9 Nov 1676
Clarke Edward s Michael, Eton, Bkm, fruiterer to Thomas Searle 6 and 12 Oct 1736
Clarke Gilbert s Humphrey, citizen and grocer to Francis Houghton 5 Mar 1693/4
Clarke Henry s Thomas, Hertford, Hrt, innholder to Thomas Obbinson 2 Oct 1705 <turned over to Thomas Tatlock, citizen and blacksmith>
Clarke James s Richard, Rotherhithe, Sry, carpenter to John Hewer 24 Jun 1659

Clarke John s John, Manthorpe Grange, Lin, gentleman to James Powell 12 Nov 1653
Clarke John s Henry, Combrook, War, yeoman to John Prick 7 Aug 1656
Clarke John s John, Buntingford, Hrt, yeoman† to Augustine Pratt 25 Feb 1657/8
Clarke John s ?, Shipwick, Som† to Brian Ailiffe 1662/3
Clarke John s Henry, Willoughby, War, husbandman to Thomas Clarke 7 Feb 1675/6
Clarke John s John, St Martin in the Fields, Mdx, gentleman† to Andrew Kipping 9 Dec 1689
Clarke John s John to his father 7 Nov 1692
Clarke Joseph s Thomas, citizen and grocer† to Richard Smith 7 Apr 1674
Clarke Joseph s Lawrence, Stoke, Sry, victualler to Thomas Wigg 22 Oct 1686
Clarke Joseph s Francis, Deptford, Ken, gardener to Samuel Withers 5 Dec 1715
Clarke Joseph s Robert, Cloth Fair, St Bartholomew the Great, tailor to Nathaniel Might 7 Nov 1726
Clarke Joseph s James, Hawarden, Fln, labourer to Thomas Searle 12 Jun 1762
Clarke Martin s Miles, Doddinghurst, Ess, yeoman† to John Harrison 1 Nov 1703 <turned over to Daniel Andrewes, citizen and draper>
Clarke Mathew s Isaac, citizen and dyer to John Hunt 2 Nov 1689
Clarke Oliver s James, Tiverton, Dev, innholder to John Sampson 10 Nov 1668
Clarke Patience d Wheatly, Southwark, Sry, glazier† to Edward Clarke 19 Feb 1756
Clarke Philip s Philip, Potsgrove, Bdf, grazier† to Richard Ingram 17 Jan 1677/8
Clarke Robert s Robert, Holborn, Mdx, porter† to Robert Butcher 10 Nov 1668
Clarke Robert s Henry, Craven, Yks, gentleman† to Henry Burton 7 Jun 1688
Clarke Thomas s Humphrey, Willoughby, War, husbandman to Robert Watson 29 Sep 1654
Clarke Thomas s Richard, Doulting, Som, blacksmith† to John Edden 10 Apr 1671
Clarke Thomas s Anthony, Ely, Cam, butcher to James Horton 24 Nov 1684
Clarke Thomas s Joseph, citizen and broderer to George Patridge 4 Sep 1727 <5 Jul 1731 turned over to Henry Marple, citizen and carpenter; 6 Nov 1732 to Alexander Christie, citizen and carpenter>
Clarke William s John, Burnham Norton, Nfk, gentleman† to James Powell 29 Nov 1638
Clarke William s William, Dover, Ken, gentleman† to Francis Marshall 8 Nov 1649 <bond from Ruth Clarke, the mother>
Clarke William s William, citizen and ?† to Edward Tomkins 19 Feb 1673/4
Clarke William s John, Fulham, Mdx, victualler to Richard Fulwood 14 Mar 1702/3
Clarkeson Ann d Alexander, St Clement Danes, Mdx, tailor† to Grace Clare, widow 3 Aug 1730
Clarkson Peter s John, Stepney, Mdx, calico printer to Mary widow of William Allen 13 Jun 1720 <7 Nov 1726 turned over to William Cottrill, citizen and feltmaker>
Clarrow John s Thomas, Ripple, Wor, yeoman to Hugh Miller 1 Nov 1658
Clarson Joseph s Timothy, Breedon on the Hill, Lei, yeoman to John Coker 23 Nov 1686
Claudius John s Christopher, Shoreditch, Mdx, tallow chandler to Samuel Radley 7 Feb 1725/6 <8 Mar 1729/30 turned over to Thomas Radley>
Clay Robert s Robert, Kelham, Ntt, gentleman† to Richard Wooding 11 Jun 1689
Clayton Thomas Lacey s John, Nightingale Lane, Mdx, tallow chandler to David Hippen 3 Jul 1798
Cleadon Peter s Hugh, Hunningham [? *in Ms* 'Huningdon'], War, tailor to Bartholomew Cadle 24 Oct 1660
Cleaver William s Samuel, Oxford, Oxf, mealman to John Bowden 20 Dec 1692
Cleeve John s Giles, Blunsdon, Wil, gentleman to John Turner 20 Apr 1687
Clegg John s Thomas, Liverpool, Lan, mariner† to Thomas Cave 17 Jun 1765
Clement Richard s Robert, Wantage, Brk, yeoman to William Gurney 31 Aug 1687
Clement Thomas s John, English Batch, Som, yeoman to Thomas Roffe 29 Apr 1635
Clements William s Robert, Wantage, Brk, tallow chandler to William Wickins 20 Sep 1680
Clendon William s James, St Martin in the Fields, gentleman to Samuel Belchambers 6 Jun 1667
Clent John s John, Minsterworth, Gls, gentleman† to Richard Worgan 11 Jul 1673
Cletherow David s William, Cirencester, Gls, maltster to Andrew Partridge 21 Mar 1663/4
Cleveland Samuel s Thomas, Hinckley, Lei, clerk to Thomas Rose 7 Jun 1641
Clever Thomas s William, Wavendon, Bkm, gentleman to Roger Price 15 Aug 1638
Clewes John s Robert, Toddington, Gls, yeoman to Edward Flood 17 Mar 1651/2
Clifford Isaac s Peter, St George Southwark, Sry, cordwainer to William Lowen 12 May 1679
Clifford John s John, St Dunstan in the West, Lnd, shoemaker† to Hugh Lake 3 Feb 1747/8
Clift Edward s Edward, Chertsey, Sry, barber chirurgeon† to William Haydon 4 Mar 1705/6
Clifton Francis s Francis, citizen and baker† to Henry Pullen 3 Oct 1720

Clifton Joseph s Joseph, 'Old Bramford', Bkm, yeoman to Thomas Gardner 16 Feb 1642/3
Clinton John s John, Braughing, Hrt, yeoman to John Fisher 3 Nov 1681
Clinton Richard s John, Peasemore, Brk, yeoman to Noah Pilcorne 4 Nov 1634
Close John s Joseph, St Giles Cripplegate, Mdx, yeoman to William Hulls 6 Feb 1698/9
Close John s Thomas, St James, Mdx, coal merchant to John Dickens 9 Jul 1756 <18 Jun 1760 master† turned over with consent of Ann, his widow to William Baker, citizen and draper>
Closs William apprentice to Samuel Closs, citizen and barber surgeon turned over to William Russell 24 Feb 1764
Clothier John s Richard, St Saviour Southwark, Sry, porter to Jeremiah Settle 25 Feb 1639/40
Cludd William s Richard, Uttoxeter, Sts, tallow chandler† to Randolph Watson 2 Nov 1696
Cluffey Thomas s William, Shrivenham, Brk, husbandman to William Hayden 6 May 1680
Clutterbuck Thomas s Nathaniel, Eastington, Gls, gentleman† to William Gurney 15 Jul 1685
Coales Edward s John, Sturminster Marshall, Dor, yeoman to Edward Mathewes 18 Jun 1668
Coare Francis s John, Gawcott, Buckingham, Bkm, butcher to John Merrydale 29 Jun 1688
Coates James s Humphrey, Byfield, Nth, yeoman to Edward Copeland 13 Jun 1720
Coates James s Benjamin, Aynho, Nth to Edward Butcher 5 Jul 1738
Coatham Robert s Thomas, St Giles in the Fields, Mdx, butcher to Anthony Chestroe 7 Nov 1712
Cobb John s John to his father 5 Mar 1676/7
Cobbett Michael s Richard, St James Westminster, Mdx, glazier to Jeremiah Ridge 7 Jun 1736
Cobden John s John, St Clement Danes, citizen and merchant tailor to William Allett 2 Oct 1649
Coching Joseph s Leonard, Wing, Bkm, yeoman† to Thomas Dowdswell 19 Jul 1687
Cock Caleb s John, St Saviour Southwark, Sry, tobacconist to Job Wright 4 Mar 1679/80
Cock Colborne s William, Kingston, Sry, apothecary to Roger Stevens 10 Mar 1726/7 <1 Dec 1729 turned over to Richard Ireland>
Cock Edmund s Richard, Colchester, Ess† to John Jeanes 18 Aug 1664
Cock John s Francis, St Botolph Aldgate, Lnd, yeoman to Henry Cock 3 Dec 1646
Cock John s William, Chesham, Bkm, maltster to Daniel Clarebutt 24 Jun 1655
Cock William s William, Shoreditch, Mdx, brewer to Henry Cock 20 Dec 1647
Cock William s William, Chadwell, Ess, yeoman to Thomas Hasted 28 May 1651
Cock William s Nathaniel, Lea Green, Chesham, Bkm, yeoman to John Bryan 9 May 1673 <struck through>
Cock William s John to his father 6 Sep 1708
Cocke John s John, Baldock, Hrt, maltster† to John Halsey 4 Nov 1695
Cocker Francis s Francis, Edmonton, Mdx, to William Haydon 19 Oct 1691
Cocking George s William, St Giles Cripplegate, Mdx, distiller to Francis Robins 1 Mar 1730/1
Cockram William s David, Cullompton, Dev, gentleman to Nicholas Beckett 24 Mar 1662/3
Cockrie Timothy s James, citizen and barber chirurgeon to John Burgis 29 Jun 1663
Cockshutt John s John, St Botolph Aldgate, Lnd, sawyer to Giles Doyley 4 Dec 1660
Cockupp John s John, Kings Langley, Hrt, yeoman to Joseph Clifton 20 Feb 1671/2
Cogan William s Thomas, citizen and plaisterer to Elizabeth widow of Robert Gresswell 6 Jan 1723/4
Cogdell William s Thomas, St Martin in the Fields, Mdx, bricklayer to John Ayscough 29 Jul 1679
Coggins Thomas to George Goodwin 4 Dec 1798
Coggs John s John, Ruislip, Mdx, gentleman to Daniel Kirton 2 Aug 1697
Coggs Joseph s John, Ruislip, Mdx, yeoman to William Wiggins 2 Feb 1632/3
Coker John s William, St Martin in the Fields, Mdx, gentleman to Mathew Walker 16 Feb 1675/6
Coker Thomas s William, Pollicott, Ashendon, Bkm, husbandman† to William Mickins 24 Jan 1638/9
Colchester Caleb s Caleb, Clerkenwell, Mdx, vintner† to William Cogan 9 Oct 1739 <2 Aug 1743 turned over to John Holsman, citizen and goldsmith>
Colcott Elizabeth d John, Denton, Bkm, butcher to William Mayne 30 Jun 1687
Colcraft John s Robert, Lincoln, Lin, tallow chandler to Hannah widow of William Hill 4 Nov 1740 <6 May 1745 turned over to Francis Slater, citizen and scrivener>
Cole Edward s Edward, citizen and blacksmith to Richard Joyce 4 Feb 1679/80
Cole Isaac s David, Merton, Sry, labourer to William Ansell 1 Jun 1730
Cole James s Andrew, Hertford, Hrt, mealman† to Joseph Taylor 4 May 1790
Cole John s Edward, Chichester, Ssx, yeoman to Daniel Child 2 Sep 1682
Cole John s Solomon, Bermondsey, Sry, anchorsmith† to Aurelius Hodson 6 Jun 1771

Cole John s William, Newgate Street, engraver (citizen and leatherseller) to John Bryan 6 Feb 1781
Cole Stephen s Thomas, Twickenham, Mdx, miller? to John Syms 5 Mar 1676/7
Cole Thomas s Thomas to his father 25 Apr 1683
Coleman Henry s John, citizen and leatherseller to Henry Clarke 16 Apr 1713
Coleman Richard s Richard, Boldre, Ham, gentleman to William Roll 18 May 1669
Coleman Thomas s John, Isle of Wight, Ham, gentleman† to John Palmer 29 Nov 1655
Coles Benedict s Benedict, Leighton Buzzard, Bdf, tallow chandler to William Lucas 8 Jul 1668
Coles Christopher s John, Sturminster Marshall, Dor, yeoman† to Edward Coles 20 Dec 1676
Coles Richard s Thomas, Adderbury, Oxf, clerk† to William Allen 16 Jun 1681
Coles Robert s Eustace, Bix, Oxf, blacksmith to Daniel Dale 28 Feb 1693/4
Coles Thomas s Mathew, St Saviour Southwark, Sry, bricklayer† to John Warman 28 Jun 1686
Coles Thomas s ..., Nth, yeoman† to Mary widow of William May 4 Nov 1706
Coles Thomas s Edward, Faringdon, Brk, gentleman to Joseph Lane 21 Jul 1738
Coles William s Thomas, citizen and cutler to Philip Pickering 3 Oct 1715
Coleson Robert s Nicholas, St Giles in the Fields, Mdx, tailor to John Rutt 4 Sep 1693
Collett John s John, citizen and coach harness maker† to John Dyer 8 Apr 1717
Collett Joseph s John, Wendover, Bkm, yeoman to William Bowyer 7 Jul 1654
Collett Robert s ?, Badbury [Chisledon], Wil, yeoman to William Gurney 9 Aug 1676
Collier Edward s Thomas, Potsgrove, Bdf, grazier to John Tipping 19 Jun 1668
Collier James s Daniel, citizen and fishmonger to John Harrison 26 Jun 1704 <turned over to Daniel Collier, citizen and fishmonger>
Collier James s William to his father 7 Oct 1706
Collier John s William to his father 1 May 1732
Collier Mathew s Henry, Stoke, Sry, husbandman to Richard Collier 13 Jan 1700/1
Collier Richard s Thomas, citizen and goldsmith to Thomas Kelke 16 Nov 1652
Collier Richard s John, Trowbridge, Wil, cordwainer to William Collier 4 Jun 1683
Collier Timothy s Jeremiah, Bradfield, Ess, clerk† to William Greenupp 18 Aug 1648
Collier William s Richard, Trowbridge, Wil, clockmaker to William Bateman 21 Nov 1667
Collier William s William, Trowbridge, Wil, cordwainer to William Collier 24 Sep 1677
Collier William s Richard, Trowbridge, Wil, grazier to William Collier 3 May 1697
Collier William s William to his father 1 Jul 1700
Collier William s William, St James Clerkenwell, trussmaker to Samuel Mackerness 7 Feb 1725/6
Collin Thomas s Thomas, Mortlake, Sry, carpenter to his father 26 Jun 1682
Collin William s William, Peterborough, Nth, grocer to Samuel Wheeler 1 Nov 1708
Collins John s Henry, Ladbroke, War, yeoman to Andrew Partridge 25 Feb 1635/6
Collins John s John, citizen and merchant tailor to William Gurney 26 Feb 1676/7
Collins John s Thomas, citizen and blacksmith to William Clark 1 Nov 1684
Collins John s John, Chelsea, Mdx, tallow chandler to John Pew 7 Apr 1712 <6 Sep 1714 turned over to Robert Thornell>
Collins John s George, Peter Street, Sry, glazier to Ann widow of William Tomkins 4 Aug 1741
Collins John s John, St Saviour Southwark, Sry, millwright to Richard Higgins 19 Apr 1773
Collins Nicholas s Valentine, Hougham, Lin, grazier to William Heather 6 May 1723
Collins Richard s Thomas, Cottesbrooke, Nth, butcher to William Lucas 6 May 1734
Collins Robert s Robert, Cranham, Ess, yeoman to John Keywood 27 Jun 1695
Collins Robert s Robert, Waltham Abbey, Ess, victualler to William Cave 5 Jul 1725
Collins Thomas s Thomas to his father 3 Jul 1664
Collins William s Nicholas, East Garston [? *in Ms* 'Eregeston'], Brk, husbandman to Simon Dawson 15 Jan 1647/8
Collins William s Valentine, Syston, Lin, gentleman to John Wiggley 6 Dec 1708
Collins William s John, Sutton, Sry, maltster† to Anthony Chester 13 Jan 1716/7
Collinson Richard s Thomas, Hanney, Brk, yeoman to John Hulcup 5 Oct 1702
Collis George William s Thomas, Stangate, no county given, butcher to John Hilliard 2 Sep 1783 <turned over to John Pearce>
Colls Benjamin s Brit?, Norwich, Nfk, butcher to Benjamin Howard Merriman 7 Jan 1794
Colverhous John s John, Easthampsted, Brk, husbandman to Robert Fawcett 26 Oct 1671
Comans Lewis s Edward, Stepney, Mdx, tobacconist to Isaac Buttew 3 Apr 1721
Combes John s Robert, Harmondsworth, Mdx, maltster to William Alexander 1 Jun 1730
Combes Joyce s Thomas, Tisbury, Wil, yeoman to Roger Mustian 2 Dec 1639

Combes Miles s James, citizen and butcher† to John Townesend 5 May 1692
Combes Robert s Robert, Harmondsworth, Mdx, maltster to William Alexander 6 Dec 1725
Comfort William s John, St Margaret Westminster, Mdx, coachman to John Sibley 10 Jul 1746
Comport Joseph s Nicholas, Stepney, Mdx, shipwright to William Gaunt 18 Jun 1681
Compton George s George, Gaddesby, Lei, woolcomber† to John Compton 7 Apr 1741
Compton John s George, Whitechapel, Mdx, carpenter to Robert Wyrell 5 Apr 1725
Compton Peter s Peter, Westminster, Mdx, baker to Daniel Man 19 Jun 1679
Compton William s Robert, Deptford, Ken, shipwright to Edward Worgan 7 Nov 1715
Comyne Thomas s Thomas, Medmenham, Bkm, yeoman to John Ayscough 28 Sep 1689
Constable Philip s William, Withyham, Ssx, yeoman to Joseph Sibley 20 Feb 1670/1
Convers Christopher s William, St Martin in the Fields, beltmaker to Richard Ayres 10 Mar 1697/8
Conway William s Thomas, Witney, Oxf, mason to William Smith 13 Apr 1685
Coocoe Christopher s Thomas, Hillesden, Bkm, carpenter to Thomas Hatton 10 Jul 1638
Cook John s Henry, Lnd, packer† to Egerton Henshaw 1 Jun 1719
Cook Thomas s Thomas, St James Westminster, Mdx, victualler to John Johnson 6 Aug 1722
<13 Apr 1724 as late apprentice to Samuel Withers master† turned over to Joseph Withers - struck through>
Cooke Andrew s Thomas, St Margaret Westminster, Mdx, glover to Andrew Godwin 9 Mar 1681/2
Cooke Deodatus s John, Potterne, Wil, gentleman to George Bowyer 29 Jul 1647
Cooke Edmund s Samuel, Waltham Abbey, Ess, gentleman to Thomas Woolhead 1 Apr 1706
Cooke Giles s Thomas, Wood Stanway, Gls, yeoman† to Daniel Wayne 7 Aug 1704
Cooke John s Jonathan, Hendon, Mdx, mealman† to Edward Taylour 18 Apr 1671
Cooke John s John, Hillesden, Bkm, gardener† to John Yarling 10 Aug 1677
Cooke John s Daniel, Holborn, Mdx, yeoman to Richard Ingram 13 Aug 1684
Cooke Julius s Henry, Coventry, War, clothier to Nathaniel Messinger 4 Feb 1684/5
Cooke Peter s Christopher, Misterton, Ntt, woollen draper to Edmund Cooke 30 Apr 1640
Cooke Richard s Richard, Christ Church Southwark, Sry, sawyer to Henry Batten 27 Mar 1683
Cooke Thomas s Francis, Cublington, Bkm, grazier† to Samuel Withers 5 Aug 1717
Cooke Thomas s Thomas, Rotherhithe, Sry, mariner to George Wane 13 Jul 1737
Cooke Thomas William s Thomas, Penington Street, St George in the East, Mdx, butcher to John Phillips 5 Aug 1777 <2 Dec 1777 turned over to Isaac Phillips>
Cooke William s Thomas, Oakley, Bkm, husbandman to Henry Cooke 17 Oct 1639
Cooke William s William, Holborn, Mdx, gardener to John Toms 4 Feb 1640/1
Cooke William s William, St John Street, Mdx, gardener to George Kayman 16 Feb 1657/8
Cooke William s William, Lnd, woollen draper to Gilbert Brandon 15 Jan 1695/6
Cookson John s Edward, Carshalton, Sry, gentleman to William Allen 10 Jul 1767
Cookson John s Edward, Carshalton, Sry, bricklayer to John Cookson 5 Apr 1791
Coombes Thomas s William, St Thomas Southwark, Sry, butcher to William Kelly 6 Dec 1738
Coombs George s George, Spitalfields, Mdx, tallow chandler to William Goble 6 Nov 1800
Cooper David s Francis, citizen and cooper to William Alexander 3 Apr 1732
Cooper Gabriel s John, St James Clerkenwell, Mdx, bricklayer† to Henry Deane 6 Nov 1710
Cooper George s George, 'Elestam', Sal, husbandman† to Thomas Hayes 29 Jul 1663
Cooper Henry s Thomas, Winwick, Lan, husbandman to Ralph Humphries 13 Oct 1647
Cooper John s Thomas, Halsted, Ken, gardener to Mary widow of George Bellis 6 Jun 1744
Cooper Joseph s Joseph to his father 8 Oct 1724
Cooper Richard s Edward, Brasted, Ken, husbandman to Samuel Brooker 17 May 1639
Cooper Robert s Robert, Stowmarket, Sfk, turner† to Thomas Lenton 25 May 1660
Cooper Thomas s William, 'Weedon', Brk, yeoman to Robert Thompson 26 Dec 1692
Cooper Thomas s Isaac, Princes Square, Mdx, gentleman to Samuel Bury 7 Apr 1789
Cooper William s Joseph to his father 2 Feb 1729/30
Cooper William s James, St Botolph Aldgate, Lnd, tinman to his father 17 Apr 1764
Cooper William s John, Tottenham, Mdx, yeoman to John Bailey 30 Jun 1772 <19 Jun 1773 turned over to John Chapman, citizen and weaver>
Cooter Mathew s Richard, Cobham, Sry, husbandman to Thomas Wall 6 May 1656
Cope Joseph s Joseph, St Katherine by the Tower, Mdx, labourer† to George Carpenter 16 Jan 1766 <10 Jul 1770 turned over to John Cogdell, citizen and joiner>
Cope William s John, St Peter Cornhill, Lnd, butcher† to Phineas Patershall 27 Sep 1763
Copeland Andrew s William, Hammersmith, Mdx, tailor to Nathaniel West 5 Jun 1732

Copeland Edward s Edward, citizen and carpenter to Richard Collier 2 May 1698
Copeland James s Edward to his father 7 Jan 1722/3
Cordell William s William, Chigwell, Ess, butcher to John Tovey 10 Dec 1740
Corfeild Thomas s Richard, Whitechapel, Mdx, glass maker to Thomas Bowers 6 Dec 1708
Corne Thomas Denet s John, St Olave Southwark, Sry, mariner† to Ralph White 7 Jul 1708
Cornelius Joseph s Whitwell, Ilminster, Som, glazier to Humphrey King 21 Aug 1678
Cornelius Peter s Peter, Whitechapel, Mdx, draper to Gilbert Cornelius 24 Jul 1644
Cornell Andrew s Samuel, Honeybourne, Gls, yeoman to William Paine 26 Jul 1680
Corney Charles s Daniel, Shelford, Cam, miller to Samuel Dare 9 Nov 1737
Cory Humphrey s Thomas, citizen and goldsmith† to Edward Leaver 17 Jul 1690
Cory John s John, citizen and haberdasher to John Brian 27 Aug 1635
Cosins Nicholas s Nicholas, Byland Abbey, Yks, mason to John Cosins 19 May 1635
Coster Edward s Richard, Walthamstow, Ess, yeoman to Thomas Eve 20 Feb 1688/9
Cotes John s Jeremiah, Foots Cray, Ken, yeoman to Humphrey Rogers 17 Oct 1682
Cotes Nicholas s Jeremiah, Foots Cray, Ken, yeoman to William Massey 8 Oct 1683
Cottell Nathaniel s John, Monkton Farleigh, Wil, yeoman to George Gerard 7 Jun 1714
Cotterell James s Thomas, Twyford, Brk, farmer to Benjamin Mattingly 6 Oct 1789
Cotterell John s Philip, Teffont, Wil, yeoman to Edward Fitz 27 May 1747
Cotterell John s John, St Mary Woolchurch Haw, Lnd, chinaman to John Colcraft 1 Jul 1762
Cotton Nathan s Nathan, Bovingdon, Hrt, yeoman to Thomas Hill 1 Sep 1707
Cotton Philip s Philip, Whatcote, War, yeoman to Mary widow of John Hall 1 May 1635
Cotton Thomas s John, Thame, Oxf, vintner† to Anthony Munn 1 Jul 1675
Cottrell Edmund s George, Fulham, Mdx, gardener to Thomas Bankes 6 Apr 1736
<5 Feb 1739/40 turned over to Henry Wintle>
Couppee Jacob s Francis, Stepney, Mdx, weaver to Isaac Buttew 7 Jan 1711/12
Course William s Thomas, Shabbington, Bkm, husbandman to Noel Whiting 3 May 1681
Court William s Matthias, Waltham, Ken, yeoman to John Harrison 13 Jul 1680
Cousins William s Thomas, Kingsclere, Ham, husbandman to Thomas Sequens 27 Jan 1663/4
Covell John s Thomas, Shoreditch, Mdx, labourer to Thomas Noble 14 Apr 1642
Coveney Thomas s Thomas, citizen and mason† to Thomas Bedell 9 Jun 1640
Coventon John s William, London Colney, Hrt, labourer to George Smith 7 Jul 1741
Coventry Henry Bond s Francis, Carshalton, Sry, esquire to Nicholas Charlton 6 Mar 1672/3
Covert Robert s Richard, Cork, Ire, merchant† to Nathaniel Porter 9 Jan 1687/8
Cowdell George s George, Bacton, Hef, yeoman to John Hunt 9 Feb 1707/8
Cowley Thomas s Samuel, citizen and mercer† to Oliver Gery 22 Nov 1650
Cowling John s John, St James Westminster, Mdx, wine cooper† to Nathaniel Might 7 Mar 1750/1
Cowper Thomas s John, Northcote [Aynho], Nth, gentleman to Joseph Lane 28 Aug 1724
<4 Apr 1726 turned over to William Kentish, citizen and woolman>
Cowsey Thomas s Francis, St James Garlickhythe, Lnd, vintner† to Charles Breed 6 Sep 1748
Cox Ambrose s Edward, Berwick St Leonard, Wil, yeoman to Francis Dyson 25 May 1657
Cox Andrew s Edward, Funtill? [? Fonthill, Wil] yeoman† to William Nelson 27 Apr 1669
Cox Edward s Edward, Mitcham, Sry, gentleman to Richard Hughes 6 Dec 1714
Cox Isaac s John, 'Leningston', Ken, yeoman to Henry Miles 23 Apr 1680
Cox Isaac s Isaac, Newington, Sry, grocer to Henry Miles 12 Oct 1708
Cox, Warrinor alias Richard s Richard, Clatford, Ham, yeoman to William Minchin 16 Feb 1646/7
Cox Samuel s Timothy, citizen and carpenter to John Warman 6 Oct 1680
Cox Thomas s Thomas, Ashton Keynes, Wil, gentleman to Robert Rodway 28 Dec 1648
Cox Thomas s ..., East Sheen, Mortlake, Sry, husbandman† to Mathew Walker 5 Feb 1686/7
Cox William s Henry, citizen and innholder† to William Nickolson 8 Jul 1669 <struck through - 'not bound being under age'>
Coxon John s John, 'Towsey', Oxf, tailor† to Ralph Arnold 8 Sep 1670
Cozens John s John, Beeston [Sandy], Bdf, yeoman to John Delan 29 Nov 1677
Crabb Thomas s John, London Colney, Hrt, yeoman to John Burby ? Oct 1662
Crabball Alexander s Alexander, Lambeth, Sry, cheesemonger to Henry Eastland 4 May 1737
<23 Feb 1742/3 turned over to George Churcher, citizen and glover>
Crabtree James s John, Stepney, Mdx, yeoman to William Badham 28 Nov 1700
Cracknell James s John, Stepney, Mdx, mariner to Phineas Patershall 5 Oct 1742
Cradock John s John, citizen and grocer† to William Cornley 2 Nov 1714

Crafts John s ..., Oxf, husbandman to John Moncke 2 Apr 1638
Craggs Joseph s Edward, Hanbury, Chs, yeoman to Philip Constable 24 May 1699
Crakanthorp Benjamin s John, Foulmere, Cam, clerk to William Smith, jnr. 6 May 1695
Crane Francis s John, Northampton, Nth, yeoman to William Smith 15 Sep 1649
Cranwell William s Edward, Little Paxton, Hun, yeoman to John Luger 22 May 1638
Cranwell William s Bennett, Colne, Hun, yeoman to William Gurney 6 Nov 1654
Cranwell William s William to his father 7 Aug 1688
Crasse John s Thomas, Pattishall, Nth, maltster to Samuel Randolph 15 Oct 1674
Crawley John s William, Lambeth, Sry, dyer to James Tilley 7 May 1733
Cressall Thomas s George, Whitechapel, Mdx, painter to John Makin 6 May 1794
Cresswell Richard s John, Dedham, Ess, grazier† to Sarah widow of Thomas Chambers 4 Feb 1689/90
Crichlowe Richard s Samuel, Cheapside, Lnd, draper to William Cave 6 Jul 1730
Crick John s Thomas, Denton, Nth, yeoman to Thomas Nicholls 15 Jul 1634
Crier Thomas s Alan, Sevenoaks, Ken, yeoman to David Morris 19 Sep 1651
Crittenden Daniel s John, Edenbridge, Ken to Edward Parott 7 Nov 1720
Croft James s Edward, Tredington, Wor, gentleman to James Church 19 Feb 1676/7
Crofts Richard s John, Lnd, gentleman to Robert Kirke 4 Oct 1703
Crofts Richard s Thomas, Darfield, Yks, husbandman to John Knowles 3 Nov 1712
Crofts Thomas s John, Stepney, Mdx, weaver† to Edward Mortimer 1 Feb 1737/8
Crofts Timothy s Timothy, Stratford le Bow, Mdx, scrivener† to Sarah widow of Thomas Chambers 21 Jan 1696/7 <22 Oct 1702 turned over to Thomas Chambers>
Croke William s Alexander, Hartwell, Bkm, clerk to Rollinson Eyans 13 Oct 1720 <12 Nov 1722 turned over to John Wyatt, citizen and haberdasher>
Crompon John s Daniel, Bishops Stortford, Hrt, labourer† to Richard Tirrell 3 May 1725
Crone Hugh s John, St Martin in the Fields, Mdx, surgeon† to John Burgis 20 Oct 1653
Crook Henry s Henry, Rotherhithe, Sry, mariner† to John Hill 3 Feb 1723/4
Crook James s John, St Katherine by the Tower, Mdx, boat builder to Charles Burkett 5 Aug 1777 <turned over to William Abbott, citizen and shipwright>
Crosier Charles s John, citizen and merchant tailor† to Benjamin Speering 14 Nov 1692
Cross William s Charles, Oxford, Oxf, schoolmaster† to John Newman 8 Dec 1712 <3 Dec 1716 turned over to Ralph Parker, citizen and clothworker>
Crosse John s John, St Mary Cray, Ken, husbandman to Thomas Hayes 28 Dec 1668
Crosse John s William, citizen and founder† to Randolph Watson 23 Sep 1674
Crosse William s William, Hornton, Oxf, yeoman to John Moncks 5 Nov 1634
Crouch John s John, Deptford, Ken, yeoman to John Mathew 23 Nov 1648
Crouch John s Thomas, Paddington, Mdx, carpenter† to John Davenport 7 Aug 1721
Croudson Silcox s John, St Saviour Southwark, Sry, blacksmith to William Alexander 4 Oct 1725
Crow Thomas s William, citizen and glazier to Richard Yorke 5 Mar 1721/2
Crowther Thomas s Henry, Sedburgh, Yks, yeoman to William Bowyer 31 Jan 1638/9
Crowther William s Joseph, Staplehurst, Ken, doctor in divinity† to John Warman 4 Oct 1704 <5 Jul 1708 turned over to Ralph Feild>
Crowther William s Edward, Newcastle on Tyne, Nbl, gentleman† to Bartholomew Wimberly 5 May 1712
Crudge Willoughby s Alexander, citizen and vintner to Catherine Woolhead 21 Mar 1744/5
Crump Edward s Ralph, Greenwich, Ken, blacksmith† to Samuel Gulliford 7 Jul 1735
Cuell William s William, St Martin in the Fields, Mdx, shoemaker† to Giles Harris 5 Sep 1734 <5 Jan 1735/6 master† turned over with consent of Edmund Harris, an exec. to William Killingworth>
Culchetch Benjamin to Richard Bedwell 1661/2
Cummins Thomas s Christopher, 'Virges', Bkm, yeoman to Richard Towne 27 Apr 1703
Cunditt Joseph s Sacheverel, St John Horsleydown, cabinet maker† to Aurelius Hudson 7 Mar 1766
Cuningham Joseph s Joseph, Sherington, Bkm, butcher to John Watts 14 Jan 1684/5
Cunningham Joseph s Joseph, Wapping, Mdx, tallow chandler to Thomas Page 7 Mar 1708/9
Curdy John s Robert, Enford, Wil, yeoman to William Knight 20 Feb 1654/5
Curtis Stephen s John, Chatham, Ken, butcher to William Stanley 5 Jul 1703
Cutbert Thomas s Thomas, North Marston, Bkm, yeoman to William Gurney 21 Apr 1666
Cutburte John s Stephen, St Andrew Holborn, Lnd, carpenter to Vincent Fletcher 25 Sep 1673

Cuthbert Samuel s Walter, Gladestry, Rad, yeoman to Elizabeth widow of John Hastings 6 Dec 1703
Cuthbert Thomas s Walter, Gladestry, Rad, gentleman to John Hastings 29 Jun 1688
Cutler James s James, Lnd, factor† to John Ewer 7 Feb 1703/4
Cutt Edmund s John, Wheathampstead, Hrt, mealman† to Mathew Woodward 18 Nov 1672
Cuttler Richard s William, Iver, Bkm, butcher† to William Hunt 12 Jan 1691/2

Dagley Giles s Paul, Merton, Oxf, mason to Andrew Partridge 1 Mar 1646/7
Dagnall William s Richard, Bermondsey, Sry, feltmaker to Henry Myles 14 Jul 1673
Daking George s John, Cavendish, Sfk, farmer to John Gray 6 Aug 1745
Dalby John s Andrew, Stepney, Mdx, butcher to Benjamin Fary 11 May 1660
Dale Caleb s Daniel to his father 5 Jan 1707/8
Dale Daniel s Francis, 'Dorrington', Nth, yeoman to Josiah Ragdale 25 Nov 1669
Dale Richard s John, Wigmore, Hef, yeoman to William Bird 3 Oct 1698
Dale Robert s Robert, Parwich, Dby, gentleman to Charles Loveioy 23 Feb 1685/6
Dale Robert s John, citizen and clothworker to Mathew Barwell 29 Aug 1690
Dale Thomas s Richard to his father 5 Dec 1720
Dalston John s John, Heath Hall, Yks, baronet to Benjamin Tomlinson 26 Apr 1704
Damerell James s Thomas, Stepney, Mdx, mariner to John Sole 3 Feb 1668/9
Dancer Thomas s Thomas, South Mimms, Mdx, husbandman to Thomas Pratt 31 May 1659
Dandridge Thomas s John, Brooks Wharf, Lnd, malt factor to Robert Ekins 9 Feb 1707/8
Dane Edward s Thomas, Horne, Sry, yeoman to Thomas Dane 15 Feb 1649/50
Daniell Jeremiah s William, Colchester, Ess, bagmaker to Jeremiah Daniell 16 Apr 1685
Daniell Jeremy s Jeremy, Colchester, Ess, draper to Henry Hawkes 4 Nov 1653
Daniell Richard s Thomas, Tortworth, Gls, clothier to Richard Backhouse 22 Jun 1680
Daniell Thomas s John, St Olave Southwark, Sry, gentleman to Martin Wheatly 2 May 1715 <3 Feb 1717/8 turned over to Richard Pountney>
Darbey Thomas s Nathaniel, South Ockenden, Ess, gentleman to John Radley 19 Mar 1687/8
Darby James s Richard, Beaminster, Dor, yeoman to George Kitchinman 13 May 1633
Darby James s James to his father 21 Jun 1660
Darby John s James to his father 21 May 1663
Darcheville Isaac s Peter, Bethnal Green, Mdx, weaver to John Axe 7 Apr 1762
Dare Charles s Samuel to his father 20 Feb 1749/50
Dare Charles Wayte s Charles to his father 3 Jul 1798
Dare John s John, Newington, Sry, butcher to William Stayner 2 Sep 1794
Dare Samuel s Mathew, citizen and distiller to Thomas Rawlinson 6 Dec 1725
Dargent James s James, Lnd, merchant to James Rondeau 11 Mar 1740/1
Darker Richard s John, Stoughton, Lei, yeoman to William Cowley 6 Oct 1707
Darker William s Edward, Scalford, Lei, gentleman to William Rice 17 Jul 1641
Darknall Phineas s Phineas, Titsey, Sry, clerk to Richard Rotheram 27 Sep 1647
Darmon Robert s John, Ardington, Brk, husbandman to Thomas Pratt 6 Jul 1648
Darrant Simon s William, St Botolph Bishopsgate, grocer to Mary widow of John Jackson 27 Mar 1663
Darwin Richard s John, citizen and lorimer to William Hutchins 5 Jun 1710 <20 Oct 1711 turned over to John Ellis, citizen and haberdasher; 4 Aug 1712 to Giles Harris; 12 Nov 1716 to Roger Gale>
Daubrine Daniel s Joseph, Stepney, Mdx, merchant to Richard Jannaway 8 Sep 1682
Davenport John s Robert, Paddington, Mdx, yeoman to William Reynolds 4 Sep 1693
Davenporte Bartholomew s Isaac, Smeeton Westerby, Lei, farmer to James Byard 2 May 1665
Davidson James s James, Middle Temple Lane, Lnd, gentleman to Thomas Bord 19 Feb 1762
Davie John s George, Rickmansworth, Hrt, yeoman† to John Burgis 1 Mar 1696/7
Davies John s John, Edmonton, Mdx, tallow chandler to John Dickins 5 May 1752 <1 Apr 1756 turned over to Griffith Pattenden, citizen and merchant tailor>
Davies William s Nicholas, Much Hadham, Hrt, gentleman to Thomas Greene 23 Aug 1654
Davis Benjamin s Benjamin, Holborn, Mdx, tallow chandler to Mary widow of James Greatrix 6 Nov 1744
Davis Henry s John, Redbourne, Hrt, innholder to William Davis 17 Feb 1641/2
Davis Henry s Henry, St Katherine by the Tower, Mdx, mariner† to Richard Fullwood 11 Nov 1685
Davis John s John, Broughton, Fln, yeoman to Ralph Hunterton 4 Nov 1635

Davis John s William, Basildon [? *in Ms* 'Bassingden'], Brk, gentleman to Francis Marshall 17 Jan 1645/6
Davis John s Thomas, Southwark, Sry, feltmaker to Thomas Allen 24 Nov 1652
Davis John s Baldwin to his father 18 Jul 1677
Davis John s Nehemiah, Compton, Brk, clerk to Thomas Burge 8 Jan 1693/4
Davis John s Philip, Monmouth, Mon, currier† to William Lucas 5 Aug 1746
Davis John Bradford s James, Newington, Sry, planemaker to John Bush 4 Sep 1787
Davis Richard s Richard, Stanstead, Hrt, yeoman† to Robert Bedell 29 Feb 1655/6
Davis Richard s John, citizen and salter to Richard Waight 18 Apr 1670
Davis Richard s John, Shutford, Oxf, yeoman to Robert Fawcett 19 Nov 1673
Davis Roger s Nicholas, citizen and clothworker to John Richbell 5 Oct 1637
Davis Samuel s Bartholomew, Newport Pagnell, Bkm, clothier† to John Tipping 19 Jun 1665
Davis Thomas s Thomas, Maidstone, Ken, vintner to Andrew Walker 12 May 1637
Davis Thomas s Thomas, St Luke Old Street, Mdx, weaver to William Johnson 4 Nov 1747
Davis William s William, St James Westminster, Mdx, fruiterer to Thomas Bennett 5 Jul 1708 <9 Feb 1711/12 turned over to William Vaston, citizen and broderer>
Davis William s Robert, Nightingale Lane, East Smithfield, Mdx, smith to Isaac Phillips 5 Mar 1782
Davison Robert s William, Holborn, Mdx, coal merchant to Samuel Snape 18 Nov 1746
Davys Robert s Richard, Colchester, Ess, yeoman to Edward Francklin 30 Mar 1635
Dawbarn Francis s Thomas, citizen and weaver† to William Lowen 9 Sep 1706
Dawson Benjamin s Thomas, citizen and armorer to John Blizard 3 Aug 1686
Dawson George s Thomas, citizen and brewer† to Robert Jackson 8 Jul 1673
Dawson George s Thomas, citizen and feltmaker to Jeremiah Ridge 6 Apr 1696
Dawson John s John, Strand, Mdx, yeoman to Thomas Dane 18 Feb 1649/50
Dawson John s John, citizen and merchant tailor to John Thompson 1 Aug 1709
Dawson Joseph s Thomas, Pulford, Chs, yeoman† to Randolph Watson 28 Aug 1671
Dawson Thomas s Thomas, citizen and salter† to John Brian 9 Jan 1649/50
Dawson William s John, Garsdale, Yks, yeoman to Thomas Kelke 10 Nov 1635
Dawson William s George, Hertford, Hrt, gentleman to Thomas Bugby 31 May 1675
Day Edward s Thomas to his father 5 Mar 1676/7
Day Richard s Nathaniel, Bolnhurst, Bdf, yeoman to Thomas Paine 17 May 1639
Day Robert s William, Wymondham, Lei, yeoman† to William Woollerton 4 Feb 1722/3 <5 Dec 1726 turned over to Francis Robotham, citizen and merchant tailor>
Day Thomas s Thomas, Croydon, Sry, maltster to Henry Pullen 7 Nov 1715
Day William s Samuel, Harmondsworth, Mdx, yeoman to Christopher Leake 19 Jan 1654/5
Day William s Isaac, York, Yks, woollen draper† to Francis Molyneux 11 Apr 1695
Deabunck William s Arthur, Terling Place, Ess, gentleman to Theophilus Folkingham 16 May 1666
Deacrow Benjamin s Benjamin, Enfield, Mdx, gentleman† to Mary widow of William Minchin 26 Nov 1667
Deale William s William, Newbury, Brk, clothier to Thomas Mirriman 1 Oct 1722
Deane Francis s John, Fetcham, Sry, yeoman to Mathew Almey 21 Dec 1634
Deane Henry s Richard, Hampstead, Mdx, yeoman to William Pannet 7 Sep 1691
Deane John s John, citizen and painter stainer to Giles Harris 13 Jun 1720 <6 May 1723 turned over to John Lamplee>
Deane Richard s Thomas, Over Peover, Chs, yeoman to Anthony Moseley 12 Nov 1635
Deane Thomas s Thomas, Burstow, Sry, yeoman to Thomas Lenton 18 Mar 1640/1
Dearmer Elizabeth d Francis, Hitchin, Hrt, maltster to Daniel Hurst 7 Nov 1671
Debat James s John, St Margaret Westminster, Mdx, victualler to Samuel Ellcock 1 May 1721
Dee Thomas s Thomas, citizen and tinplateworker to Peter Grinaway 9 Apr 1716
Deedy John Christian s John Christian, Shoreditch, Mdx, gentleman to Robert French 1 Dec 1795
Deely Samuel s John, Bicester, Oxf, shoemaker to Henry More 10 Nov 1677
Dehew Isaac s Isaac, Southwark, Sry, glass bottlemaker to John Phillips 15 Jul 1752
Deighton William Scott s John, Long Lane, Mdx, tallow chandler† to Saunderson Turner Sturtevant 5 Jul 1796
Dekewer John s John, Sandwich, Ken, weaver to Joseph Lane 1 Nov 1731
Delaney Hezekiah s Elias, St Saviour Southwark, Sry, dyer† to John Meddowes 22 Aug 1656
Delas James s James, St Martin le Grand, Mdx, silversmith† to John Gourd 14 Nov 1748

Delfes Thomas s Thomas, citizen and clothworker† to Francis Rawkestraw 5 May 1690
Delight Peter s Moses, North Hill, Colchester, Ess, scrivener to Daniel Scott 6 Nov 1693
Delivet Thomas s Thomas, Stepney, Mdx, feltmaker† to Isaac Butewe 3 May 1725
Delke Francis s Edward, Dadlington, Lei, gentleman to John Gazeley 7 Jul 1653
Dell Benjamin s Benjamin, Bermondsey, Sry, gentleman to Robert Collins 3 Aug 1748 <7 Jun 1753 turned over to Thomas Nash>
Dell George s John, St Dionis Backchurch, Lnd, butcher† to Thomas Merriman 8 Sep 1763
Dell John s Jonathan, Chesham, Bkm, yeoman† to John Davey 2 Jul 1722
Dell William s Benjamin, Stepney Green, Mdx to his father 2 Dec 1777
Demonsdom Isaac s Peter, Old Artillery Ground, Mdx, weaver† to Isaac Beten 3 Oct 1726
Denby John s Richard, Blackfriars, Lnd, yeoman to William Lucas 7 Feb 1659/60
Denn Andrew s Andrew, Stepney, Mdx, mariner† to William Fowler 25 Jan 1748/9
Denn John s John, St Ives, Hun, gentleman to Richard Reaynolds 20 Jan 1674/5
Denn John s Clement, citizen and joiner to William Coles 4 May 1742
Dennett Thomas s Henry, citizen and joiner† to Philip Pickering 7 Feb 1708/9
Denney Samuel s Nathaniel, Tewkesbury, Gls, mercer to Thomas Heydon 5 Feb 1676/7
Dennis Henry s Henry to his father 2 Apr 1673
Dennis John s Robert, Stepney, Mdx, mariner† to Thomas Hasted 9 Jul 1667
Dennis Robert s John, Enfield, Mdx, tailor to Joseph Cooper 5 May 1712 <2 Mar 1718/9 turned over to Joseph Webb, citizen and baker>
Dennison John s William, 'Anderby Steeple', Yks, farmer to John Scollough 21 Jun 1759
Dennison William s John, Holborn, Mdx, tailor to Thomas Searle 18 Nov 1746
Dersely Walter s Thomas, Kirtling, Cam, tanner to William Wright 5 Jan 1718/9
Desburrowe Richard s Richard, Newton, Nth, husbandman to Walter Clerke 29 Apr 1637
Desortemboc John s Paul, Bethnal Green, Mdx, feltmaker to John Axe 15 Oct 1765
Dettmar William David s Christopher, Oxford Road, Mdx, musical instrument maker† to Samuel Bury 2 Jan 1787
Dew John s Thomas, St Martin in the Fields, Mdx, yeoman† to Richard Wooding 31 Jul 1688
Dew William s Bernard, Shoreditch, Mdx, innholder to Mary Bellis 7 Jan 1777
Dewcem David s Henry, Lambourne, Brk, yeoman to Richard Ingram 1 Aug 1682
Dewick John s Anthony, Mansfield, Ntt, yeoman† to Thomas Hayes 17 Aug 1676
Dexter George s George, East Leake, Ntt, farmer to James Westall 3 Jun 1754 <16 Jun 1758 turned over to Joseph Cowper, citizen and weaver>
Dexter Thomas s John, Wellingborough, Nth, dyer† to Henry Hawkes 7 Dec 1696
Dibley Roger s William, Thatcham, Brk, yeoman to John Turner 11 Sep 1690
Dickenson James s John, Wormley, Hrt, maltster to Lancelot Brewer 1 Apr 1783
Dickenson John s John, St George Southwark, Sry, gentleman to Lancelot Vibert 8 Apr 1727
Dickenson Robert s Mathew, Halton, Lan, yeoman to Daniel Man 20 Dec 1647
Dickeson Francis s William, Spratton, Nth, husbandman to Richard Harding 28 Jul 1683
Dickins Daniel s John, citizen and merchant tailor to William Mellor 7 Jul 1690
Dickinson John s John, 'The Rowe', Eccleston, Lan, gentleman to Peter Pickering 10 Jul 1652
Dickinson Richard s Richard, Abbots Bromley, Sts, yeoman to Richard Parrott 10 Jul 1668
Dickinson Stephen s William, St Andrew Holborn, Lnd, poulterer to John Ballard 14 Nov 1639
Diggle Edmund s John, Chiddingfold, Sry, clerk to Robert Harvy 17 Jul 1658
Diglin William s Thomas, Windsor, Brk, clothier to Thomas Murden 24 Mar 1667/8
Dine Richard Shepherd s William, Weston Street, Southwark, Sry, carpenter to Hannah widow of John Close 1 Apr 1783
Dingley Charles s Charles, Redmarley, Wor, gentleman to Samuel Belchamber 4 Feb 1678/9
Dison Francis s Francis, Kensington, Mdx, yeoman to John Toson 17 May 1642
Diston Jacob s Isaac, Evesham, Wor, gentleman to John Phelps 10 Jun 1656
Diston John s John, Tewkesbury, Gls, yeoman† to Edmund Millton 15 Nov 1669
Ditcher John s Thomas, Wapping, Mdx, victualler† to Thomas Vaughan 5 Oct 1660
Ditcher John s Henry, St Botolph Aldersgate, Lnd, cook to William Johnson 1 Mar 1737/8
Dix George s George, Hardwick, Nth, clerk to George Stretton 28 Feb 1655/6
Dixie William s Beaumont, Bosworth, Lei, baronet to Thomas Price 4 Aug 1685
Dixie Wolstan s Wolstan, Normanton, Dby, knight and baronet to William Perkins 17 Jan 1649/50
Dixon John s George, St Thomas Apostle, Lnd, perukemaker† to John Pattinson 2 Aug 1768

Dixon Robert s Lewis, St Giles in the Fields, surgeon to Mary widow of William Flower 12 Jul 1660
Dixon William s John, St Katherine by the Tower, Mdx, mastmaker to John Phillips 25 Mar 1774
Dixon Zachary s Zachary, Hornchurch, Ess, gentleman to Edmund Barcock 15 Apr 1670
Dobbins William s Thomas, Poplar, Mdx, shipwright to Charles Dare 20 Apr 1773
Dobson Christopher s Thomas, Sutton, Lin, innholder to John Fist 6 Mar 1726/7
Dobson John s John, Bishopsgate Street, Lnd, stationer† to Hugh Lake 7 Jul 1763
Dobson William s William, Styford [Bywell], Nbl, yeoman to Thomas Pitman 7 Nov 1633
Dodd Edmund s James, Tandridge, Sry, yeoman† to Richard Badwell 29 Nov 1658
Dodd George s George, St Giles in the Fields, Mdx, yeoman to John Hooker 3 Jun 1659
Dodd John s William, Enfield, Mdx, tanner to Nathaniel Billings 8 Aug 1655
Dodford Francis s John, 'Chilworth', Nth, yeoman to Samuel Wheeler 15 Dec 1686
Dodington Thomas s Francis, High Barnet, Hrt, yeoman† to William Smith, jnr. 11 Mar 1691/2
Dodson Charles s William, St James Westminster, brandy merchant to Herbert Homan 5 Sep 1739
Dodson James s John, citizen and merchant tailor to Philip Pickering 6 Mar 1726/7
Dodson John s Thomas, Ravenstonedale, Wes, clerk to William Greenupp 6 Nov 1647
Dodson John s Anthony, Ulverston, Lan, husbandman to Ellen Noble, widow 9 May 1650
Dodson Moses s George, citizen and clothworker to Thomas Hodges 17 Oct 1650
Doe John s John, South Lopham, Nfk, baker† to Mathew Barwell 9 Feb 1686/7
Doggett John s Daniel, St Albans, Hrt, felmonger to Richard Joyce 9 Mar 1687/8
Dolafeild William s Francis, St Botolph Billingsgate, labourer† to Ralph Humfreys 10 Sep 1642
Dolby Edward s Edward, Reigate, Sry, gardener to Richard Glyd 14 Dec 1652
Dolby John s William, Galby, Lei, grazier to Thomas Johnson 1 Apr 1728
Dollin Richard s Robert, Wargrave, Brk, yeoman to John Bigg 29 Sep 1634
Dolphin Humphrey s John, Sutton Coldfield, War, gentleman† to Thomas Hawes 5 Aug 1700
Dolphin John s John, citizen and plaisterer to John Rumball 25 Mar 1675
Dommett James s James, West Hatch, Som, farmer to John Cowling 21 Jun 1764 <19 Nov 1766 (master having left trade) turned over to Henry Soames
Donington Thomas s William to his father 4 Nov 1706
Donington William s Thomas, Barking, Ess, yeoman to Thomas Watts 31 Oct 1678
Dorman Joseph s James, St Saviour Southwark, Sry, mariner† to John Sussex 3 Nov 1691
Dorrell Edward s William, Wooburn, Bkm, gentleman to Jasper Geery 28 Oct 1679
Dorrell Joseph s Robert, Mongewell, Oxf, yeoman to James Prince 3 Jun 1717
Dorrell Richard s Richard, St Saviour Southwark, Sry, yeoman to John Palmer 23 Feb 1658/9
Dorrell Robert s Thomas, North Stoke, Oxf, farmer† to Jonathan Leigh 5 Aug 1756
Dorrington Humphrey s William, citizen and tallow chandler† to Elizabeth widow of William Dorrington 1 Mar 1707/8
Doughty James s Edmund, St Sepulchre, Lnd, butcher† to Thomas Nash 3 Dec 1733
Dove Robert s Francis, Covent Garden, Mdx, tallow chandler to Walter Hoare 28 Mar 1672
Dove Robert s Thomas, Shadwell, Mdx, shipwright† to Joseph Barlow 8 Apr 1766
Dover Francis s Henry, Horwood, Bkm, gentleman to James Harding 1 Oct 1652
Dow Robert s John, Little Queen Street, Lnd, hairdresser† to Carter Cook 3 May 1796
Dowbleday Jonathan s Oliffe?, Whitechapel, Mdx, ? to Andrew Halford ? Mar 1672/3
Dowdswell Benjamin s Anthony, 'Kainton', Gls, yeoman to Jegon Mandevill 8 Apr 1678
Dowdswell Thomas s ?, 'Itney', Gls, husbandman to Robert Mathewes 14 Oct 1664
Downes Henry s Henry, St Botolph Aldersgate, Lnd, yeoman to Henry Pauncefoote 25 Nov 1661
Downes Henry s Henry, Bishopsgate Street, Lnd, haberdasher† to John Russell 4 Jan 1780
Downes James s John, Whitechapel, Mdx, collarmaker† to John Compton 1 May 1764
Downes John s John, New Brentford, Mdx, baker† to Richard Butterfeild 10 Aug 1637
Downing Robert s Richard, Putney, Sry, farrier to Peter Leigh 5 Jan 1712/3
Downing William s Joseph, Dunchurch, War, yeoman to Henry Turnish 13 Jun 1715
Dracot Richard s William, Kirby Bellars, Lei, grazier to Sarah widow of Thomas Chambers 24 Jan 1698/9 <22 Oct 1702 turned over to Thomas Chambers; 22 Jun 1703 to William Callcott, citizen and butcher; 4 Jun 1704 to Thomas Taylor, citizen and broderer>
Drage John s Lawrence, Great Easton, Lei, yeoman to Mathew Barwell 8 Mar 1682/3
Draper Daniel s Daniel, Hitchin, Hrt, maltster to John Perrin 20 Nov 1640
Draper James s Francis, Fulham, Mdx, victualler† to Robert Munden 7 Aug 1704
Draper John s John, Lewes, Ssx, yeoman to Richard Hill 8 Apr 1651

Drewett Edward s Edward, St Olave Southwark, Sry, waterman to Samuel Belchamber 30 Sep 1661
Drinckwater Francis s William, Comberton, Wor, gentleman to William Bowyer 22 Dec 1654
Drinkwater Joseph s Timothy, citizen and pewterer† to John Ford 12 Sep 1695
Driver Edward s Edward, Ladbroke, War, yeoman to Andrew Partridge 22 Jan 1637/8
Driver John s John, Ashton Keynes, Wil, yeoman to Thomas Cox 15 Jan 1656/7
Driver Robert s Robert, Gosport, Ham, mariner to Walter Hunt 28 Aug 1673
Drudge Richard s Thomas, citizen and merchant tailor to Robert Tilbury 28 Apr 1635
Drury James s Walter, Market Downham, Nfk, maltster to Robert French 12 Jan 1756
Dry Benjamin s Benjamin, citizen and cooper to Nathaniel Ragdale 13 Jul 1703
Dudeney John s George, Reigate, Sry, baker to Thomas Wall 14 Feb 1649/50
Dudeney William s George, Reigate, Sry, baker to Thomas Wall 17 Feb 1647/8
Dudman John s Thomas, St Nicholas Guildford, Sry, husbandman to John Bromfeild 9 Aug 1671
Duffell George s James, Charterhouse Lane, Mdx, victualler to Henry Soames, jnr. 6 Sep 1791
Dukes William s Francis, Shoe Lane, Lnd, tallow chandler to Henry Soames 3 Nov 1779
Dukeson John s John, citizen and barber chirurgeon to Samuel Hamond 3 May 1683
Dunbar Charles Stewart s Robert, Houndsditch, Lnd, gentleman† to James Wilkie 6 May 1794
Dunbar William to John Bryan 5 Dec 1799
Dunckley James s James, Charwelton, Nth, grazier to Francis Coare 4 Oct 1697
Dunn William s Thomas, Richmond, Sry, gardener to William Alexander 3 Dec 1716
Dunnage Thomas s Thomas, Burnham, Ess, farmer† to Henry Case 5 Jan 1796
Dunton William s James, Ruislip, Mdx, tailor to John Ferne 22 Oct 1673
Dupier Francis Henrie s Lewis, Perrardie, France, yeoman to John Symes 2 Feb 1682/3
Dupuis John s John, Jermyn Street, Mdx, wax chandler† to Henry Soames 6 Nov 1787
Durant Edmund s William, Burnham, Bkm, cook to Richard Bedwell 5 Jun 1651
Durban Henry s Christopher, citizen and vintner to Edward Leman 17 Feb 1675/6
Durdant George s William, Staines, Mdx, gentleman† to Thomas Durdant 16 Apr 1714
Durdant Thomas s George, Cobham, Sry, gentleman† to Mathew Barwell 28 Feb 1695/6
Durnford Thomas s Clark, Whitefriars Wharf, Lnd, potter to John Willoughby 2 Jan 1787
Durvill Henry s William, citizen and blacksmith to Jonas Watts 4 Feb 1711/12 <turned over to Edward Tomkins, citizen and cutler>
Dust Thomas s Thomas, Northampton, Nth, haberdasher to John Ford 18 Nov 1702
Duthort James s John, Grays, Ess, gentleman to Charles Dare 6 Oct 1778
Dutton John s Thomas, Chinnor, Oxf, farmer to Ann Hedges Gardner wife of Valentine Warner 3 May 1750
Dutton Thomas s Edward, Chinnor, Oxf, yeoman to Edmund Belson 4 Feb 1679/80
Dutton Thomas s Leonard, Chinnor, Oxf, yeoman to William Freer 3 May 1682
Dutton William s John, Withington, Gls, gentleman to Samuel Bedwell 3 Dec 1655
Dwight Bernard s Bernard, Colyton, Dev, merchant to William Dwight 14 Aug 1633
Dyer Richard s John, Old Street, Mdx, glazier to Tabitha widow of John Mansell 7 Oct 1783
Dyer Thomas s Richard, citizen and clothworker† to Richard Elsmere 10 Jun 1724
Dyer William s Thomas, Bermondsey, Sry, victualler† to Joseph Carroll 6 Jun 1786
Dyke Peter s Jeremiah, citizen and vintner† to Daniel Kerton 28 Aug 1691
Dymock John s Joseph, Woking, Sry, gentleman to William Parker 4 Sep 1721
Dyne John s Thomas, ...tle, Ssx, shoemaker to John Syms 8 May 1678
Dyson John s Ralph, Leicester, Lei, gentleman to Richard Norwood 1 Dec 1671

Eade William s Jonathan, citizen and merchant tailor to Thomas Shrimpton 8 Sep 1762
Eade William s John, Walthamstow, Ess, esquire to Thomas Shrimpton 1 Jul 1774
Eades William s John, Southwark, Sry, butcher† to Elizabeth widow of Benjamin Free 1 Mar 1735/6
Eadrop Thomas s Abraham, Rotherhithe, Sry, waterman to John Flight 1 Mar 1702/3 <9 Mar 1708/9 turned over by Mary Bowtell, relict and exec. to Mary Rencher, widow>
Eakins Robert s Alexander, Weston Favell, Nth† to William Fenny 24 Oct 1650
Eames John s Daniel to his father 24 Jun 1690
Early Alexander s William, Froxfield, Wil, yeoman to James Patey .. Feb 1706/7
East Charles *see* Charles Ace
East Robert s William, Deptford, Ken, brewer to John Carter 20 Oct 1657
East William s Edward, St Botolph Bishopsgate, Lnd, carpenter to William Eyres 3 May 1676
Eastland Henry s Henry, Epsom, Sry, yeoman to Bartholomew Wimberly 7 Sep 1724

Eastman Joshua s Thomas, citizen and haberdasher to Robert Wilkins 1 Oct 1722
Easton Joseph s William, Bankside, Sry, waterman to William Easton 7 Nov 1786
Easton Thomas s William, Bankside, Sry, waterman to William Easton, jnr. 7 Oct 1783
Easton William s William, St Saviour Southwark, Sry, waterman to Charles Burkett 3 Sep 1776
Eaton George s William, Etwall, Dby, yeoman to William Hulls 30 Sep 1680
Eaton Samuel s Richard, Ampthill, Bdf, farrier† to John Mogridg 27 Nov 1671
Eaton Thomas s Thomas, Digswell, Hrt, yeoman to Thomas Hill 15 Oct 1680
Eaton William s Richard Abbot, High Wycombe, Bkm, cabinet maker to William Lucas 4 Apr 1751 <1 Oct 1755 turned over to Thomas Whitton>
Eborall Richard s William, Warwick, War, saddler to Stephen Champion 4 Feb 1711/12 <2 May 1715 master† turned over by Matthias Goodfellow, merchant and administrator to John Radburne>
Eborall Thomas s Richard, citizen and tallow chandler† to Elizabeth widow of Richard Eborall 30 Aug 1749
Eborne Edmund s Edward, Kington, War, husbandman to Martin Gardner 11 Apr 1661
Eborne Edward s John, Kington, War, mercer† to Martin Gardiner 16 Sep 1669
Eborne John s Edward, Kineton, War, yeoman to Martin Gardner 3 Feb 1641/2
Eccleston William s William, Lynn, Nfk, innholder† to Thomas Ansell 4 Mar 1733/4
Ecopp Robert s George, Lnd, clerk† to John Palmer 14 Apr 1654
Edden John s William, Brailes, War, yeoman to William Minchin 31 Oct 1655
Edden William s Richard, Brailes, War, maltster to Thomas Hopkins 7 May 1679
Edes John s James, Wimbledon, Sry, victualler to Robert Kirby 5 Apr 1725 <2 Aug 1731 turned over to Joseph Olife, citizen and dyer>
Edes Michael s Michael, St Giles in the Fields, Mdx, yeoman to Hugh Daniell 1 Jul 1680
Edge James s James, Lnd, goldsmith† to John Ham 1 Oct 1711
Edgerley Herbert s Herbert to his father 1 Apr 1717
Edgerley Thomas s Nicholas, St Mary Oxford, Oxf, tailor† to Giles Chandler 7 Dec 1658
Edgerly Richard s Michael, Beaconsfield, Bkm, innholder to Brian Ayliffe 24 Sep 1661
Edgerly Richard s Bartholomew, Eynsham, Oxf, gentleman† to Ferdinand Ladbrook 2 Jan 1720/1
Edgley William s William, St Luke Old Street, Mdx, labourer to Ann Hedges Gardiner 20 Jul 1772
Edlin Richard s Richard, Harrow, Mdx, yeoman to Henry Robince 28 Mar 1672
Edmonds George s Thomas, Oxford, Oxf, brewer† to Richard Williams 7 Apr 1718
Edmonds John s Thomas, Buntingford, Hrt, yeoman to Robert Beadell 20 Feb 1632/3
Edmonds Mathew s Thomas, Buntingford, Hrt, yeoman to Thomas Edmonds 20 Feb 1632/3
Edmonds Thomas s Thomas, citizen and tallow chandler to Anthony Philp 4 Dec 1655
Edmonds William to William Butler 1661/2
Edmonds William s Robert, Maidstone, Ken, mariner to John Pike 15 Jul 1695
Edmonson John s William, Manchester, Lan, dyer† to Peter Leigh 7 Oct 1706
Edowes Wakefield s John, citizen and fletcher to John Jemmett 7 Sep 1724
Edsaw Richard s John, Fittleworth, Ssx, yeoman to William Janeway 1 Nov 1639
Edwards Edward s Richard, Henllan, Den, gentleman to Richard Edgerley ? Feb 1670/1
Edwards Henry s Thomas, St James Westminster, Mdx, yeoman† to Jeremiah Ridge 6 Dec 1714
Edwards John s William, Okeford Fitzpaine, Dor, yeoman to Nicholas Morris 24 Jan 1637/8
Edwards Magdalen d Roger, Overton, Fln, gentleman to John Tuer 22 Jul 1669
Edwards Ockenden s Thomas, Warnham, Ssx, yeoman† to Robert Walker 27 Feb 1646/7
Edwards Thomas s Alexander, 'Hampton Corley', War, yeoman to Robert Williams 11 Sep 1646
Edwards Thomas s John, Westbury, ? ? to John Tyson 30 Nov 1668
Eeles John s Nathaniel, Harpenden, Hrt, clerk to Francis Billing 11 Apr 1666
Eeles Nathaniel s Nathaniel, Harpenden, Hrt, clerk to Thomas Hodges 17 Mar 1663/4
Eger Edward s John, Old Alresford, Ham, yeoman to John Hooker 3 Apr 1643
Egerton William s William, Adstock, Bkm [? *in Ms* 'Brk'], yeoman to William Grove 10 Feb 1690/1
Egger Eling s Thomas, Richmond, Sry, baker to John Johnson 6 Oct 1729
Eglin Septimus s Lawrence, South Kelsey, Lin, clerk† to Richard Pepys 1 Sep 1789
Eglington James s James, Hanwell, Oxf, mason to Richard Williams 3 Dec 1711
Eightshillings Jeremy s Jeremy, St Botolph Aldgate, yeoman† to James Waggoner 26 May 1653
Ekins Robert s Thomas, Chester [Irchester], Nth, gentleman† to Abel Ward 9 Nov 1698
Elborough Thomas s Jacob, Islington, Mdx, baker to Robert Goddard 2 Oct 1792

Elcock John s Thomas, Bermondsey, gardener† to Eleanor widow of Thomas Dubber 5 Dec 1671
Elderton James s Edward, Whitechapel, Mdx, yeoman to John Willford 4 Aug 1707 <7 Jun 1714 turned over to Daniel Collier, citizen and fishmonger>
Eldridge David s John, St Giles, Mdx, haberdasher to John Ayscough 19 Jul 1688
Eldridge William s John, Lambeth, Sry, labourer to Daniel Mason 3 Dec 1751
Eliott Joshua s John, Horsham, Ssx, gentleman to Gervase Beckett 11 Jun 1674
Elisha James s James, Houndsditch, Lnd, victualler to Phineas Pateshall 5 Oct 1790
Ellard Thomas s Richard, citizen and dyer to Francis Robins 3 Dec 1722
Ellen Daniel s George, Cork, Ire, shearman to Thomas Dubber 27 Nov 1666
Elliott Prospero s Thomas, Woolwich, Ken, gentleman† to William Middlemore 4 May 1669
Elliott Richard s Ralph to his father 11 Nov 1700
Elliott Samuel s John, Woolstrop [Quedgeley], Gls, yeoman to William Knight 5 May 1686
Elliott Thomas s Thomas, Stone, Ken, yeoman to William Etheridge 14 Feb 1639/40
Ellis Edmund s Edmund, citizen and haberdasher to Rebecca widow of Joseph Muston 5 Jan 1663/4
Ellis Henry s William, 'Kiddall', Yks, esquire to Joseph Sheldon 23 Feb 1663/4
Ellis James s William, St Saviour Southwark, Sry, butcher to Mathew Peirce 25 May 1680
Ellison John s John, Lnd, gunsmith to John Osgood 5 May 1712
Ellitt Mark s John, citizen and grocer† to Richard Bromfeild 15 Apr 1679
Ellwick Nathaniel s John, citizen and mercer to Benjamin Brownesmith 8 Aug 1692
Elmehurst Benjamin s Joshua, Bosbury, Hef, clerk† to Thomas Obbinson 7 Aug 1710 <turned over to William Perkins, citizen and wheelwright>
Elmer William s William, Weldon, Nth, yeoman to Thomas Roberts 13 May 1650
Elmes George s John, Shirburn, Oxf, cook† to William Dutton 16 Oct 1671
Elsemore Richard s Richard, St Margaret Westminster, farrier† to William Reynolds 5 May 1701
Elwick John s Timothy, citizen and mercer† to John Woods 22 Oct 1649
Elworthy John s Robert, George Nympton, Dev, husbandman to Benjamin Dell 7 May 1760
Ely John s Robert, Old Lynn, Nfk, yeoman to John Broadstreete 27 Jun 1635
Emerton Giles s William, Steppingley, Bdf, victualler† to Nathaniel Perkins 5 Jan 1736/7
Emerton John s Francis, Stondon, Ess, yeoman to Thomas Piers 30 Nov 1632
Emery Solomon s Robert, Lewes, Ssx, gentleman† to Thomas Rippen 8 Feb 1658/9
Emes Edward s Richard, Pershore, Wor, gentleman to Thomas Tyler 19 Aug 1656
England William s Robert, Lambeth, Sry, sawyer to Edward Leman 7 Aug 1693
Englesfield John s Robert, St Nicholas Cole Abbey, Lnd, citizen and cooper to Benjamin Merriman 13 Nov 1770 <2 Apr 1776 turned over to Robert Fitz>
Ennis James s Richard, Liberty of the Rolls, Mdx† to Thomas Hopkins 4 Sep 1704
Ensor Jacob s Jacob, Whitechapel, Mdx, baker† to John Furnis 6 Feb 1699/1700
Ensor John s Joseph, Atherstone, War, butcher† to Edmund Hall 17 Nov 1686
Erpe John s Francis, Lynn [Stonnall], Sts, gentleman† to Thomas Smalridge 25 Mar 1648
Errow Robert s Giles, Savoy, Mdx, tailor to Robert Udall 21 Oct 1653
Erwin John s Richard, Cobham, Sry, shopkeeper† to Samuel Woodfeild 1 Jul 1734 <1 Apr 1740 turned over with consent of Abraham Lawrence, an exec. to Jonas Lawrence>
Estell John s William, Whitechapel, Mdx, tallow chandler to John Perry 6 Jun 1739
Estwick William s Thomas, Staines, Mdx, tanner† to Isaac Saffell 13 Mar 1673/4
Eustace Richard s Hugh, Milton, Oxf, yeoman to Robert Bristo 29 Sep 1632
Euster John s Edmund, Maids Moreton, Bkm, yeoman to Andrew Partridge 22 Oct 1653
Evans Edward s William, Llanrwst, Den, husbandman to Abraham Brooke 13 Feb 1635/6
Evans Hugh s Henry, Bruton, Som, yeoman to William Allett 25 May 1653
Evans John s John, Lnd, hosier to William Cave 5 Aug 1734
Evans Maurice s James, St James Clerkenwell, spectaclemaker† to Herbert Homan 14 Oct 1765
Evans Philip s John, St James Westminster, Mdx, tallow chandler to Thomas Obbinson 19 Jun 1714 <1 Sep 1718 turned over to William Haydon, citizen and blacksmith>
Evans Richard s Richard, citizen and clothworker to James Holworthie 26 Oct 1655
Evans Theophilus s Richard, Lewisham, Ken, yeoman to William Massey 3 Oct 1699
Evanson William s William, Hackney, Mdx, yeoman to John Newporte 22 Nov 1670
Eve Henry s Henry, Dorchester, Oxf, yeoman† to Benjamin Leasinby 6 Sep 1738
Eve Richard s Richard, Mundon, Ess, yeoman† to William Collier 1 Jul 1723
Eve Thomas s Andrew, citizen and butcher† to John Clarke 6 Apr 1676
Everard John s Hugh, Worsborough, Yks, clerk to Robert Wilcock 30 Aug 1647

Everard Marmaduke s John, Croft, Lei, gentleman to Thomas Everard 7 May 1679
Everingham William s Charles, Mitcham, Sry, linen draper to James Jenner 5 May 1789
Evershed John s Thomas, Cuckfield, Ssx, tallow chandler to Cleophas Comber 5 Dec 1797
Eveston John s Richard to his father 4 Oct 1738
Evington Robert s James, Offord, Hun, knight to Roger Price 7 Oct 1635
Ewer Edward s Francis, Watford, Hrt, maltster to John Pratt 3 Nov 1679
Ewer James s John, Ingatestone, Ess, clerk to John Meridale 31 May 1683
Ewer John s Francis, Watford, Hrt, maltster to John Burges 23 Oct 1668
Ewer John s Jonathan, Watford, Hrt, maltster† to John Ewer 13 Oct 1718 <2 Nov 1724 master† turned over by Ann Deakin, exec. to Edward Olive>
Ewer Mathew s John to his father 30 Oct 1705
Ewer Samuel s Samuel, St Albans, Hrt, gentleman† to John Hide 12 Aug 1748
Ewes John s John to his father 20 Mar 1700/1
Ewster William s William, citizen and carpenter† to Samuel Shakemaple ? Nov 1665
Eyans Rollinson s Richard, Enstone, Oxf, esquire to Charles Thatcher 12 Mar 1704/5
Eyle Nathaniel s John, Hardingstone, Nth, ? to Richard Bedwell 7 Jan 1668/9
Eyre John s William, Blackwell, Dby, yeoman to Nicholas Beckitt 5 Feb 1678/9
Eyre William s T?, Blackwell, Dby, yeoman to Thomas Eyre 18 Mar 1679/80
Eyton John s Thomas, Chester, Chs, gentleman to William Thatcher 1 Mar 1670/1
Eyton Thomas s Thomas, Eccleston, Chs, gentleman to Peter Pickering 7 Jul 1668

Fagg Benjamin s Robert Harding, Bermondsey, Sry, tallow chandler† to Joshua Joyce 5 Oct 1790 <2 Nov 1790 turned over to William Prior, citizen and saddler>
Fairbrother William s Roger, Southampton, Ham, clerk† to John Kerby 3 Nov 1701
Faircliff Zephaniah s Humphrey, citizen and broderer† to Lawrence Carter 11 Aug 1684
Fairclough Daniel s Richard, Bishops Hatfield, Hrt, yeoman to William Pheasant 6 Dec 1650
Fairefeild Thomas s Joseph, Stanton by Bridge, Dby, yeoman to Henry Painsfoote 4 Nov 1634
Faires Job s William, Overbury, Wor, yeoman† to William Gaunt 14 Sep 1676
Faithwaite Henry s Henry, Caton [Lancaster], Lan, yeoman† to George Bowyer 2 Dec 1638
Fare Benjamin s William, Flitwick, Bdf, yeoman to John Soule 9 Jul 1650
Farenden Benjamin s John, Shadwell, Mdx, tobacco cutter to Richard Cooke 2 Aug 1708
Farey Joseph s Edmund, Flitwick, Bdf, yeoman to Thomas Cuttlett 14 Jun 1651
Farmer Christopher s John, Holborn, Mdx, tallow chandler to William Gurney 17 Mar 1678/9
Farmer William s John, Faringdon, Brk, currier to Thomas Thatcher 4 Oct 1714 <4 Jul 1720 turned over to Thomas Woolhead>
Farndon Thomas s Edward, Coventry, War, feltmaker† to John Gill 8 Jul 1702
Farraine Thomas s Thomas, St James Westminster, tallow chandler to Joseph Callcott 12 Nov 1722
Farren Abraham s Abraham, Tewkesbury, Gls, plumber† to Robert Hancock 6 Jun 1739
Farren George s Abraham, Tewkesbury, Gls, plumber† to Abraham Farren 2 Feb 1746/7
Farren Samuel s Abraham, Tewkesbury, Gls, glazier to Anthony Chestroo 16 Nov 1703
Farrow Joseph s Benjamin, St Olave Southwark, Sry, hatmaker to John Ford 6 Dec 1708
Fasby John s John, Lambeth, Sry, waterman to George Searles 7 Oct 1777
Faukner Nicholas s Lancelot, Lewes, Ssx, gentleman to Stephen Kersinhall 24 Jan 1632/3
Favell Methusaleh s Robert, St Giles in the Fields, schoolmaster to Nathaniel Chandler 7 Nov 1715
Fawcett Christopher s Thomas, St Luke Old Street, Mdx, tailor to John Lambert 23 Apr 1765
Fawcett Robert s Daniel, Peckham, Sry, shipwright† to Francis Wardner 6 Mar 1659/60
Fawconer John s Henry, Daventry, Nth, husbandman to Simon Dawson 3 Nov 1637
Fawnce Edward s Richard, citizen and haberdasher to Thomas Greene 22 Jul 1652
Fawson Richard s Richard, citizen and innholder to Joseph Gibbons 6 Sep 1697
Fawson Stephen s George, Weston, Nth, yeoman† to Henry Cowper 7 Mar 1660/1
Fawson William s Richard, Hanslope, Bkm, labourer† to John Gill 5 Jan 1712/3
Fearne George s George, Aldenham, Hrt, yeoman to Edward Harris 4 May 1683
Fearne John s Thomas, Ruislip, Mdx, yeoman to John Hooker 21 May 1663
Feast Thomas s Felix, City Road, Mdx, brewer† to Mary Bellis, sp. 7 Jul 1778
Feesey John s Edward, St Giles in the Fields, Mdx, carman† to William Jeanes 16 Feb 1693/4
Feild Enoch s William, Covent Garden, Mdx, sempster to Richard Bedwell 29 Oct 1664
Feild Joseph s John, Welford, Brk, yeoman to Thomas Stiver 27 Mar 1654
Feild Joseph s Joseph, Watford, Hrt, husbandman to Samuel Withers 9 Oct 1689

Feild Ralph s Ralph, Hemel Hempstead, Hrt, yeoman to John Turner 27 Feb 1683/4
Feild Richard s William, Covent Garden, Mdx, gentleman to Joseph Watts 1 Apr 1659
Feild Richard s Thomas, Woodstock, Oxf, tailor to William Cranwell 7 Nov 1698
Feild Thomas s William, Hampstead, Mdx, farmer to Nathaniel Chandler 6 Mar 1731/2
Fellowes Benjamin Daniel s Benjamin, citizen and bowyer† to Mary widow of William Thredder 3 Aug 1702
Fellowes Jeremiah s William, citizen and clothworker to Richard Ward 2 Oct 1671
Fellows George s Benjamin, citizen and bowyer† to Joseph Calcott 4 Feb 1705/6
Fells Thomas s Thomas, citizen and leatherseller to Richard Backhouse 9 Mar 1670/1
Felsted Abraham s Abraham, Great Chesterford, Ess, gentleman to John Maunder 25 Mar 1656
Fenn Edward s Anthony, Limehouse, Mdx, mariner† to John Newporte 13 Mar 1672/3
Fenn John s John, Low Leyton, Ess, carpenter† to William Young 18 Jun 1772 <6 May 1777 master† turned over to John Phillips; 2 Dec 1777 to Isaac Phillips>
Fenney John William to John Stephens 5 Dec 1799
Fennymore John s Edward, Woodstock, Oxf, gentleman to Thomas Roll 2 Oct 1727
Fenton John s William, citizen and clothworker to Peter Prince 7 Apr 1669
Fenton Samuel s Thomas, Astbury, Chs, mason to Robert Leake 18 Jul 1671
Fenwick John s John, St George Hanover Square, Mdx, whitesmith to William Coles 11 Sep 1764
Ferman Roger s John, Gray Lane [Halam], Ntt, yeoman to Luke Lane 13 Nov 1635
Ferrall John s John, Lewes, Ssx, labourer to Thomas Ferrall 7 Jul 1707
Ferrall Thomas s Edward, 'Lenfield', ? ? to Edward Radliffe .. Sep 1669 <19 Dec 1701 changed to Ferrall from Verrall>
Ferrant John s Henry, Rotherhithe, Sry, shipwright to Nicholas Ferrant 28 Sep 1663
Ferren John s John, Tewkesbury, Gls, maltster to Nathaniel Chandler 29 Jul 1692
Ferrers Robert s William, Savoy, Mdx, gardener† to Richard Ingram 4 Sep 1693
Ferriss Thomas s Francis, Lnd, gentleman to John Back 11 Apr 1694
Fewtrell Robert s Thomas, Highworth, Wil, husbandman to Edward Barker 14 Feb 1638/9
Field Dalby s Richard to his father 1 Aug 1726
Field Daniel s Ralph, Hemel Hempstead, Hrt, yeoman† to Ralph Field 3 Dec 1695
Field Daniel s Francis, Green End, Hrt, yeoman to Mary widow of Ralph Field 2 Nov 1724
Field Elisha s Elisha, Watford, Hrt, corn chandler to William Shepherd 5 Jan 1779
Field Isaac s Isaac, Lnd, cheesemonger to Thomas Prentice 6 Apr 1730
Field Nathaniel s Thomas, Offley, Hrt, yeoman† to Daniel Scott 5 May 1701
Field Robert s Mathew, St Luke Old Street, Mdx, founder† to Richard Alexander 12 May 1767 <3 Oct 1767 turned over to William Hornblow, citizen and joiner>
Field William s William, citizen and draper to Nathaniel Field 7 Mar 1743/4
Fielding Willoughby s Willoughby, Whitefriars, Lnd, joiner† to John Beaumont 2 Apr 1717
Fieldwick Francis s William, Hackney, Mdx, bricklayer to Robert French 6 Feb 1798
Figg Robert s Robert, Farnham, Sry, smith to Thomas Cryer 5 Jul 1669
Filby Edward s James, Droitwich, Wor, gentleman to Bartholomew Wimberly 5 Dec 1720
Filce John s Francis, Staines, Mdx, husbandman to John Pratt 17 Jan 1670/1
Filer Felix s William to his father 6 Aug 1711
Filler William s William, Portsmouth, Ham, mariner† to William Gurney 6 Feb 1679/80
Finch Christopher s Christopher, Egham, Sry, yeoman to Thomas Kender 4 Sep 1693
Finch John s John, Stratford Langthorne, Ess, yeoman† to Richard Pitman 19 Sep 1640
Finch John s John, Ipswich, Sfk, yeoman to Mathew Woollward 6 Sep 1671
Finch John s Robert, Barnes, Sry, farmer to Egerton Henshaw 6 Jun 1733
Finch Thomas s Robert, Northaw, Hrt, yeoman to Daniel Giles 4 Jul 1642
Finch William s William, Henley, Oxf, apothecary† to Benjamin Brownesmith 28 Aug 1672
Finney William s Edward, Lichfield, Sts, mercer to Thomas Smallridge 25 Jul 1635
Fish Ambrose s Cradock, Warwick, War to Francis Banister 31 Jul 1679
Fish Samuel s Robert, Finedon, Nth, gentleman to Peter Pickering 31 Mar 1690
Fish Thomas s Thomas, Halstead, Ess, tanner to Andrew Thorowgood 23 Oct 1678
Fish Thomas s Thomas, Ware, Hrt, maltster to John Halsey 21 Nov 1693
Fish William s Robert, Finedon, Nth, gentleman† to Peter Chesshyre 22 Jan 1690/1
Fishe William s David, Axholme, Lin, yeoman to John Prichard 2 Feb 1634/5
Fisher Anthony s John, Greenwich, Ken, baker to Edward Walker 30 Sep 1687
Fisher Charles s Charles, Christ Church Southwark, Sry, waterman to John Chatfeild 7 Jul 1741

Fisher John s William, Tewkesbury, Gls, yeoman to John Wibnell 19 Jun 1671
Fisher John s John, Liberty of the Rolls, Mdx, tallow chandler to Robert Matthews 15 Feb 1686/7
Fisher John s John, St Martin in the Fields, Mdx, labourer to William Wickins 6 Dec 1697
Fisher John s John, St Sepulchre, Lnd, waterman to Edward Williams 21 Feb 1766 <22 Nov 1769 master† turned over to Daniel Butler, citizen and joiner>
Fisher Joseph s William, Holborn, Mdx, tailor to George Shelley 18 Mar 1707/8
Fisher Stephen s Stephen, Westminster, Mdx, tailor to John Tyson 30 Nov 1668
Fisher Theophilus s Theophilus, Newington, Sry, blacksmith to Edward Burgis 16 Jul 1684
Fisher William s John, citizen and broderer to Thomas Styles 27 Feb 1655/6
Fisher William s Henry, Wartling, Ssx, clerk to Samuel Hamond 2 Aug 1667
Fisher William s Joseph, St Olave Southwark, Sry, upholder to Nathaniel Field 10 May 1727
Fisher William s William, Stepney, Mdx, pattenmaker to Jonas Lawrence 17 Feb 1743/4
Fishwicke Richard s Richard, Knaresborough, Yks, gentleman to Henry Burton 14 Feb 1669/70
Fist John s John, Reigate, Sry, carrier to Robert Lamb, jnr. 5 Jun 1710 <7 Jan 1716/7 turned over to Benjamin Ludlow>
Fitch Samuel s Samuel, Wethersfield, Ess, grocer† to Richard Joyce 25 Jan 1674/5
Fitch Thomas s Samuel, Havering atte Bower, Ess, yeoman to Samuel Fitch 2 May 1720
Fitch Zachariah s Jeremy, St Albans, Hrt, innholder to Francis Wardiner 3 Jul 1660
Fitz Edward s Robert, Teffont, Wil, gentleman to Vincent Walker 5 Jun 1721
Fitz Edward s Robert, Teffont, Wil, shopkeeper† to Edward Fitz 7 Sep 1742
Fitz Edward s Edward to his father 16 Jan 1749/50
Fitz Robert s Edward, St Giles, Mdx to his father 22 Jul 1761
Flaxman Thomas s John, Maidstone, Ken, flaxman to Robert Southwood 3 Sep 1746
Fleming Thomas s Matthias, St Clement Danes, Mdx, tailor to George Smeeton 22 Mar 1774
Fletcher Edward s John, Green, Cul, yeoman to Thomas Steevenson 5 Jun 1683
Fletcher Henry s John, Over Norton, Oxf, husbandman† to Samuel Holford 14 May 1691
Fletcher Thomas s Thomas, Kingswood, Sts, yeoman to William Powell 21 Feb 1680/1
Fletcher Vincent s Anthony, Little Milton, Oxf, yeoman to Richard Eustis 9 Jul 1649
Fletcher William s William, Christs Hospital, Lnd, fishmonger† to James Tilley 2 Jun 1729
Flight John s Thomas, Kingston, Oxf, maltster to William Gaunte 8 Nov 1667
Flight John s John, citizen and tallow chandler† to Thomas Rencher 3 Apr 1693
Flight Joseph s Joseph, Henley, Oxf, baker to John Stent 4 Jul 1751
Flindall Samuel s Thomas, Northaw, Hrt, feltmaker† to Samuel Moses 1 Mar 1753 <27 Mar 1759 master† turned over with consent of John Atkins surviving exec. to Edward Man, citizen and wheelwright>
Flindall Stephen s Thomas, Northaw, Hrt, tilemaker† to Samuel Flindall 5 Sep 1763
Flindall Stephen s Stephen, Fleet Street, Mdx to his father 5 Sep 1786
Flint John to Thomas Agate 4 Apr 1799
Flower Francis s Robert, St Giles in the Fields, Mdx, farrier to Thomas Obbinson 4 Dec 1710 <turned over to Thomas Higgins, citizen and leatherseller>
Flower Henry s William, Melksham, Wil, barber to Thomas Grover 18 Mar 1660/1
Flower Richard s Adam, West Lavington, Wil, cordwainer to John Maxfeild 24 Jun 1670
Flower Richard s John, Whissendine, Rut [? *in Ms* 'Lei'], yeoman† to Thomas Smith 25 Sep 1671
Flower Robert s Robert, Lnd, tailor† to Jegon Mandevill 9 Oct 1690
Flower Stephen s Thomas, Frostenden, Sfk, yeoman† to William Flower 14 Feb 1648/9
Flower William s Thomas, Frostenden, Sfk, yeoman to Thomas London 20 Jul 1635
Floyd William s Thomas, St Clement Danes, Mdx, tobacconist to Thomas Radley 4 Oct 1708
Floyde David s John, Llanycil, Mer, yeoman to Robert Walker 14 Apr 1670
Floyde William s Francis, Kilby, Lei, yeoman† to William Gibson 3 Jul 1655
Flutter Henry s Henry, Guildford, Sry, tallow chandler to Ann widow of Nathaniel Messenger 6 Mar 1703/4
Flye Dorothy d William, Norwood, Mdx, clerk† to William and Elizabeth Roll 28 Jul 1677 <by her grandmother Mary Yearsby, Hammersmith, Mdx, widow>
Flye John s William, Crondall, Ham, yeoman to John Hooker 7 Jul 1653
Fokes William s Francis, Houghton Street, Clare Market, Mdx, copper plate printer to John Lambert 4 Oct 1785
Folkingham Theophilus s John, Burton on Trent, Sts, clerk to Thomas Palmer 24 Apr 1638
Folly John s John, Oxford, Oxf, dyer† to Richard Bedwell 8 Oct 1660

Foltrop William s William, Lnd, weaver† to Thomas Hayes 13 Nov 1665
Foorde James s James, Hurley, Brk, yeoman to Gabriel Binion 3 May 1654
Foorde John s William, citizen and clothworker† to Henry Burton 13 Sep 1672
Foote Francis s Thomas, Cambridge, Cam, innholder† to George Leaman 11 Nov 1673
Forbes Thomas s Abraham, Strelley, Ntt, clerk† to John Meddowes 27 May 1658
Ford Benjamin s Richard, citizen and barber chirurgeon to Robert Ayliffe 3 Oct 1711
Ford Henry s John, Southwark, Sry, tallow chandler to Thomas Sutton 24 Sep 1754
Ford John s Henry to his father 7 May 1722
Ford Paul s Paul, Lichfield, Sts, miller† to Thomas Smalredge 27 Oct 1655
Ford Richard s Walker, Chippenham, Wil, butcher to Thomas Stephens 10 Feb 1686/7
Ford Samuel s Henry to his father 2 May 1720
Ford William s William, citizen and grocer† to John Eyre 4 Nov 1690
Forde Henry s John, citizen and merchant tailor to John Parker 5 Oct 1686
Fores William s James, Rosamond Street, Clerkenwell, Mdx, vintner to Edward Palmer 4 May 1779 <4 Feb 1783 turned over to Alan Parsons>
Forman Thomas s Henry, Wapping, Mdx, brewer to William Thatcher 29 May 1679
Forod William s Henry, Stepney, Mdx, ?labourer to George Carr 30 Dec 1667
Forster Daniel s Thomas, Cheshunt, Hrt, farmer† to John Tovey 6 May 1755
Forster John s George, Leighton Buzzard, Bdf, currier to William Gibson 17 Dec 1641
Forster John s Thomas, St John Street, Mdx, gentleman† to John Bryan 27 Oct 1673
Forth Thomas s Charles, Holborn, Mdx, haberdasher and hosier to Thomas Ansell 18 Oct 1760
Fortune Robert s Humphrey, Henley, Oxf, woodmonger to Ezekiel Page 8 Jun 1665
Forty John s Stephen, Yarnton, Oxf, yeoman to John Forty 11 May 1669
Foscett John s Thomas, Milbourne [Malmesbury], Wil, yeoman to John Moncke 16 Mar 1635/6
Fossard Francis s Francis, Wakefield, Yks, clothier† to Thomas Tully 7 Nov 1749
Fossey Edward s Bernard, Bradwell, Bkm, yeoman to John Tipping 29 Dec 1658
Fossey Thomas s Daniel, Hemel Hempstead, Hrt, draper to Nathaniel Might 3 Mar 1711/12
Fossey Thomas s Joseph, citizen and salter to William Hayden 1 Sep 1712
Fossey Thomas s Joseph, St Sepulchre, Mdx, watchmaker to John Dickins 1 Dec 1741
Foster Anthony s Anthony, Bermondsey, Sry, dyer to Thomas Bromsell 2 Jul 1711
Foster Edmund s Henry, Shadwell, Mdx, biscuit baker to Richard Thorneton 20 Dec 1686
Foster Henry s Henry, St Albans, Hrt, brewer† to Thomas Kelke 30 Jul 1635
Foster Richard s John, South Leigh, Oxf, husbandman to John Pritchard 8 Nov 1641
Foster Timothy s Thomas, Leighton, Bdf, butcher† to Joseph Gregory 31 Oct 1689
Foster William s William, Lnd, cordwainer to Timothy Foster 9 Feb 1707/8
Fothergill George s Thomas, York, Yks, gentleman to Henry Hildyard 30 Sep 1712
Fothergill George s Thomas, York, Yks, gentleman† to Henry Hildyard 3 Nov 1712
Fothergill John s Anthony, Ravenstonedale, Wes, yeoman to Daniel Giles 14 Mar 1650/1
Fothergill John s John, Whitechapel, Mdx, saddler† to William Alexander 4 Oct 1743 <3 Apr 1744 turned over to Robert Bringhurst, citizen and founder>
Foulkes Richard s Edward, Denbigh, Den, yeoman† to Richard Jannaway 22 Jun 1678
Fountaine Lewis s Lewis, Lnd, merchant† to James Rondeau 5 Feb 1734/5
Fountayne John s R?, Cottingwith, Yks, yeoman† to Edward Foss 31 Oct 1682
Fowler John s William, citizen and leatherseller to Samuel Beasly 28 Nov 1676
Fowler John s Roger, Holborn, Mdx, cordwainer† to John Gill 5 Mar 1704/5
Fowler Joseph s William, Whitechapel, Mdx, yeoman† to John Ballard 9 Jan 1636/7
Fowler Stephen s Daniel, Stonehouse, Gls, clothier to Richard Barnard 6 Mar 1647/8
Fowler William s Thomas, Goadby, Lei, gentleman to Richard Weston 4 Dec 1732
Fowler William s William, Great Missenden, Bkm, farmer† to William Hoare 3 Nov 1764
Fox Edward s Edward, Croft, Lin, yeoman† to George Kitchinman 4 Nov 1641
Fox Richard s John, Farnham, Sry, yeoman to John Wyburd 12 Sep 1698
Frampton John s Stephen, Blandford, Dor, cordwainer to Henry Knowles 12 Jun 1693
Frances Agard s H?, Derby, Dby, gentleman† to William Garfoote 26 Jan 1673/4
Frances George s Fulk, Lnd, cloth draper† to William Adams 25 May 1668
Francis George s John, Wellesbourne, War, yeoman to Benjamin Russell 4 Apr 1698
Francis Nicholas s Philip, St Botolph Aldgate, Lnd, yeoman to Robert Asple 20 May 1641
Francis Robert s Samuel, Chelsea, Mdx, gentleman to John Lambert 6 Oct 1778
Francis Samuel s Samuel, Walton on Thames, Sry, yeoman† to Humphrey King 30 Jul 1667

Francklin Aaron s Moses, Southwark, Sry, carpenter† to Edward Masters 23 Aug 1677
Francklyn William s William, citizen and currier† to John Collington 24 Nov 1636
Frankes James s John, Bishopsgate Without, Lnd, shoemaker† to John Cheaney 5 Oct 1742
Franklin James s James, Putney, Sry, lighterman to John Packman 6 May 1788
Franklin John s Thomas, Chelsea, Mdx, butcher† to Daniel Mason 19 Jun 1754
Fray John s George, Kingston, Sry, innholder to Eliza widow of Benjamin Free 27 Oct 1729
Frederick Isaac s Isaac, Greenwich, Ken, cooper† to Richard Wells 1 Jul 1717
Free Benjamin s Michael, St Saviour Southwark, Sry, joiner† to Andrew Godwin 8 Jan 1688/9
Free Thomas s Benjamin, citizen and tallow chandler to Henry Ventrice 6 May 1723
Freeman John s Thomas, Soho, Mdx, tallow chandler to Bartholomew Wimberly 5 Mar 1704/5
Freeman John s Charles, Twyning, Gls, gentleman† to Robert Ekins 7 Feb 1717/8
Freeman Nathaniel s Cornelius, Uttoxeter, Sts, tailor to William Prince 5 Jul 1686
Freeman Robert s Thomas, citizen and upholder to William Hulls 26 Oct 1693
Freeman Thomas s John, Beckley, Oxf, yeoman to Thomas Dubber 29 May 1654
Freeman Thomas s Thomas, St George Southwark, Sry, miller to William Clements 18 Jul 1681
Freeman Thomas s Joseph, Stepney, Mdx, waterman to John Freeman 6 Jun 1726
Freeman Thomas s Thomas, Westminster, Mdx, gentleman† to John Freeman 2 Jun 1729
Freeman Thomas s Barzillin, Netteswell, Ess, schoolmaster to Robert Goddard 7 Sep 1784
Freeman William s John, Little Dalby, Lei, husbandman† to Sarah widow of Thomas Chambers 21 Oct 1691
Freemantle Nicholas s Walgrave, Moreton Pinkney, Nth, gentleman to John Smith 2 Apr 1722
French Francis s George, Stanmore, Mdx, farmer to John Lambert 7 Nov 1780
French John s Henry, Oxford, Oxf, hosier to Samuel Shakemaple 27 Apr 1648
French Robert s Thomas, South Newington, Oxf, farmer to John Perry 15 Nov 1748
French Robert s Robert, Barbican, Lnd to his father 3 Jun 1777
French Thomas s William, Smithfield Bars, Mdx, butcher† to John Furness 7 Jul 1741
French Thomas s Thomas, South Newington, Oxf, husbandman to Robert French 21 Mar 1760
Frewen Samuel s John, Northiam, Ssx, gentleman† to Nicholas Beckitt 18 Nov 1656
Frier Henry s William, Dunton, Bkm, yeoman to Samuel King 3 Jul 1655
Frisbee John s John, Whitechapel, Mdx, shoemaker to William Fowler 1 Jun 1742
Frodsall Thomas s Thomas, St Giles Cripplegate, Lnd, wine porter to Samuel Wheeler 5 Jan 1712/3
Fromanteel Jonathan s John, citizen and clockmaker to John Smith 7 Oct 1686
Frost William s William, Merton, Sry, husbandman to Thomas Nash 6 Jul 1730
Frument Robert s Simon, Stratford, Ess, farrier to John Compton 3 Jan 1758
Fry Gilbert s William, Bristol, Gls, soapmaker to John Ayre 7 Nov 1709
Fry Thomas s William, Lambeth, Sry, cordwainer† to Joseph Massey 26 Oct 1674
Fryance Thomas s Edward, Lnd, mariner† to Esther widow of Thomas Hill 2 Apr 1722
<13 Apr 1724 mistress† turned over by Mathew Dean, exec. to William Hill>
Fryer John s John, St Dunstan in the West?, Lnd, victualler to Robert Rodway 13 Oct 1669
Fryer John s George, St ... in the Fields, Mdx, innholder† to Valentine Warner 10 Sep 1722
Fryer Peter s Richard, citizen and fruiterer to Philip Constable 23 Jun 1681
Fryer William s Richard, High Wycombe, Bkm, yeoman to Edmund Rumball 23 Jun 1674
Fudgell William s John, Charlcombe, Som, yeoman to William Pope .. Mar 1650/1
Fuller Francis s John, Eynsford, Ken, husbandman to Thomas Haies 25 Feb 1660/1
Fuller James s John, Colnbrook, Bkm, tanner† to Samuel King 1 Jun 1659
Fuller Richard s William, Sevenoaks, Ken, yeoman to William Hill 12 May 1646
Fullmore John s Joseph, Colnbrook, Bkm, mealman to Thomas Stimson 5 Jul 1725
Fullwood George s John, Dulwich, Sry, victualler to Humphrey Wood 2 Jan 1798
Fulwood Richard s Sampson, St Giles in the Fields, Mdx, labourer to Thomas Vaughan 13 Jun 1659
Furinfold Geoffrey s Richard, 'Clarlton', Bkm, yeoman to John Ayscough 21 Jul 1687
Furnell James s William, Ealing, Mdx, gardener to John Parker 3 May 1703
Furnell John s William, Ealing, Mdx, yeoman to John Parker 6 Nov 1710
Furnice John s John, citizen and clothworker† to James Packett 8 Jan 1684/5
Furnis James s James, citizen and vintner to Samuel Gerard 9 Sep 1723
Furnis Joseph s Jonas, Almondbury, Yks, clothier to John Furness 4 Feb 1733/4
Fussell John s Peter, Winchester, Ham, grocer to Henry Hawkes 16 Jun 1687

Gad Charles s Joseph, Spitalfields, Mdx, fellowship porter to Charles Ace 1 Nov 1735

Gadd William s John, Stepney, Mdx, maltster† to Samuel Reeves 12 Nov 1750
Gadsby Francis s Thomas, Islington, Mdx, wheelwright to John Wyberd 10 Apr 1685
Gadsby George s Francis to his father 3 Dec 1722
Gage John s John, Raunds, Nth, esquire to Robert Hicks 12 Sep 1659
Gaggs John s Richard, 'Pomfrett', Ntt, husbandman to Richard Jannaway 5 Aug 1684
Gaines Philip s Philip, Streatham, Sry, yeoman† to Samuel Bedwell 13 Mar 1699/1700
Gainey Joseph s John, Stroud, Gls, clothier† to Francis Leech 15 Sep 1756 <15 Dec 1758 turned over to Nathaniel Bellis>
Gainford John s Christopher, St Andrew Holborn, Lnd, gardener to Francis Barber 10 Dec 1764
Gainsford Tobias s Nicholas, Holborn, Lnd, cheesemonger to Charles Hoppe 4 Mar 1794
Gale John s Thomas, Hatton Garden [Holborn], Mdx, victualler to Edward Coles 3 Oct 1677
Gale Roger s Robert, St Saviour Southwark, Sry, butcher† to Jacob Packett 12 Nov 1698
Gale Samuel s Thomas, York, Yks, clerk to Benjamin Tomlinson 18 Dec 1699
Galloway William s Ambrose, Lewes, Ssx, merchant to Robert Ingram 18 Jul 1698
Gally William s John, Grafton Street, St Marylebone, Mdx, victualler to James Pateshall 7 Dec 1790 <3 Jul 1792 turned over to Samuel Neville, citizen and skinner>
Gamble John s William, Loughborough, Lei, blacksmith to Elizabeth widow of Nathaniel Billing 1 Apr 1668
Gamon Richard s Thomas, Kirton in Lindsey, Lin, gentleman to John Banckworth 1 Aug 1635
Ganderton Joseph s William, Elmley, Wor, yeoman to William Gaunt 5 Sep 1677
Gard Peter s Thomas, Ringmer, Ssx, gentleman to Samuel Isted 17 Oct 1677
Gardener Peter s John, Silverstone, Nth, yeoman to Elizabeth widow of John Hastings 5 Feb 1699/1700
Gardiner Christian s Thomas, citizen and mercer to Richard Joyce 18 Apr 1664
Gardiner John s Isaac, Annandale, Sco, shoemaker† to John Dickins 27 Oct 1749
Gardner Benjamin s Thomas, St Luke Old Street, Mdx to Robert Hopkins 5 Feb 1793
Gardner Brian s Brian, Rolleston, Sts, yeoman to John Caldwall 6 Apr 1654
Gardner Edward s Edward, Stonesfield, Oxf, clothier to Richard Reynolds 7 Feb 1682/3
Gardner James s John, Charlbury, Oxf, joiner† to Benjamin Leasinby 15 Mar 1748/9
Gardner John s John, Buckingham, Bkm, yeoman to Humphrey Butcher 4 Nov 1673
Gardner John s Robert, Covent Garden, Mdx, victualler to Richard Ingram 17 Aug 1681
Gardner John s Zachariah, St Botolph Bishopsgate, Lnd, gentleman† to Mary Smith 15 Nov 1770
Garey John s John, Lambeth, Sry, millwright† to James Bague 2 Jul 1745 <26 Jul 1750 turned over to James Spring, citizen and hatbandmaker>
Garfott William s William, Ingatestone, Ess, gentleman† to Daniel Binion 9 Oct 1657
Garment Edward s Edward, Lambeth, Sry, carpenter to James Church 1 Jul 1687
Garment John s Edward to his father 6 Feb 1715/6
Garmson John s James, St John Street, Mdx, yeoman to William Alden 22 Oct 1674
Garnam Petley s William, Sutton at Hone, Ken, gentleman to Petley Wybourne 4 May 1648
Garne John s John, Gloucester, Gls, shoemaker† to Samuel Reeves 7 Dec 1756 <30 Jul 1760 turned over to James Filewood, citizen and wheelwright>
Garnett Edward s Mathew, Hounslow, Mdx, innholder† to Thomas Dowdeswell 28 Nov 1690
Garnham George s George, Portsmouth, Ham, mariner† to Francis Nash 20 Aug 1659
Garnish William s John, Crayford, Ken, yeoman to Robert Moore 1 Apr 1641
Garnons Roger s John, Glemsford, Sfk, doctor in divinity† to John Tewer 3 Jan 1656/7
Garrard Thomas s James, Trafford, Chs, gentleman† to Peter Chesshyre 29 Jun 1703
Garrett John s Thomas, Uxbridge, Mdx, to Edward Barker 3 Oct 1656
Garrett Philip s Philip, Doddinghurst, Ess, gentleman to Henry Miles 7 Apr 1682
Garrett Thomas s John, South Mimms, Mdx, victualler to Samuel James 15 May 1683
Garrett Thomas s Thomas, citizen and bricklayer to Randolph Watson 21 Feb 1688/9
Gartwright Robert s Robert, Kings Langley, Hrt, yeoman to William Greenehead 11 Oct 1638
Garway Nathaniel s Nathaniel, Weybridge, Sry, gentleman to Roger Price 16 Dec 1645
Gascoine Ralph s William, Heath, Yks, yeoman† to Richard Brice 14 Nov 1637
Gash John s John, Southwark Borough, Sry, lighterman† to George Searle 6 Jul 1784
Gates Richard s Thomas, Shermanbury, Ssx, yeoman to William Coltstock 16 Feb 1648/9
Gatliffe Thomas s James, Hertford, Hrt, grocer† to Caleb Talbot 7 Feb 1775
Gatton Edward s Thomas, Shere, Sry, yeoman to Richard Heather 3 Jul 1655

Gaulton James s James, Islington, Mdx, gentleman to Joseph Lane 6 Feb 1720/1 <1 Sep 1724 turned over to William Wood, citizen and clothworker>
Gaunt Thomas s Thomas, Shoreditch, Mdx, cooper to Richard West 3 Dec 1733
Gawler Samuel s Samuel, Stretton, South Petherton, Som, yeoman to George Bowyer 13 Jun 1648
Gawler Thomas s William, Lambeth, Sry, gentleman† to John Lindsey 7 Jul 1778
Gawthorne James s Edward, Hardingstone, Nth, shoemaker† to Stephen Flindall 1 Dec 1789
Gaylor John s John, Denham, Bkm, farmer to Joseph Wedgbrough 2 Mar 1741/2
Gazelie Daniel s Robert, St Paul's Walden, Hrt, yeoman to John Gazelie 1 May 1658
Geare Benjamin s John, St Giles in the Fields, Mdx, glover to Anthony Mosley 31 Oct 1673
Geeary Henry s Jasper to his father 23 Oct 1701
Geerey Thomas s Thomas, Riseley, Bdf, husbandman† to William Wright 1 Aug 1637
Geery Jasper s Henry, Wigginton, Oxf, yeoman† to Daniel Child 22 Nov 1670
Geery John s Stephen, citizen and dyer to Simon Durant 22 Jul 1679
Geirle John s William, Buckingham, Bkm, yeoman to Robert Southwood ? Nov 1667
George Richard s Thomas, Croydon, Sry, yeoman† to John Garland 26 Sep 1690
George Thomas s Thomas, citizen and merchant tailor to Edward Burgis 17 Jan 1675/6
George William s William, Kingsclere, Ham, labourer to Richard Tyrrell 6 Dec 1732
Gerrard George s George, citizen and joiner to John Bowden 5 May 1685
Gerrard John s John, Wimborne Minster, Dor, tailor to John Radley 7 Aug 1690
Gesner Henry s William, Cranford, Mdx, yeoman to Richard Conaway 7 Mar 1641/2
Gethin John s Edward, Llandyrnog, Den, gentleman to Joseph Rideout 9 Jul 1687
Gewers John s John, Little Baddow, Ess, yeoman to Edward Broomsill 3 Jun 1644
Gibb John s Edward, 'Hethorp', Oxf?, ? to John Merick 6 Jul 1667
Gibberd Thomas s Robert, Grimsbury [Warkworth], Nth, yeoman† to Edmund Barcock 29 Oct 1649
Gibbins Joseph s William, Oscot [Perry Barr], Sts, yeoman to Richard Bull 3 Jul 1655
Gibbons John s William, Denham, Bkm [? *in Ms* 'Mdx'], tanner† to John Childe 6 Mar 1703/4 <19 Jun 1704 turned over to David Haynes>
Gibbons Robert s Robert, Sunbury, Mdx, husbandman to Richard Parker 10 Dec 1753
Gibbons William s John, Lambeth, Sry, lath render8 to Thomas Northover 5 Jan 1686/7
Gibbs James s Daniel, Islington, Mdx, coachman to Henry Clarke 3 Aug 1730 <26 Apr 1733 turned over to Joseph Tovey>
Gibson Jeremy s Thomas, citizen and fruiterer to Robert Hunt 4 Oct 1661
Gibson John s Barnaby, Little Stonham, Sfk, gentleman to William Prince 16 Aug 1680
Gibson John s Robert, Bermondsey, Sry, tailor to George Carpenter 23 Aug 1728
Gibson Robert s George, St Andrew Holborn, Lnd, gentleman to Gabriel Bulter 10 Jul 1771
Gibson Samuel s Robert, Holborn, Mdx, tallow chandler to Thomas Sawtell 8 Jan 1771
Gibson Thomas s Thomas, Lnd, tailor to John Ayscough 27 Jul 1683
Gibson Thomas s Anthony, St Katherine by the Tower, Mdx, butcher to Elizabeth widow of Robert Gresswell 22 Dec 1708
Gibson William s William, St George Hanover Square, cheesemonger to Caleb Talbot 8 Oct 1770
Gidden Charles s Thomas, Lambeth, Sry, cooper to William Martin 27 May 1754 <3 Aug 1756 turned over to Thomas Stinnett, citizen and cooper>
Giddens Thomas s Thomas, Linton, Cam, gentleman† to Thomas Rigby 4 Feb 1733/4
Gielbe Thomas s John, Staines, Mdx, miller to William Payne 8 Aug 1688
Gifford Benjamin s John, Fordingbridge, Ham, weaver to Josiah Ragdale 1 Mar 1681/2
Gigner Francis s William, citizen and tinplateworker to James Ennis 15 Jul 1731
Gilbert Peter s Benjamin, Southall, Mdx, farmer to Nathaniel West 9 Dec 1731
Gilbert Thomas s William, citizen and clockmaker† to George Shelley 4 Mar 1724/5 <6 Mar 1726/7 turned over to Benjamin Durnford, citizen and goldsmith>
Gilbert William s Thomas, West Malling, Ken, tanner to Robert Roe 12 Aug 1656 <bond from William Jordan, West Malling, Ken, tanner>
Gilbird Hugh s John, Hatfield, Hrt, yeoman to Daniel Warren 5 Jul 1708
Gilderson John s George, Edmonton, Mdx, yeoman to John Wilford 6 Feb 1726/7
Gildon John s Joseph, 'Gaspord', Som, gentleman† to Benjamin Spering 1 May 1693
Gilebrand John s John, Beckenham [? *in Ms* 'Beck'], Ken, fruiterer to George Harling 17 Apr 1643
Giles Daniel s Daniel to his father 27 Mar 1656
Giles John s Richard, Ravenstonedale, Wes, yeoman to John Harrison 2 Jul 1698

Giles Richard s Richard, Newington, Sry, yeoman† to Edmund Carpenter 2 Jul 1705 <5 Dec 1709 turned over to Elizabeth widow of Robert Grosswell>
Giles Thomas s Simon, citizen and farrier to Robert Marchant 25 Feb 1659/60
Gill John s Thomas, Hampton, Gls, carrier to Thomas Hill 5 Jan 1680/1
Gill Mark s Henry, St Thomas Southwark, Sry, hatbandmaker to John Pigeon 5 Sep 1659
Gill William s William, Whitechapel, Mdx, dyer to Mary Smith 19 Nov 1765
Gillett William s Robert, Rotherhithe, Sry, caulker† to George Carpenter 31 Aug 1758
Gillgrest John s Thomas, citizen and painter stainer† to John Davenport 7 Mar 1708/9
Gillham George to Joseph Harris 5 Dec 1799
Gillmore Richard s Edward, citizen and vintner† to John Eyre 6 Oct 1710
Gingall Thomas s John, Charlton, Wil, gardener to Maurice Jarvis 27 Sep 1677
Girard Joseph s Paul, Lambeth, Sry, watch chaser to Thomas Searle 27 Aug 1772
Gird Mary d Christopher, Exeter, Dev, tucker† to John Carter 7 Feb 1714/5 <turned over to Eleanor widow of Stephen Parker, citizen and haberdasher>
Gislingham Robert s James, Ipswich, Sfk, mariner to Philip Haden 1 Nov 1758
Gittens Walter s Walter, Brentwood, Ess, gentleman† to Francis Marshall 18 Jul 1648
Gladman Bartholomew s Richard, Westminster, Mdx, butcher to John Smith 3 Dec 1733
Gladman Michael s Thomas, Uxbridge, Mdx, tallow chandler to Brian Ayliffe 25 Jul 1687
Glanvill Richard s Thomas, Shadwell, Mdx, surgeon† to Francis Briscoe 5 Jan 1712/3
Glascock Thomas s William, Jenningsbury, Hrt, gentleman to Thomas Lawrence 3 Mar 1655/6
Glass Abigail d Alexander, Cannon Street, Lnd, grocer† to Gabriel Poulter 3 Sep 1776
Glover Jonathan s Robert, Hatfield, Hrt, farmer to James Ennis 5 Jun 1727
Glover Mathew s Mathew, Croydon, Sry, mercer† to Philip Constable 26 Feb 1685/6
Glover William s Robert, Dartford, Ken, innholder† to William Thatcher 24 Sep 1694
Glue James s Stephen, Axholme, Lin, yeoman to Abraham Brock 25 Jul 1633
Glyn Thomas s Thomas, Southwark, Sry, weaver to George Carpenter 9 Feb 1761
Goble James s James, Arundel, Ssx to his father 2 Jul 1678
Godbee Edward s William, citizen and merchant tailor† to John Wood 29 Dec 1687
Goddard Anthony s Robert, citizen and ? to William Cranwell ? Oct 1662
Goddard Daniel s Daniel, Burghfield, Brk, yeoman to Giles Harris 1 May 1710 <6 Aug 1711 turned over to John Herbert; 4 Apr 1715 master† by Martha Herbert, administrator to William Williams>
Goddard John s Howell, Somerford Keynes, Wil, clothier to Thomas Searle 13 Apr 1749
Goddard Michael s Robert, Southwark, Sry, whitster† to John Hill 6 Jul 1730
Goddard Robert s William, Edmonton, Mdx, yeoman to Henry Soames 6 Feb 1770
Goddard Robert s Robert, Fleet Market, Lnd to his father 7 Apr 1795
Goddard William s Thomas, Long Marston, Hrt, yeoman to William Butler 17 Mar 1651/2
Godden Robert s George, Andover, Ham, currier† to Henry Wyne 25 Nov 1687
Godfrey George s John, Lnd, gentleman to Alexander Weedon 7 Jun 1743 <4 Jul 1749 turned over to John Sibley>
Godfrey Savil s Savil, Lambeth, Sry, turner to Thomas Searle 12 May 1758
Godlington Joseph s Thomas, citizen and salter to Edward Tomlins 11 Oct 1670
Godsane William s William, Blackmore, Ess, turner to Thomas Chambers 24 Jan 1688/9
Godwin Benjamin s Samuel, Lnd, oilman to Thomas Burge 6 Sep 1708
Godwin Charles s William, Bath, Som, clothworker† to Andrew Godwin 17 Nov 1679
Godwin John s John, Clerkenwell, innholder to Elizabeth widow of Robert Bradley 24 Mar 1651/2
Godwin Peter s John, Lnd, merchant to John Greening 1 Sep 1684
Godwin Thomas s John, Swanbourne, Bkm, yeoman to John Bavin 8 Feb 1650/1
Godwyn Mathew s John, Swanbourne, Bkm, yeoman to John Bavin 15 Jan 1648/9
Goff William s Thomas, Alresford, Ham, yeoman to Bartholomew Wimberly 12 Nov 1716
Gold John s John, Eton, Bkm, brewer to Robert Driver 11 Jun 1684
Goldham Thomas s William, Boreham Street, Ssx, mercer to Thomas Cooper 28 Feb 1651/2
Golding Francis s William, Burnham, Bkm, husbandman to Thomas Hatton 16 Jun 1657
Golding Robert s Robert, Chatham, Ken, carpenter† to Robert French 17 May 1763
Goldsmith Abraham s Richard, Barton, Bdf, yeoman† to Richard Parrott 27 Dec 1649
Goldsmith Fuller s Thomas, Penshurst, Ken, yeoman to Hugh Daniel 29 May 1673
Goldsmith John s Richard, Dartford, Ken, blacksmith† to Thomas Ferrall 11 Dec 1713
Goldsmith Joseph s Joseph, Bermondsey, Sry, mariner† to John Willoughby 7 Nov 1786

Goldsmith Thomas s Edward, St Giles in the Fields, Mdx, victualler to Thomas Bennett 5 Jun 1699
Goldstone Henry s Thomas, Lambeth, Sry, waterman† to William Hunt 12 Jan 1691/2
Good Robert s William, Nicholas Hospital, Salisbury, yeoman to William Thompson 28 Jul 1646
Goode Henry s William, Napton on the Hill, War, husbandman to Ralph Humferson 3 Jul 1637
Goode John s Robert, Ufton, Brk, clerk to Joseph Smith 20 Jun 1637
Goode John s Robert, Ufton, Brk, clerk to John Goode 15 Nov 1649
Goode Marmaduke s John to his father 30 Sep 1675
Goode Richard s Richard, Warwick, War, tallow chandler to Samuel Wheeler 19 Jul 1707
Goode Thomas s Robert, Ufton, Brk, clerk to John Goode 12 Aug 1650
Goodeman Edward s William, Market Harborough, Lei, flaxman to John Shuter 3 May 1708
Goodinge Thomas s John, Cavendish Square, Mdx, brewer to Edward Myers 6 Nov 1787
Goodman Charles s John, Llanelidan, Den, gentleman to William Goodman 2 May 1642
Goodman Edward s William, Arthingworth, Nth, butcher to Joan widow of John Noble 15 Nov 1653
Goodman William s William, Arthingworth, Nth, yeoman to Joan widow of John Noble 22 Jun 1654
Goodreg Robert s John, Snitterfield, War, yeoman to Simon White 22 Aug 1642
Goodson Benham s Robert, Thame, Oxf, cooper† to Thomas Higgins 10 Sep 1716
Goodson Seth s Robert, Wotton, Bkm, yeoman to John Pratt 28 Nov 1687
Goodwin John s Richard, West Ham, Ess, yeoman† to John Bodle 20 May 1679
Goodwin Philip s Philip, Rotherhithe, Sry, clerk to Anthony Palmer 10 May 1667
Goodwin Thomas s Robert, Clapham, Sry [? *in Ms* 'Mdx'], butcher to William Newman 21 Jun 1709
Goodwinn Richard s Richard, Portsmouth, Ham, ropemaker† to William Stanley 2 Aug 1697
Goodyeare James s John, Langley, Bkm, yeoman to Robert Fewtrell 28 Feb 1660/1
Goore Edmund s Richard, Altcar [? *in Ms* 'Alker'], Lan, gentleman† to Joseph Callcott 12 Nov 1722
Gopsill George s John, St Olave Southwark, Sry, blacksmith to Thomas Cryer 6 Dec 1697
Gorroway Manuel s James, St Giles in the Fields, carpenter† to Benjamin Speering 1 Feb 1691/2
Gorstelow John s Walter, citizen and painter stainer to Henry Pauncefoote 19 Jan 1652/3
Gorsuch John s William, Woodstock, Oxf, gentleman to Richard Cooper 3 Mar 1679/80
Gosden John s John, Ash, Sry, yeoman to William Smith 22 Jul 1668
Gosfright Daniel s Solomon, citizen and haberdasher to Benjamin Brownesmith 18 Nov 1681
Gosling Isaac s Richard, Hammersmith, Mdx, brickmaker† to Humphrey King 4 Dec 1671
Gossen Robert s William, Burford, Oxf, innholder† to Thomas Cole 17 Jun 1708
Gould Every s John, Upwey, Dor, esquire† to Nicholas Gould 12 Oct 1682
Gould James s John, Upwey, Dor, esquire† to Nicholas Gould 17 Dec 1688
Gould John s John, citizen and tallow chandler† to Cornelius Woolley 1 Feb 1731/2
Gould Samuel s John, citizen and goldsmith† to Richard York 2 Aug 1714
Goulding Joseph s John, Kirkoswald, Cul, grocer to John Phillips 4 Nov 1777 <2 Dec 1777 turned over to Isaac Phillips>
Gouldstone Thomas s Henry, Scawton, Yks, farmer to Thomas Crowther 6 Jul 1772
Goulston Maurice s Mary, Wrexham, Den, Wal to Charles Thatcher, snr. 24 May 1717
Grace Henry s William, Weston Turville, Bkm, tailor to Joseph Huntman 7 Sep 1685
Graime Richard s Richard, citizen and merchant tailor to Edward Wright 28 Oct 1670
Grane Robert s William, Bicker, Lin, yeoman to Bartholomew Wimberley 1 Nov 1731
Grange William s Edward, citizen and cutler† to William Payne 19 Oct 1686
Granger William s Samuel, St Botolph Aldgate, Mdx, pattenmaker to William Gurney 3 Nov 1679
Graves Humphrey s William, Kirton, Lin, gentleman to William Gurney 4 Dec 1676
Graves Robert s Robert, Stratford, Ess, glazier to Benjamin Merriman 24 Mar 1763
Gray Christopher s Christopher, citizen and plaisterer† to Benjamin Lazinby 2 May 1739
Gray John s Thomas, Romford, Ess, yeoman to Thomas Chambers 9 Jun 1687
Gray John s John, Newbury, Brk, mealman to John Ham 1 Oct 1711
Gray John s John, Chipping Ongar, Ess, farmer to Thomas Baynes 1 Jul 1728 <1 Oct 1733 master† turned over with consent of Mary Baynes, widow and administrator to Edward Fitz>
Gray John s Michael, Romford, Ess, yeoman† to John Gray 5 Mar 1759
Gray Ralph s John, St Clement Danes, Mdx, gentleman to George Bowyer 6 Apr 1648
Gray Simon s Simon, 'Pryall?', Lin, butcher† to John Edden 7 Jun 1670
Gray Thomas s Thomas, Stainton, Yks, yeoman to William Winney 12 Jul 1660

Gray Thomas s Richard, Shoreditch, Mdx, brickmaker to John Wyburd 6 Apr 1682
Gray Thomas s Thomas, St Martin in the Fields, Mdx, butcher to Harris Gregory 1 Jun 1784
Greatalder John s John, Whitechapel, Mdx, butcher to Thomas Chambers 6 Mar 1682/3
Greaves Thomas s Thomas, Stepney, Mdx, shipwright to Benjamin Brownsmith 9 Oct 1699
<10 Feb 1701 cancelled>
Green Henry s Edward, Westminster, gentleman to Mary widow of George Belliss 5 Aug 1746
Green James s Robert, Wakefield, Yks, clothworker to William Yalden 17 Nov 1756
Green William s William, Lnd† to John Furnis 2 Jul 1722 <13 Apr 1724 turned over
to Richard Baker, citizen and merchant tailor>
Greenall Thomas Wells s Robert, Banbury, Oxf, maltster to Martin Wheatly 10 Apr 1718
<6 Aug 1722 turned over to Richard Burgis, citizen and draper>
Greenbrough Robert s Robert, Crowell, Oxf, gentleman to Thomas Smalridge 5 Jul 1652
Greene Edward s Richard, Minety, Gls, yeoman† to John Williams 20 Jul 1668
Greene Francis s Hatton, Faringdon, Brk, glover to Thomas Taylor 5 Jun 1699
Greene Giles s Henry, Lower Slaughter, Gls, yeoman† to William Miller 14 Dec 1668
Greene Henry s William to his father 31 Jan 1704/5
Greene John s Giles, Waltham Holy Cross, Ess, yeoman to John Dell 31 May 1649
Greene John s Lawrence, Hillingdon, Mdx, victualler to Thomas Allen 8 Apr 1700
Greene John s John, Kirtlington, Oxf, yeoman† to John Gilgrest 9 Feb 1718/9 <5 Aug 1723
turned over to John Davenport>
Greene John s William, citizen and painter stainer† to Nathaniel West 2 Apr 1723
Greene Joshua s Joshua, citizen and vintner to Simon Darrant 26 Mar 1686
Greene Richard s John, Warwick, War, gentleman† to John Clarke 21 Feb 1669/70
Greene Sawdrey s Giles, Waltham Abbey, Ess† to John Greene 6 Jun 1664
Greene Thomas s Abraham, Warwick, War, chandler to Andrew Walker 25 Jan 1635/6
Greene Thomas s Thomas, Sutton, Sry, yeoman† to Mathew Peirce 23 Feb 1687/8
Greene William s John, Ratley, War, yeoman to Robert Greene 15 Dec 1633
Greene William s John, Hawkshead, Lan, gentleman† to William Davis 13 Jul 1638
Greene William s William, Clerkenwell, Mdx, gentleman to Josiah Ragdale 25 Dec 1678
Greenehill Elizabeth d William, Grays Inn, Mdx, gentleman† to Simon Greenehill 15 Aug 1672
Greeneing Nathaniel s John to his father 7 Feb 1708/9
Greening John s John, Didbrook, Gls, yeoman† to Joseph Watts 23 Dec 1671
Greening Norton s Peter to his father 5 Jan 1741/2
Greensmith Richard s Ignatius, Ravenstone, Dby, yeoman to William Plomber 20 Feb 1677/8
Greenway Griffin s Richard, Cassington, Oxf, yeoman to Richard Bedwell 4 Nov 1647
Greenway John s Thomas, Walton, Gls, yeoman† to Nathaniel Chandler 22 Jun 1676
Greenwood Abraham s John, citizen and weaver to Richard Hodgkin 10 Nov 1673
Greenwood Moses s Robert, Corby, Nth, gentleman to John Waters 11 Nov 1679
Gregg Thomas s Edward, St Olave Southwark, Sry, tallow chandler† to Edward Horne 22 Dec 1691
Gregorie Robert s John, Ufton, Brk, husbandman to William Thompson 30 Mar 1655
Gregory Hains s Edward, citizen and baker† to Nathaniel Might 5 Apr 1758
Gregory Humphrey s Joshua, St Giles Cripplegate, Lnd, cheesemonger to John Bryan 3 Aug 1791
Gregory James s Samuel, Berkhamstead, Hrt, smith† to Daniel Child ? Dec 1670
Gregory James s Joseph, Hitchin, Hrt, gentleman to John Hide 24 Jun 1742
Gregory Joseph s Joseph, Leighton Buzzard, Bdf, baker to Edmund Belson 7 Oct 1680
Gregory Rebecca d William to his father 15 Oct 1795
Gregory Richard s Richard, St Giles in the Fields, Mdx, gentleman to John Hooker 30 Oct 1670
Gregory Thomas s Thomas, Wavendon, Bkm, yeoman to Thomas Hill 8 May 1694
Gregory William s William, Nicholas Lane, Lnd, tailor to Richard Collins 14 May 1772
Gresham Jeremiah s Nehemiah, Haworth, Yks, yeoman to William Gurney 25 Sep 1676
Gressingham Thomas s Thomas, Teddington, Mdx, gentleman† to John Eyre 4 Aug 1703
Gresswell Robert s George, Waddingworth, Lin, yeoman† to John Shuter 8 Nov 1692
Greswold John s Henry, Solihull, War, clerk† to Henry Lyell 18 Dec 1701
Grevile William s Henry, Gloucester, Gls, woollen draper† to Nathan Payne 11 Jul 1700
<3 Mar 1706/7 turned over to Joseph Cooper>
Gridley Joseph s John, Whitechapel, Mdx, linemaker to John Furnis 3 Apr 1721
Griffin Benjamin s Benjamin, Drayton, Mdx, miller to Robert Udall 20 Apr 1646

Griffin Benjamin s John, Brook Market, Mdx, butcher to John Gould 4 Apr 1786 <6 Mar 1800 master† freedom refused>
Griffin David s William, Stroudwater, Gls, clothier to William Wood 16 May 1653
Griffin John s George, Walthamstow, Ess, coachman† to Thomas Burrow 3 Jan 1697/8
Griffin Samuel s Samuel, Lnd, gentleman to Thomas Tolderey 5 Feb 1755
Griffin William s John, Henley, Oxf, butcher to Ezekiel Page 5 Jul 1660
Griffith James s James, 'Clandessen', Mgy, clerk to William Gaunt 7 Jan 1697/8
Griffith James s James, Bermondsey, Sry, tanner† to John Stent 4 Oct 1743
Griffith Samuel s John, Ludlow, Sal, glover to Samuel Wheeler 6 Jan 1723/4
Griffiths Griffith s David, Knockin, Sal, yeoman† to Mathew Snabling 21 Dec 1682
Griffiths Nathaniel s William, St Giles in the Fields, labourer to Thomas Stephenson 4 May 1696
Grigby Edward s Edmund, 'Bayton', Sfk, gentleman† to Peter Pickering 5 Dec 1674
Grigg Edward s Edward, St Olave Southwark, Sry, tallow chandler† to Thomas Rust 16 Mar 1697/8
Grigg Thomas s Thomas, Limehouse, Mdx, chirurgeon† to William Winney 18 Jun 1668
Griggs George s Daniel, Waltham Abbey, Ess, husbandman to James Lunn 12 Apr 1649
Grimes John s John, Winslow, Bkm, clerk† to John Hamnett 11 Sep 1724
Grimes Ralph Errington s Richard, All Hallows the Great, carver† to Thomas Searle 3 Apr 1744
Grinaway Peter s Peter, citizen and butcher to Elizabeth widow of John Hastings 1 Jul 1706
Grinley George s John, Lnd, brewer† to Philip Constable 30 Jul 1695
Grinter George s Simon, Chard, Som, clothier† to John Newport 12 Oct 1677
Grinter Thomas s Robert, East Harptree, Som, yeoman to William Simcock 20 Jan 1634/5
Grove Arthur s Richard, Tingewick, Bkm, yeoman† to William Smith 20 Jul 1669
Grove George s John, Stowe, Bkm, gardener to John Child, snr. 2 Oct 1699
Grove John s John, Marsh Gibbon [? *in Ms* 'Mash'], Bkm, yeoman to Margaret widow of Leonard Turner 30 Apr 1655
Grove Richard s George, Penn, Bkm, yeoman to Richard Wilkinson 13 Jun 1648
Grove William s Francis, Steventon, Brk, gentleman to Richard Parret 7 Aug 1662
Grove William s Joseph, Harmondsworth, Mdx, farmer to William Alexander 26 Nov 1751
Grover Thomas s Andrew, Aldenham, Hrt, yeoman to Thomas Harris 8 Apr 1669
Groves Joseph s William, Highgate, Mdx, baker to Jonathan Watts 7 Dec 1719 <turned over to Edward Tomkins>
Groves Richard s George, Cirencester, Gls, clothier† to Joseph Lane 4 Jun 1733
Growndes Thomas s Thomas, Sherborne, Dor, gentleman to Robert Thompson 4 Sep 1699
Guenin Thomas s James, Spitalfields, Mdx, weaver to Richard Carter 3 Nov 1736
Guilford Francis s Francis, Cuddington, Bkm, mason to Benjamin Free 7 May 1700
Gulliford Samuel s William, citizen and tallow chandler† to Mary widow of William Gulliford 5 Jul 1725
Gulliford William s John, Fifehead Magdalen, Dor, yeoman to William Gurney 3 Sep 1679
Gulliford William s John, Fifehead Magdalen, Dor, serge weaver to William Gulliford 1 Aug 1709
Gummershall William s John, Woodford, Ess, yeoman to John Bryan 4 Feb 1777
Gunne Thomas s William, Edgware, Mdx, yeoman to Thomas Pratt 20 Nov 1638
Gunson John s Thomas to his father 3 Oct 1659
Gunson Thomas s Thomas to his father 8 May 1654
Gunter William s John, 'Kembrieagle', Brk, yeoman† to William Bateman 22 Dec 1646
Gurdon John s Alexander, citizen and broderer to Henry Lille 3 Aug 1663
Gurling Bassum s Thomas, Lynn, Nfk, mercer to Samuel James 18 Jan 1682/3
Gurnel William s Stephen, Ambleside, Wes, mercer† to James West 4 Nov 1673
Gurney Charles s Leonard, North Mimms, Hrt, tailor to John Gardner 9 Feb 1761
Gurney Charles s John, Wokingham, Brk [? *in Ms* 'Oakingdon, Mdx'], farmer to John Lambert 3 Nov 1779
Gurney Christopher s Ralph to his father 6 Jun 1650
Gurney Daniel s George, Dartford, Ken, surgeon† to Phineas Patershall 6 Feb 1752 <3 Feb 1758 turned over to John Packman>
Gurney Thomas s John, Wokingham, Brk [? *in Ms* 'Mdx'], grazier to John Lambert 1 Jun 1771
Guttereg William s John, Shrewsbury, Sal, husbandman† to Thomas Hatton 8 Jan 1646/7
Guy Edward s William, citizen and dyer† to Benjamin Culcheth 14 Feb 1669/70
Guy William s William, Northampton, Nth, wiredrawer to Edward Mathewes 20 Jul 1669
Guye Thomas s Thomas, Tytherington, Som, clothworker to James West 12 Jul 1692

Gwyn Thomas s John, Silsoe, Bdf, tailor to Joseph Swift 2 Jun 1701

Haddon Richard s Richard, Barking, Ess, gentleman to John Orsby 24 Oct 1638
Hadson James s John, citizen and vintner to James Packett 11 Jul 1688
Hagger James s Thomas, Chrishall, Ess, yeoman to Bernard Block 21 Jul 1669
Haile Jonathan s Arnold, citizen and weaver to John Tyson 28 Dec 1667
Haines Henry s Thomas, Fyfield, Brk, yeoman† to Josiah Ragdale 5 Aug 1695
Halbut Richard s John, Shadwell, Mdx, cooper to Philip Haden 11 Jul 1750
Hale John s John, Broadwell, Gls, yeoman to Edward Kingsley 10 Feb 1690/1
Hale William s Christopher, St Botolph Aldgate, Lnd, victualler to John Tomkins 21 Mar 1770
<4 Feb 1777 turned over to Thomas Merriman>
Hales Anthony s George Mason, Southwark Borough, Sry, gentleman to Anthony Hales 6 Oct 1795
Halfepenny William s William, Pirton, Hrt to William Ashman 8 Dec 1718
Halford Andrew s Andrew, Harborough, Lei to James Horton 25 Nov 1662
Halford Anthony s John, citizen and fishmonger to Henry Burton 7 Jul 1701
Halford Joseph s Joseph, Richmond, Sry, grocer† to Robert Wyrill 12 Nov 1711 <9 Sep 1715 turned over to George Gerrard>
Halford Thomas s Thomas, Halford, War, gentleman to Thomas Wigg 8 Sep and 8 Dec 1692
Hall Benjamin s Michael, Whitton, Twickenham, Mdx, maltster to John Hunt 5 Sep 1698
Hall Benjamin s Samuel, Ratcliffe Highway, Mdx, shoemaker to Philip Haden 1 Sep 1762
Hall Brandon s George, citizen and feltmaker to Gilbert Brandon 25 May 1720 <turned over to John Dell, citizen and merchant tailor>
Hall Christopher John s Christopher, Bagnige Marsh, Mdx, yeoman to Thomas Jarvis 6 Feb 1787
Hall Edmund s Henry, St Giles in the Fields, Mdx, bricklayer to Edmund Hunt 8 Nov 1670
Hall Edmund s William, Bourton on Water, Gls, gentleman to John Fist 1 Apr 1740
Hall Edward s Robert, Haddenham, Cam, yeoman to Gilbert Cornelius 14 Apr 1641
Hall George s John, citizen and tallow chandler† to George Wilcox 13 Nov 1646
Hall Henry s Henry, Whitechapel, Mdx, poulterer to William Minchin 1 Feb 1654/5
Hall Hugh s Hugh, citizen and joiner† to Humphrey King 27 Apr 1667
Hall James s James, citizen and plaisterer† to Thomas Pickett 2 Mar 1723/4
Hall James s Sanders, Ayrshire, Sco, mariner† to Thomas Searle 9 Jul 1756
Hall John s William, Arlingham, Gls, tallow chandler† to William Brewis 1 Dec 1707
Hall John s Thomas, Greenwich, Ken, cheesemonger to Thomas Williams 6 Sep 1725
Hall Nathaniel s John, Reddish [Stockport], Lan, flaxman to James Church 17 Jul 1685
Hall Nathaniel s Nathaniel to his father 12 Jan 1709/10
Hall Owen s Bartholomew, Barkham, Brk, esquire to Nathaniel Ragdale 2 May 1709 <9 Mar 1709/10 turned over by Hippsley Merchant, exec. to William Tanner, citizen and cordwainer>
Hall Peter s Jacob, Shadwell, Mdx, merchant† to Lancelot Vibart 19 Mar 1727/8
Hall Richard s William, Ash Prior, Som, bricklayer† to Edmund Hall 10 Jan 1708/9
Hall Robert s Richard, citizen and cook† to Peter Delight 2 Mar 1712/3
Hall Thomas s John, Greenwich, Ken, gentleman† to James Harding 3 Apr 1710
Hall William s William, Bampton, Oxf† to Margaret widow of Leonard Turner 20 Jun 1650
Hall William s William, Churchover, War, innholder to Robert Bly 1 May 1721
Halsey Henry s Robert, Edmonton, Mdx, tanner to Thomas Beadle 10 Jun 1646
Halsey John s Edward, citizen and weaver to John Jellings 6 Mar 1677/8
Halsted Thomas s John, Walworth [Newington], Sry, gentleman† to John Lindsey 4 Apr 1786
Ham John s John, Bentworth, Ham, blacksmith to Joseph Huntman 15 Apr 1684
Ham Moses s John, Bentworth, Ham, blacksmith† to John Ham 19 May 1692
Hamand Thomas s Thomas, West Haddon, Nth, husbandman† to Robert Belson 24 Nov 1679
Hamblen Mathew s Anthony, Hungerford, Brk, husbandman† to Nicholas Catkill 14 Jul 1669
Hamersly Charles s Thomas, Lnd, linen draper† to John Kingston 12 Nov 1705
Hamett John s John, Isleworth, Mdx, cheesemonger to Thomas Hamett 20 Mar 1689/90
Hammant Tobias s John, Bildeston, Sfk, yeoman† to John Church 11 Jul 1671
Hammet Edward s Thomas to his father 6 Apr 1703
Hammon Giles s Giles, Wick Street [Painswick], Gls, yeoman† to Richard Bull 2 Apr 1672
Hammond Thomas s Thomas, Deptford, Ken, carpenter† to John Ayscough 2 Oct 1704
<4 Feb 1705/6 turned over to Mary Andrewes, widow>
Hamnett John s John, Shadwell, Mdx, cheesemonger to John Tilley 7 Mar 1714/5

Hamon Jonathan s Richard, Wokingham, Brk, clothier to John Prichard 3 May 1641
Hamond Henry s Giles, Dorchester, Dor, carpenter† to Thomas Allin 5 Oct 1646
Hamond John s William, Battersea, Sry, yeoman to Leonard Turner 19 Nov 1635
Hamond John s Thomas, St Margaret Westminster, tallow chandler† to John Ayliffe 1 Mar 1707/8
Hamond Samuel s Thomas, Hurstmonceaux, Ssx, yeoman to John Tyson 6 Feb 1649/50
Hampsheire Thomas s John, Eynsham, Oxf, yeoman to William Flower 8 Nov 1653
Hampton Edward s John, Bridge Yard, Southwark, Sry, victualler† to Joseph Flight 3 Oct 1780
Hampton John s John, St John Horsleydown, Sry, tanner to John Packman 10 Sep 1773
Hampton Richard s Richard, Great Neston, Chs, yeoman to Thomas Allen 29 Jul 1650
Hanckes Samuel s Thomas, citizen and cordwainer† to Robert More 16 May 1648
Hancock John s Richard, Reading, Brk, clothier to Josiah Ragdale 29 Oct 1659
Hancock John s James, Deptford, Ken, tailor† to George Carpenter 16 Oct 1766 <9 Jan 1771 turned over to John Crook, citizen and joiner>
Hancock Robert s Isaac, St Martin in the Fields, Mdx, painter to Jeremy Ridge 4 Feb 1722/3
Hand Martha s Jeremiah, Aldworth, Brk, gentleman to John Tuer 17 Jun 1669
Hands John s Clement, Greenwich, Ken, husbandman to Jacob Packett 6 May 1700 <17 Jan 1704/5 master† turned over by Samuel Nellham, administrator to Robert Gresswell>
Hankin George s George, citizen and haberdasher to Richard Weste 3 Nov 1707 <6 Aug 1711 turned over to Thomas Walter, citizen and dyer>
Hankin John s William, Chelsea, Mdx, lighterman† to Joseph Benson 14 Jun 1729 <4 Jun 1733 master† turned over with consent of James Hill, administrator to Samuel Mackerness>
Hankinson John s John, citizen and butcher† to William Miller 20 Jul 1675
Hankinson Robert s John, St Giles, Mdx, carpenter to Stephen Harris 5 Jun 1667
Hanks Thomas s James, Hatton Garden, Mdx, tailor to Charles Dare 7 Feb 1792 <turned over to John Stephens, citizen and salter>
Hankson Richard s John, Dalbury [? *in Ms* 'Daberles'], Dby, carpenter to Francis Pittman 15 Nov 1641
Hannis Esther d Joseph, Nibley, Gls, clothier† to Thomas Humphries 6 Jun 1698
Hanson Edward s Thomas, citizen and grocer† to John Skepper 28 Mar 1670
Hanson Robert s ?, citizen and fishmonger† to William Dutton 3 Jan 1670/1
Hanson Samuel s Samuel, citizen and haberdasher to Jonathan Hicks 6 Aug 1716
Hanson William s William, citizen and grocer to Richard Potter 8 Apr 1639 <bond from Robert Hanson, Thomas Hanson and Francis Hanson>
Hapgood Richard s Richard, Charlton, Dor, yeoman to William Surman 15 Dec 1674
Harbart Philip s Richard, Brailes, War, clerk to John Edden 30 Sep 1669
Harbert Philip s George, Porton, Wil, slater to Walter Lewer 13 Jan 1700/1
Harding Gilbert s John, citizen and cordwainer† to John Hooker 22 Apr 1663
Harding John s Henry, St Martin in the Fields, Mdx, gardener† to Thomas Cole 2 Oct 1662
Harding John s Giles, Painswick, Gls, innholder† to John Ayliffe 18 Nov 1699
Harding John s William, Trowbridge, Wil, clothmaker to Richard Collier 7 Oct 1706
Harding Joseph s James, citizen and mercer to John Bedwell 5 Dec 1720
Harding Richard s Richard to his father 29 May 1678
Harding Richard s Richard, Greenwich, Ken to Benjamin Skelton 2 Jul 1793
Harding Simon s John, citizen and joiner to Joseph Wedgeburrough 2 May 1715
Harding Thomas s William, Stafford, Sts, husbandman to Simon Dawson 24 Apr 1647
Hardy John s Bartholomew, Barningham, Yks, gentleman to William Bowyer 23 Nov 1648
Hardy John s Thomas, Bridport, Dor, yeoman to Thomas Radley 7 Nov 1709
Hardy Thomas s William, Stodday, Lan, yeoman to ... Dalock 18 Nov 1641
Hare John s Benjamin, Edmonton, Mdx, gentleman† to John Osgood 2 Oct 1704
Harebottle William s Robert, Highgate, Mdx, chirurgeon to James Wakeham 6 Jan 1706/7
Harford Samuel s Samuel, Spitalfields, Mdx, stationer to Edward Palmer 3 Dec 1776
Harison John s John, Hurst, Brk, gentleman to Joseph Sheldon 9 Jun 1656
Harlow Francis s George, St John Horsleydown, Sry, waterman to George Harlow 13 Jun 1770
Harlow George s George, Fulham, Mdx, waterman† to Thomas Rigby 4 Aug 1740 <11 Dec 1745 turned over to Ann widow of Peter Archer, citizen and haberdasher>
Harlow Thomas s George, St John Horsleydown, Sry, waterman to George Harlow 27 Oct 1772
Harper Charles s William, Westminster, Mdx, grocer† to William Cogan 7 Jun 1732
Harper John s Leonard, St Martin in the Fields, Mdx, joiner† to Thomas Stephenson 29 Aug 1687

Harper Timothy s William, Stepney, Mdx, shoemaker to John Smith 31 Mar 1690
Harpur William s John, citizen and salter† to Joseph Lane 9 Jun 1718
Harriman William s Thomas, Tooley Street, Southwark, Sry, yeoman to Daniel Webb 2 May 1780
Harrington Richard s Richard, Enfield, Mdx, surgeon† to John Chatfield 3 Feb 1746/7
Harrington William s Robert, Ipswich, Sfk, husbandman† to Thomas Hatton 26 Oct 1663
Harris Barkley s Barkley, Clapham, Sry, vintner† to Robert Kerby 7 Aug 1727
Harris Daniel s Daniel, Weston Favell, Nth, yeoman† to Nathaniel Winchester 23 Jul 1684
Harris Edward s Edward, Aldenham, Hrt, yeoman to John Harris 5 Jun 1651
Harris Edward s John, Ramsbury, Wil, husbandman† to William Haydon 19 Oct 1691
Harris Edward s Edward, Holborn, Mdx, gentleman to John Wilford 4 Apr 1715
Harris Franklin s Benjamin, Hackney, Mdx, gentleman† to Joseph Woodward 27 Jun 1726
Harris George s George, Thorpe Mandeville, Nth, grazier† to Edward Butcher 1 Nov 1738
Harris Giles s Thomas, Charlbury, Oxf, yeoman to William Proudman 22 Mar 1691/2
Harris Henry s George, Thorpe, Nth, grazier† to Edward Butcher 1 Apr 1734
Harris James s James, Hereford, Hef, feltmaker to William Allen 3 Jul 1682
Harris James s Robert, East Indies, gentleman to Robert French 8 Jul 1767
Harris John s Thomas, Witney, Oxf, clothier to William Minchin 25 Feb 1651/2
Harris John s Edward, Aldenham, Hrt, yeoman to Edward Harris 22 Nov 1661
Harris John s Robert, Bishops Waltham, Ham, yeoman to Robert Ayliffe 6 Dec 1714 <2 Nov 1719 master† turned over by Mary Ayliffe, mother and administrator of Robert to Matthias Wheatley>
Harris John s George, Thorpe Mandeville, Nth, grazier† to Edward Butcher 2 Nov 1742
Harris Jonathan s Jonathan, East Molesey, Sry, blacksmith to Robert Stevens 2 Nov 1713
Harris Joseph s Robert, Bradford, Wor, yeoman to Josiah Ragdale 3 Mar 1685/6
Harris Joseph s Joseph, Chiswick, Mdx, labourer to James Coates 1 Jan 1739/40
Harris Mathew s Uriah, Weston, Hrt, yeoman to Henry Lathwell 30 Oct 1678
Harris Michael John s George, Great Marlborough Street, St James Westminster, Mdx, minister to John Price 16 Apr 1762
Harris Thomas s John, Long Marston, Gls, yeoman to John Bryan 9 Dec 1637
Harris Thomas s George, Salisbury, Wil, haberdasher to Andrew Goodwin 5 Oct 1686
Harris William s Henry, Duston, Nth, blacksmith† to Thomas Clarke 21 Oct 1675
Harris William s Peter, Dorking, Sry, baker to Thomas Broadbank 4 Jan 1724/5
Harrison Benjamin s Joseph, Lambeth, Sry, yeoman to Samuel Reeves 1 Sep 1773
Harrison George s Andrew, citizen and horner to Joseph Cooper 1 Mar 1707/8 <2 Jul 1711 turned over to Mary widow of John Cotes, citizen and broderer>
Harrison Henry s Thomas, Allerthorpe, Yks, esquire to Francis Molyneux 20 Jan 1685/6
Harrison Henry s Thomas, Sefton, Lan, yeoman to William Collier 8 May 1693
Harrison Henry s Henry, York, Yks, esquire† to Benjamin Tomlinson 3 Jul 1721 and 16 Jun 1722
Harrison John s Thomas to his father 4 Aug 1648
Harrison John s Richard, citizen and stationer† to Daniel Benyon 20 Jan 1663/4
Harrison John s George, St James Westminster, Mdx, gentleman to William Lucas 4 Apr 1720
Harrison Richard s Richard, Caxton, Cam, yeoman to Thomas Day 18 Apr 1684
Harrison Thomas s Thomas, citizen and tallow chandler to John Rumball 4 Sep 1648
Harrison William s Thomas, Waddesdon, Bkm, grazier to John Meridale 19 Nov 1678
Harrison William s William, Waddesdon, Bkm, maltster to Robert Bly 15 Oct 1703
Harrod Daniel s Daniel, Islington, Mdx, joiner to Timothy Foster 2 Nov 1724
Harrold Edward s Richard, Woolwich, Ken, strong waterman to Daniel Jeffs 6 Dec 1682
Hart George s Thomas, Clerkenwell, Mdx, yeoman to Thomas Weaver 17 Mar 1651/2
Hart Joseph s Mathew, Northolt, Mdx† to Thomas Hodges 16 Oct 1645
Hart William s William, 'Holmideane', Hrt, yeoman to Thomas Nettleton 10 Jul 1656
Hart William s William, Westminster, Mdx, mariner to William Alexander 1 Nov 1731 <6 Mar 1731/2 turned over to Robert Bringhurst, citizen and founder>
Hart William s William, Kingston, Sry, gardener to Thomas Searle 1 Nov 1735
Harte John s Mathew, Northolt, Mdx, yeoman† to Samuel Wilkin 17 Jan 1636/7
Harton John s Hugh, Horton, Ken, gentleman† to William Gurney 19 Jun 1677
Harton Thomas s John, citizen and tallow chandler† to Rebecca widow of John Harton 6 Aug 1716
Harton Thomas s John, citizen and tallow chandler† to Samuel Wheeler 3 Mar 1717/8
Hartree Robert s John, St Stephen, Hrt, carpenter to John Rumball 1 May 1668

Hartwell James s Francis, Langley, Bkm, yeoman to Thomas Kender 5 Aug 1700 <9 Sep 1702 turned over to Robert Belson, citizen and haberdasher; 1 Jul 1706 (by Mary Belson, widow and exec. to David Salter, ironmonger>

Hartwell John s William, Wellingborough, Nth, innholder to John Wilford 4 Oct 1735 <6 Apr 1742 turned over to William Fisher, citizen and plaisterer>

Harvey Edward s William, Fulmer, Bkm, husbandman to Henry Cox 20 Jul 1643

Harvey Richard s John, Baldock, Hrt, maltster to Thomas Wilson 20 Nov 1667

Harvey Robert s Robert, Warwick, War, gentleman to Thomas Smalridge 4 Feb 1644/5

Harvey Thomas s Thomas, 'Selson', Eastry, Ken, gentleman to Ralph Wilson 8 Nov 1683

Harvey William s William, Rearsby, Lei, gentleman to James Miller 22 Jul 1664

Harwood George s John, citizen and merchant tailor to John Radburne 5 Jul 1686

Haseler Edward s William, Wells, Som, haberdasher to John Burton 24 Dec 1633

Haselton (Haseldine in freedom) Daniel s Daniel, Stroud, Gls, clothier to Stephen Holland 6 Apr 1790

Hasie Henry s Hasie, Salisbury, Wil, innkeeper to Thomas Parker 23 Jul 1651

Hasie John s Hasie, Salisbury, Wil, yeoman to Thomas Allen 24 Oct 1655

Haskell John s Stephen, Bermondsey, Sry, yeoman to Aurelius Hodson 14 Feb 1772

Hasler John s John, Rotherhithe, Sry, ropemaker to George Carpenter 5 Jan 1736/7 <5 Jan 1741/2 turned over to James Walker, citizen and joiner>

Hastings Edward s John, Charlbury, Oxf, woolman to William Gaunt 25 Mar 1697

Hastings Hugh s Martin, Hindringham, Nfk, esquire to John Wich 15 Mar 1652/3

Hastings Jacob s John, citizen and tallow chandler† to Elizabeth widow of John Hastings 6 Mar 1698/9

Hatch John s John, Mortlake, Sry, gentleman† to Thomas Nettleton 1 Sep 1647

Hatch John s Henry, Rainham, Ken, brickmaker† to John Gilgrest 6 Jan 1723/4

Hatley Richard s Thomas, citizen and carpenter to Robert Fewtrell 28 Jan 1659/60

Hatree William s John, St Stephen, Hrt, carpenter to John Harris 25 Mar 1671

Hatton Frederick s Thomas, citizen and joiner to James Packett 21 Jan 1679/80

Hatton Jabez s Mathew, Crutched Friars, Lnd, innkeeper† to Phineas Pateshall 2 Aug 1785

Haughton Robert s Robert, Hackney, Mdx, yeoman to John Cock 22 Jan 1701/2

Havens William s Robert, Colchester, Ess, clothier to John Ayre 20 Dec 1705

Haward Robert s Thomas, Redbourne, Hrt, yeoman† to Nicholas Hawett 30 May 1671

Hawes Edward s Francis, Risborough, Bkm, gentleman† to Richard Towne 12 Oct 1708

Hawes John s Thomas, Hereford, Hef, gentleman to Robert Hicks 6 Feb 1649/50

Hawes John s Thomas, White Waltham, Brk, maltster to Thomas Hawes 6 Jan 1679/80

Hawes John s John, citizen and cordwainer to Henry Lathwell 18 Nov 1681

Hawes John s John, Wooburn, Bkm, yeoman to Joseph Flight 5 Aug 1700

Hawes Mary d Samuel, Shadwell, Mdx, gentleman to Grace Clare, sp. 6 Sep 1725

Hawes Thomas s Thomas, White Waltham, Brk, yeoman to John Denby 18 May 1671

Hawes Thomas s Thomas to his father 3 Aug 1696

Hawett Nicholas s Thomas, Ormskirk, Lan, gentleman to Joseph Coggs 28 Jul 1657

Hawkes John s John, Whitefriars, Lnd, tailor to John Darcey 29 May 1678

Hawkins Edward s Thomas, citizen and butcher† to Thomas Allen 15 Oct 1677

Hawkins George s Henry, Southwark, Sry, tallow chandler† to Mary widow of Thomas Higgins 6 Nov 1732

Hawkins Henry s Francis, Harrow, Mdx, farmer to Thomas March 5 Apr 1748 <30 Nov 1753 master† turned over with consent of Latham Arnold, an exec. to George Scott, citizen and ironmonger>

Hawkins John s John, Colchester, Ess, weaver to James Storer 23 Jan 1690/1

Hawkins John s Henry, citizen and tallow chandler to Daniel Weale 1 Jul 1723 <7 Sep 1724 turned over to Dinah widow of Henry Hawkins>

Hawkins John s John, Cloth Fair, Lnd, victualler to John Doble Hillier 3 Nov 1789 <7 May 1793 turned over to John Stephens, citizen and salter>

Hawkins Joseph to William Stayner 3 Oct 1799

Hawkins Richard s Simon, Marlborough, Wil, cordwainer to John Botton 7 Aug 1674

Hawkins Samuel s William, Keynsham, Som, yeoman to Andrew Makepeace 14 Feb 1645/6

Hayden John s Richard, Croydon, Sry, blacksmith to William Haydon 7 Nov 1704

Hayden Joshua s William to his father 1 Sep 1712

Hayden Samuel s Henry, Rowley, Sts, gentleman† to Robert Hayden 1 May 1693
Hayden William s William, Whitechapel, Mdx, gentleman to Samuel Wardel 5 Jun 1792
Haydon Anthony s Nicholas, Durrington, Wil, weaver to Robert Moore 21 Feb 1641/2
Haydon Nicholas s Nicholas, Durrington, Wil, weaver to Robert Moore 1 Jun 1641
Haydon Robert s Henry, Rowley Regis, Sts, gentleman to John Dolphin 29 Apr 1685
Haydon Thomas s Richard, Oddington, Gls, yeoman to John Selan 7 Dec 1668
Hayer Peter s Peter, Soho, Mdx, linen draper to Isaac Beatew 1 Aug 1709
Hayes Daniel s Robert, citizen and haberdasher to William Peale 5 Dec 1699
Hayes James Arthur s Charles, Chelsea, Mdx, gentleman to Nathaniel Perkins 6 Jun 1739
Hayle John s Arnold, citizen and weaver to John Tyson 6 Mar 1655/6
Hayle William s William, St Albans, Hrt, innholder to Michael Hayle 6 Oct 1656
Haynes Joseph s John, Horton, Bkm, yeoman to Thomas Haies 25 Jan 1676/7
Haynes Richard s John, Burford, Oxf, maltster to Elizabeth widow of Samuel Harris 11 Nov 1700 <27 Jul 1704 turned over by Mary Smith, exec. of Elizabeth to John Fisher, citizen and cutler; 1 Apr 1706 to Joseph Lathwell, citizen and currier>
Haynes Thomas s Thomas, Worndritch, Hun, husbandman† to John Velan 18 Feb 1670/1
Haynes Thomas s Thomas to his father 7 Oct 1723
Hayre John s John, Greenwich, Ken, brewer to John Tockfield 5 Feb 1699/1700
Hayter John s John, Chelsea, Mdx, cordwainer to Joseph Taylor 6 Apr 1784
Haythorne John s David, Lambeth, Sry, yeoman† to William Gurney 28 Jan 1673/4
Hayward James s Joseph, Bruton, Som, cordwainer to John Harding 4 Aug 1718
Hayward Joseph s Thomas, Tangley, Oxf, yeoman to Jeremy Ridge 3 Apr 1688
Hayward William s Decimus, Southwark, gentleman to Hannah widow of John Close 3 Apr 1792
Head Roger s John, Purleigh, Ess, clerk to Thomas Oliver 13 Oct 1671
Heap John s John, Tottenham Court Road, Mdx, stablekeeper to George Soames 2 Sep 1794
Heard Robert s William, Little Holland, Ess, yeoman to William Butler 18 Jul 1654
Heard Robert s John, St Margaret Westminster, Mdx, butcher† to Richard Collier 2 May 1698
Hearn George s Thomas, Soho, Mdx, gentleman† to Elizabeth widow of James Byard 20 Nov 1701
Hearn John s William, St Giles Cripplegate, Lnd, tailor to Jonathan Leigh 4 Apr 1764 <4 Jul 1769 master† turned over with consent of Mary Leigh, his widow and exec. to Charles Dare>
Hearne George s George, White Waltham, Brk, labourer to Robert Boucher 2 Jan 1692/3
Heath Charles s William, Wootton Bassett, Wil, shopkeeper to Rebecca widow of Samuel Dare 9 Dec 1760
Heath James s ?, Inner Temple, Lnd, esquire to John Yeomans 20 Jan 1674/5
Heath John s John, Richmond, Sry, gardener to Egerton Henshaw 6 Jul 1736
Heath Joseph s John, Lilley, Hrt, yeoman to William Carr 17 Jan 1658/9
Heath Joseph George s George, Shoreditch, Mdx, brickmaker to John Hill 6 Nov 1732
Heath Judah s Thomas, citizen and goldsmith to John Wilford 31 Oct 1700
Heath William s Edward, Hayes, Ken, yeoman to George Harling 1 Aug 1642
Heath William s Henry, Mansfield, Ntt, innholder to Thomas Haies 8 Jul 1667
Heather Ephraim s Ephraim, Dorking, Sry, baker to Charles Godwin 21 Jul 1692
Heather Richard s John, Worplesdon, Sry, yeoman† to Samuel West 5 May 1646
Heather Thomas s Thomas, Puttenham, Sry, husbandman to Mary widow of Richard Howse 20 Mar 1647/8
Heather William s Edward, citizen and baker to William Jeanes 1 May 1704
Hebb Joseph s Thomas, Loughborough, Lei, gentleman to John Wich 23 Jul 1647
Hebbart John s Edward, Buckland, Sry, mercer† to Thomas Cole, jnr. 10 May 1698
Hedderwick George s James, St John Clerkenwell, Mdx, blacksmith† to Daniel Gurney 5 Apr 1772 <7 Jun 1774 master† turned over by William Shepherd, exec. to Alan Parsons>
Hedgeland William s Richard, Exeter, Dev, weaver to Felix Rickard 9 Nov 1750
Hedger Elizabeth d William, St Saviour Southwark, Sry, waterman to Henry Batten 13 Nov 1684
Hedges Joseph s Joseph, Newbury, Brk, cooper† to Robert Ayliffe 6 Aug 1705
Hedges Thomas s John, Stonesfield, Oxf, yeoman to Daniel Dale 1 Aug 1677
Heiron John s Henry, Duffield, Dby, clerk to William Gurney 25 Mar 1675
Helder Thomas s Thomas, Bow Brickhill, Bkm, tanner to William Cocke 2 May 1664
Helder William s Richard, Great Staughton, Hun, gentleman to Henry Andrew 30 Jul 1657
Heli Thomas s John, Tonbridge, Ken to William Williams 7 Feb 1714/5
Hemings Christopher s Mathew, St Bride, Lnd† to Richard Cooke 24 Oct 1704

Hemming Edward s Edward, Fifield, Oxf, gentleman† to Mary widow of William Allen 7 Nov 1715 <17 Dec 1719 turned over to Edmund Harris, citizen and feltmaker>

Hemmons John s Richard, Barking, Ess, yeoman† to Richard Parker 7 Apr 1762

Hemsley John s Charles, citizen and vintner† to Richard Joyce 4 Nov 1695

Henderson Geoffrey s Geoffrey, St James Westminster, Mdx, victualler to William Loveage 24 Jan 1749/50 <25 Jun 1750 turned over to William Charles Hutchins>

Henderson Robert s William, Hoddam, Dfs, Sco, weaver† to Sarah widow of William Renolds 1 Dec 1707 <6 Jul 1713 mistress† turned over to Robert Wooding, citizen and joiner>

Hendey John s John, St James Westminster, Mdx, innholder† to John Tilley 4 Mar 1723/4

Henley Anthony s Edward, Mitcham, Sry, carpenter to Thomas Noble 12 Jul 1637

Henley William s John, Mursley, Bkm, yeoman† to Edward Fossey 11 Jul 1673

Henly James s James, Stepney, Mdx, yeoman to James Harding 7 Nov 1655

Henn Edward s James, Risborough, Bkm, yeoman to John Browne 12 Dec 1655

Henshall Egerton s Egerton, citizen and cook to Thomas Obbinson 1 Apr 1706 <turned over to Henry Lathwell, citizen and currier; 12 Oct 1711 to Sarah widow of John Cleave>

Hensly Charles s John, Deptford, Ken, tallow chandler† to Francis Tunsted 12 Feb 1676/7

Herbert James s William, Strood, Ken, gentleman† to Joseph Gibbons 22 Jun 1670

Herbert Peter s Thomas, Bankside, Sry, lighterman to Thomas Easton 1 Nov 1796

Herbert William s Thomas, Newton Blossomville, Bkm, yeoman† to Joseph Clifton 28 Nov 1664

Heriott Charles s Andrew, College Hill, Lnd, gentleman† to George Teague 7 Oct 1740 <17 Dec 1741 turned over to Daniel Town, citizen and fruiterer>

Herne John s William, Abingdon, Brk, haberdasher† to Giles Rodway 26 Dec 1647

Herne John s John, St Clement Danes, Mdx, gentleman to John Hooker 9 Jul 1655

Heron James s Patrick, Towcester, Nth, clothier to Richard Backhouse 1 Jul 1684

Hesterly John s Obadiah, Atherstone, War, husbandman to John Michell 13 Jan 1672/3

Heughs Griffin s Hugh Lewis, Nevin, Cae, husbandman to John Millard 24 Jun 1647

Hevill John s Peter, Norley, Chs, butcher† to Thomas Flamnore 21 Aug 1660

Hewer Thomas s Thomas, citizen and merchant tailor to James Harding 20 Oct 1653

Hewett Richard s Josiah, Bermondsey, Sry† to Mary widow of William Allen 7 Oct 1717

Hewitt Edward s William, Hillmorton, War, smith to John Johnson 6 Mar 1726/7

Hewittson William s Edward, St Luke Old Street, Mdx, labourer to Ann widow of William Farmer 6 Jan 1734/5

Hewlett William s William, St Mary Magdalen Southwark, Sry, farrier to Thomas Mills 24 Jul 1651

Heyden John s John, St Martin in the Fields, Mdx, perfumer† to William Reynolds 7 Aug 1699

Heydon William s William, Hounslow, Mdx, cordwainer to Anthony Bunn 4 Dec 1678

Heyward David s Richard, Lnd, gentleman to William Perkins 10 Jul 1662

Heywood John s William, Lnd, sawyer† to Peter Champney 2 Mar 1636/7

Hickman Benjamin s Benjamin, citizen and clothworker to Thomas Fossey 3 Jul 1721

Hickman Hugh s Henry, Bushey, Hrt, yeoman to Richard Tailer 29 Sep 1632

Hickman Samuel s William, Limehouse, Mdx, gentleman to William Edmonds 30 Aug 1671

Hickman Thomas s Thomas, Heston, Mdx, gentleman† to John Caddy 6 Dec 1697

Hicks George s Valentine, Blockley, Wor, cordwainer† to John Garnson 23 Oct 1684

Hicks Hugh s Hugh, citizen and blacksmith† to George Wilcocks 14 Jul 1647

Hicks Jonathan s Thomas, Chesterton, Oxf, yeoman to John Bowden 8 May 1678

Hicks Robert s John, Medstead, Ham, yeoman† to Mathew Woodward 5 Jun 1694

Hickson John s John, Hendon, Mdx, tailor to Richard Higby 18 Sep 1675

Hide John s Richard, Milborne Port, Som, baker to Samuel Brooker 4 Sep 1646

Hide John s Daniel, Abingdon, Brk, bargeman† to John Hulme 7 May 1719

Hide Richard s William, citizen and clothworker† to Benjamin Tomplinson 6 Nov 1693

Hierne John s Richard, Salford Priors, War, husbandman to James West 21 Feb 1680/1

Hierne Richard s Richard, Salford Priors, War, husbandman to John Hierne 7 Jan 1690/1

Higbey Abraham s Abraham, Aldenham, Hrt, yeoman† to Thomas Harris 15 Apr 1668

Higby Richard s Abraham, Aldenham, Hrt, yeoman to Edward Harris 6 Jan 1667/8

Higby William s William, Aldenham, Hrt, mealman† to Thomas Harris 30 Nov 1674

Higdon William s Peter, Marston, Som, yeoman† to Edmund Barcock 15 Jan 1660/1

Higgins Richard s John, Bermondsey, Sry, dyer to Edward Clarke 16 Aug 1749

Higgins Thomas s Thomas to his father 19 Nov 1707

Higgins Thomas s Thomas, St Dunstan in the West, Lnd, tallow chandler† to Mary Higgins, widow 21 Sep 1744
Higgs Francis s Simon, Lnd, gentleman† to Humphrey King 20 Apr 1680
Higgs Robert s Samuel, Paddington, Mdx, labourer to John Davenport 5 Mar 1721/2
Hightor John s John, South Mimms, Mdx, gentleman to James Holworthy 10 May 1665
Hilam Jonathan s Nicholas, Yks, yeoman to Robert Wilcock 1 May 1641
Hilbord Thomas s James, Soho, Mdx, gentleman to Robert Day 19 Nov 1755
Hildyard Henry s Christopher, Winestead, Yks, esquire† to Benjamin Tomlinson 11 Nov 1700
Hill Adam s John, Chigwell, Ess, yeoman to Henry Miles 29 Apr 1687
Hill Edward s Edward, Ashby de la Zouch, Lei, gentleman to Thomas Young 19 Sep 1672
Hill Henry s Henry, Woburn, Bdf, mercer to Francis Tunsteed 3 Feb 1667/8
Hill Henry s Edward, Buckingham, Bkm, innholder to James Gregory 28 Jan 1678/9
Hill James s Edward, St Martin in the Fields, Mdx, poulterer to Jane widow of William Kelly 31 Jan 1743/4 <13 Mar 1745/6 turned over with consent of Aaron Newbolt to whom Jane is married to Vincent Peach; 23 Dec 1746 to Thomas Spenceley, citizen and glover>
Hill John s Ralph, Houghton, Yks, yeoman to William Hill 13 Jun 1638
Hill John s Humphrey, St Olave Southwark, Sry to Humphrey Hill 8 Jan 1643/4
Hill John s Francis, 'Glytheford', Sal, gentleman to William Edmunds 30 Jan 1672/3
Hill John s John, Putney, Sry, yeoman to William Hunt 3 Oct 1683
Hill John s Christopher, Enfield, Mdx, yeoman to Samuel Osborne 7 Apr 1718
Hill John s John, Joy Lane, Lnd, tallow chandler to Richard Wiggins 18 Oct 1764
Hill John s John Tottenham Court Road, Mdx, cheesemonger to Charles Dare 3 Jun 1794
Hill John s John, Lambeth, Sry, waterman to George Searle 3 Feb 1795
Hill Jonathan s Humphrey to his father 21 Apr 1652
Hill Oliver s Oliver to his father 30 Apr 1640
Hill Richard s Thomas, Ashleworth, Gls, gentleman to Giles Rodway 20 Nov 1638
Hill Richard s Richard, Leicester, Lei, brewer to Richard Warren 20 Apr 1665
Hill Richard s Richard, Plaistow, Ess, carpenter to James Slatford 2 Nov 1742
Hill Robert s Robert, Nuneaton, War, yeoman to Simon Butterton 30 Jun 1634
Hill Robert s Humphrey to his father 25 Sep 1654
Hill Thomas s Roger, Streatham, Sry, yeoman to Thomas Tapp 11 Apr 1636
Hill Thomas s John, Kempston, Bdf, yeoman to John Rumball 26 Apr 1669
Hill Thomas s Thomas, Woburn, Bdf, mercer to Henry Hill 9 Mar 1674/5
Hill Thomas s Thomas, Limehouse, Mdx, grocer to Samuel Reeves 8 Dec 1748
Hill Thomas s Thomas, St John Horsleydown, Sry, porter to Henry Dunkin 5 Dec 1786
Hill William s Thomas, citizen and tallow chandler to Thomas Nettleton 30 Apr 1640
Hill William s William, Holborn, Mdx, gentleman to Simon White 24 Jul 1648
Hill William s Thomas, citizen and tallow chandler† to Thomas Hill 7 Aug 1704
Hilldrupp Thomas s John, Maidenhead, Brk, farmer to Nathaniel Perkins 7 Mar 1725/6
Hiller Richard s Mathew, citizen and mercer† to James Horton 25 May 1669
Hilliard Daniel s Henry, Mendham, Sfk, carpenter to George Kitchinman 31 Dec 1655
Hilliard Francis s Robert, 'Berds Watering', Mdx, yeoman to Arthur Trumplin 5 Sep 1650
Hillier John Double s Stephen, Deptford, Ken, sawyer to Thomas Underwood 25 Jul 1770
Hillman William s James, Devizes, Wil, victualler to Richard Tirrell 8 Aug 1706
Hills John s John, Margate, Ken, blacksmith† to Thomas Rakestraw 9 Nov 1696
Hilton Samuel s John, Warrington, Lan, feltmaker to Isaac Saffell 24 Jul 1668
Hinde Michael s Michael, Chelmsford, Ess, shopkeeper to Egerton Henshaw 4 Nov 1717
Hinde William s William, St Dunstan in the West, Lnd, tailor to Anthony Bunn 21 Nov 1704 <6 Aug 1711 master† turned over to Thomas Wheeler, citizen and brewer>
Hindes Jacob s Zachariah, Woodstock, Oxf, apothecary to John Gibbons 9 Feb 1713/4
Hindes Jacob s Zachariah, Woodstock, Oxf, apothecary to Thomas Wyment 9 Feb 1718/9
Hinsby Joseph s John, Norwich, Nfk, hotpresser to James Wilkie 3 Jul 1792
Hinson William s James, Harwich, Ess, shipwright to Robert Driver 5 Dec 1683
Hinton Joshua s Ralph, Berrick, Oxf, tailor to John Yarling 19 Jul 1677
Hinwood Edward s William, Teffont Magna, Wil, blacksmith to Vincent Walker 3 Feb 1728/9
Hiorne James s John, citizen and clockmaker to Thomas Taylor 7 Apr 1741
Hipkins John s Edward, St James Clerkenwell, Mdx, combcasemaker to James Wakeham 2 Jun 1701
Hitchman George s Thomas, Groundwell [Blunsden], Wil, yeoman to John Cleave 3 May 1708

Hitchman William s Richard, Enstone, Oxf to Robert Goddard 5 Jun 1800
Hoan James s Gabriel, Limehouse, Mdx, gardener to Jonas Lawrence 25 Mar 1746
Hoane Jonathan s James, Soho, Mdx, baker to Jonas Lawrence 26 May 1757 <10 Aug 1761 turned over to Redburn Tomkins, citizen and butcher>
Hoare Hopewell s Walter, Tewkesbury, Gls, yeoman† to Walter Hoare 30 Nov 1668
Hoare John s John, Great Missenden, Bkm, baker to Thomas Rowles 2 Jul 1722
Hoare Walter s Walter, Tewkesbury, Gls, yeoman† to Daniel Clarebutt 15 May 1648
Hoare William s John, Great Missenden, Bkm, baker to John Hoare 1 Jul 1734
Hobbes Josias s Josias, Hitchin, Hrt, mercer† to Mathew Hobbes 21 Nov 1638
Hobbs Anthony s Anthony, Bromley, Ken, gentleman to George Wilcocks 13 Jan 1645/6
Hobbs Mathew s John, Hitchin, Hrt, clothier† to Edward Bromsall 14 Jan 1646/7
Hobbs Thomas s Richard, Abingdon, Brk, barber to William Jefferys 6 Oct 1729 <13 Jul 1732 turned over to Richard Warter, citizen and dyer>
Hobcrafte John s John, M...?, Nth, yeoman to William Gurney 26 Sep 1671 <turned over to Henry Hanslopp>
Hoddilow John s John, citizen and girdler to John Watts 5 Jun 1727 <4 Nov 1727 turned over to Hannah widow of John Hoddilow, citizen and girdler>
Hodge Daniel s Daniel, Hitchin, Hrt, butcher to John Harrison 5 Dec 1692
Hodges Richard s Richard, Kensington, Mdx, carpenter† to Joseph Wedgbrough 3 Dec 1733
Hodges William s William, Croscombe, Som, clothier to Thomas Hodges 20 Jun 1654
Hodges William s Charles, Holborn, Mdx, hatter† to Benjamin Munn 12 Jan 1748/9
Hodgkin Samuel s George, citizen and carpenter to Richard Bull 1 Jul 1675
Hodgkins John s Edward, citizen and cooper† to Thomas Watts 25 Sep 1701
Hodgskinson Richard s Robert, Walthamstow, Ess, monyer to Richard Haddon 6 May 1646
Hodgson John s Peter, 'Berwick Field', Cul, gentleman† to John Smith 10 Sep 1705
Hodgson Thomas s William to his father 22 Feb 1741/2
Hodgson William s Samuel, Scarborough, Yks, mariner† to William Ingram 15 Oct 1698
Hodgson William s William to his father 7 Apr 1729
Hodsden Henry s Henry, Willington, Ssx, clerk to Rollinson Eyans 3 Nov 1718 <12 Nov 1722 turned over to Miles Halsey, citizen and glass-seller>
Hoford Samuel s William, Plumstead, Ken, husbandman to Robert Walker 30 May 1667
Hoggins Samuel s Samuel, St Pancras, Mdx, innholder to William Lucas 5 Oct 1747
Hoggsflesh Thomas s Thomas, Kentish Town, Mdx, gentleman to John Richbell 13 Apr 1652
Holbeech Mathew s Mathew, Cold Newton, Lei, yeoman to William Bowyer 25 Jan 1637/8
Holden Charles s Edward, Mortlake, Sry, gentleman† to Robert Lamb 6 Sep 1714
Holden Edmund s Thomas, Petworth, Ssx, carpenter† to Robert Butcher 6 Jul 1677
Holding John s Richard, Southwark Borough, Sry, baker to Richard Holding, jnr. 4 Jun 1793
Holding Richard s Richard, Borough High Street, Southwark, baker to Thomas Forth 5 Mar 1782
Holdsworth Thomas s William, Broad Sanctuary, Westminster, grocer to Edward Myers 4 Nov 1771
Holgate Thomas s Thomas, Hackney, Mdx, corn chandler† to Mathew Woodward 6 Feb 1698/9
Holland John s William, Chesterfield, Dby, flaxman† to Benjamin Brownesmith 6 Sep 1683
Holland Mathew s Mathew, citizen and blacksmith to Thomas Hill 29 Sep 1686
Holland Robert s Richard, Lincoln, Lin, innholder† to Nicholas Bull 5 Feb 1667/8
Holliar Richard s William, Shustoke, War, yeoman to John Townesend 5 May 1701
Hollingshed Ralph s Ralph, 'Odford', Chs, gentleman to John Child 16 Nov 1681
Hollingworth John s John, Islington, Mdx, grazier to Thomas Eyre 5 Mar 1676/7
Hollis Nathaniel s Thomas, citizen and draper to Henry Burton 17 Jun 1679
Hollister Robert s Samuel, Maidstone, Ken, brewer to Joseph Fisher 29 Aug 1737
Holloway Ambrose s John, St James Westminster, Mdx, vintner to John Townesend 2 Jul 1711
Holloway John Andrew s Richard, Witney, Oxf, cooper† to Edmund Carpenter 7 Apr 1707
Holloway Stephen s William, Barkham, Brk, yeoman to William Knight 4 Jan 1642/3
Hollowell James s John, Westminster, Mdx, yeoman to Robert Maybanck 8 Jan 1647/8
Hollyday Esther d Henry, Lambeth, Sry, carpenter to Thomas Smith 2 Feb 1670/1
Holman Robert s Michael, Whitton, Mdx, gentleman to Robert Hicks 29 Oct 1649
Holman Robert s William, Andover, Ham, saddler to Robert Southwood 22 May 1672
Holmden John s John, Oxted, Sry, maltster† to William Newman 1 Sep 1718
Holmes John s Francis, Steventon, Brk, cordwainer to Samuel Bedwell 3 Jul 1693
Holmes John s Edward, Chelsea, Mdx, plumber† to Samuel Hoggins 15 Apr 1762

Holmes Philip s John, West Ham, Ess, gardener† to Richard Morris 12 Apr 1711
Holmes Samuel s ..., Winslow, Bkm, victualler† to Nathaniel Perkins 13 Nov 1747
Holmes Thomas s Robert, Keele, Sts, yeoman to William Spencer 3 Feb 1641/2
Holmewood Gabriel s Henry, Nutfield, Sry, yeoman† to John Collington 13 Nov 1646
Holney Richard s John, Woodmancote, Ssx, clerk to William Goodman 11 Oct 1658
Holoway William s John, St George Southwark, Sry, cheesemonger to William Steward 28 Oct 1690
Holt Richard s Walter, citizen and musician to David Heywood 1 May 1693
Holton William s William, Hampton, Mdx, glazier to Giles Harris 5 Jan 1729/30
Holway Richard s William, Marcham, Brk, gentleman to John Velan 11 Apr 1676
Holworthie James s Nicholas, Nynehead, Som, yeoman to Edward Holworthie 20 Sep 1649
Holworthy Edward s Nicholas, Nynehead, Som, gentleman to Edmund Barcock 9 Jun 1640
Homan Herbert s Herbert, citizen and cooper to Robert Dove 2 Aug 1725
Homan John s Herbert, St James Clerkenwell, Mdx, glazier† to Herbert Homan 5 Nov 1733
Homan William s William, citizen and cooper to Charles Dare 6 Jun 1799
<turned over to his father>
Homer John s Thomas, Water Orton, War, gentleman to Charles Berdoe 7 Nov 1695
Hood John s Peter, Lnd, factor to Thomas Kelke 19 Mar 1650/1
Hook John s John, Walthamstow, Ess [*in Ms* 'Mdx'], gardener† to Samuel Otrage 2 Dec 1700
Hooke John s William, Wolston, War, yeoman to William Mayne 11 Oct 1686
Hooker Daniel s William, Redbridge [? *in Ms* 'Redbeach'], Ham, yeoman to Christopher Leake 26 Feb 1656/7
Hooker John s John, St Giles in the Fields, Mdx to John Hooker 3 Apr 1645
Hooker Peter s Henry, Chilworth, Ham, yeoman to Edward Hooker 23 Jan 1633/4
Hooker Samuel s Benjamin, Great Ealing, Mdx, surgeon to John Bright 22 Dec 1773
Hooper Francis s Francis, Hammersmith, Mdx, yeoman† to Robert Rodway 7 Oct 1668
Hooper William s Benjamin, citizen and salter to Benjamin Brownesmith 5 Mar 1690/1
Hooper Zacheus s Zacheus, Bridgewater, Som, innholder to Samuel Coleman 23 Apr 1691
Hopkins Abraham s William, citizen and vintner to John Harrison 21 Jun 1693
Hopkins Benjamin s Samuel, Pulloxhill, Bdf, clerk to William Putnan 24 Aug 1633
Hopkins Clement s Hugh, Warwick, War, husbandman to Thomas Knight 28 May 1660
Hopkins Francis s Francis, Wokingham, Brk, yeoman to David Morris 23 Jul 1656
Hopkins Francis s ?, 'Cooten Magna', ? glazier to Francis Houghton 6 Aug 1667
Hopkins James s John, Llanvihangel-ystern-Llewern, Mon, gentleman to John Greene 17 Aug 1671
Hopkins John s ..., Hef, yeoman to Zachariah Dixon 7 Nov 1692
Hopkins Richard s Francis, Wokingham, Brk, yeoman to John Hamond 26 Mar 1668
Hopkins Robert s John, Harwell, Brk, farmer to Charles Dare 18 Jun 1771
Hopkins Thomas s Geoffrey, Kinwarton, War, yeoman† to John Eden 30 Apr 1668
Hopkins Thomas s Geoffrey, Kinwarton, War, yeoman to Thomas Hopkins 7 Nov 1709
Hopkins William s William, St Martin in the Fields, Mdx, drawer to Edward Walcott 15 Dec 1652
Hopkins William s Edmund, Silsoe, Bdf, gentleman† to Richard Weight 14 Sep 1672
Hoppe Charles s John, St Pauls Churchyard, Lnd, shoemaker to Henry Soames 3 Dec 1782
<turned over to Lewis Ducroq, citizen and upholder>
Hoppen Henry Christian s Henry Andrew, St Martin in the Fields, Mdx, piece broker to William Stephens 4 Mar 1772
Hopperton Bowack John s Robert, Fulham, Mdx, gardener to Thomas Rigby 7 Apr 1741
<1 Mar 1744/5 turned over to William Masters, citizen and joiner>
Hopwood John s James, Oldham, Lan, maltster to William Gurney 5 Sep 1677
Hore Mathew s Christopher, Croydon, Sry, tailor to Robert Udall 6 Sep 1648
Hore Philip s Caesar, St Giles in the Fields, Mdx, tallow chandler to John Jordaine 21 Jun 1764
Hore Thomas s Caesar, St Giles in the Fields, Mdx, tallow chandler to Philip Hore 13 Dec 1771
Horlock John s Richard, Hammersmith, Mdx, farrier† to John Townesend 3 May 1708
Horlock William s Richard, Hammersmith, Mdx, blacksmith† to John Horlock 2 Jul 1722
Horn Isaac s John, Northly† to Francis Buggey ?13 Dec 1669
Hornbey John s John, Mentmore, Bkm, clerk† to Avery Vokins 9 Sep 1700
Horne Edward s Edward, St Martin in the Fields, Mdx, shoemaker† to John Cotes 6 Jun 1678
Horne John s Augustus, Tingewick, Bkm, yeoman to Richard Hughes 3 May 1697
Horner Jeremiah s John, St Ives, Hun, innholder to William Collier, snr. 3 Oct 1715
Horner John s Jeremiah to his father 5 May 1747

Horner William s Joseph, Gloucester, Gls, gentleman to William Webb 14 May 1668
Horsey John s Peter, Clare Market, Mdx, poulterer to James Ennis 4 Sep 1740 <4 Sep 1744 turned over to John Marlin, citizen and cooper>
Horsley Thomas s John, Horton, Sts, yeoman to Thomas Smalridge 1 Nov 1664
Hort William s Robert, Malmesbury, Wil, yeoman to Thomas Lenton 6 Apr 1654
Horton James s John, Gumley, Lei, yeoman to James Wood 13 Nov 1651
Horton James s William, Cirencester, Gls, mercer to Richard Parrott 25 Oct 1675
Horton John s Thomas, Gumley, Lei, yeoman to James Horton 1 Nov 1672
Horton John s William, Cirencester, Gls, yeoman to John Ayliffe 7 Aug 1690
Horton Samuel s Samuel, Rotherhithe, Sry, cooper to Nathaniel Lyford 5 Jan 1685/6
Horton Thomas s William, Cirencester, Gls, yeoman to William Miller 1 Jul 1679
Horton Thomas s Thomas, March, Cam, yeoman† to William Alexander 3 Feb 1728/9
Horwood William s Thomas, citizen and cook to William Jordan 1 Apr 1692
Hoskin Nathaniel s Edward, Shadwell, Mdx, grocer to Thomas Cave 14 Jul 1766
Hoskin Thomas s Thomas, Oxford Street, Mdx, cordwainer to Ann Searle 3 Oct 1780
Hospitall Edward s Edward, Rushden, Nth, farrier to William Massey 3 Feb 1648/9
Hough William s Peter, Preston, Lan, yeoman† to Josiah Ragsdale 11 Mar 1667/8
Houghton Francis s Richard, Woburn, Bdf, yeoman to John Veyland 3 Mar 1655/6
Houghton Francis s Francis to his father 2 Apr 1686
Houghton Henry s Henry, Newbury, Brk, haberdasher to Thomas Capet 26 Nov 1668
Houghton John s John, Wherwell, Ham, yeoman† to William Gurney 29 Jul 1675
Houghton Martin s John, Northampton, Nth, innholder† to William Lucas 3 Apr 1744
Houlbeach Walter s Walter, Cold Newton [Lowesby], Lei, yeoman to William Bowyer 24 May 1638
House Robert s Robert, Reading, Brk, weaver to William Gaunt 5 Jun 1662
Houssam Solomon s Thomas, Margate, Ken, blacksmith to John Hills 9 Feb 1710/11
How Joseph s John, Abbotts Langley, Hrt, yeoman to William Prince 7 Apr 1707
How Joseph s Joseph, Lnd, distiller to Samuel Osborn 6 Aug 1722
Howard Christopher s Thomas, Lnd, knight† to William Badham 6 Jul 1681
Howard Henry s Henry, St Dunstan in the West, Lnd, cordwainer to Robert Walker 22 Sep 1669
Howard James s Henry, citizen and draper† to John Harbert 12 Oct 1708 <4 Jun 1711 turned over by William Williams to Richard Haines>
Howard John s John, White Cross Street, Lnd, butcher to Robert French 1 Mar 1791 <7 Jul 1795 turned over to John Johnson>
Howard Mark s Thomas, St Michael Cornhill, Lnd, perukemaker to John Townshend 20 Sep 1769
Howard William s Robert, Sutton Coldfield, War, saddler to Thomas Smalridge 28 Dec 1658
Howe John s William, Leighton Buzzard, Bdf, glover to William Osmond 5 Nov 1638
Howell Henry s Henry, Lewes, Ssx, yeoman to John Browne 23 Jul 1660
Howell Thomas s Joel, Henley, Oxf, miller to Francis Bowder 3 Apr 1693
Howes George s William, Wootton, Oxf, farmer to William Killingworth 1 Dec 1741
Howes William s Richard, Daventry, Nth, gentleman to William Gurney 18 Nov 1650
Howson Edward s Edward, St Clement Danes, Mdx, victualler to John Cleave 3 May 1703 <6 May 1706 turned over to William Parker>
Howson John s James, Dover, Ken, chandler to Peter Prince 7 Jun 1671
Hoy Edward s Edward, Ham, Ess, yeoman to Ralph Humfreys 12 Nov 1643
Hubbard John s Jonathan, Melton Mowbray, Lei, grocer to Robert Day 4 Oct 1748
Hubbard Richard s Richard, Thames Ditton, Sry, wheelwright† to William Newman 14 Sep 1694
Hubbart William s William, St James Westminster, Mdx, farrier to Henry Wyne 5 Sep 1689
Hubberd Thomas s William, Langham, Rut, yeoman to George Adams 7 Sep 1634
Hubbert John s John, Denham, Bkm, miller† to Richard Wilkinson 20 Nov 1648
Huddell William s William, Whitechapel, Mdx, innholder to John Bayrand 8 May 1770
Huddle William s Edward, St Marylebone, Mdx, gardener† to Joseph Hayward 7 Nov 1698
Hudgebutt Marigold s Charles, St Giles Cripplegate, wiredrawer† to Richard Backhouse 25 Aug 1669
Hudson Aurelius s Richard, Tower of London, gentleman to Thomas Tully 1 Sep 1747
Hudson James s Nathaniel, citizen and farrier to Samuel King 9 Oct 1679
Hudson Walter s Thomas, Witney, Oxf, yeoman† to Samuel Bedwell 9 Oct 1678
Hudson William s William, Culworth, Nth, blacksmith† to John Wilcock 18 Apr 1654
Hudson William s William, Hadley, Mdx, plumber† to Nicholas Farrant 4 Dec 1660

Hudson William s Joseph, Abchurch Lane, Lnd, plumber† to Charles Dare 7 Dec 1790
<turned over to James Elmer, citizen and skinner>
Hugett Anthony s William, Reigate, Sry, tallow chandler to Joseph Gibbons 3 Oct 1709
Huggett Richard s John, Dagenham, Ess, yeoman to Richard Morris 15 Oct 1707
Huggett William s Mathew, Reigate, Sry, labourer to James Collier 2 Dec 1734
Hughes James s John, Ware, Hrt, clerk to William Phillipps 15 Mar 1727/8
Hughes John s John, Bucklebury, Brk, husbandman to William Allen 7 Aug 1693
Hughes John s Edward, Ridge, Hrt, joiner to William Allen 28 Nov 1704
Hughes Richard s ?, Stanton, Gls, yeoman to Thomas Dowdeswell 7 Nov 1675
Hughes William s John, Lambeth, Sry, whiting maker to John Lindsey 6 Nov 1771
Hughes William s John, Enfield, Mdx, gentleman† to James Pateshall 3 Nov 1779
Hughs James s Richard to his father 9 Jan 1709/10
Hughs Richard s Richard to his father 12 Feb 1705/6
Huitson Thomas s Miles, Gatcombe, Gls, clerk to Thomas Dowdswell 20 Jun 1682
Hulbert Thomas s Thomas, Corsham, Wil, tanner† to William Lucas 4 May 1724
Hulbert William s Wilmot, St Martin in the Fields, Mdx, yeoman† to Nathaniel Might 6 May 1734
Hull Thomas s Humphrey, citizen and clothworker to William Badham 14 Nov 1687
Hull William s John, St Giles in the Fields, Mdx, yeoman to James Westall 4 Oct 1746
Hullah Edward s Edward, St Marylebone, Mdx, victualler to Richard Smith 3 Jun 1769
Hulme Hannah d Obadiah, Levenshulme, Lan, fuller to John Hulme 2 Oct 1710
Hulme John s Obadiah, Levenshulme, Lan, whitster to Nathan Hall 16 Jan 1692/3
Hulme John s John to his father 5 Apr 1725
Hulme William s Samuel, Bradford, Yks, gentleman to John Hulme 7 Feb 1738/9
Hulme Zephaniah s William, Hoxton, Shoreditch, gentleman to William Jonathan Eade 1 May 1800
Humber George s Charles, Whitechapel, Mdx, gentleman to William Proudman 4 May 1771
Hume John s John, Offord Cluney, Hun, clerk† to Benjamin Polden 20 Jul 1695
Humfreys Peter s Ellis, Northop, Fln, yeoman to Jeremiah Broadgate 27 Feb 1672/3
Humfreys Thomas s John, Somerheath, High Ercall, Sal, yeoman to Ralph Humfreys 4 Feb 1640/1
Humfreys Thomas s Thomas, Waters Upton, Sal, husbandman to Ralph Humfreys 28 Jul 1646
Humfries Thomas s John, Rodington, Sal, carpenter to Ralph Humfries 1 Sep 1656
Humfry Henry s Henry, Cranbrook, Ken, yeoman to John Jackson 13 Apr 1636
Humphrey John s John, Camberwell, Sry, farrier to William Massey 9 Apr 1725
Humphrey John s William, Stepney, Mdx, tallow chandler to David Bland 3 Jun 1777
Humphries David s Thomas, Welshpool, Mgy, husbandman to Thomas Humphries 10 Sep 1694
Humphries Thomas s Thomas, 'Trelester', Sal, husbandman to John Radburne 18 Dec 1682
Humphries William s Mathew, Charlwood, Sry, yeoman† to Richard Carter 6 Sep 1714
Hunt Charles s Charles, St James Westminster, Mdx, perukemaker to John Burbrough 6 Nov 1710
Hunt Christopher s Thomas, Wantage, Brk, innholder† to Richard Hughes 3 Aug 1691
Hunt Hugh s Ofield, Long Alley, Shoreditch, Mdx, butcher† to John Packman 11 Dec 1761
Hunt John s Edmund to his father 2 Feb 1681/2
Hunt John s Ralph, Shipston upon Stour, Wor, draper to Anthony Moseley 1 Feb 1658/9
<bond from his father and Robert Hunt, citizen and tallow chandler, his brother>
Hunt John s John, Rotherhithe, Sry, waterman† to William Wright 7 Sep 1737
Hunt John s John, Marston, Wil, doctor in physic† to Isaac Price 3 Sep 1746
Hunt Joseph s Joseph, citizen and haberdasher† to Edmund Hunt 19 Aug 1691
Hunt Robert s Ralph, Shipston, Wor, draper to Henry Pauncefoote 13 Dec 1649
Hunt Robert s William, citizen and tallow chandler† to Mary widow of William Hunt 23 May 1702
Hunt Thomas s John, St Martin in the Fields, Mdx, blacksmith† to John Ham 3 Mar 1700/1
Hunt Walter s William, Hedgerley, Bkm, clerk to Roger Rayner 28 Jan 1656/7
Hunt William s William, Hedgerley, Bkm, clerk to Walter Hunt 4 Jun 1668
Hunt William s John, St Andrew Holborn, Lnd, gentleman† to William Cogan 8 Nov 1750
Huntingford Benjamin s Benjamin, St John Horsleydown, blockmaker† to Richard Higgins 17 Feb 1762
Huntman Joseph s Robert, Bishops Hatfield, Hrt, miller to William Cock 6 Feb 1670/1
Hurd James s Thomas, Somerton, Som, maltster to Thomas Cryer 4 Sep 1693
Hurlock George s George, Ealing, Mdx, yeoman† to Samuel Wilkin 10 Jun 1646
Hurlock Joseph s George, citizen and stationer to Thomas Rosse 16 Nov 1663
Hurst Daniel s John, Henlow, Bdf, yeoman to John Berry 20 Jul 1663

Husse Thomas s Thomas, Toddington, Bdf, yeoman† to Silvester Cordey 15 Oct 1642
Hurst Thomas s Christopher, Leckhampstead, Bkm, smith to Samuel Kitchinman 27 May 1663
Hurst Thomas s Andrew, Wapping, Mdx, distiller† to Charles Carpenter 4 Aug 1713
Hussey Samuel s Samuel, St John Clerkenwell, Mdx, vellum bookbinder to John Dickins 7 Apr 1747
Hussey Samuel s William, Southwark, Sry, mason to James Mitchell 5 Mar 1752
Husston John s John, North Curry, Som, butcher to John Jordaine 17 Mar 1761
Hust Benjamin s ?, citizen and cook† to John Bryan 9 Jul 1666
Hutch Robert s Edward, Aldenham, Hrt, husbandman to John Marner 11 Oct 1638
Hutchins John s John, citizen and merchant tailor to Thomas Davies 21 Aug 1656
Hutchinson Benjamin s Edward, Newington, Sry, perfumer to Francis Zouch 3 Sep 1679 <18 Nov 1679 discharged>
Hutchinson John s John, Owthorpe, Ntt, esquire† to Nicholas Charleton 14 Jun 1678
Hutchinson John s John, Nottingham, Ntt, esquire† to William Chesshire 3 Dec 1707
Hutchinson Joseph s Thomas, Bishops Stortford, Hrt, goldsmith† to Joseph Pett 24 Mar 1672/3
Hutt Charles s John, Rickmansworth, Hrt, husbandman† to John Burbrough 7 Dec 1713
Hutt Robert s Robert, Abingdon, Brk, yeoman to Samuel Bedwell 16 Oct 1676
Hyde Edmund s Edmund, St Dunstan in the East, Lnd, chapman to James Westall 1 Sep 1735
Hyett Wm s Robert, Burford, Oxf, clothworker to Samuel Bently 7 Jan 1705/6

I'att Edward s John, St Giles in the Fields, Mdx, coachmaker to Nathaniel Chandler 6 Jul 1719
Ibbott James s John, Ramsey, Hun, gentleman† to William Gurney 3 May 1686
Ibott Thomas s Edmund, St Neots, Hun, salter to Thomas Paine 26 Jun 1637
Ingall James s Thomas, Chelsea, Mdx, gardener to Joseph Wedgbrough 4 Jun 1716
Ingold John s Jonathan, Theydon Garnon, Ess, maltster to Richard Berry 4 Jan 1652/3
Ingram John s Ralph, Whitchurch, Bkm, yeoman to Thomas Obbinson 27 Nov 1704 <turned over to Nicholas Greene, citizen and bowyer>
Ingram John s William, Clapham, Sry, coachmaster to Thomas Jarvis 2 Aug 1785
Ingram Richard s James, Whittington, Gls, doctor in divinity† to Stephen Harris 28 Oct 1670
Ingram Robert s William, citizen and tallow chandler to William Finney 21 Jan 1685/6
Ingram Samuel s Samuel, Whiteparish, Wil, maltster to George Grove 2 Jul 1711 <turned over to Mary widow of Nathaniel Guy, citizen and bricklayer>
Ingram William s Robert, St Ives, Hun, baker to William Finney 30 May 1655
Innocent Jonathan s William, East Langton, Lei, tallow chandler† to Thomas Smith 23 Dec 1673
Iredell William s Henry, St Giles in the Fields, Mdx, labourer to Richard Makepeece 12 Dec 1695
Ireland James s William, Hitchin, Hrt, maltster to William May 11 Jul 1688
Ireland Mary d Robert, 'Abcott', Nth, gentleman† to Richard Cooper 20 Dec 1671
Ireland Richard s William, Norwich, Nfk, weaver to Daniel Scott 26 Apr 1715
Ireland Thomas s Anthony, citizen and blacksmith to Samuel Bexhill 7 Mar 1714/5
Ireland William s John, Wormsley, Hef, yeoman to William Tucker 24 Feb 1678/9
Irwin Richard s Richard, Chatham, Ken† (ward of John Wildash, Hackney, Mdx, brewer) to John Makin 5 Jun 1800
Isaac James s Lawrence, Lambeth, Sry, labourer to Daniel Clarebutt 24 Nov 1669
Isaac Samuel s Thomas, St Botolph Aldgate, Lnd, brazier to Richard Carter 3 Aug 1730
Isaacke George s Daniel, Shoreditch, Mdx, yeoman to Thomas Ford 8 Oct 1640
Isard William to Robert French 4 Jul 1799
Isted Samuel s Richard, Lewes, Ssx, gentleman† to William Goodman 11 May 1657
Iverey Roger s Thomas, Rickmansworth, Hrt, brewer to Adrian Hansford 20 Jun 1633
Iverey Thomas s Thomas, Rickmansworth, Hrt, yeoman to Adrian Handford 19 Apr 1638
Ives Francis s Thomas, Whittlesey, Cam, yeoman to Robert Marchant 21 Apr 1662
Ives John s Francis, St Giles Cripplegate, Mdx, cordwainer to Samuel Jackson 5 Jun 1721
Ives William s William, Maidenhead, Brk, yeoman to John Kidd 12 Mar 1671/2
Ivory Edward s Edward, Northampton, Nth, hosier† to Thomas Claro 5 Mar 1693/4

Jackett John s Richard, Pinner, Mdx, yeoman to John Burgess 16 Sep 1674
Jackman Thomas s Thomas, St Margaret Westminster, victualler to John Radley 27 Feb 1682/3
Jackson Isaac s Isaac, Croydon, Sry, husbandman to John Pratt 2 Apr 1667
Jackson Isaac s Isaac, citizen and tallow chandler† to Isaac widow of Mary Jackson 16 Apr 1695
Jackson John s Jabez to William Jackson 7 Aug 1798

Jackson Samuel s Charles, citizen and frameworkknitter† to John Willford 12 Oct 1704
Jackson William s George, Thorpe Arnold, Lei to Thomas Chambers 11 Mar 1680/1
Jackson William s Robert, Bainbridge, Yks, innholder to John Jellings 19 Feb 1683/4
Jackson William s John, Hampton [? *in Ms* 'Lampton'], Mdx, yeoman† to William Cave 8 Dec 1714
Jackson William s William, Aldersgate Street, tallow chandler† to Joseph Blandford 5 Oct 1742
Jackson William s Clement, Tower Street, Lnd, tailor to Richard Davis 1 Jul 1788
Jacob Moses Solomon s Moses, Stepney, Mdx, limner† to Isaac Bettew 1 Jul 1728
Jacob Robert s Edmund, Buscot, Brk, yeoman to Robert Rodway 8 Dec 1664
Jacob Valentine s John, citizen and currier† to William Gurney 27 Jul 1658
Jacob William s Valentine, citizen and tallow chandler† to William Cranwell 16 Dec 1687
Jacobs William s William, Ratcliffe, Mdx, mariner to Robert Wyrill 7 Oct 1723
Jacus William s John, Tooting, Sry, shoemaker† to Robert Kerby 1 Jun 1719
James Christopher s William, Edmonton, Mdx, butcher† to Nicholas Hawett 7 May 1666
James George s Thomas, citizen and vintner to Nathaniel Perkins 21 Nov 1749
James John s John to his father 26 Jul 1679
James John s Moses, citizen and cook† to Samuel James 1 Feb 1686/7
James Richard s William, Whitechapel, Mdx, pinmaker to Francis Drinkewater 9 Jan 1666/7
James Richard s John, Didbrook, Gls, yeoman† to John Greening 2 Mar 1695/6
James Robert s Robert, Hampstead, Mdx, yeoman to William Leach 22 Jan 1639/40
James Samuel s Samuel to his father 24 May 1687
James Thomas s William, citizen and butcher† to Joseph Gregory 11 Jul 1688
Janes William s Richard, Weston on the Green, Oxf, yeoman to Richard Yates 2 May 1678
James William s John, Apsley, Bdf, shoemaker to Samuel Hussey 19 Feb 1756 <29 Nov 1757
turned over to John Bailey, citizen and pewterer>
Jange Thomas s Walter, Cheltenham, Gls, carpenter to Samuel Withers 12 Dec 1672
Jarmin John s John, Lnd, gentleman to Samuel Berry 15 Apr 1662
Jarrat George s George, citizen and salter to Richard Reynolds 24 Nov 1635
Jarrett Abraham s Timothy, citizen and draper to George Kitchinman 12 Apr 1651
Jarves William s Thomas, Guston, Ken, yeoman to Thomas Webster 8 May 1657
Jarvis Thomas s Thomas, citizen and weaver to Edward Williams 20 Jul 1758
Jarvis Thomas s Thomas, Charing Cross, Mdx, undertaker to his father 2 Mar 1784
Jeanes John s Robert, Milton, Martock, Som, yeoman to Thomas Ross 10 Feb 1647/8
Jefferies John s Richard, Adstock, Bkm, yeoman to Joseph Woolhead 7 Dec 1696
Jefferies Oliver s Oliver, Westminster, Mdx, coachman† to Henry Wine 11 Feb 1668/9
Jefferson Edward s Edward, Crown Court, Newgate Street, Lnd, porter to John Hearn 4 Aug 1778
<6 Apr 1779 turned over to Robert French>
Jefferson John s William, Romaldkirk, Yks, yeoman† to William Rayne 1 Jun 1636
Jeffery John s George, Blakesley, Nth, yeoman to John Turner 19 Apr 1686
Jeffery Robert s Thomas, Greenwich, Ken, butcher to James Scott 7 Sep 1713
Jeffery William s John, Lnd, malt factor to Robert Dove 5 Oct 1719 <2 Apr 1722 turned over
to Joseph Callcott>
Jefferys William s John, Westminster, Mdx, geographer to Joseph Carroll 21 Jan 1755
Jeffreys Henry s John, Old Woodstock, Oxf, yeoman to Philip Peirson 6 Aug 1640
Jeffries John s John, Chancery Lane, Lnd, gentleman to Samuel Belchamber 31 Oct 1651
Jeffs Timothy s Thomas, Priors Marston, War, yeoman to Daniel Jeffs 3 Nov 1680
Jellibrand Thomas s Thomas, Astley, Lan, gentleman† to Peter Pickering 17 Apr 1650
Jellings John s William, Hilton, Hun, yeoman† to Nathaniel Chandler 14 Sep 1669
Jellings William s John, citizen and tallow chandler† to Benjamin Munn 12 May 1698
Jemett Phinnis s Warham, Dover, Ken, brewer to Richard Thornton 17 Jul 1679
Jemmett William s William, Thame, Oxf, mercer to Richard Clement 2 Feb 1681/2
Jemmett William s William, Thame, Oxf, mercer to Thomas Figgins 9 May 1682
Jenings Ellis s Richard, Westminster, Mdx, glover† to Henry Burnley 31 Dec 1657
Jenings William s Richard, Codicote, Hrt, yeoman to John Mothewell 21 Oct 1637
Jenkins Benjamin s John, Daylesford, Wor, yeoman to Nicholas Cattkitt 17 Jun 1669
Jenkins Daniel s William, Nailsworth, Gls, mason to James Ennis 5 Jul 1736
Jenkins John s Henry, Toft [Dunchurch], War, yeoman to Thomas Stone 10 Jul 1667
Jenkins John s John to his father 4 Dec 1695
Jenkins Peter s William, Llanhennock, Mon, bricklayer† to Edmund Hunt 12 May 1670

Jenkinson John s George, Wandsworth, Sry, butcher to Richard Collins 25 Aug 1767

Jenks Edmund s Edmund, citizen and blacksmith† to George Wightman 3 Oct 1709

Jenner James s James, Croydon, Sry, butcher† to John Fist 5 Mar 1752

Jenner John s Robert, St Martin in the Fields, Mdx, yeoman to Richard Reynolds 19 Jan 1690/1

Jenney John s George, citizen and haberdasher to Thomas Smalridge 26 Aug 1664

Jennings James s ?, Norton, Chs to Peter Pickering 23 Sep 1662

Jennings John s Thomas, Rushall, Sts, yeoman to Brian Ayliffe 28 Mar 1684

Jennings Samuel s Samuel, St Olave Southwark, Sry, mariner† to Robert Dove 7 May 1711

Jennoway Martin s William, Coton, Nth, yeoman to Nathaniel Messinger 17 Dec 1678

Jerard Andrew s George, citizen and salter to William Thompson 20 Oct 1670

Jerard Samuel s George to his father 2 Aug 1703

Jermin Charles s John, Romford, Ess, gentleman† to David Taylor 10 Jun 1723 <1 May 1727 turned over to Agnes widow of Richard Ebrall, citizen and draper>

Jervis James s James, citizen and blacksmith to Russell Ferrall 18 Mar 1761

Jery Oliver s Richard, Bushmead, Eaton [Socon], Bdf, esquire to Robert Hooke 30 Jan 1637/8

Jesson Benjamin s Francis, citizen and merchant tailor to William Paine 15 Apr 1680

Jessop William s Thomas, Coggeshall, Ess, clerk to William Webbe 9 Sep 1670

Jeve Edward s Edward, citizen and glover† to Randolph Watson 25 Mar 1679

Jiglis John s Richard, Hackney, Mdx, labourer to Ann widow of William Smith 19 Feb 1729/30

Jobbins John s James, Knightsbridge, Mdx, bricklayer to Richard Calloway 26 Sep 1765

Jocham Joseph s Joseph, Lambeth, Sry, gardener to Edward Clarke 23 Jun 1761

Jodrell Robert s Edmund, Yeardsley, Chs, gentleman to Francis Molyneux 31 Oct 1711

Joell Dorothy s William, Southampton, Ham, labourer to Samuel Withers 11 May 1658

Johnson Abraham s Peter, Colchester, Ess, gentleman to Jeremiah Daniell 29 Oct 1678

Johnson Cornelius s Thomas, Berkhamstead, Hrt, gentleman to William Cock 16 Sep 1715 <6 May 1717 turned over to Thomas Science, citizen and stationer; 5 May 1718 to Jonathan Runt, citizen and clockmaker>

Johnson Edward s John, Lingfield, Sry, esquire to Thomas Kelke 16 Nov 1654

Johnson George s Henry, Overton [Biddulph], Sts, yeoman to Robert Thompson 2 Apr 1694

Johnson Henry s William, Beverley, Yks, gentleman† to Thomas Marsh 1 Sep 1735

Johnson Humphrey s William, Wells, Som, chirurgeon† to George Shelley 16 Jul 1697

Johnson John s John, citizen and haberdasher† to John Parker 14 Apr 1698

Johnson John s John, St James Clerkenwell, Mdx, brewer† to Joseph Swift 25 May 1699 <25 Feb 1702/3 turned over to Elizabeth Hastings, widow>

Johnson John s William, citizen and leatherseller to Thomas Obbinson 7 Jun 1714 <turned over to Daniel ..., citizen and fishmonger>

Johnson Jonathan s Henry, Broughton, Nth, yeoman to Edward Barker 21 Nov 1644

Johnson Joshua s Joseph, Richmond, Yks, butcher† to Richard Dove 4 Sep 1732

Johnson Peter s William, Colchester, Ess, bagmaker† to Jeremiah Daniell 21 Feb 1683/4

Johnson Peter s John, citizen and cooper† to John Furnis 8 Oct 1705

Johnson Thomas s William, Macclesfield, Chs, tailor to William Massey 6 Feb 1667/8

Johnson Thomas s Thomas, citizen and clothworker to George Wightman 2 May 1698 <1 Oct 1701 turned over to William Pope, citizen and broderer>

Johnson Thomas s Thomas, citizen and barber chirurgeon to Robert Thompson 11 Nov 1700

Johnson William s Thomas to his father 3 Feb 1723/4

Johnson William s James, Ratcliffe, Mdx, backmaker† to Samuel Jackson 2 Dec 1728 <1 Apr 1734 master† turned over with consent of Ann Jackson, widow and exec. to Thomas Haddon, citizen and skinner>

Johnson William s Christopher, St Katherine by the Tower, Mdx, corkcutter† to Samuel Wheeler 1 Jul 1734

Jolly Giles s Edward, Cirencester, Gls, woolcomber to Thomas Peirson 13 May 1685

Jones Daniel s John, Hatherop, Gls, clerk to James Church 13 Dec 1658

Jones Edward s Samuel, Lnd, labourer to Mathew Woodward 3 Apr 1721

Jones Eldridge s Samuel, Streatley, Brk, miller to Samuel Wheeler 6 Mar 1731/2

Jones Henry s Daniel, citizen and haberdasher to John Caddy 8 Apr 1696

Jones Job s Peter, Bath, Som, weaver† to Peter Lyme 2 Jun 1741

Jones John s William, Winchcombe, Gls, brazier to William Dutton 21 May 1663

Jones John s John, Havant, Ham, tanner to James Church 19 Aug 1680

Jones John s James, St George Southwark, Sry, weaver† to Henry Miles 17 Feb 1690/1
Jones John s Robert, Bodffordd [Heneglwys], Agy, cordwainer to Robert Boucher 6 Feb 1694/5
Jones John s James, Leominster, Hef, gardener to Benjamin Kendall 6 Sep 1697
Jones John s Josiah, Launton, Oxf, yeoman to Benjamin Sherman 4 Aug 1702
Jones John s Philip, Marlborough, Wil, tallow chandler to William Allexander 7 Apr 1718
Jones Joseph s John, Taplow, Bkm, clerk to Thomas Stone 27 Oct 1673
Jones Lancelot s Maurice, 'Smithey', Sal, yeoman to Henry Wyne 28 Jun 1669
Jones Morgan s Thomas, St Margaret Westminster, blacksmith† to Francis Gaddsbe 13 Apr 1713
Jones Robert s Richard, citizen and bricklayer to John Cadday 31 Mar 1691
Jones Thomas s John Cadwalader, Llanrhos, Cae, clerk to Thomas Palmer 26 Oct 1652
Jones Thomas s Neville, Romsey, Ham, gentleman to Thomas Gale 9 Jan 1682/3
Jones Thomas s Richard, Edvin Loach, Wor, yeoman† to Benjamin Mann 26 Oct 1693
Jones Thomas s William, St James Westminster, Mdx, gentleman† to John Lambert 1 Sep 1767
Jones William s William, Montford [? *in Ms* 'Manford'], Sal, tailor to John Palmer 20 May 1652
Jones William s George, Brockworth, Gls, gentleman to Thomas Bennett 5 Dec 1698
Jones William s John, citizen and stationer to William Coles 20 Aug 1756
Jopson Jeremiah s John, St Clement Danes, Mdx, salesman† to Jeremiah Bradgate 6 Nov 1710
Jordaine John s John, Paternoster Row, Lnd to his father 1 Jun 1767
Jordan Andrew s Andrew, Melton Mowbray, Lei, innholder to Lancelot Vibart 1 Dec 1735
Jordan Benoni s Richard, Fulbrook, Oxf, yeoman† to William Gurney 29 Apr 1675
Jordan John s Charles, St Giles Cripplegate, Mdx, glass-seller to William Reynolds 1 Feb 1702/3
Jordan John s Andrew, Melton Mowbray, Lei, innholder to Andrew Jordan 24 Feb 1745/6 <20 Jun 1749 turned over to Elizabeth widow of William Downing>
Jordan Robert s Thomas, Shadwell, Mdx, mason to Thomas Obbinson 27 Apr 1705 <turned over to Edward Tomkins, citizen and cutler>
Josling Richard s Henry, Limehouse, Mdx, waterman† to Timothy Foster 5 Dec 1720
Joyce Daniel s John, Lnd, carpenter to William Bowyer 17 Mar 1651/2
Joyce James s James, St John Horsleydown, Sry, sailmaker to Henry Dunkin 1 Apr 1788
Joyce Joshua s Jeremiah, Cheshunt, Hrt, woolcomber to William Shepherd 18 Jul 1771
Joyce Richard s Peter, citizen and merchant tailor to Anthony Moseley 11 Oct 1647
Joyce Richard s Richard to his father 29 Oct 1680
Juckes Edward s Edward, 'Elmore', Sal, yeoman to Robert Warde 5 Jul 1664
Judgson John s John, Covent Garden, Mdx, ostler to John Palmer 3 Jul 1655
Jurdine John s Robert, Edmonton, Mdx, yeoman to John Slaughter 13 Jul 1654
Jutkin Jonathan s John, Barby, Nth, yeoman to John Sutton 16 Oct 1637

Kaddey John s John, Muncaster, Cul, yeoman to James Makeham 29 May 1682
Katkett (Catkett) Nicholas s David, Salisbury, Wil, tallow chandler to Robert Rodway 15 Apr 1656
Kay James s John, St James Westminster, Mdx, corkcutter to William Johnson 3 Oct 1759
Keare Thomas s Thomas, Chatham, Ken, shipwright† to George Gerrard 3 Nov 1712
Kearshaw Robert s Abraham, Lnd, tailor to Samuel Wheeler 6 Jan 1725/6
Keasar Edmund s Edmund, citizen and ironmonger to Daniel Binion 12 Jan 1656/7
Keate Andrew s Andrew, citizen and grocer to James Lunn 31 Oct 1655
Keede Robert s Michael, Withycombe Raleigh, Dev, gentleman to Richard Makeham 25 May 1655
Keene George s Roger, St Giles in the Fields, Mdx, yeoman to Thomas Ford 29 Nov 1655
Keep Richard s John, citizen and coach harness maker† to John Gray 15 Apr 1746
Keines Francis s Thomas, Marston Moretaine, Bdf, yeoman† to John Velan 30 Jun 1674
Keirby John s Samuel, Buntingford, Hrt, felmonger† to James Scott 4 Jul 1720
Kell Charles s Robert, Queen Street, Mdx† to Robert Kell 7 Aug 1798
Kell Robert s Robert, Snow Hill, Mdx, cloakmaker† to Henry Soames, jnr. 6 Jan 1789
Kellow John s Benjamin, Little Brickhill, Bkm, yeoman to Samuel Bedwell 13 Oct 1659
Kelly Barnet s John, Rotherhithe, Sry, waterman to James Page 1 May 1781
Kelly William s William, citizen and tallow chandler to Richard West 5 Dec 1720
Kelsall Richard s William, Audley, Sts, yeoman to Edward Holworthie 23 Aug 1652
Kelsey Hannah d Thomas, citizen and draper to Susanna widow of Job Wright 14 Jun 1694
Kelway Jasper s Thomas, Windsor Castle, Brk, clerk to Jeremiah Ridge 1 Jul 1685
Kemmis John s Richard, Dunchurch, War, butcher to John Palmer 24 Jan 1703/4 <15 Aug 1706 turned over to John Cleave>

Kempe John s John, St George Southwark, Sry, gentleman to William Townsend 26 Feb 1684/5
Kempsall John s Thomas, Lewisham, yeoman to Alice widow of Edward Fletcher 26 Jan 1635/6
Kempster William s Christopher, Barford, Oxf, mason to Lancelot Vibart 7 Oct 1740
Kendall Andrew s Andrew, Shadwell, Mdx, cordwainer to Samuel Fitch 6 Jul 1724
Kendall Benjamin s Benjamin, citizen and leatherseller to Robert Butcher 4 Sep 1684
Kendall Benjamin s Benjamin to his father 4 Apr 1709
Kendall George s Edward, Stourbridge, Wor, gentleman to Thomas Marsh 19 Mar 1738/9
Kendar Thomas s Thomas to his father 30 Sep 1659
Kender Samuel s Thomas to his father 5 Oct 1667
Kennell John s Edward, Chapel Brampton, Nth, yeoman† to Thomas Addison 9 Jun 1659
Kensington William s Richard, Brentford, Mdx, innholder to Thomas Lenton 16 Jul 1647
Kent Joseph s John, Upper Wallop, Ham, maltster to Benjamin Brownesmith 1 Feb 1670/1
Kentish John s William, Redbourne, Hrt, yeoman to Nathaniel Chandler 12 Aug 1668
Kentish Samuel s William, St Giles Cripplegate, Lnd, gentleman to John Velan 28 May 1675
Kentish Thomas s Thomas, Watford, Hrt, yeoman† to John French 29 Dec 1645
Kenton Joseph s Henry, citizen and grocer† to William Wright 13 Jan 1637/8
Kenyon William s Roger, 'Poole', Lan, esquire to Francis Molyneux 14 May 1688
Kerbie Richard s Richard, Wallingford, Brk, cordwainer† to Christopher Sumner 21 Oct 1685
Kerby John s Lancelot, Winchester, Ham, gentleman† to William Cranwell 11 Sep 1686
Kerby Robert s William, Wandsworth, Sry, calico printer to Thomas Watts 3 Apr 1710
<12 Apr 1713 turned over to Thomas Woolhead>
Kerrington Francis s Robert, Bury St Edmunds, Sfk, mercer† to John Jeanes 27 May 1658
Kestian Francis s Francis, citizen and fishmonger† to Richard Wright 28 Dec 1652
Kettle John s William, Hackney, Mdx, yeoman to William Jannaway 29 Jun 1650
Keys William s Thomas, Flyford Flavell, Wor, husbandman to Thomas Baynard 13 Dec 1684
Keyte Arthur s William, Minories, Lnd† to his mother Ann Keyte 4 Mar 1788
Keywood John s Stephen, Hampton, Mdx, shoemaker† to John Treavers 15 Jun 1678
Keyzer Jasper s Jasper, St Martin in the Fields, Mdx, jeweller† to John Parker 20 Mar 1690/1
Kidd John s Francis, East Molesey, Sry, draper to William Knight 11 May 1660
Kiddar George s Robert, Blechingley, Sry, miller† to Richard Glyd 3 Oct 1662
Kidney Isaac s Michael, Rugby, War, yeoman to George Haines 24 Dec 1673
Kidwell Knightley s ?, Maidenhead, Brk, brewer to Catherine Wilkinson ? Feb 1664/5
Kift James s John, Lnd, wine cooper to Robert Jackson 24 Jul 1676
Killingly William s Henry, citizen and haberdasher† to Mary widow of Nathaniel Winchester
9 Feb 1701/2 <7 Dec 1702 turned over to Henry Ward, citizen and draper>
Killingworth William s Thomas, Wootton, Oxf, yeoman to Giles Harris 13 Apr 1724
Kimber Francis s Francis, Tubney, Brk, yeoman to Thomas Osborne 29 Jul 1679
King Benjamin s Benjamin, St Giles in the Fields, mariner† to William Thompson 27 Nov 1677
King Charles s William, Chisledon, Wil, yeoman to William King 3 Aug 1696
King Daniel s Daniel, St Saviour Southwark, Sry, threadmaker to Robert Gresswell 9 Mar 1702/3
King Edward s Edward, Tottenham, Mdx, husbandman to Thomas Carpinter 14 Jan 1655/6
King George s Thomas, Timsbury, Ham, farmer to William Goble 6 Mar 1798
King Henry s Francis, Chelsea, Mdx, gentleman to Jeremiah Bradgate 12 Feb 1690/1
King Humphrey s Chad, Westminster, Mdx, yeoman to Robert Udall 19 Apr 1652
King James s Samuel to his father 19 Mar 1674/5
King James s Henry, Cambridge, Cam, waggoner to Charles Goodier 4 Aug 1795
King John s John, Glastonbury, Som† to Peter Prince 12 Apr 1649
King John s Zachary, Watford, Hrt, clothier† to John Burgis 27 Oct 1663
King John s John, Witherby, Lei, yeoman to William Gurney 9 Jun 1676
King John s John, St Katherine by the Tower, Mdx, butcher to Thomas Gilson 5 Jan 1729/30
King Peter s Thomas, citizen and goldsmith to Thomas Andrewes 5 Jul 1687
King Richard s Richard, Bloxholme, Lin, yeoman† to Edward Floyd 30 Jul 1638
King Richard s Robert, Camberwell, Sry, yeoman to William Smith 4 Mar 1671/2
King Roger s Thomas, Crewkerne, Som, cooper to Jeremy Brodgate 12 Feb 1682/3
King Sabin s Daniel, citizen and cutler to William Wickins 12 Feb 1655/6
King Samuel s Samuel, Gravesend, Ken, yeoman to James Magener 10 May 1638
King Thomas s Thomas, citizen and clothworker to Richard Joyce 4 Mar 1674/5
King William s William, Chisledon, Wil, husbandman to William Wickins 9 Nov 1686

King William s Charles to his father 6 Dec 1725
King William Frederick s William, Fore Street, Lnd, cheesemonger to Robert French 7 Dec 1784
Kingham James s ... 1640 <not completed>
Kingham John s John, St Giles in the Fields, Mdx† to Edmund Hall 20 Oct 1685
Kingsley Edward s Edward, citizen and carpenter to John Cooper 3 Jul 1678
Kingston John s Thomas, Buscot, Brk, clerk to John Wood 2 Jul 1695
Kingston John s George, Monmouth, Mon, yeoman to Joseph Booth 4 Apr 1724
Kingstone Edward s Edward, Elton, Hun, yeoman to Edward Orley 10 May 1638
Kington Thomas s Thomas, Banbury, Oxf, butcher† to James Scott 4 May 1724
Kinns Edward s William, Fenny Stratford, Bkm, innholder to John Prick 10 Nov 1640
Kinns John s Edward, citizen and weaver? to Edward Kinns 27 Sep 1672
Kinsell Simon s Simon, Kinwarton, War, yeoman to Thomas Hopkins 12 May 1682
Kinsey John s William, citizen and ironmonger† to Thomas Shelley 23 Jan 1638/9
Kippin Nicholas s John, Wendover, Bkm, yeoman to Andrew Kippin 13 Jan 1680/1
Kipping Andrew s John, Wendover, Bkm, yeoman to William Cranwell 29 Jul 1673
Kirby Henry s William, Horley, Sry, yeoman to Thomas Gardener 19 Aug 1633
Kirby Richard s Thomas, citizen and joiner to William Mayne 1 Feb 1702/3
Kirby Thomas s Richard to his father 3 Dec 1733
Kirke Robert s Robert, Hammersmith, Mdx, butcher to Richard Fulwood 6 Aug 1683
Kirke William s John, Grantham, Lin, butcher† to Thomas Obbinson 12 Nov 1716 <turned over to William Kirke, citizen and haberdasher>
Kirton Daniel s John, Ruislip, Mdx, yeoman to Joseph Coggs 16 Feb 1673/4
Kishee Charles s Edward, Lambeth, Sry, potter to Samuel Wheeler 2 Nov 1719
Kitchingman John s John, Norwich, Nfk, clothier to George Kitchingman 17 Aug 1637
Kitchingman Samuel s George to his father 5 Jun 1651
Knight Edward s Thomas, Clapham, Sry, gardener to William Wright 7 Sep 1730
Knight Edward s Richard, St John Horsleydown, Sry, victualler to Joshua Knight 13 Sep 1770
Knight Francis s Roger, Greenham, Brk, esquire to William Palmer 18 Jun 1646
Knight John s William, citizen and joiner† to Thomas Farrant 1 Jun 1648
Knight John s John, Salisbury, Wil, coachman to William Parker 1 Sep 1712
Knight Joshua s Richard, Shad Thames, Southwark, victualler to Francis Barrell Searle 5 Jan 1763
Knight Richard s Richard, Southwark, Sry, waterman to Francis Barrell Searle 12 Nov 1756
Knight Thomas s William, Brailes [? *in Ms* 'Barrells'], War, gentleman to Robert Harvy 8 Jul 1652
Knight Thomas s Richard, Lnd, scalemaker to John Hunt 14 Dec 1676
Knight William s William, Andover, Ham, scrivener to Richard Whitcher 19 Sep 1664
Knight William s Holliday, Eastington, Gls, clothier† to Edward Terrey 21 Jul 1676
Knight William s Thomas, Eastington, Gls, cheese factor to William Knight 25 Jun 1702
Knightley Thomas s Thomas, Buckingham, Bkm, husbandman† to Robert Maybancke 15 Nov 1637
Kniveton John s Thomas, Broughton, Dby, yeoman to Edward Walker 16 Oct 1682
Knott Thomas s Thomas, St James Clerkenwell, Mdx, sawyer† to Charles Crosier 2 Jul 1711 <4 Feb 1716/7 turned over to Joseph Chamberlin, citizen and saddler>
Knowles John s John, Helpston, Nth, clerk† to William Badham 25 Mar 1689
Knowles John s William, citizen and draper† to William King 5 Oct 1702
Knowles William s Jonathan, Yarm, Yks, tallow chandler to Samuel Fitch 25 Jun 1711
Knowlton Robert s Nehemiah, Watford, Hrt, yeoman† to John Carter 5 Mar 1715/6
Knyveton Henry s John to his father 10 Jan 1708/9
Kynneston Thomas s Edward, 'Adbrightcley', Sal, esquire to Thomas Price 2 Nov 1683

Laban Jacob s Richard, citizen and haberdasher to Samuel Withers 6 Nov 1710
La Bram William s William, St Giles Cripplegate, Mdx, victualler to Daniel Eames 6 Apr 1687
Lacey Benjamin s Benjamin, Great Missenden, Bkm, laceman† to Evan Phillips 7 Mar 1786
Lacon William s Francis, 'Evengton', Hef, gentleman to William Gurney 16 Oct 1676
Ladbrooke Ferdinand s Richard, citizen and salter to William Mayne 26 Apr 1710
Ladbrooke Richard s Thomas, Upton, Bkm, corn chandler to Ferdinand Ladbrooke 4 Mar 1733/4
Lake Francis s William, citizen and apothecary† to John Warman 13 Sep 1692
Lake Henry s William, Buttsbury, Ess, yeoman to Ralph Humpherye 3 Mar 1654/5
Lake Hugh s William, Soho, Mdx, upholder to Egerton Henshaw 27 Mar 1728

Lake Joseph s Francis, Wapping, Mdx, tallow chandler† to John Bezand 5 Sep 1751 <28 Feb 1754 turned over to Henry Hawkins>
Lake Thomas s Richard, Stone, Ken, yeoman† to Thomas Hasted 6 Nov 1658
Lakin William Francis s Francis, Westminster, Mdx, yeoman† to Richard Calloway 17 Feb 1755 <4 Jul 1759 turned over to Joseph Ray, citizen and joiner>
Lamas Peter s Jeremiah, citizen and goldsmith to George Shelley 6 May 1706
Lamb James s Thomas, Lant Street, Southwark, Sry, tailor† to John Withers 4 Aug 1778
Lamb Thomas s Percival, citizen and brewer to Thomas Chewter 4 Nov 1695
Lamb Thomas s William, Jamaica, fishmonger to Eliza widow of Robert Lamb 7 Nov 1726
Lambe Nathaniel s John, citizen and clothworker† to John Greening 22 Jun 1687
Lambe Robert s John, Colchester, Ess, mercer to Henry Hawkes 7 Oct 1676
Lambe Robert s Robert to his father 6 Jun 1698
Lambert John s George, Melton Mowbray, Lei, innholder† to John Jordaine 17 Apr 1753
Lambert John s John, All Hallows the Less, Lnd, iron porter to John Packman 31 Jan 1760
Lambert William s Thomas, Bourton on Water, Gls [? *in Ms* 'Lan'], yeoman to Daniel Weale 7 Feb 1714/5
Lambford Thomas s Thomas, Hornsey, Mdx, labourer† to Timothy Foster 6 Jun 1728
Lamble John s William, Bentley, Ham, yeoman to William Wickins 17 Jul 1660
Lamplee John s Humphrey, St James Westminster, Mdx, butcher to Avery Vokins 2 Nov 1713
Lance Benjamin s James, Lewisham, Ken, baker† to George Bord 2 Apr 1776
Lance Benjamin s William, Sydenham, Ken, baker to Benjamin Lance 1 Jun 1790
Lane James s William, Lnd, poulterer† to Edward Copeland 4 Jan 1730/1
Lane John s James, St George Southwark, Sry, colourmaker to Lancelot Brewer 3 May 1785
Lane Joseph s Thomas, Lnd, alderman and knight† to John Childe 18 Oct 1710 <6 Sep 1714 turned over to Charles Greenwood, citizen and leatherseller>
Lane Joseph s Mathew, Newport Pagnell, Bkm, husbandman to John Townesend 3 Jun 1717
Lane Josiah s Francis, St Martin in the Fields, Mdx, barber to Richard Ingram 28 May 1679
Lane Nathaniel s Nathaniel, Blewbury, Brk, clerk† to William Grove 4 Dec 1678
Lane Samuel s John, Bocking, Ess, weaver† to Samuel Shakemaple 15 Jan 1666/7
Lane Samuel s Thomas, citizen and founder† to John Greening 27 Mar 1701
Lane Thomas s Thomas, Tiverton, Dev, mercer to Hugh Cholmley 19 Jul 1638
Lane Thomas s Henry, citizen and vintner to Robert Wyrill 8 Jul 1706
Lane Thomas s William, Hampstead, Mdx, yeoman to John Sibly 3 Jul 1721
Lane William s John, Hammersmith, Mdx, gardener to Thomas Hamett 16 Nov 1690
Lane William s John, St Clement Danes, Mdx, mariner† to Thomas Searle 7 Apr 1729
Langdon Farding s Joshua, Lnd, gentleman† to Thomas Haines 4 Apr 1715
Langdon Josiah s Josiah, Lnd, haberdasher of small wares† to Joseph Cotching 6 Mar 1698/9
Langford Joseph s Joseph, Wood Street, Lnd, hosier to Joseph Barlow 4 Sep 1798
Langham Thomas s John, St Giles Cripplegate, Mdx, bricklayer† to Thomas Hopkins 23 Apr 1694
Langhorne Leonard s Edward, Dalston, Cul, yeoman to Robert Briscoe 20 Feb 1654/5
Langley Henry s Adam, Radnage, Bkm, clerk to Thomas Cooper 18 Mar 1645/6
Langley Thomas s Benjamin, Mile End New Town, Mdx, mariner to John Stevens 6 Feb 1798
Langley Valentine s Richard, Marlow, Bkm, yeoman† to Richard Langley 30 Jan 1638/9
Langrish John s William, Chichester, Ssx, gentleman† to John Prick 31 May 1659
Langthorne Peter s Peter, Ashwell, Hrt, grocer† to Thomas Haines 1 Nov 1703
Langton Thomas s Oliver, Purton, Wil, gentleman† to William Langton 7 Jan 1705/6
Langton William s Oliver, Purton, Wil, gentleman to Thomas Higgins 20 Aug 1694
Langworthy Henry s Anthony, citizen and leatherseller to John Hills 24 Mar 1717/8
Lansdale Richard s Henry, St Martin in the Fields, Mdx, sawyer† to William Nicholson 3 Jul 1686
Larche James s James, Spitalfields, Mdx, weaver to James Couppe 3 Jul 1732 <6 Oct 1736 turned over to Jacob Clarke, citizen and weaver>
Larder John s John, citizen and merchant tailor to Thomas Yonge 25 Jul 1634
Lardner Hamden s Emanuel, Streatham, Sry, butcher to William Gurney 5 Mar 1659/60
Lardner William s Walter, Bampton, Oxf, gentleman to Richard Walter 29 Apr 1684
Lark Joseph s John, Great Warley, Ess, yeoman to John Radley 20 Jun 1684
Larkin William s John, Christ Church Southwark, Sry, mariner to Henry Batten, jnr. 4 Jul 1709
Larratt John s William, Stamford, Lin, gentleman† to Francis Houghton 9 Jul 1688
Larrett John s Robert, St Giles Cripplegate, Mdx, cordwainer† to William Aldersea 4 Feb 1705/6

Lasley Joseph s Joseph, citizen and fishmonger to William Lucas 4 Mar 1722/3
Latham William s Vincent, Shifnal, Sal, yeoman to Joseph Addams 17 Mar 1651/2
Lathwell Henry s Thomas, St Martin in the Fields, tallow chandler to William Gurney 30 May 1677
Lathwell Joseph s Henry, citizen and tallow chandler† to Mary widow of Henry Lathwell 23 Jul 1686
Latter James s James, Sevenoaks, Ken, victualler to Humphrey Wood 5 Jul 1796
Laurence John s Stephen, citizen and pewterer to Abel Ward 5 Jun 1691
Lavender James s Levi, Coursers Farm [Ridge], Hrt, yeoman to Evan Phillips 1 Feb 1780
Lavender Samuel s Levi, Ridge, Hrt, yeoman to Evan Phillips 6 May 1774 <5 May 1778 turned over to John Shenston, citizen and wheelwright>
Law John s John, citizen and clothworker to Mathew Snablin 9 Sep 1700
Law John s John, Hackney, Mdx, yeoman to Elizabeth widow of Egerton Henshaw 30 Jun 1743 <30 Apr 1745 turned over to Hugh Lake>
Lawman George s John, Norton, Hrt, yeoman to Thomas Noble 29 Mar 1633
Lawndey Thomas s Richard, Cauldwell [Bedford], Bdf, yeoman to William Cock 26 Jun 1656
Lawranson Peter s Thomas, Budworth, Chs, husbandman to Thomas Eyre 6 Feb 1692/3
Lawrence James s Richard, Bourton on Water, Gls, yeoman to John Skepper 23 Nov 1681
Lawrence John s John, Islington, Mdx, tanner to William Lane 2 Apr 1685
Lawrence Jonas s Abraham, Ratcliffe, Mdx, mariner to Jonas Watts 29 Oct 1728
Lawrence Robert s Thomas, Chilton, Brk, clerk to Mary widow of John Flight 2 Mar 1685/6
Lawrence Samuel s Robert, citizen and barber chirurgeon† to Benjamin Russell 8 Aug 1706
Lawrence Thomas s Thomas to his father 3 Mar 1655/6
Lawrence Vincent s Vincent, Thatcham, Brk, yeoman to Simon White 26 Mar 1642
Lawson Andrew s John, St Michael Queenhithe, Lnd, clothworker to Matthias Wrice 1 Jul 1654
Lawton Josiah s Josiah, St Saviour Southwark, Sry, grocer† to Samuel Osborne 5 May 1712
Lawton Richard s John, Newton, Bkm, husbandman to Margaret widow of William Smith 12 Nov 1659
Layton Obadiah s William, St Sepulchre, Lnd, planemaker to John Davenport 7 Apr 1729
Lea John s John, citizen and farrier to William Minchin 15 Jul 1651
Lea John s Richard, Maisemore, Gls, yeoman to Hopewell Hore 22 Jun 1696
Lea Thomas s Thomas, Clare Market, Mdx, gentleman† to Stephen Flindall 1 Sep 1778
Leach John s Richard, Leighton Buzzard, Bdf, yeoman† to Robert Thompson 6 Nov 1704
Leader Richard s George, Speldhurst, Ken, yeoman to William Steere 10 Jan 1666/7
Leake Robert s Robert, Hackney, Mdx, husbandman to Francis Tunsteed 8 Mar 1660/1
Leake William s William, citizen and innholder to Mathew Woodward 30 Aug 1689
Leasingby Joseph s Benjamin, Drayton, Oxf, yeoman to Robert Thompson 14 Feb 1704/5 <18 Apr 1709 turned over to Bartholomew Bonner, citizen and merchant tailor>
Leave Isaac s Richard, Bermondsey, Sry, feltmaker to Thomas Bromsall 3 Apr 1704
Leaver Edward s Edward, Thame, Oxf, clothier to William Finney 1 Sep 1680
Leaver Thomas s Michael, St Clement Danes, Mdx, butcher to John Smith 7 Nov 1715
Ledgingham William s William, citizen and founder to Samuel Clare 30 Nov 1649
Lee Christopher s William to his father 30 Jun 1691
Lee Francis s Thomas, Pontefract, Yks, founder† to Daniel Gurney 30 Jun 1680
Lee John s Samuel, Wapping, Mdx, mariner to Francis Brisco 6 Sep 1697
Lee John s Thomas, Broomfield, Ess, grocer† to Samuel Wright 8 Jun 1724
Lee Joseph s Abraham, Farnham, Sry, tallow chandler† to Mathew Walker 7 Sep 1686
Lee Joseph s John, citizen and carpenter to James Ellis 11 Dec 1700 <2 Nov 1713 turned over to Ann Messenger, widow>
Lee Joseph s Benjamin, Holborn, Mdx, shoemaker to William Noss 7 Aug 1710
Lee Samuel s William, Sewardstone, Ess, yeoman to Joseph Sherwin 11 Jan 1785
Lee William s Christopher, Stourmouth, Ken, yeoman to John Harrison 13 Dec 1655
Lee William s James, Basing, Ham, maltster† to Thomas Rencher 2 Feb 1691/2
Leech Francis s Roger, Hereford, Hef, butcher† to William Barrett 5 Mar 1732/3
Leech John s Thomas, West Wycombe, Bkm, yeoman to Mathew Woodward 31 May 1683
Leech, Bull alias John s Thomas, St Botolph Bishopsgate, Lnd, soap boiler to Daniel Clarebutt 14 Oct 1646
Leech Richard s John, Putney, Sry, gentleman† to Thomas Anckle 13 May 1639
Leech William s William, St Giles in the Fields, Mdx, baker to Herbert Homan 30 Jan 1771

Leeke Daniel s Samuel, Litchborough, Nth, yeoman to Samuel Randall 9 Sep 1675
Leet Isaac s Gregory, Badby, Nth, yeoman to Robert Jackson 18 Aug 1680
Lefevre John s John, Walworth [Newington], Sry, hairdresser† to Robert French 2 Jun 1795
Legg Daniel s Walter, Fulmer, Bkm, yeoman to William Alden 6 Dec 1673
Legg John s Robert, Bloomsbury, Mdx, undertaker† to John Freeman 10 Jul 1750
Legg Robert s Richard, Iron Acton, Gls, yeoman to William Simonds 9 Jun 1635
Legg Thomas s Peter, Swinford Ferry [Cumnor], Brk, maltster to Thomas Fossey 1 Aug 1720
Leggatt William s Abraham, Andover, Ham, maltster to Thomas Cole, jnr. 3 Mar 1700/1
Leichmore Edward s Edward, Hanley Castle, Wor, esquire to Hugh Cholmley 5 Jun 1638
Leigh Jonathan s Jonathan, Whitchurch, Sal, nailor to Philadelphia widow of Edward Osborn 1 Oct 1733
Leigh Peter s William, Westhoughton [Deane], Lan, gentleman to John Townesend 31 Oct 1690
Leigh Peter s Peter to his father 23 Sep 1718
Leigh William s Peter to his father 12 Nov 1716
Leir David s Thomas, St Botolph Bishopsgate, Lnd, merchant tailor to Thomas Bourne 13 Dec 1652
Lem James s Joseph, Paulerspury, Nth, yeoman to William Smyth 13 Mar 1654/5
Lem Joseph s James, Chester, Chs, distiller to William Gurney 11 May 1685
Leman Edward s William, Northaw, Hrt, esquire to Nicholas Charlton 21 Jun 1658
Leman Suckling s Mathew, Weston, Sfk, esquire† to Benjamin Tomplinson 6 Nov 1693
Lemon John s John, Bermondsey, Sry, wheelwright to Robert Preaist 1 Jun 1702
Le Nain Jacob s Juan, Stepney, Mdx, weaver to Thomas Broadbank 9 Feb 1718/9 <5 Aug 1723 turned over to John Collier, citizen and fishmonger>
Lench William s John, Doverdale, Wor, esquire† to John Childe 18 Nov 1675
Lenton William s John, citizen and fletcher to Robert Marsh 3 Oct 1715
Leopard William s William, Lnd, bricklayer† to Samuel Halford 7 Oct 1684
Lered Robert s Robert, Amersham, Bkm, cordwainer† to Isaac Saffell ? Feb 1667/8
Lernoult Herman s Adrian, Lnd, merchant to Joseph Woodward 31 May 1722
Lettas Robert s Robert, Clophill, Bdf, flaxdresser† to Samuel Withers 31 May 1698
Letton Samuel s William, Greenwich, Ken, gardener to Benjamin Skelton 2 Dec 1794
Leveridge John s William, St Luke Old Street, Mdx, leatherdresser† to Richard Smith 19 Oct 1769
Levett Samuel s John, citizen and butcher to Christopher Robotham 2 Jul 1635
Leving Charles s Richard, Parwich, Dby, esquire to John Goode 3 Oct 1677
Levington James s John, Richmond, Yks, gentleman to Peter Champney 25 Nov 1651
Lewer Henry s Walter to his father 6 May 1717
Lewer Walter s Henry, Oxted, Sry, husbandman to Richard Fullwood 1 Mar 1688/9
Lewis Benjamin s John, Liberty of the Tower, Lnd, yeoman† to Robert Howell 5 Feb 1693/4
Lewis Elton s Edward, Tetbury, Gls, mercer to William Gurney 2 Dec 1691
Lewis Henry s Thomas, Stafford, Sts, gentleman to John Child 2 Jul 1695
Lewis Hugh *see* Griffin Heughs
Lewis John s Humphrey, Ashford Carbonell, Sal, yeoman to John Poston 1 Jun 1674
Lewis John s Hugh, Hereford, Hef, clerk to Thomas Hawes 4 Apr 1698
Lewis Nathaniel s Richard, St Peter Paul's Wharf, Lnd, brewer† to Thomas Young 20 Jul 1641
Lewis Philip s Edmund, Elmington [Ashton], Nth, yeoman to William Smith 10 Dec 1656
Lewis William s John, Stevenage, Hrt, tailor† to Jeremiah Woodward 25 Nov 1685
Lewis William Walter s Walter, Swallow Street, St James Westminster, Mdx, gentleman to John Lindsey 4 Mar 1788
Lewrey William s John, Great Melton, Nfk, tailor to Thomas Ford 4 Jun 1638
Lickfold Thomas s George, Petworth, Ssx, blacksmith to Christopher Farmer 5 Jul 1703
Liddyard Thomas s Philip, Upavon, Wil, yeoman to William Clement 19 Aug 1679
Life Geoffrey s Robert, Godstone, Sry, wheelwright to Richard Bull 23 Sep 1646
Lifely William s Abel, St Sepulchre, Lnd, ropemaker to Joseph Withers 1 Apr 1740
Ligo George s Thomas, Stoke Mandeville, Bkm, gentleman to Thomas Hawes 2 Apr 1705
Limbery William s William, Essendon, Hrt, farmer to William Proudman 5 Sep 1786 <turned over to Robert Hopkins>
Limbrey Tobias s Edward, Limehouse, Mdx, mariner to John Rudson 12 Feb 1645/6
Linch Maurice s Maurice, Wapping, Mdx, mariner† to William Dorrington 28 Mar 1689
Lincoln William s Richard, Hainton, Lin, yeoman† to William Collier 9 Sep 1723

Lindsey John s John, Lambeth, Sry, gentleman to Daniel Mason 13 Oct 1762 <23 Feb 1769 turned over to Thomas Lindsey, citizen and cook>
Linfeld William s William, Framfield, Ssx, yeoman to William Coulstoke 23 Mar 1643/4
Ling Richard s Edward, Market Harborough, Lei, apothecary† to Daniel Dale 9 Feb 1685/6
Linney Iliffe s Joseph, Burton Lazars, Lei, grazier to Robert Day 3 Aug 1758
Linsdale Hannah d John, Tollerton, Ntt, husbandman† to Sarah Cock 14 Jan 1683/4
Liscombe Holland s Thomas, Exeter, Dev, clothier† to Thomas Bord 4 Jun 1770
Litchfeild John s John, Lnd, joiner to Thomas Chewter 2 Feb 1686/7
Litchfeild Mary d John, St Andrew Undershaft, Lnd† to Emma widow of William King 2 Jun 1729
Litchfeild William s John to his father 16 Feb 1718/9
Littell William s John, Southwark, Sry, woolwinder to Thomas Broadbank 7 Jun 1753
Littell William s William, Paternoster Row, Spitalfields, Mdx to his father 1 May 1781
Littlefear Gervase s Thomas, Westminster, Mdx, apothecary to John Pattinson 18 May 1757 <9 Apr 1761 turned over to James Hancock, citizen and carpenter>
Littleton George s Thomas, Hagley, Wor, knight† to Nicholas Charlton 11 Mar 1656/7
Living Richard s John, Chertsey, Sry, linen draper to James Pateshall 7 Jan 1775 <6 Jun 1775 turned over to Joseph Cowper, citizen and weaver>
Lloyd James s Humphrey, citizen and joiner† to Daniel Clarebutt 3 Dec 1662
Lloyd Robert s Jonah, Whitechapel, Mdx, victualler† to Thomas Arewater 12 Oct 1765
Lloyd William s Evan, Llanvetherine, Mon, husbandman to Thomas Rippen 30 Aug 1664
Loader Daniel s William, Lambeth, Sry, glass maker to Daniel Mason 5 Mar 1743/4
Loadman Joseph s Robert, citizen and bricklayer† to William Cranwell 26 Apr 1694
Lock John s Edward, Hounslow, Mdx, innholder to Thomas Kender 20 Feb 1686/7
Lock Samuel s William, Acton, Mdx, farmer† to Methusaleh Favell 1 Apr 1728
Lockington Stephen s Stephen, Thrapston, Nth, grocer† to William Gurney 20 Aug 1677
Lockley Richard s Thomas, Cricklade, Wil, baker to Jeremiah Ridge 16 Sep 1741
Lockyer Benjamin s John, citizen and haberdasher† to William Perkins 17 Apr 1689
Lockyer John s Thomas, Marshwood, Dor, butcher† to Edward Parsons 27 Mar 1691
Loder Edward s William, Brentford, Mdx, butcher† to Richard Fulwood 8 Sep 1684
Lodge Samuel s Samuel, Stepney, Mdx, mariner† to Thomas Hasted 25 Feb 1669/70
Lodge Thomas s Michael, Totternhoe, Bdf, gentleman to John Parker 28 Nov 1637
Loen John s Roger, Cheshunt, Hrt, yeoman to John Hewer 27 Feb 1653/4
Logan William s William to his father 17 Feb 1752
Lole Edward s Henry, Shawell, Lei, husbandman to Thomas Orley 11 May 1647
Long Benjamin s William, Portugal Street, Mdx to his father 6 Feb 1781
Long Henry s John, Stoke Orchard, Gls, farmer to John Flock Roberts 5 Jul 1771
Long Robert s William, Portugal Street, Mdx to his father 7 Oct 1783
Long William s William, St Albans, Hrt, wheelwright to Francis Gadsby 5 May 1729
Long William s William, Brailes, War, labourer to Henry Soames 2 Oct 1752
Longbothom Robert s Thomas, Barnet, Hrt to James Ring 6 Aug 1722
Longhurst John s John† to George Weatherstone 7 Aug 1798
Longstaffe Thomas s John, Hatfield, Hrt, surgeon† to John Townesend 6 Sep 1708
Looker John s Thomas, Faringdon, Brk, labourer to John Higgs 8 Nov 1695
Lord Edward s Edward, Clerkenwell, Mdx to William Gurney 2 May 1662
Lord Robert s Robert, St Martin in the Fields, Mdx, gentleman to Peter Pickering 19 Nov 1694
Lorkin Thomas s John, St John Street, Mdx, oilman to Samuel Blower 4 Feb 1794
Lovage William s William, St James Westminster, Mdx, planemaker† to Robert Higgs 7 Sep 1742 <21 Feb 1748/9 turned over with consent of William Higgs, administrator to George Carpenter>
Loveday John s John, St George Southwark, Sry, carpenter to Aurelius Hodson 24 Oct 1770
Loveday Joseph s John, Atherstone, War† to Samuel Brooker 21 Apr 1649
Low James s William, St Botolph Bishopsgate, Lnd, glover† to Edward Heming 6 Apr 1737
Low John s John, Holborn, Mdx, victualler† to Abraham Farren 23 Jan 1771 <6 May 1777 turned over to Samuel Farren>
Lowd John s George, Warbleton, Ssx, yeoman† to Samuel Hamond 7 Feb 1660/1
Lowday Thomas s Edward, Brackley, Nth, yeoman to James Harding 23 Jan 1654/5
Lowden John s Thomas, Wragmire, Cul, husbandman† to John Back 25 Jan 1671/2
Lowe John s William, Purston [King's Sutton], Nth, gentleman to Henry Durban 18 Mar 1694/5

Lowe Joseph s Edward, citizen and cutler† to Francis Houghton 7 Mar 1678/9
Lowe Lawrence s Thomas, Tewkesbury, Gls, yeoman to Thomas Dawson 22 Jan 1632/3
Lowen William s William, citizen and tallow chandler to William Gurney 2 Jun 1690
Lucas Jonathan s William, Chelmsford, Ess, butcher to Andrew Partridge 2 Sep 1657
Lucas Joseph s Joseph, Whitechapel, Mdx, labourer to Edward Copeland 2 Feb 1736/7
Lucas Michael s Thomas, St Giles in the Fields, Mdx, tobacconist to Thomas Cole, jnr. 8 Nov 1692
Lucas Richard s John, citizen and joiner to William Bowyer 24 May 1647
Lucas Samuel s Daniel, Chelmsford, Ess, tailor† to Thomas Woolhead 5 Jan 1718/9
Lucas Thomas s John, Guilsborough, Nth, gentleman to Sarah widow of John Cleave 7 Mar 1714/5 <18 Dec 1716 turned over to Elizabeth widow of John Hastings>
Lucas William s Thomas, Hollowell, Nth, yeoman to William Gibson 19 Jan 1646/7
Lucas William s William, Hollowell, Nth, gentleman† to Elizabeth widow of John Hastings 2 Jul 1711
Luckins James s James, Wicklow, Ire, gentleman to William Gaunt 14 Sep 1676
Lucock John s Roger, Seavington St Michael, Som, yeoman to Thomas King 8 Feb 1649/50
Ludlow Benjamin s Stephen, Lnd, wool stapler† to Thomas Haynes 7 Jun 1708
Luff Nicholas s John, East Meon, Ham, yeoman to William Luff 8 Aug 1698
Luff William s John, East Meon, Ham, husbandman to Jeremiah Ridge 5 Jul 1688
Lunn James s James, Aylesford, Ken, tailor† to Thomas Northover 30 Sep 1689
Lunne James s James, Hertford, Hrt, yeoman† to Gilbert Cornelius 10 Apr 1638
Lunshun Samuel Emier s George, Greenwich, Ken to Benjamin Lance 7 Aug 1798
Luther Martin s Thomas, Hoddesden, Hrt, joiner† to Kenelm Savill 12 Feb 1638/9
Lutwyche Richard s Richard, Clyro, Rad, yeoman to Thomas Watts 14 Mar 1693/4
Luxford Edward s Thomas, Houndsditch, Lnd, pinmaker† to Thomas Jarvis 7 Mar 1797 <2 Jan 1800 turned over to Edward Chandler>
Lye Cuthbert s Thomas, Shoreditch, Mdx, yeoman to Thomas Bord 20 Oct 1756
Lyford Nathaniel s Nathaniel, Windsor, Brk, butcher to Richard Hodgkin 19 Jul 1676
Lyford Thomas s Richard, Bradfield, Brk, gentleman† to Geoffrey Lyte 1 Apr 1658
Lym Mathew s William, citizen and shipwright to William Smith 18 Mar 1683/4
Lymer Giles s Giles, St Clement Danes, Mdx, saddler† to John Syms 10 Nov 1685
Lynes William s Thomas, Hellidon, Nth, maltster to Samuel Osborn 7 Feb 1738/9
Lynnell Robert s John, Duston, Nth, yeoman† to William Haydon 5 Feb 1678/9
Lynnett John s John, Terling, Ess, chandler to William Gaunt 23 Nov 1652
Lyster Jonathan s Thomas, Duncot [Atcham], Sal, yeoman to Christopher Farmer 1 Jul 1700

Mace Isaac s Joseph, Spaldwick, Hun, yeoman† to John Mace 21 Feb 1695/6
Mace John s Joseph, Spaldwick, Hun, yeoman† to Thomas Haynes 21 Jul 1680
Machell John s John, Chigwell, Ess, gentleman to Richard Cooper 20 Aug 1649
Mackey Hugh s Thomas, Wapping, Mdx, mariner† to Elizabeth widow of Cornelius Woolley 7 Jul 1735 <5 Jul 1737 turned over with consent of Henry Rawlins who married Elizabeth Woolley to John Compton>
Macky David s David, Elgin, Mor, yeoman to Thomas Hatton 6 Sep 1654
McMillan John s Daniel, Leadenhall Street, Lnd, oilman† to Phineas Pateshall 1 May 1800
Madding Robert s Robert, 'Kicker End', Mdx, butcher to John Hewer 30 Jun 1641
Maddock Humphrey s John, Osmaston, Dby, yeoman to James Collier 9 Dec 1718
Maddox Robert s William, Boxley, Ken, esquire to James Woods 2 Jul 1660
Magrath Daniel s Roger, Limehouse, Mdx, tailor to Jonas Lawrence 7 Feb 1765
Magridge John to Thomas Rippen 1661/2
Maior Adam s Hugh, Hartley [Shinfield], Brk, yeoman† to John Bury 16 Aug 1649
Maisters Edward s Edward, Bankside, Lnd, vintner† to Thomas Wall 15 Feb 1647/8
Makeham Amy d James to her father 3 Apr 1693
Makeham James s James, Bosbury, Hef, husbandman to Richard Makeham 24 Nov 1669
Makeham Paul s Richard, Bosbury, Hef, yeoman to Richard Makeham 2 Oct 1662
Makeham Richard s Richard, Bosbury, Hef, yeoman to William Goodman 18 Dec 1646
Makepeece John s Thomas, Staverton, Nth, yeoman† to Richard Makepeece 11 Jan 1697/8
Makepeace John s Richard to his father 18 Dec 1710
Makepeece Richard s Thomas, Staverton, Nth, yeoman to Richard More 28 Feb 1682/3

Makernes Samuel s John, Finedon, Nth, yeoman† to Walter Hoare 10 Jun 1689
Makin John s John, Southwark, Sry† to William Stephens 3 Dec 1781
Malcombe William s William, Ratby, Lei, bachelor of divinity to Robert Jackson 2 Oct 1678
Malkin Francis s Richard, citizen and upholder to Richard Yates 3 Apr 1704
Mall Thomas s Thomas, Prittlewell, Ess, yeoman† to Thomas Obbinson 1 Dec 1680
Malpas Thomas s Thomas, citizen and merchant tailor† to Edward Smith 28 Feb 1752
Maltman Thomas s Francis, Waterbeach, Cam, yeoman to John Palmer 18 Jun 1655
Man Daniel s Miles, Halton Green, Lan, gentleman to George Bowyer 25 Feb 1635/6
Man Joseph s Thomas, Braintree, Ess, gentleman† to William Bowyer 17 Mar 1651/2
Man Thomas s John, Swansea, Gla, gentleman to Daniel Man 13 Nov 1679
Mander John s John, Oxford, Oxf, innholder† to William Gibson 19 Jan 1646/7
Mandevell William s Jegon to his father 5 Oct 1702
Manfeild John s Edward, 'Hamsey', Ssx?, yeoman to John Browne ?27 Oct 1670
Maning James s Thomas, Christ Church, Lnd, merchant tailor† to John Goade 30 Sep 1656
Manings Josiah s John, Winchester, Ham, smith to Humphrey Hill 1 Sep 1646
Manistey Thomas s William, Peterborough, Nth, tanner to William Troughton 6 Apr 1654
Manning Bartholomew s Bartholomew, Northampton, Nth, mercer† to Philip Constable 26 Jul 1687
Manning John s John, Milton, Nth, yeoman† to Griffith Griffiths 8 Mar 1697/8
Manning Thomas s Thomas, Horsleydown, Sry, carpenter to John Gold 5 Feb 1694/5
Manning William Glyde s Henry, Stokeinteignhead, Dev to William Hodges 5 Aug 1777
Mansell John s Peter, Bethnal Green, Mdx, tallow chandler to John Hunt 9 Apr 1761
Mansell William s Walter, Shoreditch, Mdx, tanner to John Pratt 4 Jul 1687
Mansfeild Peter s John, Shoreditch, Mdx, weaver to Richard Carter 12 Jul 1737
Mapleton Mary d Jonathan, Reading, Brk, armorer† to William Hulls 24 Apr 1690
Marce William s Robert, Geddington, Nth, yeoman to William Gunston 12 Aug 1641
March Simon s Paul, Stalisfield, Ken, butcher† to Thomas Andrewes 5 Dec 1691
March Thomas s Thomas, Northallerton, Yks, gentleman to Joseph Lane 7 Nov 1726
March Thomas s Thomas, Bilbrough, Yks, gentleman to Joseph Lane 17 Jan 1726/7 <cancelled same day>
Marchant Thomas s Anthony, Ardingley, Ssx, yeoman to Thomas Parker 29 Nov 1633
Marchant William s Hugh, St Giles in the Fields, Mdx, gentleman† to Charles Thatcher 4 Apr 1715
Mardener Francis s Robert, Peckham, Sry, yeoman to Robert Udall 19 Jul 1638
Mardle Thomas s Thomas, Stanford le Hope, Ess, yeoman to Thomas Jarvis 8 Jul 1774
Mare John s Henry, Tabley, Chs to Margaret widow of Leonard Turner 30 Aug 1650
Marken John s Ewry, Old Park, Dur, gentleman† to Francis Molyneux 7 Feb 1694/5
Markland Mary d Robert, Wigan, Lan, mercer† to William Hulls 15 Oct 1688
Markwell Richard s Thomas, 'Wigham', Lin, yeoman† to Thomas Rawlinson 12 Nov 1722
Marrant William s Anthony, Putney, Sry, blacksmith to Daniel Browne 10 Apr 1671
Marriott John s William, Little Canfield, Ess, clerk to James Scott 1 Apr 1717
Marriott Nicholas s John, Harpole, Nth, yeoman to Elizabeth widow of Samuel Harris 14 Mar 1699/1700
Marriott Richard s Richard, Towcester, Nth, tanner to Richard Palmer 12 Jul 1677
Marsh Robert s Thomas, Elstree, Hrt, yeoman† to John Halsey 26 May 1704 <15 Dec 1707 turned over to William Holiday>
Marsh William s William, St Olave Southwark, Sry, yeoman to William Ragsdale 9 Jan 1689/90
Marshall Benjamin s Benjamin, Red Cross Square, warehouseman to John Doble Hillier 3 Feb 1792
Marshall Daniel s Francis, Stepney, Mdx, mariner to Roger Gale 8 Aug 1706
Marshall Francis s ..., Yks to Thomas Rosse 24 Dec 1633
Marshall James s Thomas, 'Arelake', Yks, yeoman to Francis Marshall 22 May 1655
Marshall John s William, Colly Weston, Nth, clerk to William Urmston 30 May 1650
Marshall John s John, Eynsford, Ken, yeoman† to Elizabeth widow of Robert Lamb 1 Jul 1717
Marshall John s Thomas, Colchester, Ess, weaver† to William Havens 3 Jul 1721
Marshall John s Charles, Aynho, Nth, farmer† to William Lucas 15 Oct 1756 <7 Mar 1759 master† turned over to Francis Flower, citizen and carpenter with his own consent as an exec.>
Marshall Richard s Thomas, Michelham [Arlington], Ssx, clerk to William Sheffeild 10 Jul 1633
Marshall William s Daniel, Holborn, Mdx, turner† to Thomas Mason 3 Mar 1686/7
Mart William s William, Sheering, Ess, yeoman to Joseph Wedgbrough 2 Dec 1723 <8 Nov 1728 turned over to Edward Chamberlayne, citizen and salter>

Marter Edward s John, Thatcham, Brk [? *in Ms* 'Sry'], yeoman to Thomas Greene 18 Jun 1646
Marter James s Robert, Covent Garden, Mdx, gentleman to William Mellor 2 Jul 1722 <turned over to William Kirke, citizen and haberdasher>
Martin Benjamin s Samuel, St John Horsleydown, fellowship porter to Edward Clarke 18 Jul 1764
Martin Daniel s William, Brixworth, Nth, yeoman to John Radley 21 Feb 1688/9
Martin Edward s Henry, citizen and plaisterer† to Thomas Commins 7 Jan 1714/5 <9 Jun 1718 as Henry Martin turned over to Lydia widow of Charles Burrowes, citizen and salter>
Martin Jabez s Jabez, citizen and merchant tailor to William Wright 6 May 1723 <3 Jun 1728 turned over to Henry Hall, citizen and grocer>
Martin James s Robert, Great Stanwell, Mdx, butcher† to Samuel Osborn 5 Jun 1721
Martin John s John, citizen and goldsmith to John Rumball 12 May 1682
Martin John s Henry, West Camel, Som, gentleman to Edward Parsons 2 Jun 1683
Martin John s Hugh, St Marylebone, Mdx, joiner to Thomas Crowther 4 Apr 1769
Martin Joshua s William, Billington, Bdf, yeoman to Joan Prentice widow of William Martin 12 Aug 1662
Martin Richard s Richard, Lnd, haberdasher† to Samuel Mackerness 5 Mar 1704/5
Martin Thomas s John, Bletchley, Bkm, yeoman to William Tucker 17 Jun 1653
Martin William s Thomas, Waltham, Brk, yeoman to Thomas Givers 21 Sep 1654
Martin William s William, St Martin in the Fields, Mdx, tailor to John Turner 21 Jan 1691/2
Martin William s Thomas, citizen and haberdasher† to Joshua Baldwin 7 Dec 1704
Martin William s John, Lambeth, Sry, gardener† to Thomas Searle 6 May 1734
Martland Henry s Thomas, Blackrod [Bolton le Moors], Lan, to Thomas Hatton 2 Feb 1662/3
Masingberd William s William, Brickley, Bkm, gentleman† to Thomas Rose 27 Sep 1642
Mason Daniel s John, Lnd, currier to Gabriel Whiteaker 1 Feb 1724/5
Mason Daniel s Daniel to his father 21 Nov 1759
Mason Edward s Edward, Soho, Mdx, yeoman† to George Stockdale 28 Apr 1691
Mason Edward s George, Noaks [Avonbury], Hef, gentleman to Thomas Kender 7 Oct 1695
Mason Francis s George, Noaks [Avonbury], Hef, gentleman to Edward Mason 15 Dec 1707
Mason George s Edward, Monmouth, Mon, gentleman to Thomas Kendar 30 Sep 1659
Mason Henry s John, Stepney, Mdx to James Darby 23 Jul 1662
Mason Henry s Daniel, Lambeth, Sry to his father 15 Mar 1770
Mason John s John, Bicester, Oxf, vintner to James Church 25 Apr 1672
Mason John s Daniel, Stratford on Avon, War, mercer to Josiah Ragdale 1 Aug 1683
Mason John s William, Brentingby, Lei, farmer† to Robert Day 6 Jan 1740/1
Mason John s Thomas, St Giles Cripplegate, Lnd, shoemaker to Radcliff Badily 6 Sep 1748
Mason Joseph s John, Holy Trinity Minories, Lnd, currier to William Jackson 4 Feb 1722/3
Mason Joseph s Joseph, Spitalfields, Mdx, tallow chandler† to Daniel Mason 7 Apr 1752
Mason Robert s John, Wapping, Mdx, gentleman to William Gaunte 19 Aug 1672
Mason Stephen s Benjamin, Southwark, Sry, labourer to John Hulme 9 Aug 1738
Mason Thomas s John, Hemingford Abbots, Hun, yeoman to William Cranwell 10 Feb 1670/1
Mason Thomas s William, St Clement Danes, Mdx, tailor† to John Turner 13 Sep 1679
Mason William s William, Worcester, Wor, clothier† to Samuel Wheeler 24 Aug 1680
Massey William s William to his father 8 Nov 1669
Master Thomas s Edward, 'Franc', Sfk?, clerk to Peter Prince 18 Jun 1666
Masters Benjamin s Benjamin, St Ives, Hun, yeoman to William Simcock 28 Jul 1634
Masters Elias s Elias, Deptford, Ken, mariner† to Richard Walker 1 Dec 1712
Masters George s Martin, Lnd, carver† to William Smith 9 Feb 1707/8 <7 Jun 1714 turned over to Isaac Wellings, jnr.>
Masters Nicholas s Edward, St Saviour Southwark, Sry, mercer to Thomas Wallcott 13 Dec 1652
Masters Robert s George, Walton le Naze, Ess, mariner to Catherine widow of Thomas Hiccock 10 Jan 1649/50
Mathew Richard s Nicholas, 'Holloway', Bdf, yeoman† to John Berry 18 Aug 1659
Mathewes John s Francis, citizen and weaver† to Samuel Sheriffe 5 Sep 1673
Mathewes John s John, Barrington, Gls, yeoman to Robert Mathewes 8 May 1678
Mathewes Richard s Richard, Hackney, Mdx, coachman to Robert Leake 4 Mar 1668/9
Mathewes William s William, Sherborne, Dor, yeoman to William Tucker 28 Jan 1655/6
Mathews Nathaniel s Nathaniel, St Dunstan in the West, Lnd, tallow chandler to William Shepherd 17 May 1773

Mathews Robert s Roger, Lnd, silkman to John Thompson 5 Jun 1721
Mathews Thomas s William, St Giles in the Fields, Mdx, mason to Thomas Grover 29 Oct 1656
Matley George s Anthony, St James Westminster, Mdx, victualler to James Davidson 13 Nov 1770
Matrevers Richard s Elias, Bath, Som, tanner to John Tyson 3 Nov 1674
Matthewes Charles s Thomas, Latton, Wil, farmer† to John Hill 4 Apr 1739 <2 Dec 1740 turned over to John Clarke, citizen and joiner>
Matthews Robert s Thomas, Barrington, Gls, yeoman to John Wilse 22 Jun 1654
Mattingly Benjamin s Thomas, Cirencester, Gls, farmer to Charles Dare 9 Mar 1768
Maxey Benjamin s Thomas, Wallingford, Brk, joiner to Joseph Dorrell 4 Sep 1727
Maxey John s William, East Bergholt, Sfk, clothier to John Yarling 19 Feb 1658/9
May Edwin s George, Willesborough, Ken, clerk to John Saywell 19 Nov 1657
May John s William to his father 4 Apr 1698
May Michael s William, Wing, Bkm, yeoman to Richard Johnson 8 Nov 1638
May Michael s Michael, Wing, Bkm, grocer† to William Gurney 5 Oct 1687
May Robert s John, Lambeth, Sry, labourer to James Titley 3 Jul 1744
Mayfield John s Richard, Shadwell, Mdx, victualler to Francis Gigner 7 Jul 1778
Maylin Joseph s Thomas, Bermondsey, Sry, stapler to Francis Zouch 22 Sep 1674
Maynard William s Henry, citizen and fishmonger to Gilbert Brandon 28 Nov 1678
Mayne John s John, citizen and butcher to Brian Ayliffe 5 Dec 1698
Mayo Thomas s Thomas, citizen and glazier† to Thomas Rigby 3 Aug 1702
Mazey Samuel s John, Braintree, Ess, clothier to William Buckley 6 Mar 1656/7
Mead John s John, Watford, Hrt, husbandman to Robert Maybanke 14 Nov 1636
Meade John s Richard, St Martin in the Fields, Mdx, victualler† to William Threader 22 May 1672
Meade Thomas s John, citizen and fruiterer† to John Watts 20 Oct 1686
Meadowes John s John, Chigwell, Ess, butcher to Thomas Kelke 22 Nov 1639
Meadowes John s William, Bermondsey, Sry, mariner† to Thomas Spencer 30 Apr 1669
Meager Nicholas s Francis, Croydon, Sry, farmer to John Berridge 6 Oct 1778
Meake Thomas s Joseph, Thame, Oxf, labourer to Robert Boucher 22 Jul 1703
Meakins William s Thomas, Oakham, Rut, innholder to John Brian 23 Aug 1649
Meare Joseph s Joseph, St Martin in the Fields, Mdx, victualler to Richard Kerby 7 Oct 1723
Medborne William s William, Geddington, Nth, yeoman to William Massey 18 Dec 1651
Medcalf James s James, Lnd, collier to John Hooke 5 Jul 1714
Meddens Samuel s Edward, Worcester, Wor, weaver† to George Harlow 21 May 1766
Medding William s William, Lambeth, Sry, lathmaker to Walter Hunt 20 Jan 1670/1
Meddowes Paul s Paul, Tower Hill, Lnd, factor† to Henry Cox 8 Sep 1659
Medes William Thomas s Thomas, Bridewell Precinct, gentleman to Philip Pickering 5 Jul 1731
Medlicott Cromwell s Thomas, Cheshunt, Hrt, yeoman to Abel Ward 23 Oct 1684
Meekley George s John, Dunham, Ntt, farmer to John Colcraft 3 Jul 1754
Megrah Edward s John, Church Row, St Botolph Aldgate, soapmaker to William Proudman 5 Aug 1783
Meller William s Richard, Bradley, Dby, husbandman to Samuel King 31 Oct 1671
Melton Luke s John, Woolstone, Gls, yeoman to George Kitchingman 10 Sep 1651
Mence Francis s Richard, citizen and upholder to Samuel Shepward 28 Aug 1705
Mence Thomas s Thomas, Grafton, Wor, yeoman† to Charles Beardoe 7 Dec 1686
Merat alias Tyler Robert s Robert, Ushant, Wil, yeoman† to Edward Skinner 5 Feb 1693/4
Mercer Robert s James, Greenwich, Ken, innholder to Thomas Greene 12 Jun 1643
Merefield John s Nicholas, Teffont, Wil, gentleman to Edward Fitz 4 Sep 1740
Merrett Peter s Richard, Wandsworth, Sry, calico printer to Robert Kerby 5 Aug 1723
Merrett Samuel s Francis, citizen and blacksmith to John Thompson 3 Jan 1670/1
Merrick John s John, Ruislip, Mdx, yeoman to William Pope 8 Jul 1658
Merriman Benjamin Howard s Benjamin, St Katherine Coleman, Lnd to his father 6 Feb 1776
Merriman Benjamin s Thomas to his father 4 Sep 1740
Merriman James s Henry, St Botolph Bishopsgate, Lnd, joiner† to Thomas Searle 4 Oct 1743
Merriman Thomas s Benjamin, Newbury, Brk, clerk to James Horton 2 May 1711 <4 May 1713 turned over to Richard Stonier; 5 Dec 1715 to William Collier, citizen and shipwright>
Merriman Thomas s Thomas, citizen and tallow chandler† to Martha widow of Thomas Merriman 19 Dec 1749 <11 Apr 1755 turned over to William Mascall, citizen and poulterer>

Merritt Thomas s Thomas, Wapping, Mdx, victualler† to Elizabeth widow of Robert Gresswell 7 Aug 1710 <4 Jul 1715 turned over to Joseph Cocke citizen and merchant tailor>
Merryatt Joseph s Maurice, citizen and skinner† to William Osmond 7 Jul 1654
Mersam George s Richard, Llandyrnog, Den, yeoman to William Jenkins 3 May 1636
Mervin James s John, Lnd, merchant to Benjamin Brownesmith 11 Jul 1676
Merydale William s John to his father 3 Feb 1686/7
Messinger John s John, Isham, Nth, husbandman† to John Syms 27 May 1685
Messinger Thomas s Richard, 'Shelsworth and Simpson', Wil, yeoman† to Thomas Burge 7 Jul 1701
Messingham Thomas s Thomas, Binstead, Ham, yeoman to William Tomson 10 Jul 1643
Metcalfe Edward s Edward, Osmotherley, Yks, yeoman to Samuel Fitch 1 Apr 1723
Meyers Andrew s Joseph to his father 4 Apr 1755
Meyers Thomas s Joseph to his father 7 Apr 1762 <7 Apr 1763 turned over to Thomas Sherwood, citizen and draper>
Michell John s Charles, All Hallows Barking, Lnd, waterman to William Thompson 21 Apr 1648
Middlemore William s Robert, Hazelwell, Wor, gentleman to William Allett 19 Mar 1650/1
Middleton Edward s William, Maresfield, Ssx, yeoman to William Nelson 18 May 1661
Middleton Elizabeth d Thomas, Whittlebury, Nth, gentleman to John Tuer 12 Apr 1660
Middleton Francis s Anthony, Horsham, Ssx, clerk† to Richard Bull 12 Dec 1645
Miers Benjamin s Walter, citizen and shipwright to Henry Bartan 19 Jul 1687
Might Daniel s Nathaniel to his father 6 Nov 1721
Might Nathaniel s Nathaniel, Spitalfields, Mdx, brewer to Samuel Makernis 7 Mar 1697/8
Milburne William s Robert, Warkworth, Nbl, merchant† to Samuel Fitz 1 Dec 1707
Miles Henry s John, Newington, Mdx, gentleman to Thomas Stiver 21 Jul 1659
Miles William s William, Hampton Wick, Mdx, gentleman† to Gilbert Brandon 6 Oct 1687
Millard John s William, Upleadon, Gls, husbandman to Thomas Noble 20 Jun 1638
Miller Edward s Richard, Chiddingley, Ssx, yeoman to William Nelson 25 Apr 1673
Miller Henry s Henry, Chapel Brampton, Nth, farmer to John Tilley 12 Sep 1738 <7 Nov 1739 turned over with consent of John Tilley, son and exec. to Joseph Hunt, citizen and bricklayer>
Miller Hugh s John, Staines, Mdx, yeoman to William Wickins 4 May 1649
Miller James s James, Saffron Walden, Ess, husbandman to John Crouch 23 Nov 1637
Miller James s Thomas, Ross, Hef, yeoman† to Thomas Givers 12 Aug 1641
Miller William s John, Warwick, War, yeoman to Edward Orley 1 May 1633
Miller William s William, Rearsby, Lei, yeoman to James Miller 5 Jun 1661
Milles Edward s William, Greatham, Ssx, esquire† to John Banckworth 23 Mar 1635/6
Milles John s John, 'Brickmaster', Wil, yeoman to Robert Morre 19 Apr 1638
Millis John s John, Bermondsey, Sry, tanner to John Wyburd 6 Nov 1688
Mills Alexander s Alexander, Lambeth, Sry, lighterman to Francis Barrell Searle 5 Sep 1775
Mills Humphrey s Humphrey, Reading, Brk, clothier to John Tyson 13 Oct 1640
Mills Jacob s Jacob, Belluton [Stanton Drew], Som, yeoman to William Alexander 4 Aug 1718
Mills Thomas s John, Stratfield Mortimer, Ham, yeoman to John Syms 9 May 1682
Milner Samuel s Thomas, Compton Martin, Som, yeoman to John Compton 6 Mar 1734/5
Milnes Robert s Robert, Brampton, Dby, yeoman† to William Butler 19 Feb 1666/7
Milton Edmund s John, Woolstone, Gls, yeoman to George Kitchinman 15 Jun 1646
Milton Francis s Francis, Greenwich, Ken, mariner to Thomas Thatcher 4 Jun 1722
Milword Abraham s Isaac, Derby, Dby, cordwainer to Joseph Baker 5 Oct 1702
Mimmark John s John, Newark, Ntt, gentleman to Philip Pickering 1 Mar 1730/1
Minchin John s William to his father 2 Feb 1659/60
Minchin Joseph s William to his father 24 Mar 1665/6
Missen John s John, St Botolph Aldgate, Lnd, butcher to Andrew Goodwin 25 Jul 1678
Missingham John s Thomas, Binstead, Ham, weaver to William Thompson 9 May 1650
Mitchell Edward s Edward, Abingdon, Brk, bookbinder† to Ebenezer Ambrose 4 Mar 1699/1700
Mitchell Edward s Stafford, Middle Aston, Oxf, gentleman to Joseph Lane 5 Jun 1744
Mitchell James s Edmund, Battersea, Sry, tallow chandler to Thomas Sutton 6 Jul 1742
Mitchell John s John, Watford, Hrt, yeoman to Thomas Vaughan 9 May 1656
Mitchell John s George, St Pancras, Mdx, baker† to John Pearce 5 Jun 1792
Mitton Henry s Thomas, Bedwardine, Worcester, Wor, gentleman to Samuel Belchamber 4 Nov 1654

Mock John s Alan, St Mary Cray, Ken, husbandman† to Thomas Hayes 3 Oct 1662
Moger Charles s Guy, Reading, Brk to James Brent 2 Oct 1721
Mogridge John s John, Potterne, Wil, tanner† to Thomas Rippen 16 May 1661
Molyneux Francis s Francis, Mansfield, Ntt, esquire to Nicholas Charleton 13 May 1672
Molyneux John s Darcy, Mansfield, Ntt, esquire to Peter Pickering 6 Oct 1702
Mompesson Henry s William, Eakring, Ntt, clerk to Francis Molyneux 19 Apr 1690
Monck Richard s Thomas, Bierton, Bkm, yeoman to William Hoare 4 May 1742
Monday Henry s Henry, St James Westminster, tallow chandler† to William Shepherd 9 Apr 1767
Monday Nicholas s Edward, Slimbridge, Gls, yeoman to Michael Haile 23 Nov 1634
Money Mark s Richard, Blewbury, Brk, farmer† to Thomas Sawtell 29 Oct 1766
Monk David s Jonathan, Great Bowden, Lei, husbandman to John Ham 9 Sep 1695
Monk Hatton s Hatton, Mitcham, Sry, gentleman† to Aurelius Hudson 6 May 1755
Monk James s Daniel, Westerham, Ken, yeoman to John Holmden 2 Oct 1727
Monk Thomas s Richard, Westminster, Mdx, brazier to Avery Vokins 6 Oct 1707
Monkhouse John s John, St Sepulchre, Lnd, joiner to Edward Williams 9 Mar 1767 <20 Dec 1769 turned over to Thomas Parsons, citizen and joiner>
Moody Christopher s William, Lnd, cordwainer to John Tisdale 28 Jan 1632/3
Moor Richard s Henry, Reading, Brk, cordwainer to Edward Smith 6 Sep 1725
Moore Ann d John, Shirley, Dby, yeoman to John Tewer 13 Jul 1661
Moore Edward s Nathaniel, Welford, Gls, farmer to John Tovey 2 Sep 1756
Moore George s Robert, Thorpe, Sry, gentleman to Magdalen widow of William Allett 17 Jun 1658
Moore Henry s Henry, Egham, Sry, yeoman to Samuel King 18 Nov 1664
Moore Henry s Henry, citizen and butcher to James Copeland 6 Oct 1736 <9 Apr 1742 turned over to William Wright, citizen and butcher>
Moore Hugh s Richard, 'Magnus Martin', Poulton, Lan, yeoman to Mathew Woodward 5 Jun 1721
Moore Joshua s James, St George Southwark, Sry, gentleman to Thomas Nash 13 Jan 1746/7
Moore Thomas s Stephen, Lewes, Ssx, cordwainer to John Meddowes 8 Aug 1655
Moore Thomas s Thomas, Ne...?, Sry, mariner† to Henry Miles 23 Sep 1670
Moore Thomas s George, Appleby, Lei† to Edward Leaver 27 Jul 1688
Moore Thomas s Thomas, Lambeth, Sry, tailor to William Stephens 1 Sep 1789
Moore Thomas Griffith s Thomas, Clerkenwell, Mdx, enameller† to Joseph Flight 2 Apr 1793 <6 Sep 1796 turned over to Joseph Flight, jnr.>
Moore William s William, citizen and carpenter† to John Archer 24 May 1638
More Henry s Thomas, Edmondthorpe, Lei, yeoman to Thomas Palmer 20 May 1647
More John s Henry, citizen and woodmonger to Thomas Pitman ? Apr 1666
More Luke s Richard, Streatham, Sry, yeoman to William Surman 5 Mar 1678/9
More Richard s Robert, Thorpe Green, Sry, gentleman to William Middlemore 26 Dec 1659
Moreland Joseph s Anthony, Ipsden, Oxf, farmer to Jonathan Leigh 3 Oct 1759 <16 Jun 1761 turned over to Anthony Morland, citizen and joiner>
Morgan Charles Savery s Edmund, Kempsford, Wil, yeoman† to William Cogan 21 Oct 1746
Morgan David s William, St James Westminster, tallow chandler to Henry Eastland 15 Aug 1747
Morgan James s Maurice, Whitechapel, Mdx, victualler† to Thomas Potter 5 Apr 1725
Morgan John s Robert, Bloomsbury, Mdx, smith to Richard Living 6 Nov 1792
Morgan Jonah s Morgan, Deptford, Ken, shipwright to Richard Walker 13 Apr 1713
Morgan Randolph s Thomas, Whitchurch, Sal, mercer to Daniel Scott 15 Feb 1695/6
Morgan William s William, St James Clerkenwell, Mdx, victualler† to Rebecca widow of Richard Barnard 6 Oct 1664
Moring William s Anthony, Andover, Ham, yeoman to Thomas Roberts 27 Apr 1654
Morley Edward s Edward, Colchester, Ess, corn merchant to Joseph Fisher 20 Apr 1757
Morley Henry s Henry, Ely, Cam, chirurgeon to Nathaniel Field 15 Aug 1713
Morley Richard s Francis, Winchester, Ham, esquire to Francis Molyneux 18 Feb 1685/6
Morley Thomas s William, 'Burrow', Wor, yeoman to Samuel Denney 3 Dec 1694
Morn James s Edward, Basingstoke, Ham, innholder to Richard Webster 1 Aug 1709
Morris Edward s Hugh, Porkington [Selattyn], Sal, gentleman to Thomas Dallock 13 Oct 1635
Morris John s Nicholas, 'Lidlington', Oxf, baker to Edward Hall 8 Oct 1705
Morris John s John, St Giles in the Fields, Mdx, tailor to Charles Crosier 6 May 1706
Morris Mathew s John, Bridgewater, Som, tailor† to Thomas Haies 21 Apr 1680
Morris Richard s Thomas, 'Castle Fryatt', Rad, husbandman to Silvester Carde 21 Jun 1638

Morris Richard to William Allam 1661/2
Morris Richard s Richard, citizen and grocer to William Meller 24 Mar 1686/7
Morris Richard s Richard, Oswestry, Sal, tailor† to Thomas March 21 Jan 1746/7
Morris Thomas s Henry, Pembroke, Pem, shoemaker† to Robert Hancock 4 Sep 1745
Morrisbee Thomas s Charles, Westminster, Mdx, cook† to Samuel Bedwell 28 Jul 1668
Mortimer Edward s George, Laycock, Wil, yeoman† to Robert Upington 30 Mar 1696
Mortimore Henry s William, Lnd, tailor to John Darcey 28 Jul 1690
Morton Peter s Edward, Moreton, Chs, doctor in divinity to John Jeffrey 2 Feb 1658/9
Morwent Thomas s Thomas, Eastington, Gls, gentleman† to Christopher Staniford 17 Jun 1672
Mose John s Henry, East Worldham, Ham, clerk to Richard Clements 31 May 1692
Mose Richard s John, Whitechapel, Mdx, cordwainer to Thomas Eve 3 Jun 1686
Moses Samuel s Michael, citizen and draper to Thomas Barksdale 7 Sep 1724 <4 Jun 1730 master† turned over by Sarah Barksdale, exec. to Thomas Merriman>
Moss John s Francis, Lambeth, Sry, yeoman to Walter Hunt 4 May 1676
Mosse Robert s John, Hannington, Nth, clerk to Robert Briscoe 28 Jul 1638
Moton Robert s Robert, Enfield, Mdx, husbandman to Nathaniel Billings 28 Apr 1653
Mott Henry s John, Edmonton, Mdx, clothier to Andrew Godwin 3 Apr 1684
Moulde William s Henry, Heydon, Ess, labourer† to Stephen Harris 4 Aug 1669
Mounger Thomas s Thomas, Reigate, Sry, yeoman to Richard Fullwood 6 Feb 1692/3
Mount Walter s William, Bolton, Lan, husbandman to Andrew Godwin 26 Jan 1691/2
Mountaine John s John, Chelsea, Mdx, carpenter to Thomas Seagood 7 Aug 1732
Mountfort John s John, Wroxton, Oxf, gentleman to Roger Toogood 28 Aug 1655
Mountmoungomery wm s John, Stepney, Mdx, weaver to William Langton 8 Dec 1712
Mousley Benjamin s John, St James Clerkenwell, tallow chandler to Thomas Sawtell 12 Feb 1744/5
Mowre James s Robert, citizen and grocer to Francis Tunsteed 12 Sep 1672
Much William s Thomas, St George Southwark, Sry, labourer to Robert Preist 21 Jun 1709
Muddin John s John, Wardington, Oxf, yeoman† to Robert Rayton 11 Jun 1703
Mulford William s John, Rotherhithe, Sry, sawyer to Thomas Searle 11 Jun 1754
Mullin Daniel s Tegg, 'Harby Maller', Cork, yeoman to Richard Ingram 24 Feb 1679/80
Munday George s Richard, Eastcheap, Lnd, butcher to Phineas Pateshall 2 Oct 1746
Munday John s John, St Giles, Mdx, cook† to Isaac Beatew 16 Dec 1763 <25 Feb 1765 as apprentice to Isaac Buttew turned over to John Christian, citizen and goldsmith>
Munden Robert s Robert, Chelsea, Mdx, bricklayer to Francis Vaughan 2 Jun 1675
Mundy Robert s Gilbert, Allestree, Dby, esquire to Benjamin Tomlinson 2 Dec 1691
Munn Benjamin s Ralph, Rothwell, Nth, yeoman to Mathew Barwell 29 Aug 1679
Munn Benjamin Skinner s Benjamin to his father 26 May 1756
Munsey Thomas s William, citizen and carpenter to Thomas Spencer 2 May 1662
Murden James s William, Richmond, Sry, ropemaker to John Pew 4 Dec 1699
Murden John s John, citizen and stationer to William Gurney 12 Aug 1687
Murden John s John, Welford, Nth, husbandman to Mary Flight 18 Nov 1687
Murden Thomas s Thomas, St Olave Southwark, Sry, yeoman to Henry Symonds 17 Feb 1652/3
Murdon Edward s Francis, Wapping, Mdx, carman to Sarah widow of James Downes 5 Aug 1788
Murfitt John s John, Wimbledon, Sry, victualler† to John Sibley 5 Apr 1753 <8 Nov 1753 turned over to Francis Philpott, citizen and butcher>
Murrey William s Saudri, Mortlake, Sry, husbandman to Thomas Collins 11 Jul 1667
Murton Benjamin s Benjamin, Church Lawford, War, clerk to Richard Makeham 11 Jul 1663
Myers Andrew s William, Lambeth, Sry, salesman to Thomas Searle 5 Apr 1764
Myers Edward s Robert, St James Westminster, Mdx, butcher to Richard Savage 27 Mar 1760
Mynott Joseph s Joseph, Cottenham, Cam, scrivener to James Church 23 May 1678
Myrry Gabriel s John, Heyford Warren, Oxf, yeoman to William Cranwell 17 Jan 1710/11 <24 Aug 1714 turned over to John Kerby; 12 Nov 1716 to Edward Bates, citizen and broderer>
Myson Thomas s Challoner, Plaistow, Ess, carpenter to John Cook 18 Oct 1784

Naish Francis s Thomas, Pershore, Wor, yeoman to John Woods 28 Sep 1650
Napper George s John, Cocking, Ssx, clerk to Henry Pauncefoote 18 Oct 1656
Napton William s Henry, citizen and pewterer to Simon Durrant 15 Dec 1686
Narbeth John s Maurice, ..., Pem, tailor to Mark Anthony Mister .. Apr 1639

Narbrow William s William, Norton Folgate, Mdx, butcher to William Kelly 6 Sep 1738
Nash George s Robert, Tonbridge Wells, Ken, gentleman† to Richard Tyler 1 Jan 1788
<1 May 1792 turned over to Richard Living>
Nash John s John, Hurst, Brk, wheelwright† to Robert French 8 Nov 1771
Nash Lancelot s Lancelot, Abridge, Ess, yeoman† to John Wyberd 3 Sep 1679
Nash Robert s John, Mile End Road, Mdx, tallow chandler to ... 6 Nov 1800
Nash Thomas s Nicholas Thomas Nash, Houndsditch, Lnd to his father 6 May 1783
Nash William s Nicholas, Holborn, Mdx, tallow chandler† to Thomas Nash 1 Feb 1731/2
<7 Jan 1733/4 and 27 Aug 1736 turned over to Avery Vokins>
Nashe Richard s Ralph, Windsor, Brk, miller to John Wilcox 6 Aug 1635
Neale Edmund s George, citizen and leatherseller to Edmund Carpenter 14 Feb 1703/4
Neale Edward s Edward, St Saviour Southwark, Sry, toyman to Samuel Griffiths 5 Aug 1740
Neale Isaac s Edward, Deptford, Ken, toyman to Edward Neale 16 Jan 1749/50
Neale James s John, Holborn, Mdx, laceman to Richard Wiggins 26 Apr 1770
Neale Nathaniel s John, Watford, Hrt, tallow chandler to William Hulls 5 Aug 1682
Neatby Anthony s Anthony, St Thomas Southwark, leatherdresser to Richard Pountney 13 Mar 1722/3
Neave Thomas s John, Ipswich, Sfk, clothier to William Webb 12 Feb 1656/7
Neave Thomas s David, Threadneedle Street, Lnd, victualler to James Soames 4 Dec 1800
Needham Francis s John, Monmouth, Mon, gentleman to William Lucas 2 Oct 1732
Needham James s Robert, Derby, Dby, butcher to John Higgs 20 Jan 1689/90
Needham John s John, 'Corand', Yks, gentleman† to William Webb 3 Mar 1662/3
Needham Thomas s William, St James Westminster, Mdx, victualler† to William Bly 2 Dec 1723
Neeler Edmund s Edmund, Fulham, Mdx, cordwainer to Robert Kirk 29 Jan 1704/5
Neeve Jeremiah s Edmund, Needham Market, Sfk, tanner to Francis Tegg 14 Dec 1663
Negus Thomas s Daniel, Stevington, Bdf, yeoman† to Thomas Bromsall 1 Feb 1713/4
Nelson John s Thomas, Wandsworth, Sry, butcher† to Thomas Banks 6 Nov 1738
Nelson Robert s James, Brick Lane, Mdx, weaver to Tabitha widow of John Mansell 3 Jun 1783
Nelson Thomas s George, citizen and draper to John Richbell 17 Jun 1663
Nettelton Thomas s Thomas to his father 13 Mar 1654/5
Nettlefold Samuel s Samuel, St Katherine by the Tower, Mdx† to John Wynn 7 Jan 1679/80
Nettlefold William s Edward, ?, Sry, yeoman to Humphrey King 27 Sep 1669
Neve John s Richard, Lnd, merchant† to Daniel Kirton 22 Jul 1684
New Thomas s Thomas, Bredon, Wor, yeoman to Robert New 11 Mar 1640/1
Newbold Peter s James, Redbourne, Hrt, yeoman to William Davis 19 Mar 1644/5
Newcombe Bartholomew s Bartholomew, Lnd† to William Goodman 15 Dec 1652
Newham William s Robert, Bermondsey, Sry, carpenter to Robert Dove 1 May 1787
Newhouse Abraham s Abraham, Spitalfields, Mdx, weaver† to Isaac Buttew 2 Mar 1718/9
Newington Henry s William, Beaconsfield, Bkm, innholder† to William Gurney 3 Jun 1674
Newington William s William, Beaconsfield, Bkm, merchant to William Alden 10 Jan 1671/2
Newins Robert s Robert, Aylesbury, Bkm, butcher† to William Daken 10 Jun 1664
Newins William s Robert, Aylesbury, Bkm, butcher to Henry Twyford 18 Mar 1646/7
Newlan James s John, Chipping Barnet, Hrt, victualler to John Lambert 4 Oct 1796
Newman Benjamin s William, Sundridge, Ken, gentleman† to William Newman 6 Mar 1692/3
Newman Henry s Daniel, Westminster, waterman to Martha widow of Robert Thompson 6 Jan 1728/9
Newman John s Thomas, citizen and haberdasher† to John Ewster 8 Jun 1661
Newman John s Thomas, citizen and haberdasher† to Henry Cox 1 Apr 1663
<served some time with John Ewster>
Newman John s Henry, Henley Green, Oxf, yeoman to John Halsey 4 Jul 1698
Newman Joseph s James, Ruislip, Mdx, labourer to Joseph Booth 23 Mar 1721/2
Newman Richard s Thomas, Paulerspury, Nth, butcher† to Joseph Lem 15 Jul 1692
Newman Thomas s Thomas, Clack [Lyneham], Wil, gentleman to Thomas Rosse 22 Nov 1649
Newman Thomas s Henry, Ewell, Sry, tallow chandler† to William Andrewes 8 Jul 1702
Newman William s William, Sundridge, Ken, gentleman to Christopher Sumner 28 Nov 1685
Newport Christopher s William, Grays Inn Lane, Mdx, farrier to John Stevens 6 Nov 1800
Newport John s Anthony, Limehouse, Mdx, mariner† to Thomas Hasteed 21 May 1663
Newton John s Miles, Loughborough, Lei, yeoman to John Hulcup 6 Dec 1708

Newton Thomas s John, Market Lavington, Wil, cutler to Thomas Jarvis 18 Dec 1690
Newton Thomas s Thomas, Whitechapel, Mdx, glass maker to Samuel Bury 3 Apr 1787
Niccoll Edward s Edward, Hendon, Mdx, yeoman to John Child, snr. 24 Apr 1702
Nicholas Richard s Richard, Stanford Bishop, Hef, gentleman to Charles Doyley 2 May 1638
Nicholl William s Richard, Hampstead, Mdx, tanner† to Michael Hayle 6 Oct 1656
Nicholls John s Charles, Chailey, Ssx, yeoman to George Carpenter 4 Feb 1762
Nicholls Richard s Richard, Cheltenham [? *in Ms* 'Chillingham'], Gls, yeoman to Robert Nicholls 4 May 1642
Nicholls Richard s Richard, St George Southwark, Sry, gentleman to Nathaniel Owen 7 Mar 1660/1
Nicholls William s John, 'Little Bramford', Bkm, yeoman to Thomas King 2 Aug 1641
Nicholls William s Robert, St Albans, Hrt, joiner to Thomas Hopkins, jnr. 7 Jan 1711/12
Nicholson Joseph s William, Maryland, merchant† to Joseph Woodward 8 May 1727
Nickolls Nathaniel s Richard, Watford, Hrt, yeoman to John Hooker 16 Feb 1636/7
Nicoll John s William, Cowley, Mdx, tanner to Simon Styles 24 Feb 1682/3
Nightingall John s Robert, St Olave Southwark, Sry, waterman to Henry Battin, jnr. 12 May 1699
Nightingall Robert s Robert, St Olave Southwark, Sry, waterman to Henry Battin 3 Jan 1697/8
Nipping John s William, Whitechapel, Mdx, glover to Robert Apsley 2 Apr 1647
Nix John s William, Covent Garden, Mdx, tailor to Thomas Chambers 25 Apr 1672
Nixon Francis s Francis, Wendover, Bkm, tallow chandler to Christopher Farmer 5 May 1701
Nixon John s Richard, Medbourne, Lei, mason to Jane widow of Robert More 9 Dec 1656
Nobes William s John, citizen and clothworker to John Wood 7 Apr 1674
Noble John s John, 'Chailey', Sts, gentleman to Edward Leman 4 Dec 1668
Noble Thomas s Martin, St Michael Coventry, War, butcher to Henry Miles 21 Oct 1668
Nolton James s John, Nettlebed, Oxf, poulterer† to Richard Thorneton 24 Nov 1687
Noone Arthur s William, St Bartholomew the Less, Lnd, cheesemonger† to James Jenner 7 Jan 1775
Norman Joseph s Robert, Lillingstone Dayrell, Bkm, grazier to Nathaniel Porter 7 Oct 1686
Norman Richard s John, Newton, Bkm, gentleman to John Hankinson 7 May 1684
Norman Samuel s Richard, Woodstock, Oxf, baker† to John Fist 7 May 1733
Norris Isaac s ... to John Scollough 25 Jun 1750
Norris Robert s Thomas, citizen and tinplateworker† to John Packman 11 Jun 1766
Norris Thomas s John, Lambeth, Sry, waterman to Thomas Searle 19 Dec 1755
North John s Walter, Wokingham, Brk, tanner† to William Clements 24 Aug 1680
North John s George, Christ Church, Lnd, yeoman to Philip Haydon 4 Jul 1739
Northover Francis s John, Haselbury Bryan, Dor, tallow chandler† to Thomas Northover 30 Sep 1689
Norton Gabriel s William, Sawley, Yks, esquire to Robert Lord 7 Jun 1704
Norton James s John, 'Rockway', Dor, labourer to Thomas Barwell 5 May 1712
Norton John s Henry, Tring, Hrt, yeoman to Richard Whitcher 8 Sep 1647
Norton William s Daniel, Cransley, Nth, yeoman to John Browne 13 Jun 1642
Norton William s John, Lnd, labourer to Mathew Woodward 18 Dec 1706
Norwood Francis s Francis, Beckenham, Ken, carpenter to George Carpenter 4 Mar 1739/40 <4 Nov 1740 turned over to Samuel Larkum, citizen and carpenter>
Norwood Richard s Edward, Stanmore, Mdx, gentleman to William Gibson 7 Feb 1660/1
Noss William s John, Alresford, Ham, cooper to Josiah Ragdale 19 May 1698
Nossiter Joseph s William, Chardstock, Dor, husbandman to William May 23 Sep 1689
Nowland James s Daniel, Tothill Street, Westminster, Mdx, stablekeeper to Henry Julius Anslow 2 Dec 1788 <7 Jun 1791 turned over to Samuel Barton>
Noyes George s George, Upper Clatford, Ham, yeoman to Robert Southwood 26 Jan 1673/4
Nuns Lawrence s Lawrence, Newbarns, Lan, yeoman to Thomas Roberts 24 Jan 1660/1
Nurse John s John, Clatford, Ham, fuller to Samuel Withers 4 Jun 1661
Nutt Edward s Thomas, Hollingbourne, Ken, miller to Henry Cox 18 Dec 1638
Nutting William s Robert, Impington, Cam, gentleman to Robert Fewtrell 29 Jul 1650

Oakely Ann d John, St Margaret Westminster, Mdx, gentleman† to John Tuer 26 Jun 1672
Oakely Henry s William, St Helen Worcester, Wor, ironmonger† to Thomas Hopkins 19 Jul 1687
Oakes Thomas s William?, Alpraham [Tilstone], Chs, yeoman to Samuel King 13 Oct 1674
Oateway Elisha s Elisha, Ottery St Mary, Dev, clothier to William Wright 30 Jun 1687
Oatridge Daniel s Daniel, Crudwell, Wil, yeoman† to Sarah widow of John Cleave 4 May 1713

Obourne William s Thomas, Salisbury, Wil, cutler† to Thomas Barber 24 Mar 1752
Ockley James s Robert, Reigate, Sry, butcher to James Jenner 6 May 1772
Ocklie Henry s John, Yarmouth, Nfk, yeoman to Christopher Leake 11 May 1655
Odell John s Samuel?, Hemel Hempstead, Hrt, ? to William Maycock 24 Mar 1668/9
Odell John s John, 'Stepbon', Bdf, yeoman† to James Tayler 7 Jul 1701
Offley Thomas s John, citizen and haberdasher to William Bowyer 21 Feb 1660/1
Okeley Rowland s Robert, Bishops Castle, Sal, gentleman to Henry Havell 5 Nov 1634
Oldham Thomas s Thomas, Twickenham, Mdx, gentleman† to Joseph Fisher 22 Oct 1730
Oldnall John s Edward, Leighton Buzzard, Bdf, grocer† to Simon Dauson 10 Jan 1648/9
Olive Edward s John, Buxted, Ssx, yeoman† to John Ewer 5 Feb 1712/3
Oliver John s Edward to his father 27 Sep 1738
Oliver Thomas s William, Islip, Nth, yeoman to Robert Rodway 13 Aug 1646
Oliver Thomas s Nicholas, Hoo, Ken, gentleman to John Godwin 3 Aug 1653
Oliver William s Francis, Wilburton, Cam, husbandman† to Thomas Nettleton, jnr. 13 Feb 1662/3
Onley Thomas s William, Enfield, Mdx, gentleman to William Goodman 12 May 1653
Onsley Richard s Richard, Courteenhall, Nth, esquire to Richard Miller 10 Nov 1640
Ordway John s James, citizen and joiner† to Jonathan Leigh 6 Dec 1743
Orme Elizabeth d Robert, citizen and pewterer to Job Wright 11 Apr 1678
Ormorud Richard s George, Whalley, Lan, yeoman to Thomas Hatton 31 Dec 1657
Orton Alexander Job s Job, St Gregory, Lnd to his father 22 Aug 1771
Orton Job s Job, Lnd, weaver to Joseph Blandford 8 Jan 1746/7
Orum William s James, Upavon, Wil, husbandman to John Harrison 4 Jan 1702/3 <4 Jan 1702/3 turned over to Charles Barker, citizen and stationer>
Orwell Edward s Benjamin, Great Chesterford, Ess, gentleman to George Orwell 27 Apr 1648
Orwell George s Benjamin, Great Chesterford, Ess, gentleman to Charles Doiley 25 Apr 1640
Osbaldeston Alexander s Alexander, Os...?, Lan, esquire to Thomas Burdett 19 Oct 1669
Osbaldiston Joseph s John, Lnd, milliner† to Benjamin Speering 1 Jul 1691
Osborn James s Jonas, Bocking, Ess, baker to John Prentice 7 Mar 1766 <27 Feb 1772 master† turned over with consent of Ralph Prentice, exec. to Joseph Overlove, citizen and grocer>
Osborn Samuel s Edward, citizen and tallow chandler† to Philadelphia widow of Edward Osborn 3 May 1714
Osborne Edward s Edward, citizen and leatherseller to Valentine Jacob 17 Jan 1672/3
Osborne Edward s Edward, citizen and tallow chandler† to Philadelphia widow of Edward Osborne 7 Nov 1709
Osborne George s George, Osborne, Ham, yeoman to William Spencer 13 May 1639
Osborne Henry s Thomas, Horley, Sry, yeoman to John Harris 13 Nov 1640
Osborne Richard s William, Camberwell, Sry, yeoman to William Chater 5 Dec 1709
Osborne Richard s Richard, Wapping, Mdx, mariner† to Herbert Edgerly 5 Mar 1710/11
Osborne Thomas (jnr.) s John, Walton on Thames, Sry, yeoman to William Knight 18 Oct 1652
Osborne William s Edward, Inner Temple, Lnd, esquire to Roger Price, jnr. 6 Mar 1633/4
Osburne Charles s John, Lechlade, Gls, yeoman to Benjamin Steevens 16 Feb 1681/2
Oseland John Lamkin s William, Lambeth, Sry, lighterman† to Edward Clarke 11 Jun 1766
Osey John s William, Fawley, Ham, yeoman to Anthony Moseley 25 Jan 1637/8
Osgood John s Richard, Newbury, Brk, feltmaker to John Furness 7 Nov 1692
Osgood Nathaniel s Nathaniel, citizen and tallow chandler† to John Litchfeild 7 Aug 1704
Osman John s John, Flamstead, Hrt, yeoman† to John Halsey 7 Jul 1704
Osmond Richard s John, Harrow, Mdx, yeoman to Nathaniel Sibley 8 Jan 1676/7
Osmor Adam s Chaney, St Botolph Aldgate, Lnd, brewer to Nicholas Watts 4 Aug 1642
Otley Timothy s Timothy, South Shoebury [? *in Ms* 'South Sugarly'], Ess, yeoman† to Roger Gale 6 Dec 1708
Outridge Samuel s Richard, Whitechapel, Mdx, carpenter to Richard Collier 18 May 1691
Overing John s Thomas, Lnd, haberdasher† to William Perry 1 Mar 1653/4
Overing Thomas s Thomas, Leicester, Lei, ironmonger to William Gaunt 2 Apr 1679
Overs Edward s Thomas, Cirencester, Gls, yeoman to Leonard Turner 11 May 1647
Owen Cornelius s Nathaniel, Reigate, Sry, gentleman to Jeremiah Owen 6 Oct 1718
Owen Humphrey s John, St Clement Danes, Mdx, tailor† to William Voss 9 Sep 1717
Owen Jeremiah s Nathaniel, Reigate, Sry, hop merchant to John Ayre 6 Aug 1711 <7 Dec 1713 master† turned over by Esther Ayre, widow and relict to William Hodgson>

Owen John s John, 'Salsowney', Cae, yeoman to John Prichard 22 Jun 1646
Owen John s Nathaniel, Holborn, Mdx, grocer† to Edward Leman 1 Mar 1672/3
Owen John s Nathaniel, Sevenoaks, Ken, mercer to John Turner 20 Jun 1689
Owen William s Owen Williams, St Lawrence, Cae, husbandman to Henry King 24 Jul 1679
Owen William s William, St James, Mdx, ivory turner† to Thomas Bennett 4 Dec 1704
Owen William s Jeremiah, Princes Risborough, Bkm, gentleman to William Hoare 9 Jul 1754
Ower Boyce s Daniel, Lnd, barber surgeon to James Woods 2 Nov 1697
Oxenbridge Joseph s Nicholas, Canterbury, Ken, tailor to Thomas Watts 13 May 1675
Oxenbridge Joseph s Nicholas, Canterbury, Ken, mercer to Thomas Willson 26 Jul 1675
Oxlard Robert s Robert, Great Marlow, Bkm, yeoman† to Thomas Rencher 13 Apr 1697
Oxley Edward s Elias, Barnsley, Yks, yeoman to Thomas Haits 21 Apr 1680
Oxley Richard s Francis, Hemel Hempstead, Hrt, innholder to William Hole 28 Jan 1663/4
Oxton Thomas s Thomas, Whetstone, Mdx, yeoman† to John Tipping 30 May 1671

Pace Samuel s John, Wood Street, Spitalfields, Mdx, shoemaker to William Littell 7 Aug 1765
Pack Thomas s William, citizen and woodmonger† to George Lewis 27 Nov 1658
Packer William s John, Northampton, Nth, ironmonger to Richard Yates 25 Mar 1691
Packett Jacob s Nathaniel to his father 7 Apr 1703
Packett Nathaniel s Francis to his father 12 May 1673
Packett Nathaniel s Nathaniel, citizen and tallow chandler to Jacob Packett 6 Sep 1697
Packett Richard s James, Lnd, yeoman to James Clark 7 Oct 1634
Packman John s Mathew, Bersted, Ken, farmer to Thomasine widow of John Williams 23 Jan 1749/50
Page Ezekiel s Francis, Henley, Oxf, maltster† to William Bateman 7 Apr 1651
Page Francis s William, Ashtead, Sry, yeoman to Richard Page 11 Jun 1650
Page George s Thomas, 'Abberton', Mdx, yeoman to Thomas Fish 7 Apr 1701
Page James s William, Lambeth, Sry, waterman to Thomas Searle 25 Sep 1766 <27 Sep 1768 turned over to Edward Clarke; 6 Jun 1771 to Thomas Searle>
Page James s William, *Chequers*, Tower Street, Lnd to James Page 3 Apr 1800
Page Jeremiah s Henry, T...?, Oxf, baker† to Valentine Jacob 25 May 1671
Page Jeremiah s Henry, Thame, Oxf, baker† to John Clarke 14 Sep 1674
Page John s Clement, Uxbridge, Mdx, tallow chandler† to John Cock 11 Feb 1673/4
Page John s Abraham, Folkingham, Lin, clerk† to Thomas Harris 1 Jun 1674
Page Ralph s Michael, Pinner, Mdx, gentleman to John Thomas 17 Jul 1638
Page Richard s Richard, Ashtead, Sry, yeoman to Samuel Wilkin 30 Sep 1642
Page Robert s Robert, Hackney, Mdx, gentleman† to John Hastings 6 May 1692
Page Robert s Charles, Northleach, Gls, clerk† to Joseph Phelps 1 Dec 1789 <7 Jul 1803 apprentice principally of Madeira at freedom>
Page Thomas s George, Chicheley, Bkm, clerk† to William Knight 3 Jan 1648/9
Page William s Richard, citizen and tallow chandler to Francis Drinkewater 28? May 1668
Page William s William, Tower Street, Lnd, yeoman to James Page 5 Oct 1790
Paine Ephraim s Ephraim, citizen and clothworker to William Clarke 14 Feb 1653/4
Paine John s John, Digswell, Hrt, weaver to Thomas Obbinson 6 Dec 1708
Paine Nathaniel s Nathaniel, Berkhamstead, Hrt, tallow chandler† to Mathew Walker 12 Feb 1671/2
Paine Samuel s Samuel, Grafton Regis, Nth, gentleman to Richard Jannaway 16 Oct 1682
Paine Thomas s Thomas, Hinckley, Lei, weaver to Henry Wine 22 Sep 1675
Paine Thomas s Thomas, Andover, Ham, mercer to Thomas Day 28 Jun 1677
Paine William s Nicholas, Bermondsey, Sry, tanner to John Hamond 13 Jun 1654
Painter John s John, Abbots Bromley, Sts, butcher† to Edward Mathewes 15 Aug 1660
Palmer Anthony s ...Alvingham, Lin, gentleman to ... Moseley 7 Nov 1644
Palmer Anthony s William, Leicester, Lei, gentleman† to Benjamin Solley 7 Aug 1667
Palmer Edward s James, Gosport, Ham, mariner to Walter Hunt 20 Feb 1674/5
Palmer Edward s Thomas, Melton Mowbray, Lei, shopkeeper† to John Jordaine 27 Sep 1754
Palmer John s George, Tallantire, Cul, yeoman to Thomas Peele 10 Feb 1640/1
Palmer John s John, Winthorpe, Lin, gentleman to Anthony Moseley 4 Dec 1646
Palmer John s William, Peatling Magna, Lei, yeoman to William Hulls 21 Mar 1689/90
Palmer John s John, Bath, Som, brewer to Robert Hancock 9 Sep 1757
Palmer Philip s Charles, Dorney, Bkm, esquire† to John Thompson 7 Dec 1725

Palmer Richard s Henry, Huish, Som, yeoman† to Nathaniel Payne 13 Nov 1695
Palmer Richard s William, Radway, War, yeoman† to William Plant 10 Jul 1707
Palmer Thomas s Anthony, Alvingham, Lin, gentleman to Simon White 12 Aug 1642
Palmer Walter s Thomas to his father 6 May 1662
Palmer William s Thomas, Exning, Sfk, yeoman† to Robert Walker 21 Jun 1677
Palmer William s William, Deptford, Ken, shipwright† to George Searle 22 Jun 1774
Palmer William s William, Leatherhead, Sry, cooper to Isaac Bignold 1 Sep 1795
Pancoast John s John, Whitechapel, Mdx, cordwainer to Richard Smith 10 Mar 1761
Pannett William s William, Hammersmith, Mdx, butcher to Richard Fulwood 2 Oct 1682
Pantall Thomas s William, Southwark, Sry, gentleman to William Bateman 22 Nov 1684
Pantrey William s William, Godmersham, Ken, innholder to Christopher Leake 26 Jun 1656
Parde Philip s Richard, Shoreditch, Mdx, felmonger to Nathan Hall 5 Feb 1732/3 <5 Mar 1732/3 turned over to Isaac Berryman, citizen and merchant tailor; 24 Nov 1737 to John Sibley>
Parish William s Robert, Savoy, Mdx, mathematical instrument maker to George Harlow 6 Aug 1766 <16 Jul 1770 turned over to Christopher Stedman, citizen and stationer>
Parke William s William, St George in the East, Mdx, gentleman† to James Pateshall 2 May 1775
Parker Jacob s Jacob, citizen and fishmonger to Benjamin Tomlinson 7 Mar 1708/9
Parker John s Daniel, Watford, Hrt, yeoman to James Miller 16 Nov 1670
Parker John s Richard, citizen and weaver to William Clarke 20 Oct 1681
Parker John s John, Chester, Chs, apothecary to Joseph Collier 7 Jun and 6 Sep 1725
Parker John s John, Peterborough, Nth, maltster† to William Alexander 6 Apr 1737 <1 Jun 1737 turned over to Robert Bringhurst, citizen and founder>
Parker John s Robert, citizen and weaver† to William Alexander 11 Apr 1751
Parker Ralph s Ralph, Maidenhead, Brk, victualler to Morgan Jones 6 Apr 1731 <5 Jul 1734 turned over to Humphrey Smith, citizen and wheelwright; 17 Apr 1735 to John Miles, citizen and wheelwright>
Parker Richard s John, Barton, Chs, gentleman to John Halsey 8 Aug 1706
Parker Richard s John, Brackley, Nth, yeoman to Mary Copeland 1 Nov 1743 <5 Sep 1746 turned over to William Elliott, citizen and butcher>
Parker Robert s John, Brentford, Mdx, mealman to William Parker 7 Jul 1653
Parker Thomas s Thomas, St John Westminster, Mdx, gentleman to John Davis 18 Nov 1766 <31 Oct 1772 turned over to John Flock Roberts>
Parkin William s Cuthbert, 'Watcoe', Dur, yeoman to John Cosins 23 Nov 1634
Parkins Daniel s William, Tingewick, Bkm, yeoman to Edward Garment 5 Sep 1698
Parkman Richard s Thomas, Crediton, Dev, tailor to Thomas Palmer 28 Sep 1658
Parnell Henry s Thomas, Chingford, Ess, husbandman to Richard Hodgkin 13 Aug 1684
Parnell Richard s Richard, Clatford, Ham, husbandman† to Simon Dawson 12 Oct 1650
Parratt Richard s Richard, Dunton, Bdf, yeoman to William Bowyer 18 Feb 1641/2
Parrey Edward s Edward, citizen and merchant tailor† to Thomas Gunstone 25 Jul 1663
Parrey William s Richard, citizen and weaver† to William Mickins 16 Feb 1644/5
Parrott Edward s Thomas, Shillington, Bdf, yeoman† to Joseph Huntman 15 Nov 1710
Parrott George s Thomas, Chellington, Bdf, gentleman to Richard Parrott 31 Mar 1656
Parrott John s Robert, Hanslope, Bkm, yeoman to Robert Parrott 9 Feb 1652/3
Parry John s Edward, Mimms, Mdx, innholder† to Thomas Woollhead 7 Nov 1698
Parry John s Isaac, Deptford, Ken, potter to Richard Savage 7 Oct 1754
Parry Robert s Nicholas, Oxford, Oxf, baker† to Silvester Cardy 15 Mar 1648/9
Parry Thomas s John, Nicholas Lane, Lnd, vintner† to William Hoare 2 Aug 1774
Parry William s Edward, St Margaret Westminster, Mdx, labourer to James Tetly 7 Sep 1710
Parslow Henry s Henry, citizen and upholder to Richard Weston 4 Oct 1725
Parsons Alan s Alan, Stamford Hill, Mdx, farmer† to Eliza widow of Robert Greswell 4 May 1730 <2 Mar 1736/7 turned over with consent of William Cogan, an exec. to Mary widow of Thomas Ansell>
Parsons Edward s Andrew, West Camel, Som, gentleman to William Finney 8 Jun 1669
Parsons Francis s Andrew, Camel, Som, yeoman to John Baugh 8 Oct 1675
Parsons Henry s Robert, Sampford Arundell, Som, clothier to Robert Flewellin 13 May 1664
Parsons John s Jacob, Guildford, Sry, draper to Abel Whiteing 6 Mar 1692/3
Parsons John s John, Holborn, Mdx, tallow chandler to Henry Soames 5 Dec 1775
Parsons William s William, Thame, Oxf, gentleman† to Thomas Farraine 7 Jun 1731

Parteridge John s Ezekiel, Stourbridge, Wor, tallow chandler to Josiah Ragdale 21 Oct 1668
Partridge Andrew s Andrew, citizen and tallow chandler† to Joan widow of Andrew Partridge 28 Aug 1671
Partridge Edward Lewis s Lawrence, Little Queen Street, St Giles, Mdx, oilman to Samuel Blower 6 Nov 1792
Partridge George s Richard, Dorstone, Hef, yeoman to Joseph Wedgbrough 4 Sep 1710
Partridge Humphrey s ..., ..., Lei, yeoman to James Wagener 9 Apr 1635
Pashley Andrew s Andrew, citizen and innholder to John Bryan 23 Jul 1663
Pate Daniel s Thomas, Willesden, Mdx, gentleman to Henry Twyford 14 Oct 1648
Pateshall Phineas s Joseph, Leominster, Hef, clothier to George Bellis 7 Dec 1730
Pateshall Phineas s Phineas, citizen and tallow chandler to James Pateshall 26 Nov 1767
Patey James s Thomas, Reading, Brk, maltster† to William Reynolds 13 Jan 1695/6
Patience Stephen s Rodgers, Bloomsbury, Mdx, tailor to Herbert Homan 10 Dec 1772 <8 Apr 1777 turned over to John Maynard Hanwell, citizen and draper>
Patshall Thomas s John, St Olave Southwark, Sry, leatherseller† to Ralph Peirson 27 Oct 1685
Pattinson John s Joseph, Castle Carrock, Cul, clerk† to John Fist 2 Apr 1745
Pattison John s Francis, Hampstead Norris, Brk, yeoman† to Henry Wyne 3 Jul 1672
Pattison Thomas s Rowland, Waltham Abbey, smith to Esther widow of William Paine 29 Apr 1635
Pattrick John s Robert, Witney, Oxf, yeoman to John Noble 4 Feb 1649/50
Paty Thomas s Thomas, Union Street, Old Artillery Ground, cotton merchant to his father 7 Oct 1788
Paul Robert s Samuel, Westminster, Mdx, brewer to John Bedwell 5 Jan 1701/2
Pavey Isaac s James, Epsom, Sry, shoemaker to Felix Richard 17 Mar 1757
Paxton John s William, Finmere, Oxf, yeoman to Richard Gates 6 Aug 1694
Payne James s Thomas, Blakesware [Ware], Hrt, farmer to Thomas Pickett 6 Mar 1726/7
Payne John s John, Weston on the Green, Oxf, blacksmith to Charles King 5 Jan 1736/7
Payne Robert Malthus s Malthus, Bloomsbury, Mdx, gentleman† to William Lucas 19 Feb 1756
Payne Thomas s Joseph, Binfield, Brk, tailor to Ferdinand Ladbrooke 28 Feb 1743/4
Paynter John s John, 'Stratton', Brk, yeoman to William Thredder 23 Oct 1676
Peabody John s William, Ashby Parva, Lei, yeoman to Richard Johnson 20 Nov 1634
Peace George s John, St Albans, Hrt, labourer to Thomas March 2 Oct 1738
Peace James s John, Lnd, labourer to George Kendall 1 Dec 1747 <25 Jun 1750 turned over to Jacob Gudgeon, citizen and weaver>
Peach Vincent s Thomas, Lnd, haberdasher† to William Kelly 1 Oct 1733
Peacock Edward s Abraham, Tring, Hrt, innholder to William Egerton 4 Dec 1701 <12 Jun 1706 turned over to Edward Bristur, citizen and ironmonger>
Peacock Francis s Charles, Brk, gentleman to Thomas Hawes 14 Jul 1691
Peacock Jonas s John, St Ives, Hun, clothier† to William Ingram 24 Sep 1680
Peake William s Edward, Ely, Cam, cordwainer to William Tucker 1 Oct 1667
Peal Sarah d Daniel, Hornchurch, Ess, clerk to Philip Haden 5 May 1741
Pearce Charles s John, St Giles in the Fields, Mdx, gentleman to William Gurney 7 Nov 1676
Pearce John s Robert, Spitalfields, Mdx, weaver† to Henry Stent 7 May 1776
Pearce Samuel s John, Turkdean, Gls, weaver to Thomas New 3 Feb 1652/3
Pearn William s William, citizen and joiner to Thomas Rawlinson 2 Oct 1721
Pearson Anthony s Ralph to his father 4 Jul 1698
Pearson John s John, Shelley, Ess, clerk to Joseph Booth 1 Sep 1701
Pearson Samuel s Silvester, Wolverhampton, Sts, yeoman to John Noble 5 Dec 1645
Peart Stephen s Stephen, Horsted Keynes, Ssx, clerk† to John Syms 26 Oct 1682
Pebworth Mathew s John, Witney, Oxf, fuller to William Squire 6 Oct 1712
Peck Jeremiah s Thomas, Greenwich, Ken, baker† to Robert Goddard 7 Oct 1788
Peck Robert s Robert, Hadley, Mdx, yeoman to John Yarling 3 Feb 1666/7
Pecore George s William, Deptford, Ken, shipwright to John Dickens 7 Apr 1756
Pedder John s William, Lnd, salter† to Robert Bly 8 Nov 1697 <22 May 1702 turned over to Richard Walker>
Peele Bartholomew s William, Albury, Hrt, yeoman to John Burgis 1 Jul 1646
Peele John s John, Kensington, Mdx, baker to Francis Barber 11 Nov 1769
Peell John s Francis, Albury, Hrt, weaver to Bartholomew Peell 30 Sep 1656
Peeres Francis s John, Sandhurst, Gls, yeoman to William Massey 30 Nov 1665

Pefer James s James, Poplar, Mdx, mariner to Jonas Watts 2 Feb 1735/6 <3 Feb 1741/2 master† turned over with consent of Abraham Lawrence, exec. to Jonas Lawrence>
Pegg John s Joseph, Orton, Lei, yeoman to Job Orton 11 Sep 1781
Pegler Thomas s John, Bledington, Gls, yeoman to William Gurney 8 Aug 1677
Pegler William s John, Bledington, Gls, yeoman to William Hulls 7 Mar 1707/8 <1 Nov 1708 turned over by Mary Hull, his exec. to John Close>
Peinker Thomas s Benjamin, Ilsley, Brk, weaver to John Sussex 4 May 1702
Peirce Mathew s Thomas, Hever, Ken, miller to Samuel Wilkin 9 Apr 1657
Peirson James s Robert, Kildale, Yks, yeoman to Thomas Shipton 4 Feb 1636/7
Peirson Thomas s Thomas, Hadley, Mdx, husbandman to Robert Apsley 8 Apr 1658
Peirson William s William, Ealing, Mdx, carpenter to Thomas Kender 5 Dec 1698
Pell William s Martin, Moulton, Nth, yeoman to Ralph Field 4 May 1692
Pemberton William s Samuel, Greenwich, Ken, gentleman to Henry Stent 1 Dec 1795
Pemerton William s Henry, Shrivenham, Brk, yeoman to William Grove 18 Nov 1675
Pendelebury Edward s ?, Morton, Ess, gentleman† to Joseph Sibley 6 Jul 1670
Pennant Edward s Peter, Halkin, Fln, gentleman to William Smith 21 Nov 1653
Pennant Richard s Edward, Drury Lane, Mdx, gentleman† to William Allett 20 Nov 1656
Pennell Robert s Nicholas, St Saviour Southwark, Sry, waterman to Richard Walker 18 Nov 1651
Penny John s John, St Clement Danes, Mdx, coal merchant to Richard Turner 6 Dec 1756
Penord Thomas s William, Hillingdon, Mdx, yeoman to Robert Maybanck 19 Nov 1641
Penrice William s William, Norton Canon, Hef, gentleman† to Elizabeth widow of Richard Wooding 23 Oct 1693
Pepys George s John to John Cheaney 22 May 1750
Percival Thomas s George, Little Salkeld, Cul, cordwainer to Ann widow of Isaac Phillips 2 Jul 1793
Perkins Edward s Moses, St Margaret Westminster, Mdx, gentleman to Philip Peirson 17 Apr 1667
Perkins George s John, Bethersden, Ken, husbandman to Thomas Stonestreete 3 Feb 1647/8
Perkins James s Thomas, 'Barbert', Oxf, butcher to Timothy Foster 7 Apr 1707
Perkins Richard s Richard, Burton, War, gentleman to Thomas Stone 9 Aug 1653
Perkins Thomas s Thomas, St Giles in the Fields, Mdx, victualler† to Vincent Walker 13 Jun 1715
Perkins William s ?, Edmonton, Mdx, smith to Thomas Dabber ? Feb 1662/3
Perkins William s William, citizen and tallow chandler to William Perkins 28 Feb 1673/4
Pernell Thomas s Robert, citizen and fishmonger to John Dawson 2 Nov 1719
Perrott Caleb s Robert, citizen and haberdasher to John Greening 20 Nov 1684
Perry Elias s John, Edvin Ralph, Hef, yeoman to Christopher Leake 1 Aug 1650
Perry John s Richard, Camberwell, Sry, farmer to Samuel Gerard 4 Oct 1731
Person Rudolph s Anthony?, St Botolph, Lnd, yeoman to John Bryan 11 Apr 1668
Pestell John s Thomas, Shillington, Bdf, yeoman to Robert Udall 31 Jul 1658
Pett John s John, Hertford, Hrt, tailor† to William Parker 4 Aug 1707
Petter John s Christopher, South Petherton, Som, yeoman to William Bavin 12 Jun 1648
Pettie John s Ulysses, Marlborough, Wil, scrivener to Thomas Lawrence 7 Nov 1637
Pettitt Jasper s Thomas, Ware, Hrt, yeoman to Joseph Callcott 8 Jan 1721/2 <4 Mar 1722/3 turned over to Elizabeth widow of Robert Grosswell>
Petts Joseph s Henry, 'Alholland', Hrt, yeoman to James Cutts 22 Apr 1656
Petty John s John, citizen and joiner to Nathan Hall 1 Apr 1695
Petty William s John, Gainsborough, Lin, gentleman† to John Ewer 24 Jun 1696
Pew John s Michael, Richmond, Sry, brewer to William Gurney 16 Oct 1683
Pew John s Michael, Richmond, Sry, carpenter to Thomas Gerrard 6 May 1707
Phelpe Thomas s Anthony to his father 20 Oct 1662
Phelps John s Joseph, Evesham, Wor, yeoman to William Knight 7 Oct 1635
Phelps Joseph s Joseph, Dursley, Gls, cooper to Thomas Merriman 3 Oct 1759
Philipps William s William, Lnd, gentleman to William King 10 Sep 1694
Philips John s Roger, Baschurch, Sal, yeoman to Samuel Osborne 15 Aug 1744
Phillipps John s Thomas, Hillingdon, Mdx, butcher† to William Pannett 4 May 1696
Phillipps Richard s Richard, Wanborough, Wil, draper to Richard Wilkinson 28 Nov 1655
Phillipps Richard s Robert, Ham, maltster to Anthony Moseley 17 Jun 1668
Phillips Evan s John, Rosemarket, Pem, clerk to Jonas Lawrence 30 Jul 1753
Phillips Isaac s John, St Botolph Aldgate, Lnd to his father 8 Oct 1770

Phillips Isaac s Isaac, Goodman Fields, Mdx, tallow chandler† to Ann Phillips 4 Oct 1796
Phillips James s Benjamin, Wandsworth, Sry, gardener to Thomas Cave 2 Feb 1763
Phillips John s Walter, Yateley, Ham, gentleman to Gilbert Brandon 24 Aug 1703
Phillips John s Robert, Edmonton, Mdx, baker to John Gilderson 6 Aug 1747
Phillips John s John, St Botolph Aldgate, Lnd to his father 12 Jan 1764
Phillips John s Jonathan, Westminster, Mdx, clerk† to Saunderson Turner Sturtevant 3 Sep 1793
Phillips Samuel s Barnaby, Ashton, Hef, gentleman to Richard Bach 15 Jan 1676/7
Phillips Samuel s Adrian, citizen and grocer† to Joseph Collier 4 Apr 1720
Phillips Thomas s Isaac, Whitefriars, Lnd, brewer to Nathaniel Winchester 19 Oct 1681
Phillips William s William, Kington, Hef, tailor to Francis Rakestraw 9 Nov 1703
Phillips William s Owen, Southwark, Sry, mariner to Edward Butcher 4 May 1746
Phillips William s Roger, Baschurch, Sal, farmer† to John Phillips 4 Jul 1759
Phillips William s William, Cloth Fair, Mdx to his father 7 Dec 1784
Philpot Roger s Roger, Margate, Ken, shoemaker to Joseph Carroll 16 Jan 1765 <7 Sep 1767 turned over to John Bowley, citizen and musician>
Pickering Edmund s Henry, Bermondsey, Sry, broker to William Russell 1 Sep 1747
Pickering Peter s John, Warford, Chs, gentleman to Richard Dunbabin 7 Jan 1639/40
Pickering Peter s Peter to his father 9 Mar 1671/2
Pickering Peter s Peter to his father 26 Aug 1696
Pickering Philip s John, Grays Inn, Mdx, esquire to George Shelly 23 Oct 1699
Pickering Richard s Richard, Bugbrooke, Nth, yeoman to Mathew Snablin 1 Aug 1692
Pickering William s Thomas, Church Honeybourne, Wor, clerk to Peter Leigh 29 Nov 1703
Pickett Thomas s Thomas, Stoke Newington, Mdx, yeoman† to William Mellor 4 Jan 1698/9
Pickett William s John, Edmonton, Mdx, husbandman to Thomas Pickett 6 May 1717
Pickring George s Nicholas, citizen and tinplateworker to John Cotes 3 Mar 1684/5
Pierce Joseph s Joseph, Rye, Ssx, ironmonger† to Samuel Savage 14 Jan 1752
Piers Isaac s Geoffrey, Sowe, War, yeoman to Gabriel Benion 6 Feb 1633/4
Piggott Richard s Nicholas, Chiddingstone, Ken, yeoman to Richard Fullwood 4 Nov 1695
Pike John s Michael, St Martin in the Fields, Mdx, chandler to Richard Parratt 30 Apr 1655
Pike John s Richard, citizen and poulterer to Francis Zouch 28 Oct 1669
Pilcorne Walter s Henry, Badgworth, Som, blacksmith to Noah Pilcorne 2 Feb 1633/4
Pilfold Henry s John, Warnham, Ssx, yeoman to Richard Bull 22 Dec 1645
Pilgrim Philip s Richard, St Olave Southwark, Sry, merchant† to Robert Roe 15 Sep 1669
Pilgrim Walker s Thomas, Putney, Sry, merchant† to William Hodgson 16 Mar 1720/1
Pilson Nathaniel s William, St Mary Magdalen Colchester, grocer to Robert Rowe 10 May 1665
Pincke Thomas s Thomas, St Olave Southwark, Sry, butcher† to Charles Godwinn 7 Sep 1697
Pinckney William s William, 'Nether Celton', Yks, gentleman to Thomas Oliver 11 Aug 1665
Pinder Peter s Henry, Ravenstonedale, Wes, yeoman to William Gurney 4 Mar 1674/5
Pinder Peter s John, Sheffield, Yks, gentleman to William Cogdell 29 May 1691
Pirie George s George, Fetter Lane, Lnd, baker to George Soames 4 Aug 1795
Pitchard Thomas s John, Greenwich, Ken, baker† to William Chater 4 Feb 1716/7 <7 Sep 1719 turned over to Samuel Jackson>
Pitman Avery d Richard, citizen and tallow chandler to Samuel Withers 11 May 1658
Pitman Francis s Thomas to his father 2 Jan 1650/1
Pitt William s William, St Martin in the Fields, Mdx, cook to John Freeman 6 Nov 1717 <7 May 1722 turned over to Thomas Haynes>
Pittman Thomas s Thomas, Barking, Ess, shopkeeper† to John Tovey 7 Jan 1745/6
Pitts Felix s Silas, Kentish Town, Mdx, yeoman to Thomas Pratt 15 Jul 1651
Pitts Joshua s ..., Southwark, Sry, weaver† to William Terrell 5 Jun 1717
Pittson William s George, Chertsey, Sry, yeoman to Josiah Ragdale 8 Jun 1691
Plant William s William, Great Bourton, Oxf, yeoman to Thomas Higgins 10 Aug 1699 <6 Aug 1705 turned over to Henry Davis, citizen and cutler>
Plat Thomas s Richard, Islington, Mdx, yeoman to Robert Udell 18 Jul 1643
Plomber James s Thomas, Alrewas, Sts to Edward Archer 7 Jul 1647
Plomer John s John, Stone, Bkm, gentleman to William Maine 28 Nov 1684
Plowman Henry s John, St Giles in the Fields, Mdx, coal seller to John Merydale 1 Sep 1693
Pluckington Richard s Richard, Hampton, Mdx, yeoman† to John Wood 1 Jun 1702
Pluckwell George s George, citizen and cordwainer to William Goodman 7 Mar 1649/50

Pluckwell John s John, Fulham, Mdx, cooper to George Pluckwell 3 Sep 1678

Plush William s George, Martock, Som, yeoman to Richard Fullwood 7 Apr 1701

Pocock John s John, Brenchley, Ken, clothier to Robert Davies 3 Nov 1654

Pocock John s John, Watlington, Oxf, labourer to Thomas Rolles 5 Jan 1729/30 <2 Jul 1734 master† turned over with consent of Christiana Rolles, widow and exec. to John Hoare>

Podger James s John, Bradninch, Dev, gentleman to Charles Dare 4 Mar 1788

Podger Thomas s James, Donyat, Som, potter to John Cowling 6 Aug 1761

Pollard James s Ralph, Thornborough, Bkm, yeoman to John Hastings 13 Aug 1696

Pollard Thomas s William, St Giles Cripplegate, Lnd, glover to William Gurney 25 Mar 1680

Polter William s Mathew, Reading, Brk, tanner† to Thomas Allen 8 Mar 1640/1

Pond Henry s Henry, citizen and cooper to Giles Harris 5 Aug 1717

Pond William s John, Purleigh, Ess, yeoman† to Nathaniel Billings 1 Jun 1647

Ponde Francis s ?, Harrow, Mdx, butcher† to Richard Cooper ? Mar 1663/4

Poole Miles s Thomas, Kingston, Sry, mercer to William Newman 4 Jul 1698

Poole Richard s James, Upavon, Wil, cordwainer to Edmund Hunt 27 Jun 1670

Poole Richard s Richard, 'Chayneast', Mer, esquire† to John Hopkins 23 Jan 1700/1

Poole William s Francis, Farndon, Ntt, gentleman† to Anthony Mosely 30 Oct 1663

Poolhampton Stephen s Stephen, St Katherine by the Tower, mariner† to John Dent 5 Mar 1683/4

Poore Thomas s ?, Goodworth Clatford, Ham, yeoman† to Robert Southwood 10 Nov 1668

Pope Samuel s Thomas, Braintree, Ess, clothier to Thomas Tew 4 Jan 1652/3

Pope Samuel s Henry, Rugby, War, innholder to Mathew Harris 15 Feb 1704/5 <4 Sep 1710 turned over by Thomas Burgis, citizen and cooper exec. of Elizabeth Harris, widow of Mathew to Edward Jeanes, citizen and bowyer>

Pope William s William, Weston, Som, yeoman to William Phesant 14 Apr 1642

Popular John s Samuel, St Saviour Southwark, Sry, yeoman to James Waggoner 24 Apr 1656

Porland Henry s Robert, Warham, Nfk, gentleman to Roger Price 16 Sep 1648

Porter James Edward s David, citizen and leatherseller to Henry Pullen 30 Sep 1751 <2 Dec 1756 master† turned over to Thomas Sudger, citizen and baker - struck through 'not done'>

Porter John s John, Holborn, Mdx, tailor† to Jegon Mandevill 10 Sep 1684

Porter John s William, Woodbridge, Sfk, shipwright† to Mary widow of Henry Lathwell 28 Jan 1685/6

Porter John s Thomas, St Saviour Southwark, Sry, gentleman to Mathew Snablin 8 Oct 1689

Porter John s John, Liberty of the Tower, Lnd, porter to Joseph Flight 26 Aug 1767

Porter Nathaniel s John, 'Milbert', Ham, gentleman† to Nicholas Beckett 8 Dec 1664

Porter Samuel s James, Liverpool, Lan, tailor to Thomas Cave 16 Apr 1762

Portresse John s John, citizen and leatherseller to John Shuter 3 Nov 1685

Pory Robert s Robert, doctor of theology to Joseph Sheldon, knight 7 Nov 1667

Poston John s Roger, Knightwick, Wor, yeoman to Robert Dickenson 18 Dec 1663 <turned over to John Burg>

Potengar James s Richard, Burghfield, Brk, gentleman† to Thomas Lawrence 17 Apr 1660 <bond from Mary Potengar and Richard Potengar, Burghfield, Brk>

Pott John s John, Blechingley, Sry, gentleman to William Parker 2 Jul 1716 <6 Feb 1720/1 turned over to Francis Robins>

Potter Thomas s George, Wapping, surgeon† to Elizabeth widow of Robert Gresswell 5 Mar 1715/6

Potts James s John, Blechingley, Sry, surgeon to Mary widow of Richard Webster 2 Jun 1735

Potts Samuel s Edward, St Margaret Westminster, Mdx to William Killingworth 6 Nov 1746

Poulden Robert s Robert, Whitechapel, Mdx, yeoman† to Nicholas Thomas Nash 2 Nov 1790

Poulter Gabriel s Gabriel, Covent Garden, Mdx, saddler† to Peter Rainser 6 Apr 1731

Poulter Robert s Jacob, St Giles, Mdx, cordwainer to Mary widow of Edward Steele 5 Jul 1687

Pountney Richard s John, 'Milleham', Wil, baker to Robert Lamb 7 Oct 1706

Pout William s Edward, White Horse Street, Ratcliffe, Mdx, coachmaster to John Humphery 3 Dec 1793 <2 May 1799 turned over to Mathew Peter Davies>

Powell Elizabeth d John, Dublin, Ire† to Edward Mathewes 13 Feb 1664/5

Powell Jeremiah s Henry, Clun, Sal, gentleman to Thomas Crowther 16 Sep 1664

Powell Richard s Richard, citizen and barber surgeon to John Banckworth 26 Oct 1635

Powell Richard s Joseph, Balsham, Cam, clerk to William Thatcher 4 Mar 1695/6

Powell Roger s Roger, Wrexham, Den, yeoman to Thomas Dubber 3 Jul 1655

Powell Thomas s Joseph, Rugeley, Sts, collarmaker to William Alexander 4 Sep 1740

Pratt Augustine s Augustine, Wilby, Nth, tailor to John Prick 6 Dec 1648
Pratt James s James, St Ann Blackfriars, Lnd, cooper to George Harlow 19 Dec 1769
Prentice John s Thomas, St Paul's Walden, Hrt, farmer to Thomas Prentice 1 Dec 1735
Prentice John s William, Tewin, Hrt, farmer to Thomas Prentice 27 Jan 1746/7
Prentice Thomas s Thomas, St Paul's Walden, Hrt, yeoman to Nathaniel Field 7 Aug 1721
Prentice William s Henry, Dunstable, Bdf, husbandman† to Richard Tayler 27 Nov 1640
Prentice William s William, Hovend, Paul's Walden, Hrt, farmer to Thomas Prentice 16 Nov 1758
Preston William s Richard, St Clement Danes, Mdx, tailor† to William May 6 Jun 1698
Pretty Richard s Richard, Lnd, gentleman to Richard Joyce 13 Feb 1665/6
Price Daniel s James, citizen and pinmaker to Jonathan Hicks 5 May 1712 <7 May 1716 turned over to John Warman>
Price Daniel s Nicholas, Beckford, Gls, yeoman† to Richard Trevell 31 May 1641
Price Isaac s John, Stepney, victualler to John Quatermayne 12 Sep 1711 <8 Dec 1712 master† by Thomas Quatermayne, adm. to Harward Wilton, cit. & bowyer; 4 Apr 1715 master† by Mary, relict & exec. to Elizabeth widow of Robert Gresswell; 7 Nov 1715 to William Squire>
Price James s Richard, Dublin, Ire, shoemaker to Henry Soames 20 Aug 1765
Price John s John, citizen and barber surgeon† to William Parker 6 Sep 1714
Price Richard s Richard, Great Burstead, Ess, yeoman to George Evans 13 Mar 1649/50 <bond from father and James Watts, Writtle, Ess, yeoman>
Price Roger s Roger, Westbury, Bkm, esquire to Joseph Shildon 6 Jun 1671
Price William s William, St Olave Southwark, Sry, feltmaker to Ann Adie 5 Oct 1646
Price William s Thomas, St Andrew Holborn, Lnd, cutler to Charles Breed 15 Sep 1762
Price William s James, Worcester, Wor, glover to William Walton 3 Jul 1800
Priest Robert s Robert, St George Southwark, Sry, butcher† to Charles Godwin 20 Nov 1688
Priest William s William, Ealing, Mdx, yeoman† to Joseph Rideout 18 Sep 1691
Priest William s Robert to his father 2 Mar 1718/9
Priestley John s John, Westminster, Mdx, gentleman† to Francis Billing 28 Apr 1665
Prince James s George, Basingstoke, Ham, ironmonger to Thomas Thatcher 19 Sep 1707
Prince John s Bartholomew, Dorchester, Oxf, yeoman to Richard Tailer 2 Feb 1634/5
Prince Peter s John, West Garforth, Yks, yeoman to William Spencer 27 Jan 1634/5
Prince Thomas s John, West Garforth, Yks, yeoman† to Peter Prince 19 Oct 1658
Prince William s William, Spitalfields, Mdx, throster† to Mathew Woodward 6 Sep 1743
Prior Thomas s Nicholas, St Saviour Southwark, Sry, butcher† to William Nelson 27 Apr 1669
Pritchard David s Richard, Ellesmere, Sal, felmonger to Joseph Huntman 26 Oct 1681
Pritchard Philip s David, Glascwm, Rad, yeoman to David Morris 2 Oct 1649
Pritchard Richard s John to his father 16 Feb 1640/1
Pritchard William s Richard Griffin, Boduan, Cae, husbandman to Thomas Parker 30 Dec 1658
Procter John s William, Claycoton, Nth, yeoman† to Thomas Kelke 2 Feb 1637/8
Proctor Bucknall s Stephen, Aldersgate Street, Lnd, mariner to David Prudom 6 Jan 1740/1 <24 Jan 1746/7 turned over to Thomas March>
Prosser Andrew s John, Axminster, Dev, shoemaker to Thomas Allen 20 Sep 1656
Prou John s John, citizen and clockmaker to John Johnson 5 Jun 1744
Proudelove Christopher s John, Knipton, Lei, yeoman to Thomas Butterfeild 19 Jun 1669
Proudman John s William, Appleby, Dby, yeoman to William Proudman 1 Aug 1689
Proudman William s William, Appleby, Dby, yeoman to Edward Steele 26 Jun 1682
Proudman William s John, Appleby, Dby, yeoman† to William Proudman 2 Jul 1716
Prowett William s Anthony, Lilbourne, Nth, grazier to William Mayne 7 Dec 1719
Prudom David s David, 'Burlington', Yks, merchant† to Nathaniel Feild 29 Aug 1731
Pryor Daniel s Daniel, Great Gaddesden, Hrt, tallow chandler† to John Turner 5 Jul 1689
Puckle John s Thomas, Lewes, Ssx, gentleman to Thomas Addison 10 Aug 1654
Puckle Thomas s Samuel, Norwich, Nfk, alderman to Francis Marshall 19 Sep 1655
Pulford William s Richard, 'Connington', Chs, yeoman to John Halsey 4 Jun 1689
Pull James s James, Dalton in Furness, Lan, husbandman to Gabriel Binion 1 Jul 1647
Pullen Christopher s Christopher, Devizes, Wil, cordwainer to Thomas Burton 8 Mar 1668/9
Pullen Henry s John, Croydon, Sry, maltster to Joseph Booth 26 Nov 1707
Pullin Robert s Robert, citizen and shipwright† to Thomas Rakestraw 30 Oct 1705
Punn Thomas s Thomas, Ridge, Hrt, husbandman to William Allen 5 May 1712
Purchase Andrew s Andrew, Dorchester, Dor, maltster to Humphrey King 27 May 1678

Purdue Richard s John, Winchester, Ham, ironmonger to Brian Ayliff 12 Aug 1686
Purkiss William s Francis, Old Bethlem Court, Mdx, yeoman to John Pitman 6 Jun 1797
Purser Thomas s William, Hidcote, Gls, husbandman to William Winney 21 May 1661
Putland John s John, Hurstmonceaux, Ssx, yeoman to John Tyson 10 Sep 1656
Putnam John s Gabriel, Edlesborough, Bkm, yeoman to Simon Greenhill 26 May 1653
Putt William s William, Savoy, Mdx, joiner to Edward Harris 6 May 1662
Puzey Robert s Joseph, Wantage, Brk, feltmaker† to Francis Robins 1 Jun 1724
Pyrke Samuel s Lazarus, Houndsditch, Lnd, pattenmaker to Henry Case 7 Oct 1788

Quarles Benjamin s John, Lnd, carpenter to Henry Knyveton 5 Feb 1721/2 <turned over to Michael Adams, citizen and skinner; 5 Oct 1724 to Roger Gale>
Quarles William s Charles, Wanstead, Ess, yeoman to Gilbert Cornelius 4 Feb 1649/50
Quarterman John s Francis, Henley, Oxf, maltster to Francis Rakestraw 15 Apr 1695
Quarterman John s Thomas, Cuddesdon [? *in Ms* 'Cursdon'], Oxf, yeoman to Thomas Watts 12 Apr 1703
Quarterman Robert s Robert, 'Chagrave' [? Chalgrove, Oxf], yeoman to Daniel Hurst 26 May 1680
Quelch Andrew s Henry, citizen and draper to John Church 11 Feb 1674/5
Quinsey Joseph s Robert, St George Southwark, Sry, broker to Joseph Barlow 5 Feb 1768
Quinton Nathaniel s Nathaniel, citizen and cutler to William Barrett 3 Nov 1741
Quyno Stephen s Stephen, St Martin in the Fields, Mdx, tailor to William Plomber 6 Feb 1677/8

Radburne John s John to his father 2 May 1698
Radcliffe Edward s Ralph, Walthamstow, Ess, gentleman to Thomas Smalridge 6 Nov 1649
Radford William s John, citizen and vintner to Jeremiah Ridge 13 Jan 1717/8
Radley John s ?, Lambeth, Sry, tallow chandler† to Simon Greenehill 27 Apr 1670
Radley Joseph s John to his father 3 Dec 1705
Radley Samuel s John to his father 3 May 1714
Radley Thomas s John to his father 5 Aug 1701
Radley Thomas s Thomas to his father 2 Feb 1729/30
Radly John s Weston, Hornchurch, Ess, yeoman to William Wiggins (Wickins) 28 Nov 1673
Rae William s William, Stratford, Ess, yeoman to William Littell 6 Jun 1786
Ragdale Josiah s Andrew, citizen and cutler to Josiah Ragdale 2 Dec 1700
Ragdall Joshua s Robert, Wilby, Nth, yeoman to John Prick 13 Nov 1651
Ragesdale William s William, East Bridgeford, Ntt, yeoman to Ann widow of John Richards 20 Aug 1634
Ragsdale Richard s William, citizen and tallow chandler† to William Tucker 2 May 1667
Rainborow Mytton s Edward, Cranford, Mdx, gentleman to Thomas Kendar 9 Jul 1679
Rainforth William s Sampson, St Clement Danes, tallow chandler to William Shepherd 30 Oct 1772
Rainsford Robert s Henry, Tewin, Hrt, clerk† to John Goode 22 Dec 1653
Rakestraw Francis s J?, Henley, Oxf, yeoman† to John Turner 25 Jun 1677
Rakestraw John s Francis to his father 7 Apr 1707
Rakestraw Joseph s Thomas to his father 5 Jan 1707/8
Rakestraw Thomas s William, Henley, Oxf, maltster to John Flight 6 Sep 1678
Rakins Thomas s Thomas, Mortlake, Sry, oarmaker† to Richard Sparrow 25 Jun 1662
Ramsay James s Alexander, East Smithfield, Mdx, gentleman to George Searle 19 Jul 1786
Ramser Peter s Thomas, Gresley, Dby, weaver† to William Proudman 7 May 1711
Rance Richard s Richard, Kingston, Sry, yeoman† to Thomas Smith 9 Nov 1667
Rand James s Thomas, 'Lillingstone Russell', Oxf, tallow chandler to John Burbrough 7 Jun 1719
Rand Thomas s Thomas, Silverstone, Nth, tallow chandler to Nathaniel West 4 May 1724
Randall John s Samuel, Radnage, Bkm, yeoman to Joseph Casbert 20 Jan 1675/6
Randall John s Edward, Hayes, Mdx, cordwainer to Thomas Randall 6 Nov 1676
Randall John s John, St John Horsleydown, Sry, carpenter† to Joseph Carroll 5 Mar 1767
Randall Robert s John, St John Horsleydown, Sry, carpenter† to Joseph Carroll 6 Jun 1775
Randall Thomas s Jonathan, St Botolph Bishopsgate, Lnd, mariner to Thomas Cutlet 6 Apr 1654
Randall Thomas s Edward, Marlborough, Wil, cordwainer to Gervase Beckett 29 Oct 1667
Randall William s Thomas, Witney, Oxf, clothworker† to Nicholas Kipping 19 Feb 1690/1
Randolph Samuel s William, 'Ashcott', Nth, yeoman to Joseph Coggs 27 Nov 1664
Randolph William s Samuel, citizen and tallow chandler to Joseph Woolhead 5 Mar 1704/5

Ranolds William s William, Bicton Township, Sal, yeoman to Richard Ingram 21 Aug 1686
Raper Humphrey s Lancelot, Bromfield, Cul, yeoman† to Humphrey King 26 Sep 1676
Rasberry Francis s Francis, Lambeth, Sry, waterman to William Hunt 14 Aug 1691
Rash John s Simon, citizen and dyer† to Robert Linnell 10 Jun 1691
Rasine George s George, Doncaster, Yks, apothecary† to Nathaniel Chandler 24 Dec 1689
Ratcliffe Peter s Ralph, Walthamstow, Ess, gentleman to Edward Ratcliffe 1 Apr 1658
Rathbone George s Martin, Farnborough, War, gentleman to Thomas Burdett 1 Sep 1675
Raven John s John, St Martin in the Fields, Mdx, labourer† to Edward Harris 13 Aug 1685
Raven Thomas s Thomas, St Sepulchre, Lnd, butcher† to Timothy Foster 12 Sep 1718
Rawbon Joseph s Joseph, citizen and leatherseller to William Ingram 27 Mar 1701
Rawley Edward s John, Winsham, Som, yeoman to Mathew Woodward 2 Mar 1684/5
Rawling John s Luke, Great Smeaton, Yks, yeoman to Samuel Fitch 3 May 1697
Rawling Ralph s Luke, Welbury, Yks, yeoman to Henry Burton 14 Mar 1693/4
Rawlings Michael s John, Lichfield, Sts, esquire† to Francis Molyneux 1 Jan 1700/1
Rawlins Daniel s John, Lichfield, Sts, gentleman† to Edward Parsons 18 Jul 1690
Rawlins Henry s Henry, Brooke, Rut, gentleman to Cornelius Woolley 17 Dec 1717
Rawlins John s Nicholas, Hanslope, Bkm, yeoman to William Davis 13 Dec 1648
Rawlins Joseph s William, All Hallows Barking, Lnd, victualler to Richard Parker 20 Nov 1766
Rawlins William s John, St Botolph Aldgate, Lnd, labourer to Gilbert Cornelius 21 Apr 1642
Rawlins William s Henry to his father 2 Dec 1751
Rawlinson John s William, Sheffield, Yks, instrument casemaker† to Benjamin Kendall 7 Sep 1702
Rawlinson Thomas s Richard, South Witham, Lin, gentleman† to Thomas Obbinson 29 Jun 1687
Rawson Samuel s Samuel, Lincoln, Lin, gentleman† to John Jefferies 9 Feb 1707/8 <5 May 1712 turned over to Richard Burgis, citizen and draper>
Ray Giles s Thomas, Henley, Oxf, maltster to William Gurney 21 Mar 1675/6
Ray John s John, Headington, Oxf, gentleman to John Mahew 7 Aug 1647
Raymond Robert s Charles, Spitalfields, Mdx, weaver to William Coles 3 Jan 1748/9
Rayne Joseph s Joseph, citizen and pewterer to Leonard Ansell 5 Feb 1710/11
Rayner Thomas s Godfrey, Barnet, Hrt, husbandman to Bernard Block 3 May 1650
Rayner William s Samuel, Hillingdon, Mdx, yeoman to Thomas Pratt 11 Mar 1640/1
Rayner William s John, Shoreditch, Mdx, weaver to George Searle 7 Apr 1789
Raynham John s John, Raydon, Sfk, yeoman† to Jeremiah Daniell 28 Apr 1680
Rayton Robert s John, citizen and plaisterer† to John Byrd 6 Apr 1696
Rea William s William, 'Laborton', Gls, yeoman to John Richbell 17 Dec 1639
Read Geoffrey s Thomas, Sutton Cheyney, Lei, yeoman to William Proudman 2 Dec 1701
Read John s John, citizen and plaisterer† to Thomas Higgins 4 May 1688
Read Richard s Richard, Woodstock, Oxf, butcher to John Mouncke 1 Jul 1635
Read Samuel s Francis, Lambeth, Sry, feltmaker† to Peter Greening 9 Oct 1725
Reade Edward s Edward, Stevington, Bdf, lacemaker to William Gurney 9 Nov 1685
Reade George s George, Faccombe, Ham, gentleman to Peter Pickering 21 Jun 1653
Reading Barnett s Barnett, St Giles in the Fields, Mdx, vintner† to George Shelley 2 Dec 1717
Reading William s John, Hardwick, Bkm, yeoman† to Nicholas Beckett 18 Apr 1650
Reading Zachariah s Edward, Watford, Hrt, mercer† to Nathaniel Payne 6 Dec 1708
Reames William s John, citizen and carpenter† to Henry Rutland 17 Nov 1669
Redding James s John, Ruislip, Mdx, yeoman to Richard Redding 18 Feb 1638/9
Redding John s John, Ruislip, Mdx, yeoman to Richard Redding 8 Mar 1636/7
Redding John s John, Sutton Coldfield, War, gentleman to John Hastings 13 Jul 1687
Redding William s William, citizen and leatherseller to Thomas Haines 12 Sep 1695
Redmire Samuel s John, Gulston Square, Whitechapel, staymaker and tailor to James Collier 6 Dec 1725
Reede William s John, Plymouth, Dev, gentleman† to William Perkins 29 Aug 1682
Reeve Anthony s Fowler, Eynsford, Ken, yeoman to William Trevill 1 Dec 1637
Reeve Thomas s William, Wimberry, Chs, gentleman† to John Ayliffe 18 Jul 1690
Reeves James s Jonathan, West Ham, Ess, clerk to John Gould 9 Apr 1782
Reeves William s William, Sherfield, Ham, blacksmith† to Robert Driver 9 Jun 1696
Reily Mathew s John, Rotherhithe, Sry, cheesemonger to Edward Clarke 17 May 1756
Rencher Thomas s Robert, Welford, Nth, labourer to William Gurney 8 Jan 1678/9
Renton Lancelot s John, Lnd, clerk† to Thomas Paine 10 Jan 1632/3

Resteau Elias s John, Soho, Mdx, linen draper to Thomas Burrow 15 Dec 1696
Revell George s John, Greenwich, Ken, innholder† to John Townsend 5 Dec 1763
Rewbeard Thomas s John, Ratcliffe, Mdx, mariner† to John Palmer 26 Feb 1656/7
Reyner Roger s Rowland, Hillingdon, Mdx, yeoman to Robert Maybanck 11 Mar 1640/1
Reynolds James Lott s James Edward, Tooley Street, Southwark, Sry, to Edward Knight 7 Dec 1790
Reynolds Richard s Thomas, Faringdon, Brk, yeoman to Richard Hill 12 May 1675
Reynolds Thomas s Richard, citizen and tallow chandler† to Priscilla widow of Richard Reynolds 6 Sep 1703
Rhodes Lawrence s Lawrence, St Mary Magdalen Southwark, feltmaker to Thomas Allen 5 Jul 1652
Rhodes William s William, citizen and butcher to James Bague 9 Feb 1718/9
Rich Richard s John, Southwark, Sry, gentleman† to Thomas Harris 10 Feb 1658/9
Rich William Barnaby s William Nathaniel, Christ Church Southwark, Sry, boat builder to William Nathaniel Rich 2 May 1797 <4 Apr 1799 turned over to George Martin, citizen and joiner>
Rich William Nathaniel s Henry, St John Horsleydown, sailmaker to Thomas Searle 17 Jun 1766
Richards Abraham s ?, St Albans, Hrt, gentleman to Thomas Obinson 10 Feb 1669/70
Richards George s John, 'Laydon', Ssx, yeoman† to William Nelson 18 Jan 1676/7
Richards Robert s Charles, St James Clerkenwell, Mdx, butcher to Charles Richards 7 Feb 1725/6
Richards Thomas s Thomas, Croft, Lei, yeoman† to Nathaniel Fidd 1 Aug 1720
Richardson Charles s Randall, Cork, Ire, haberdasher† to Peter Citty 21 Jul 1647
Richardson Edward s John, Southwark, Sry, labourer to Francis Norwood 7 Dec 1749
Richardson Edward s Edward, Fish Street Hill, Lnd, carpenter to his father 3 Apr 1787
Richardson James s Edward, Fish Street Hill, Lnd, carpenter to his father 2 Apr 1793
Richardson John s John, Colchester, Ess, linen draper† to Peter Chesshyre 19 Feb 1700/1
Richardson Richard s Richard, St Margaret Westminster, gardener to John Ayliffe 11 Apr 1691
Richardson Robert s Winstanley, Leadenhall Street, Lnd, optician to Robert Morrell 4 Oct 1791
Richardson William s John, citizen and dyer to Zachariah Dixon 4 Dec 1699
Richardson William to William Walton 5 Sep 1799
Riches Andrew s William, 'Eucheries', Ely, Cam, yeoman to Francis Pitman 15 Jun 1665
Richman Edward s John, Woodham Mortimer, Ess, yeoman to Thomas Pratt 13 Mar 1650/1
Richmond Oliffe s Henry, Christian Malford, Wil, gentleman to Arthur Trumplin 17 May 1649
Rickard Felix s Felix, Lnd, gentleman† to Thomas Rigby 1 Sep 1735
Rickard William s William, Westminster, Mdx, cook† to Henry Bullock 11 Dec 1652
Rickards Henry s Henry, 'Glasshouse', Hef, yeoman to George Partridge 6 Dec 1736 <9 Sep 1740 turned over to John Cooke, citizen and carpenter>
Rickets Stephen s Richard, Broadway, Wor, labourer to John Beyzand 9 Apr 1761
Ricketts John s Edward, St Saviour Southwark, Sry, wine porter to Richard Elliott 8 Dec 1712
Ricketts Robert s Richard, Broadway, Wor, farmer to John Bayzand 1 Dec 1755
Ricketts William s Nicholas, 'Sedburdfaris', Oxf, husbandman to George Kitchinman 30 Apr 1655
Rickson John s John, Nettleden, Bkm, carpenter to Francis Pittman 28 Feb 1653/4
Rideout James s George, Shadwell, Mdx, barber chirurgeon† to Joseph Rideout 17 Sep 1691
Rideout John s John, St James Clerkenwell, Mdx to James West 2 Nov 1666
Rideout Joseph s Thomas, Stalbridge, Dor, yeoman† to Richard Thornton 1 Oct 1669
Rider John s John, citizen and joiner† to John Parker 8 Aug 1690
Ridge Jeremiah s Thomas, Chertsey, Sry, grocer to Brian Ayliffe 7 Mar 1675/6 <bond from Jeremiah Ridge>
Rigbey Richard s Thomas, 'Rennell', Lan, husbandman to Nathaniel Billing 5 Aug 1664
Rigby Thomas s William, Holland, Lan, yeoman† to Lawrence Carter 22 Sep 1685
Rimington William s William, Watford, Hrt, weaver to James Shepard 4 Sep 1678
Ring James s Matthias, Barnet, Hrt, innholder† to Samuel Jackson 16 Jul 1714 <16 Dec 1718 turned over to Richard Darker>
Ringwood George s Humphrey, Fownhope, Hef, innkeeper to Thomas Hatton 7 Feb 1648/9
Ripley Samuel s James, citizen and turner† to Mary widow of Thomas Bennett 6 Jul 1719 <3 Feb 1723/4 turned over to Richard Collett, citizen and painter stainer>
Rippen Lawrence s Thomas, Hampstead, Mdx, yeoman to Thomas Rippen 20 Nov 1656
Rippin Thomas s Thomas, Hampstead, Mdx, husbandman to Thomas Carr 22 Jul 1646
Rivers Richard s Richard, St James Westminster, Mdx, yeoman† to John Johnson 7 Mar 1738/9

Rivett John s John, citizen and cooper to Robert Dove 1 Jul 1723 <3 May 1725 turned over to Samuel Mackerness>
Roane Ornys s Anthony, Newent, Gls, gentleman to Robert Marchant 26 May 1652
Roberts Adrian s Thomas, Chesterton, Oxf, yeoman to Jonathan Hicks 5 Jul 1697
Roberts Charles to George Martin Bird 6 Nov 1798
Roberts Francis s Philip, Wapping, Mdx, goldsmith† to Jonas Lawrence 14 Sep 1758
Roberts James s Edward, citizen and haberdasher to William Gurney 31 Jul 1684
Roberts John Flock s Flock, Lye, Gls, farmer to John Davis 18 Aug 1762
Roberts Robert s Robert Ellis, Criccieth, Cae, gentleman to William Owen 3 Nov 1691
Roberts Thomas s William, Edgware Road, Mdx, cowkeeper to Nathaniel Mathews 2 Oct 1787
Roberts William s William, Great Warley, Ess, yeoman to John Sole 4 Nov 1647
Roberts William s John, South Mimms, Mdx [? *in Ms* 'Hrt'], yeoman† to Mathew Woodward 1 Aug 1709
Roberts William s John, citizen and joiner to William Allexander 10 Jun 1723
Robins Edmund s Edmund, Clerkenwell, Mdx, butcher† to Christopher James 23 Oct 1678
Robins Francis s Francis to his father 6 Oct 1736
Robins Henry s Henry, Ruislip, Mdx, yeoman to Joseph Coggs 24 Oct 1651
Robins James s James, Ruislip, Mdx, yeoman to William Watridge 4 Dec 1710
Robins Snow s Richard, Strand, Mdx, buttonseller† to Edward Holsey 7 Mar 1725/6
Robins William s William, East Hanney, Brk, yeoman to Francis Robins 7 May 1722
Robinson Charles s Charles, Bermondsey, Sry, musician to Joseph Carroll 19 Nov 1767 <23 Dec 1767 turned over to Starling Goodwin, citizen and musician>
Robinson Henry s Thomas, Feckenham, Wor, yeoman to William Simons 7 Oct 1635
Robinson Henry s John, Thornton, Yks, yeoman to William Gurney 1 Aug 1677
Robinson John s John, Petworth, Ssx, yeoman to Henry Arris 30 Nov 1635
Robinson John s Thomas, Shoreditch, Mdx, brickmaker to Robert Apsley 1 Apr 1647
Robinson John s John, Leighton Buzzard, Bdf, joiner to John Robinson 28 Jan 1656/7
Robinson Joseph s Joseph, Heyford, Nth, farrier to Mary Copeland, sp. 10 Oct 1744
Robinson Richard s Jacob, Tideswell, Dby, yeoman to John Richbell 31 Mar 1634
Robinson Samuel s John, Lnd, warehousekeeper to Philadelphia widow of John Blackbourne 1 Apr 1740
Robinson Thomas s William, St Botolph Bishopsgate, yeoman to Egerton Henshaw 23 Nov 1728
Robinson William s William, Car Colston, Ntt, yeoman to John Slater 10 Jun 1634
Robinson William s Thomas, Stony Stratford, Bkm, gentleman† to Thomas Bennett 3 Apr 1704 <turned over to Thomas Woolhead>
Robinson William s James, St Clement Danes, Mdx, farrier† to Henry Pullen 7 Jan 1745/6 <5 Jul 1747 turned over to Arthur Vincent, citizen and baker>
Robrough Nathaniel s Henry, St Leonard Eastcheap, Lnd, clerk to Giles Rodway 11 Feb 1648/9
Roch Robert s Peter, Southwark, Sry, feltmaker† to Richard Whitcher 18 Sep 1649
Rocke John s Richard, citizen and merchant tailor† to John Blizard 25 May 1688
Rodes Henry s Henry, citizen and cordwainer to Joseph Hurlock 15 Jan 1671/2
Rodes John s George, citizen and barber surgeon to John Richbell 28 Jul 1635
Rodway George? s William, Cherington, Gls, yeoman to Robert Reding 31 Jul 1640
Rodway William s George, Witcome, Badgeworth, Gls, yeoman to Robert Rodway 30 Aug 1658
Roe John s John, St Margaret Westminster, Mdx, farrier† to Francis Buggy 14 Aug 1673
Roe John s Thomas, St Saviour Southwark, Sry, undertaker to Francis Barrell Searle 27 Nov 1767
Roe Robert s John, Kingston, Sry, yeoman to John Davis 14 Feb 1642/3
Roe William s Thomas, St Saviour Southwark, Sry, undertaker to Aurelius Hodson 12 Jul 1771
Roe William s Thomas, St Saviour Southwark, Sry, undertaker† to Francis Barrell Searle 9 Jan 1773
Roffey ... s Christopher, Horley, Sry, gentleman to Richard Bull 24 Mar 1637/8
Roffey Anthony s Christopher, Horley, Sry, gentleman to Richard Bull 21 Dec 1638
Roffey Edmund s Christopher, Horley, Sry, gentleman to Anthony Roffey 7 Feb 1647/8
Roffey James s Christopher, Horley, Sry, gentleman† to Anthony Roffey 26 Aug 1647
Roffey Robert s Robert, Banstead, Sry, yeoman to Andrew Kipping 13 Jul 1687
Rogers Francis s John, Christ Church Southwark, Sry, waterman to Richard Cooke 1 Aug 1692
Rogers Francis s Humphrey to his father 25 Nov 1695
Rogers George s Robert, Malden, Sry, carpenter to Edmund Hunt 15 Nov 1678
Rogers Humphrey s John, Erdington, War, yeoman to Richard Whight 20 Nov 1660

Rogers James s Morgan, Llanwenarth, Mon, husbandman to David Morris 22 Oct 1640
Rogers John s Henry, Walworth [Newington], Sry, shopkeeper to Joseph Barlow 5 Jul 1791
Rogers Moses s Moses, Soho, Mdx, butcher to John Ayliffe 6 Jul 1713
Rogers Richard s Richard, Dunstable, Bdf, barber chirurgeon to John Osgood 4 Aug 1707
Rogers Rowland s Robert, St Benet Fink, Lnd, scrivener to Nathaniel Ragdale 7 Apr 1701
Rogers Samuel s William, St Clement Danes, Mdx, tailor† to George Johnson 6 May 1728
Rogers Samuel s John, Tillington [Burghill], Hef, sawyer to Thomas Hill 7 Jul 1795
Rogers Thomas s David, Oswestry, Sal, husbandman† to William Bromwich 6 Oct 1712
Rogers Thomas s William, Lampeter, Cgn, farmer† to Thomas Bord 2 Jun 1778
Rogers William s Morgan, Abergavenny, Mon, yeoman to David Morris 28 Mar 1638
Rogers William s Thomas, Coventry, War, threadmaker to William Gurney 30 Nov 1675
Rogers William s William, citizen and leatherseller to Humphrey Johnson 7 Oct 1728
Rogers William s Henry, Walworth [Newington], Sry, cheesemonger to Joseph Barlow 2 Feb 1796
Role William s William, Yetminster, Dor, maltster to Philip Peirson 26 Aug 1659
Rolfa John s Guy, Alton, Ham, victualler to John Hain 12 Nov 1705
Rolls Daniel s Samuel, Lnd, doctor of medicine to John Hill 25 Nov 1678
Rolls Peter s William, Lewknor, Oxf, yeoman to William Andrews 2 May 1709
Rondeau James s James, Rochester, Ken, gentleman to William Havens 6 Mar 1726/7
Rood John s Robert, Portsmouth, Ham, wine merchant to John Gould 6 Nov 1787
Rooke John s John, St Olave Southwark, Sry, feltmaker† to Edward Steele 26 Jun 1682
Roome Samuel s Samuel, St James Westminster, Mdx, corn chandler to Jeremiah Ridge 8 Jun 1743
Roper Richard s William, Evesham, Wor, felmonger to Edward Tomlins 8 Aug 1692
Rose James s William, Lambeth, Sry, gardener† to Thomas Searl 1 Apr 1723
Rose John s Richard, St Clement Danes, Mdx, carpenter to Samuel Smith 6 Jun 1709
Rose Richard s Richard, Warrington, Lan, yeoman to Thomas Bedell 5 Feb 1635/6
Rose Robert s James, Kensington, Mdx, carpenter to Richard Calloway 2 Dec 1746
Rose Thomas s John, citizen and vintner† to John Coates 3 Sep 1689
Ross Thomas s Thomas, Haddenham, Bkm, yeoman to William Luffe 7 May 1705
Rosse John s Richard, St Giles Cripplegate, Mdx, baker to Philadelphia widow of Edward Osborne 7 Mar 1725/6
Rosse Joseph s John, Osgathorpe, Lei, clerk to Thomas Rosse 30 Nov 1670
Roswell John s John, St Margaret Westminster, Mdx, lorimer† to John Hastings 2 Mar 1690/1
Rotheram Edmund s Edmund, Caddington, Hrt, gentleman† to Richard Rotheram 18 Dec 1646
Rotheram Ralph s Ralph, Sundon, Bdf, gentleman to Richard Rotheram 30 Jul 1646
Rotheram Richard s Ralph, Toddington, Bdf, gentleman to Robert Bradley 26 Feb 1637/8
Rothwell William s Nicholas, Warwick, War, yeoman to Henry Woolhead 3 Jan 1703/4
Roundell Ralph s Marmaduke, Westminster, Mdx, chandler† to Thomas Tapp 5 Jul 1650
Rouse Thomas s Robert, Brentwood, Ess, husbandman to Thomas Haines 1 Sep 1736 <3 Feb 1740/1 turned over with consent of his widow Elizabeth Haines to Edmund Popplewell, citizen and haberdasher>
Roward William s Henry, Croydon, Sry, baker to Samuel Reeves 14 Jul 1766
Rowe Thomas s William, Norton, Nth, labourer to John Williams 12 Feb 1637/8
Rowland John s Thomas, Hathersage, Dby, gentleman to Samuel Shakemaple 17 Jun 1658
Rowland Peter s ?, Hagley, Wor?, husbandman to Robert Jackson 3 Jun 1672
Rowland Thomas s Thomas, Haughley, Sfk, yeoman to Robert Jackson 27 Feb 1667/8
Rowles Thomas s Henry, Turville Heath, Bkm, husbandman to Nathaniel Chandler 8 Jan 1704/5
Rowley William s George, Norton, Sts, yeoman to Francis Marshall 23 Apr 1650
Rowley William s William, citizen and tallow chandler to Elizabeth widow of James Byard 7 Aug 1678
Rowse Thomas s William, Newington Green, Mdx to Thomas Hatton 12 Apr 1651
Royle John s Charles, Bond Street, Mdx, upholsterer to George Goodwin 5 Mar 1793
Rudd Henry s Thomas, Pedwardine [? *in Ms* 'Petherton'], Hef, yeoman† to John Hunt 11 Dec 1704
Rudd John s Daniel, Kings Walden, Hrt, farmer to Nathaniel Field 11 Dec 1740
Rudge Francis s Michael, Shere, Sry, gentleman to John Burgis 12 Dec 1654
Rudler Henry s George, Battersea, Sry, gardener to John Johnson 16 Dec 1746
Rule Thomas s Robert, Colchester, Ess, shoemaker to Robert Bristoe 28 Apr 1653
Rumball Daniel s Mathew, Wootton, Bdf, yeoman to William Alden 6 Dec 1666
Rumball John s John to his father 1 Dec 1656

Rumbold William s Richard, Rye, Hrt† to Daniel Scott 23 Feb 1685/6
Rundall Robert s Robert, Battersea, Sry, husbandman to Robert More 15 Sep 1647
Rushworth Cornelius s John, Wroot, Lin, yeoman† to William Buckler 31 Dec 1674
Ruspy Thomas s Thomas, Leather Lane, Mdx, corn chandler to Thomas Jarvis 11 Jul 1780
Russ George s William, St Clement Danes, Mdx, tallow chandler to Henry Bernard 11 Jul 1682
Russell Benjamin s William, Broadway, Wor, yeoman to Robert Matthewes 3 Apr 1683
Russell Edward s Joseph, Hounslow, Mdx, innholder† to Thomas Dowdswell 7 Aug 1685
Russell John s George, Aston Abbots, Bkm, esquire† to Edward Hitchcock 26 Nov 1686
Russell John s John, Tottenham, Mdx, butcher† to Daniel Kirton 22 Dec 1702
Russell John s Michael, Dover, Ken, esquire to Thomas Shrimpton 7 Feb 1770
Russell John s Joseph, Little Britain, Lnd, butcher to William Marsh 4 Aug 1795 <1 Dec 1795 turned over to Margaret widow of John Deacon, citizen and baker>
Russell Robert s William, Brilley, Hef, gentleman to Edward Walker 1 Feb 1702/3
Russell Thomas s Mathew, Hayes, Mdx, yeoman† to Joseph Archer 14 Apr 1703
Russell William s Stephen, Wooburn, Bkm, butcher to Edward Mortimer 9 Oct 1705
Russell William s Benjamin to his father 5 Mar 1710/11
Russhen John s John, citizen and dyer to William Watridge 31 Dec 1706 <4 Oct 1708 turned over to Benjamin Russell>
Rust Thomas s Edward, East Ham, Ess, clerk to Richard Thorneton 13 May 1672
Rusted Robert s Robert, Barley, Hrt, yeoman† to John Jemmett 4 Mar 1722/3
Rutland Henry s Peter, Quainton, Bkm, husbandman to John Hooker 6 Nov 1657
Rutland William s John, Ripley, Sry, yeoman† to Francis Zouch 16 Sep 1685
Rutt John s Richard, St Giles in the Fields, Mdx, chandler to John Ayscough 3 Jun 1686
Rutterford William s William, Shadwell, Mdx, mariner† to John Newman 4 Jun 1680
Rycroft Gerard s William, Dukes Place, Lnd, gentleman to William Townsend 23 Mar 1684/5
Ryme Peter s Peter, citizen and merchant tailor to Nicholas Howett 13 Nov 1665

Sabin Joseph s Nathaniel, Buntingford, Hrt, yeoman to Mathew Woodward 27 Jan 1676/7
Sabisford John s Thomas, Watford, Hrt, yeoman to John Turner 15 Jun 1687
Sadler John s John, Thoralby, Yks, yeoman to Edward Guy 6 Dec 1677
Sadler John s Orgar, Graveley, Hrt, labourer† to Evan Phillips 9 Dec 1765
Saffell Abraham s Jacob, Barking, Ess, weaver to Margaret widow of Isaac Saffell 2 Oct 1675
Saffell Isaac s Thomas, Barking, Ess, brewer to Samuel Bedwell 30 Jun 1654
Safford Thomas s Edmund, Hoxton, Mdx, yeoman to William Jordan 30 Aug 1681
Sale Richard s John, Arborfield, Brk, gentleman to Henry Clarke 28 Nov 1719
Sale Robert s Geoffrey, Woodbridge Hasketon, Sfk, yeoman to Peter Prince 27 Feb 1653/4
Sale William s William, St Botolph Bishopsgate, Lnd, miller to John Radburne, jnr. 7 May 1716 <3 Apr 1721 turned over to Richard Eborall>
Salisbury Charles s ?, Lnd, gentleman to William Perkins 28 Sep 1680
Salisbury Hugh s Piers, Ruthin, Den, gentleman to Stephen Kersinhall 24 Apr 1634
Sallaway Richard s Richard, Stepney, Mdx, labourer to Richard Morris 7 Feb 1708/9
Sallock William s ?, Whitechapel, Mdx, carpenter to Isaac Saffell 12 Sep 1672
Salmon John s John, St Olave Southwark, Sry, cheesemonger to Elizabeth widow of Benjamin Free 6 Jan 1734/5 <22 Jan 1735/6 turned over to John Pantree; 1 Dec 1736 to Thomas Catterns, citizen and saddler>
Salmon John s John, St Andrew Holborn, Lnd, gentleman to Robert Collins 6 Nov 1745
Salmon John s Daniel, Coggeshall, Ess, bay fuller to Thomas Nash 2 May 1797
Salt Thomas s Thomas, St Sepulchre, Mdx, watchmaker to Edward Palmer 15 Nov 1770
Salte John s William, Butterton, Sts, yeoman to Thomas Smalridge 12 Oct 1669
Sam John s John?, Newport Pagnell, Bkm, innholder† to Isaac Jackson 10 Jul 1674
Sampson Isaac s Thomas, citizen and upholder to John Sampson 1 Sep 1684
Sampson James s John to his father 1 Sep 1684
Sampson John s John, Butterleigh, Dev, clerk to Thomas Kelke 31 May 1655 <bond from John Uppington, Butterleigh, Dev, yeoman>
Samuel Richard to Thomas Paty 6 Jun 1799
Sanders Brian s Brian, Stepney, Mdx, joiner to Herbert Edgerly 7 Mar 1708/9
Sanders John s John, Kidlington, Oxf, yeoman to Valentine Warner 18 Dec 1706
Sanders John s Robert, Loughton, Bkm, innholder to Benjamin Wheeler 1 Mar 1708/9

Sanders Nicholas s Nicholas, Soho, Mdx, baker to John Fist 7 Aug 1721 <26 Jul 1727 turned over to Thomas Belson, citizen and draper>
Sanders Thomas s Robert, Holborn, Mdx, cook† to Bartholomew Wimberly 9 Jun 1707
Sanderson Richard s William, Billesdon, Lei, yeoman† to Andrew Partridge 12 Dec 1664
Sanderson Thomas s Thomas, Newmarket, Sfk, innholder to Richard Kirby 6 Apr 1730
Sandes John s John, citizen and carpenter† to Peter Citty 2 Dec 1656
Sandford Joseph s John, Buckby, Nth, clerk to Daniel Scott 11 Dec 1699
Sandiford William s William, Chelsea, Mdx, victualler† to George Goodwin 7 Dec 1790
Sandle Henry s Edmund, Hinton on the Green, Gls, yeoman to Brian Ayliffe 23 Jul 1660
Sandwell Edgate s Joseph, Stepney, Mdx, gentleman to John Jemmett 2 Dec 1717
Sanford Thomas s William, Stepney, Mdx, potter† to Thomas Clark 4 Mar 1691/2
Sanney John s Robert, Finchley, Mdx, yeoman to Robert Ayliff 10 Sep 1702
Sapster William s William, Orsett, Ess, yeoman to William Flewellyn 29 Aug 1653
Sargeant William s Thomas, Welham, Lei, grazier† to George Bird 5 Feb 1793
Sargent George s George, Blandford, Dor, innholder to Isaac Cox 15 Jun 1714
Sargent Robert s George, College Hill, looking glass manufacturer to George Sargent 6 May 1794
Sarjant Daniel s Joseph, Calne, Wil, woollen draper† to Edward Halsey 2 Jul 1733
Sarjant John s John, St James Westminster, gentleman† to Elizabeth widow of John Hastings 1 Jun 1713
Satterthwaite Clement s Henry, Hawkhurst, Ken, tanner to William Davis 13 Jun 1654
Saunders John s Thomas, Chaddleworth, Brk, clerk† to Francis Zouch 13 May 1686
Saunders Robert s Robert, Hankerton, Wil, husbandman to John Moncke 2 Apr 1638
Saunders Thomas s ?, Walton on Thames, Sry, schoolmaster† to Nicholas Katkitt ? Aug 1668
Saunders Thomas s Thomas, 'Anglisham', Brk, gentleman to John Turner 3 May 1688
Saunders Thomas s William, Cricklade, Wil, yeoman to Joseph Lane 11 Mar 1725/6
Saunders William s Robert, Lnd, gentleman to William Parker 3 Dec 1716 <6 Jan 1716/7 turned over to Edward Tratt, citizen and draper>
Savage John s Richard, Bury Street, St James Westminster, Mdx to his father 4 Nov 1777
Savage Richard s John, Wrenbury Wood, Chs, farmer† to Samuel Dare 6 Apr 1742
Savage Richard s Richard, Bury Street, St James Westminster, Mdx to his father 5 Jan 1779
Savage Samuel s James, Maidstone, Ken, yeoman to Benjamin Crackinthorpe 4 Nov 1717
Sawdrey Nathaniel s John, Waltham Abbey, Ess, yeoman to John Greene 20 Oct 1669
Sawford John s Samuel, Heston, Mdx, yeoman to Benjamin Jenkins 7 Sep 1676
Sawtell Thomas s Thomas, Lnd, gentleman to Ferdinand Ladbrooke 4 Mar 1722/3
Sawyer John s Thomas, Bicester, Oxf, yeoman to Thomas Kirton 20 Dec 1637
Sawyer John s Alan, Cheshunt, Hrt, weaver to Daniel Giles 11 Jun 1661
Sawyer Joseph s Thomas, Bicester, Oxf, felmonger to Thomas Higgins 12 Jun 1689
Saxbee Thomas s Richard, citizen and salter to Peter Prince 6 Mar 1677/8
Saxbes Richard s Richard, Westerham, Ken, yeoman to Thomas Fuller 4 Jun 1638
Saxon John s Samuel, Ashton [? *in Ms* 'Ashen'], Lan, yeoman to William Gurney 1 Jun 1686
Saxon Samuel s John, Betley, Sts, yeoman to Thomas Smalredge 9 Apr 1639
Saywell John s Samuel, Nazeing, Ess, yeoman to John Parker 10 May 1638
Saywell Samuel s Samuel, Nazeing, Ess, yeoman to John Saywell 5 Jan 1646/7
Scarborow John s John, 'Nulton', Ham, joiner to John Edden 28 Feb 1669/70
Scardefield John s Thomas, St Clement Danes, tallow chandler† to Thomas Cole 17 Feb 1673/4
Scatterford Michael s Michael, Westminster, Mdx, smith? to Henry Wyne 25 Jun 1668
Scedamine Henry s James, Longstone, Dby, yeoman to Edward Harris 26 Dec 1678
Scoles James s William, Westminster, Mdx, barber to John Tyson 5 May 1670
Scollough George s John, St Sepulchre, Lnd to his father 30 Mar 1764
Scollough John s John, St George Hanover Square, Mdx, victualler to Richard Kirby 2 May 1739
Scoones Henry s Thomas, Tonbridge, Ken, clothworker† to Martin Wheatly 23 Dec 1709
Scott Daniel s Samuel, Little Hadham, Hrt, yeoman to Joseph Watts 4 Feb 1668/9
Scott Daniel s Daniel to his father 7 Jun 1708
Scott James s Thomas, Hadham Hall, Hrt, yeoman to Thomas Cole 20 Dec 1705
Scott Lewis s John, Kempsford, Gls, clerk† to Nathaniel Chandler 4 Mar 1699/1700
Scott Peter s John, Camberwell, Sry, gentleman† to John Skeale 16 Oct 1637
Scott Robert Mitchell s John, Bermondsey, Sry, mariner† to William Stephens 6 Dec 1774
Scott Samuel s Joseph, Bishops Stortford, Hrt, ironmonger to Mathew Woodward 15 Oct 1705

Scott Samuel s Samuel, Smithfield, Lnd, butcher to John Sibley 6 Jul 1730
Scotton Moses s Edward, Daventry, Nth, yeoman to John Rutt 8 Jul 1706
Scratton John s Daniel, Broomfield, Ess, gentleman† to Philip Constable 27 Jan 1762
Seabrooke William s William, Soho, Mdx, collier to Robert Bly 3 Apr 1710
Seager Joseph s Joseph, Southwark, Sry, shipwright to John Hills 1 Nov 1735
Seagood Thomas s Stephen, citizen and lorimer to Thomas Johnson 7 Mar 1708/9
Seakins John s Mathew, citizen and tallow chandler† to Elizabeth widow of Mathew Seakins 3 Dec 1716
Seale Robert s Robert, Great Marlow, Bkm, yeoman to William Jenkins 29 Sep 1633
Seamer Stephen s Thomas, Oxford, Oxf, maltster to William Gibson 20 Jul 1652
Searle John s Fulk, Epping, Ess, yeoman to Samuel Hamond 30 Jul 1673
Searle Thomas s Edward, Chatham, Ken, gunner to James Tetly 1 Sep 1712
Searle Thomas s Francis Barrell, Lambeth, Sry, shipwright to Thomas Searle 18 Oct 1764
Sears Thomas s William, St Katherine by the Tower, pattenmaker† to Thomas Gilson 6 Dec 1736
Seaward Tobias s John, Somerton, Som† to Thomas Davis 27 Apr 1648
Sebbon John s Walter, Islington, Mdx, farmer to William Johnson 2 Jan 1749/50
Secker Edward s Michael, York, Yks, merchant† to Thomas Smalridge 22 Mar 1658/9
Sedgly Robert s James, citizen and fruiterer to Francis Haughton 23 Sep 1680
See Abraham s Abraham, Canterbury, Ken, weaver to William Malebarr 18 Dec 1656
Seer Thomas s William, Addington, Bkm, yeoman to Thomas Noble 4 Oct 1639
Selden William s John, Holywell Street, Mdx, tailor† to William Hoare 3 Aug 1779
Sell William s Roger, 'Cartner [? Catmore]', Brk, yeoman to Thomas Relews 6 Sep 1641
Senhouse Wrightington s John, Seascale, Cul, esquire to Peter Pickering 17 Jun 1656
Senior John s John, St Clement Danes, Mdx, clothier to Thomas Hayes 4 Dec 1678
Senskall John s Charles, citizen and fishmonger† to John Rumball 3 Apr 1654
Sequens Thomas s Thomas to his father 22 Apr 1656
Serjeant John s James, citizen and skinner to Jeremiah Gibson 8 Jun 1674
Serle George s Edward, Newbury, Brk, gentleman† to Bartholomew Wimberley 5 Jul 1714
Serman William s Richard, Croydon, Sry, yeoman† to William Smith 23 Mar 1664/5
Setall William s William, Skelsmergh, Wes, husbandman to Robert Fewtrell 21 Oct 1662
Seymar Edward s Thomas, Woolster, Yks, yeoman to William Smith, jnr. 25 Jun 1683
Seymour James s John, Charles Street, St John Horsleydown, tallow chandler to John Randall 1 Jul 1783
Seymour John s John, St John Horsleydown, Sry, tallow chandler to John Randall 5 Mar 1782
Seyton Edward s Richard, Kislingbury, Nth, yeoman to John Babbin 16 Jun 1663
Shackerly William s William, citizen and dyer to Thomas Hasted 28 May 1674
Shakemaple John s John, citizen and woodmonger to William Parry 5 Feb 1654/5
Shakemaple Samuel s Jeremy, citizen and joiner† to John Rudson 26 Jan 1635/6
Shampain James s James, Hampstead, Mdx, victualler to Michael Lucas 4 Dec 1699 <5 May 1702 turned over to Elizabeth widow of Michael Lucas>
Sharpe John s John, Yks, gentleman to Charles Doilie 24 Apr 1651 <bond from Robert Clarkson, citizen>
Sharpe John s Thomas, Hurley, Brk, yeoman† to Thomas King 17 Dec 1645
Sharpe Philip s Philip, Islington, Mdx, clerk† to George Clare 16 Jun 1670
Sharpe Robert s John, Little Horton, Yks, gentleman† to John Sharpe 24 Oct 1672
Sharpe Thomas s George, Eastwell, Lei, weaver to Henry Collett 1 Aug 1633
Sharpe Thomas s Thomas, Winchester, Ham, yeoman† to Richard Whitcher 18 Aug 1660
Sharples Robert s Robert, Balderstone, Lan, husbandman† to Thomas Flaxmore 5 Nov 1657
Shaw Henry s William, Crooks Beck, Ravenstonedale, Wes, yeoman to Thomas Buggbie 7 Nov 1692
Shaw John s John, St George Hanover Square, Mdx, victualler to William Wright 2 Sep 1756
Shaw William Michael s Michael, citizen and cooper to Thomas Nash 8 Mar 1742/3
Shaylor Joseph s Martin, Shipton, Oxf, blacksmith to Thomas Ball 2 Oct 1683
Sheale Walter s Richard, Bilston, Sts, blacksmith to William Peale 18 Nov 1697
Sheen Michael s Thomas, Aylesbury, Bkm, dealer in wool to Samuel Hoggins 11 Mar 1755
Sheerman Benjamin s George, Bicester, Oxf, saddler to William Powell 7 Aug 1679
Sheldon Charles s Francis, Woolwich, Ken, gentleman to John Tuer 6 Apr 1654

Sheldon Joseph s Ralph, 'Wadley', Dby, gentleman to Roger Price, jnr. 7 May 1647
<bond from Gilbert Sheldon, University of Oxford, doctor of theology>
Sheldon William s William, Broadway, Wor, esquire to Nicholas Charlton 23 Aug 1667
Shelley Joseph s John, citizen and merchant tailor to William Langton 1 Feb 1719/20
Shelley Nicholas s George, Nazeing, Ess, yeoman to Thomas Shelley 5 Sep 1645
Shelmerdine Josiah s Daniel, Findern, Dby to Joseph Watts 30 Jul 1691
Shelton Benjamin s Richard, Greenwich, Ken, linen draper to George Bird 6 May 1777
Shenston John s Samuel, Wellclose Square, Mdx, silk dyer to Thomas Charles Arewater 4 Mar 1783
Shepard Samuel s John, Towcester, Nth, yeoman to Richard Palmer 3 May 1682
Sheperd William s Richard, Hitchin, Hrt, tailor† to Nathan Hall 13 Apr 1702
Shepheard Richard s Francis, citizen and scrivener to John Collington 21 Feb 1654/5
Shepheard William s William, Midhurst, Ssx, blacksmith to William Massey 4 Dec 1660
Shepherd Joseph s Joseph, Hellingly, Ssx, gentleman to William Shepherd 4 Jul 1780
Shepherd Thomas s Thomas, Beech Lane, Lnd, baker to Henry Soames, jnr. 2 Oct 1781
Shepherd William s Joseph, Aldbourne, Wil, cotton spinner to William Shepherd 8 Feb 1773
Sheppard James s Robert, Tickhill, Yks, dyer† to Richard Wright 6 Jan 1667/8
Sheppard John s Edward, St Martin in the Fields, Mdx, gentleman to Thomas King 7 Jul 1646
Sheppard Mary d Samuel, Loughborough, Lei, cordwainer† to Samuel Withers 2 Nov 1681
Sheppard Mathew s Mathew, Radbourne Hall, Dby, cook to Thomas Hamett 16 Jan 1683/4
Sheppard Thomas s Richard, Great Bookham, Sry, husbandman to John Clant 31 Jul 1637
Sherard Bennett s Bennett, Whissendine, Rut, esquire† to Francis Molyneux 7 Jan 1701/2
Sherborne Miles s Miles, citizen and stationer† to James Clarke 2 Apr 1638
Sheriff John s Thomas, Diss, Nfk, yeoman to Thomas Lawrence 29 Apr 1665
Sheringham John s John, Woolwich, Ken, joiner to Mary Andrews 4 Dec 1710 <19 Jul 1714
master† turned over by Mary Andrews exec. to William Hayden>
Sherley Charles s William, citizen and bricklayer to Thomas Stephenson 3 Nov 1687
Sherman Ezekiel s Ezekiel, Dedham, Ess, clothier† to Jeremiah Daniell 26 Aug 1668
Sherman Francis s Benjamin to his father 3 Dec 1705
Sherman John s William, Croydon, Sry, gentleman to Joseph Sheldon 15 Aug 1660
Sherman John s Richard, citizen and armorer† to Benjamin Clarke 6 May 1723
Sherman William s Mathew, Weedon, Nth, yeoman to Nathaniel Butterton 10 Jul 1633
Sherwin Joseph s Robert, St Martin in the Fields, tallow chandler to Herbert Homan 1 Nov 1774
Sheward Richard s William, Southwark, Sry, clogmaker to John Griffiths 3 Feb 1734/5
Shilton Samuel s William, Nuneaton, War, yeoman to Richard Redding 28 Sep 1638
Shipp Edmund s John, Needham Market, Sfk, draper to Bernard Block 13 Nov 1657
Shippard Michael s Samuel, Edgware, Mdx, maltster to John Jefferie 4 Jun 1663
Shipside George s George, citizen and grocer to Henry Woollhead 26 May 1696
Shipton Joseph s Richard, Kingsclere, Ham, tanner† to Brian Alyff 22 Jul 1669
Shipton Thomas s John, citizen and grocer to William Smith 17 Jun 1647
Shittler William s Thomas, Blandford, Dor, gentleman to Richard Fullwood 4 Nov 1717
Short John s John, St James Westminster, Mdx, gentleman to Lancelot Vibart 2 Mar 1718/9
Short Joseph s William, St Clement Danes, Mdx, tailor to George Sweeton 4 Feb 1777
Short Mathew s John, Wellow, Ham, husbandman to Silvester Cardy 4 Nov 1647
Short Richard s Thomas, Wardington, Oxf, yeoman to Edmund Barcock 22 Jun 1654
Short Thomas s Henry, Culworth, Nth, yeoman to Alexander White 31 Oct 1639
Shorter James s George, Witney, Oxf, gentleman† to William Gurney 23 Feb 1685/6
Shorthoose Robert s Henry, Stretton, Sts, husbandman† to John Ford 17 Nov 1690
Shortland Edward s John, Weston by Welland, Nth, yeoman to Francis Ardinton 28 May 1703
<3 Jun 1706 turned over to William Vaston, citizen and broderer>
Shouler John s Nathaniel, Edgiock [Inkberrow], Wor, salter to Humphrey Hill 11 Mar 1640/1
Showell Arthur s William, Deptford, Ken, shipwright to Samuel Redmire 7 Sep 1748
Shrewsbridge John s Thomas, St Giles Cripplegate, Lnd, cooper to Richard Markhall 2 Sep 1746
Shrimpton John s Joseph, Chipping Wycombe, Bkm, gentleman to Thomas Shrimpton 16 Aug 1758
Shrimpton Thomas s Joseph, High Wycombe, Bkm, ironmonger to William Alexander 8 Aug 1748
Shrimpton William s Thomas, Iver, Bkm, tanner† to Robert Briscoe 11 Jul 1656
Shrubb Thomas s John, Farnham, Sry, weaver to John Collington 1 Jun 1658
Shurley Michael s James, Lnd, gentleman to John Browne 17 Feb 1655/6
Shuter John s Robert, Harborough, Lei, shoemaker† to John Newington 12 Nov 1677

Shutt Francis s William, St Giles Cripplegate, Lnd, refiner to Thomas Johnson 4 Apr 1715
Shuttlewood John s Joel, ?, Lei, yeoman to John Church 7 Jul 1669
Shuttleworth Barnabas s Robert, St Olave Southwark, victualler to Thomas Allen 16 Feb 1663/4
Sibley Nathaniel s Joseph to his father 23 Jul 1657
Sibley Robert s John, citizen and tallow chandler to John Johnson 2 Feb 1735/6
Sibly John s ..., Lnd, wine cooper† to William Mayne 4 Feb 1705/6 <2 Jun 1712 turned over to Ralph White>
Siddall Nathaniel s James, Hereford, Hef, gentleman to Jeremiah Dranton 6 Feb 1677/8
Silver John s William, High Wycombe, Bkm, maltster to William Alden 27 Oct 1669
Silver William s William, Wargrave, Brk, maltster to Nathaniel Perkins 3 Aug 1730
Simes Isaac s Isaac, St Margaret Westminster, Mdx, cook to Henry Soames 5 Oct 1757
Simes Thomas s William, St Giles, Dev, keeper† to John Simes 11 Nov 1675
Simes William s William, citizen and blacksmith to John Bowden 4 Jan 1696/7
Simmonds Daniel s Thomas, Hadley, Mdx, carpenter to James Parrot 9 Jul 1695
Simmonds James s John, Lnd, beadmaker to William Coles 1 Sep 1735
Simonds James s James, Egham, Sry, husbandman to Samuel King 28 Nov 1670
Simonds Thomas s John, Wokingham, Brk, felmonger to James Prince 7 Nov 1715
Simpson Edward s Thomas, Loughborough, Lei, yeoman† to Humphrey King 7 Jul 1675
Simpson Edward s William, Farndon, Chs, labourer† to John Keywood 3 Aug 1702
Simpson John s Thomas, Fishlake, Yks, gentleman† to Samuel Fitch 3 Jan 1708/9
Simpson Richard s John, Cheshunt, Hrt, carpenter to George Staines 30 Oct 1674
Simpson Richard s Benjamin, citizen and stationer to William Roberts 7 May 1733
Simpson Samuel s Samuel, Grub Street, Lnd, tobacco cutter† to John Chambers 6 Dec 1774
Simpson Thomas s Andrew, St Margaret Westminster, tailor to William Threadher 23 Jul 1688
Simpson Thomas s Thomas, citizen and haberdasher to Philadelphia widow of Edward Osborne 13 Jan 1700/1
Sims James s James, St Olave Southwark, Sry, waterman to Benjamin Free 2 May 1709 <8 Mar 1714/5 turned over to Jonathan Randall, citizen and leatherseller; 13 Jun 1715 to William Mayo, citizen and butcher>
Sims Thomas s William, Chard, Som, husbandman to John Pritchard 5 Apr 1647
Sindry William s John, citizen and haberdasher to John Childe, jnr. 2 Dec 1706
Siritt John s Simon, Brentford, Mdx, cheesemonger to George Wightman 10 Jun 1691
Sitlington Richard s John, St George Hanover Square, victualler† to Herbert Homan 6 Jul 1757
Skelton William s William, citizen and weaver to Edward Copeland 11 Feb 1709/10
Skepper John s Richard, Lincoln, Lin† to Thomas Kelke 21 Jul 1647
Skepper John s ?, Mavis Enderby, Lin, gentleman to Richard Smith 28 Feb 1670/1
Skerrett James s Michael, Galway, Ire, gentleman to Elizabeth widow of James Byard 5 Jun 1678
Skinner Edward s John, Trowbridge, Wil, butcher to William Collier 31 Jul 1682
Skinner Edward s Thomas, Reigate, Sry, butcher to John Fist 10 Dec 1718 <5 Jun 1721 turned over to William Kirk, citizen and haberdasher>
Skinner John s Thomas, Little Hinton, Wil, farmer† to Jonathan Leigh 9 Jan 1752
Skinner Robert s Robert, Penshurst, Ken, yeoman to John Church 29 Aug 1672
Skinner William s William, Chatham, Ken, tobacconist to Richard Webster 3 Feb 1728/9
Skipp Samuel s Judah, Spitalfields, Mdx, tallow chandler to Richard Carter 3 Aug 1730
Skreene William s William, Pucklechurch, Gls, glover to Henry Wyne 26 Mar 1684
Sky William s William, Deptford, Ken, mariner to John Chatfield 16 Dec 1728
Slack Noah s Hugh, Elstow, Bdf, husbandman to Elizabeth widow of Thomas Barwell 7 Oct 1717
Slade John s Anthony, St Saviour Southwark, Sry, fisherman to John Hooke 5 Feb 1712/3
Slade Nicholas s John, Worplesdon, Sry, husbandman to Nicholas Farrant 23 Mar 1657/8
Slater Benjamin s Thomas, Wrexham, Den, Wal to Edward Palmer 7 Sep 1784 <2 Jan 1787 turned over to John Treacher, citizen and wheelwright>
Slater John s William, Goswell Street, Mdx, wheelwright to Richard Savage 3 Dec 1782
Slatter Samuel s Giles, Abingdon, Brk, weaver to Nathaniel Chandler, snr. 15 Aug 1706
Slaymaker John s Thomas, Clifton, Oxf, victualler to Robert Hopkins 5 Aug 1788 <4 Jan 1791 turned over to Richard Davies>
Sleate Jonathan s Richard, St Sepulchre, Mdx, carpenter† to Charles Leveings 6 Oct 1687
Sleath Gabriel s Richard, Friern Barnet, Mdx, yeoman to James Waggoner 8 Dec 1657
Sledd Lawrence s Thomas, citizen and ironmonger to John Skepper 26 Nov 1674

Sleigh Jonathan s Thomas, Ratcliffe, Mdx, mariner† to John Bowden 20 Feb 1688/9
Slemaker John s Henry, citizen and mason to Robert Butcher 7 May 1689
Slifer Benedict s Robert, Aston upon Carrant, Gls, gentleman to Robert New 28 Sep 1657
Slifield William s John, Cobham, Sry, cordwainer to Edward Sargeant, Kingston, Sry, citizen and cordwainer free 3 May 1796
Slowe Joseph s Hugh, Luton, Bdf, yeoman to Joseph Slowe 7 Jun 1654
Slynett John s Richard, Kensington, Mdx, labourer to Giles Harris 3 Aug 1713 <1 Jul 1717 turned over to Elizabeth widow of Francis Rakestraw>
Smalcomb Thomas s Thomas, citizen and feltmaker to William Squire 6 Oct 1718
Smales Joseph s John, St Katherine by the Tower, Mdx, mariner† to Richard Holbert 2 Jan 1776
Smales Richard s John, St Katherine by the Tower, Mdx, mariner† to Richard Holbert 1 Feb 1780
Smales Thomas s John, St Katherine by the Tower, Mdx, mariner† to Richard Holbert 7 Mar 1780
Small Christopher s George, Stepney, Mdx, mariner† to Francis Briscoe 13 Feb 1698/9
Small George s George, Newark, Ntt, mercer† to Nathaniel Owen 3 Mar 1653/4
Smallbourn John s William, Finchley, Mdx, farmer to Thomas Charles Arewater 7 Nov 1780
Smalridge John s John, Lichfield, Sts, shoemaker to Thomas Smalridge 23 Jul 1656
Smalwood James s Mathew, Lnd, haberdasher† to Francis Marshall 2 Feb 1640/1
Smart William s John, Holborn, Mdx, yeoman to Anthony Bunn 1 Dec 1691
Smedley Richard s Thomas, St Olave Southwark, Sry, labourer† to Nathaniel Burchett 6 Dec 1750
Smeeton George s William, St Martin in the Fields, tallow chandler to William Shepherd 27 Jun 1765
Smenbey John s William, 'Ursiter Woodland', Sts, carpenter to Edward Brandreth 20 Oct 1637
Smith Anthony s Anthony, Vernhams, Ham, husbandman† to John Pritchard 2 Nov 1646
Smith Anthony s Anthony, Braintree, Ess, grocer to John Adams 16 May 1683
Smith Benjamin s Daniel, Merevale, War, gentleman to Richard Worgan 14 Nov 1694
Smith Benjamin s George, Moreton, Bkm, grazier to George Page 6 Nov 1721
Smith Christopher s Christopher, Brompton, Yks, yeoman to Samuel Fitch 6 Oct 1718
Smith Clement s William, Marlborough, Wil, yeoman† to Thomas Hawes 8 Oct 1684
Smith Edward s Richard, Whetstone, Mdx, gentleman to Richard Dunbarton 24 Jun 1634
Smith Edward s ... to Peter City 8 Aug 1634
Smith Edward s William, Edmonton, Mdx, husbandman to Thomas Smith 15 May 1672
Smith Edward s Ralph, St Ann Blackfriars, Lnd, merchant to Samuel Cox 19 Jul 1709
Smith Edward s Richard, Reading, Brk, mealman† to Richard West 3 Oct 1709
Smith Edward s Edward, Spitalfields, Mdx, weaver to Thomas Radley 2 Mar 1736/7
Smith Edward s Edward, citizen and tallow chandler† to Richard Moore 4 Jan 1742/3
Smith Francis s Francis, Cogenhoe, Nth, clerk† to Thomas Harris 29 Jan 1656/7
Smith Francis s Arthur, Hemel Hempstead, Hrt, doctor in physic† to John Jellings 11 Dec 1690
Smith Francis s Edward, Richmond, Sry, clockmaker to Richard Collins 16 Jan 1765 <28 Mar 1767 turned over to Richard Savage>
Smith Gabriel s George to his father 7 Feb 1750/1
Smith George s William, Shutlanger, Nth, yeoman to John Velan 22 May 1679
Smith George s William, citizen and leatherseller to John Coates 17 Jul 1691
Smith George s Gabriel, Waterham, Ken, yeoman to Richard Feild 5 Feb 1710/11
Smith George s Peter, St Giles Cripplegate, Lnd, founder to Silcox Croudson 4 Aug 1743
Smith Gervase s John, citizen and weaver to Thomas Chewter 7 Dec 1713 <7 Feb 1714/5 master† turned over by Thomas Hains, exec. to John Chewter>
Smith Harman s Richard, St James Westminster, Mdx, coachman to Samuel Traunter 7 Sep 1697 <turned over to Ralph Field; 15 May 1702 to William Haydon>
Smith Henry s Miles, Guildford, Sry, yeoman† to Joseph Gibbons 4 Mar 1689/90
Smith Henry s Henry, St Giles in the Fields, Mdx, cutler to Edward Heming 7 Dec 1730
Smith Isaac s James, Bedford, Bdf, wool stapler to Evan Phillips 5 Oct 1779
Smith James s William, Coventry, War, clothier to Christopher Gurney 26 Nov 1661
Smith James s John, Thornton, Yks, grocer† to Mathew Snablin 1 Aug 1677
Smith James s William to his father 18 Dec 1688
Smith James s William, Melton Mowbray, Lei, woolcomber to Samuel Fitch 2 Aug 1725 <turned over to Robert Baughurst, citizen and founder>
Smith John s Richard, Ealing, Mdx, yeoman to Adrian Harford 27 Feb 1639/40
Smith John s Edward, Newington, Sry, yeoman to John Pritchard 24 Aug 1653

Smith John s John, Goodworth Clatford, Ham, clothworker to Richard Whitcher 18 Jan 1658/9
Smith John s ?, citizen and merchant tailor to Henry Cox ? Oct 1663
Smith John s William, Ashton under Lyne, Lan to John Palmer ? Jun 1664
Smith John s William, Coventry, War, cordwainer† to Robert Udall 17 Mar 1673/4
Smith John s Henry, Banbury, Oxf, ironmonger to John Greene 3 Jul 1676
Smith John s William, Barton, Gls, yeoman to Thomas Dowdswell 20 Oct 1682
Smith John s Thomas, St Giles Cripplegate, Mdx, innholder to Edward Stroud 21 Jul 1685
Smith John s Richard, Stanton St Bernard, Wil, yeoman to Robert Uppington 21 May 1686
Smith John s George, St George Southwark, Sry, cordwainer to William Clarke 10 Jan 1686/7
Smith John s John, St Giles Cripplegate, Mdx, victualler to Thomas Obbinson 2 May 1709
<turned over to William Gown, citizen and blacksmith>
Smith John s Abraham, citizen and haberdasher to John Davey 3 May 1714
Smith John s Henry, St Margaret Westminster, Mdx, butcher to Timothy Foster 7 Feb 1714/5
Smith John s Daniel, Westminster, Mdx, innholder to William Alexander 1 Nov 1725
<turned over to Robert Bringhurst, citizen and founder>
Smith John Gould s Thomas, citizen and turner to William Tally 5 Apr 1738 <6 Feb 1743/4 master† turned over with consent of Esther Tally his widow to Charles Cartwright, citizen and skinner>
Smith Joseph s John, citizen and haberdasher to John Darcy 8 Feb 1674/5
Smith Joseph s John, Birtsmorton, Wor, yeoman to Samuel Hanson 1 Mar 1730/1
Smith Joseph s John, Wootton Bassett, Wil, saddler to John Woodward 7 Dec 1742
Smith Joseph s John, St Botolph Aldgate, Lnd, grocer† to John Butts 5 Oct 1770
Smith Joseph s Thomas, South Benfleet, Ess, farmer to John Chadsey 6 Feb 1800
Smith Maurice s Thomas, Geddington, Nth, chandler to Gilbert Cornelius 2 Sep 1645
Smith Michael s Michael, Blechingley, Sry, husbandman to Robert Maybanke 1 Aug 1636
Smith Michael s Giles, Bicester, Oxf, mason to Robert Boucher 3 Aug 1696
Smith Nicholas s Edward, Ampthill, Bdf, gentleman to William Smith 10 Aug 1653
Smith Reuben s Henry, Marlborough, Wil, tanner to Catherine widow of Thomas Woollhead 6 May 1728 <3 Dec 1733 turned over to Samuel Osborne>
Smith Richard s Edward, Moreton Pinkney, Nth, yeoman† to Christopher Leake 1 Feb 1650/1
Smith Richard s ?, Emberton, Bkm, yeoman to Thomas Kelke 23 Sep 1662
Smith Richard s John, Wibsey, Yks, clothier to Thomas Lawrence 25 Sep 1668
Smith Richard s John, Wokingham, Brk, linen draper† to John Ragdale 2 Oct 1693
Smith Richard s William, Chalfont St Peter, Bkm, mealman to Giles Harris 8 Oct 1705
Smith Richard s Edward to his father 13 Sep 1739
Smith Richard s Robert, Campden, Gls, yeoman to John Cheany 14 May 1741
Smith Samuel s Robert, citizen and dyer† to John Ayscough 2 Aug 1697
Smith Samuel s Samuel, citizen and shipwright to William Noss 5 Jul 1725
Smith Thomas s William, Edmonton, Mdx, husbandman to William Minchin 7 Nov 1660
Smith Thomas s Thomas, St Martin in the Fields, Mdx, coachman to John Parker 16 Jul 1689
Smith Thomas s John to his father 7 Apr 1712
Smith Thomas s Thomas, Claycoton, Nth, clerk† to Thomas Johnson 12 Aug 1720
Smith Thomas s George, St Giles Cripplegate, Lnd, carman† to Thomas Wilkinson 7 Aug 1737
Smith Thomas s John, Thames Ditton, Sry, coal merchant to Robert French 6 Mar 1787
Smith Timothy s Charles, citizen and stationer to John Scollough 8 Dec 1772
Smith Valentine s Valentine, Bonby, Lin, yeoman to Thomas Kelke 23 Apr 1667
Smith William s Thomas, Weston, Hef, yeoman† to Edward Hooker 25 Jan 1637/8
Smith William s Edward, citizen and merchant tailor to Robert Bradley 23 Jul 1645
Smith William s John, Harlington, Mdx, yeoman† to Henry Twyford 2 Apr 1649
Smith William s John, Goodworth Clatford, Ham, clothworker to Richard Whitcher 11 Feb 1650/1
Smith William s John, Westcote, Gls, yeoman to John Collington 7 Oct 1652
Smith William s William, Mitcham, Sry, yeoman to Richard Bull 13 Jul 1654
Smith William s William, Lnd, merchant to Thomas Smalridge 16 May 1661
Smith William s William, Bermondsey, Sry, feltmaker† to Thomas Allen 8 Jun 1664
Smith William s William, East Meon, Ham, husbandman† to Thomas Hayes 13 Nov 1665
Smith William s William to his father 27 Feb 1676/7
Smith William s Richard, St Thomas Southwark, Sry, victualler to Thomas Dowdswell 2 Jun 1701
<2 Mar 1702/3 turned over to John Harbert>

Smith William s Benjamin, citizen and carpenter to Samuel Mackerness 5 Feb 1712/3
Smith William s Richard, Burstow, Sry, yeoman† to Richard Walker 15 Jun 1719
Smith William s John, Horsleydown, Sry, victualler to Sarah Downes 4 Nov 1794
Smitheman William s William, Bromley, Ess, clothier to Nicholas Beckett 15 Dec 1664
Smithen Richard s William, citizen and weaver to Bartholomew Peele 13 May 1658
Smithman John s John, Barking, Ess, clothier† to Edmund Barcock 13 Dec 1652
Smithyman Joseph s William to his father 3 Feb 1695/6
Smythe Edward William s William, Bury St Edmunds, glazier† to Robert Mitchell Scott 5 May 1795
Snape John s Charles, St Saviour Southwark, Sry, waterman to Richard Cooke 19 Jan 1690/1
Snape Samuel s William, St Pancras, Mdx, cowkeeper to Ferdinand Ladbrooke 1 Dec 1735
Snape Thomas s Samuel, Fleet Market to his father 5 Sep 1780 <turned over to Charles Dare>
Snaxton Stephen s George, St Andrew Wardrobe, woollen draper to William Hunt 12 Jan 1680/1
Snelling Young s Thomas, Fleet Street, watchmaker to Charles Breed 15 Aug 1755 <21 Jan 1761 turned over to Thomas Snelling, citizen and clothworker; 22 Jan 1761 to Charles Breed>
Snook Isaac s Clement, Shoreditch, Mdx, weaver to Charles King 3 Jul 1744
Snowden Thomas s Thomas, Kingsbury, Mdx, yeoman to Adrian Handforth 29 Sep 1633
Soame Henry s George, Edmonton, Mdx, weaver to Jeremiah Ridge 2 Aug 1708
Soame Richard s Bartholomew, citizen and goldsmith to Benjamin Browne 11 Oct 1687
Soames George s Henry, Holborn, Mdx to his father 4 Feb 1783
Soames Henry s Henry, St Andrew Holborn, Lnd to his father 6 Sep 1774
Soames Henry Aldwin s Henry to his father 6 Feb 1800
Soames James s Henry, Holborn Hill, Lnd, tallow chandler to Henry Soames, jnr. 7 Mar 1786
Solley Benjamin s Stephen, Ash, Ken, gentleman to Charles Doilie 12 Oct 1654 <bond from father and Joshua Pordage, draper>
Solte John s George, Flitwick, Bdf, tanner to Thomas Cutlett 21 Nov 1639
Souch Francis s Henry, Amport, Ham, clerk to Richard Wilkinson 29 Dec 1657
Soundy John s John, Henley, Oxf, maltster to Joseph Flight 1 Mar 1770
Soundy Joseph Johnson s Thomas, Queen Street, Southwark, undertaker† to William Littell, jnr. 3 May 1796
South William s Stephen, Kingston, Sry, wheelwright to John Palmer 12 Apr 1708
Southam Thomas s John, Bicester, Oxf, tallow chandler† to William Gurney 21 Nov 1676
Southwood Robert s Robert, Goodworth Clatford, Ham, gentleman to Richard Whitcher 17 Nov 1657
Sowerby John s John, St Marylebone, Mdx, butcher to Nathaniel Mathews 4 Sep 1787
Sowthen Henry s John, Stanwell, Mdx, yeoman to Samuel Harris 6 Nov 1678
Spackman Richard s Richard, Wroughton [? *in Ms* 'Roton'], Wil, husbandman to John Skepper 27 Jun 1661
Sparke Edward s Andrew, Witham, Ess, gentleman to Ralph Bigland 18 May 1767
Sparke Richard s John, citizen and grocer† to William Badham 20 Sep 1686
Sparrow Benjamin s John, 'Benton', Sal, gentleman to Charles Beardoe 7 Nov 1692
Sparrow Henry s Robert, St Clement Danes, Mdx, tailor to Edward Clarke 6 Nov 1759
Sparrow William s John, St Benet Paul's Wharf, Lnd, inkmaker to John Willoughby 7 Oct 1794
Spearing Richard s Richard, Gosport, Ham, baker to Joseph Collier 7 Feb 1715/6
Speede George s John, citizen and cordwainer† to Samuel Deely 10 Mar 1690/1
Speede William s William, citizen and leatherseller to Joseph Woolhead 2 Apr 1679
Speering Benjamin s Benjamin, Fordington, Dor, gentleman† to James Makeham 14 Jul 1683
Speller John s James, Mile End, Mdx, corn chandler to Elizabeth widow of Robert Gresswell 6 Nov 1732 <2 Mar 1736/7 turned over with consent of William Cogan, an exec. to Richard Norman, citizen and joiner>
Spenceley George s George, St Botolph Aldersgate, Lnd, butcher to Aurelius Hodson 14 Mar 1770
Spencer Henry s William to his father 31 Jan 1656/7
Spencer John s John, Holborn, Mdx, gentleman to Stephen Flindall 19 Feb 1772
Spencer John s Humphrey, Queen Street, Cheapside, Lnd, grocer to William Gregory 3 Nov 1779
Spencer Samuel s Edward, Daventry, Nth, gentleman to William Leggatt 12 Feb 1711/12
Spencer Thomas s William, Lnd, clerk† to William Spencer 11 Mar 1640/1
Spencer William s William, Ripley, Yks† to Thomas Kinglebey 20 May 1642
Spencer Zachariah s Thomas, New Brentford, Mdx, joiner† to John Hulcupp 11 Jul 1695
Sperry John s Thomas, St Katherine by the Tower, Mdx, corn factor to Isaac Jackson 3 Jul 1721

Spicer Theophilus s John, Standon, Hrt, esquire to Richard Ingram 14 Jun 1678
Spikernell James s James, Chichester, Ssx, gardener to Silvester Carde 10 Aug 1647
Spilsbury James s James, Alcester, War, gentleman to Roger Stevens 5 Jun 1732 <5 May 1735 turned over to Joseph Delafeild, citizen and leatherseller>
Spincks William s Michael, Hackney, Mdx, cordwainer to William Tucker 11 Jul 1667
Spragg William s William, St Giles in the Fields, Mdx, yeoman to Thomas Hayes 16 Apr 1684
Spratley Richard s John, Cookham, Brk, butcher† to Edward Skinner 3 Dec 1690
Spratt Henry s Henry, St John Horsleydown, Sry, mariner to Francis Barrell Searle 6 Sep 1774
Spriggs Richard s Richard, Brixworth, Nth, yeoman† to Thomas Claro 13 Sep 1688
Springell Ralph s Richard, Hardwick, Bkm, husbandman to Richard Draydge 6 Nov 1645
Spry William s Nathaniel, St Mary Axe, Lnd, gentleman to John Gardner 26 May 1761
Spurling Eric s Nicholas, Thames Street, Lnd, carman† to Richard Markwell 7 Jan 1733/4
Spurling James s ..., Tower Hill, Mdx, linen draper† to William Smith 13 Aug 1680
Spurrier Samuel s Samuel, Shad Thames, Sry, victualler to Joseph Collier 5 Sep 1739
Squibb Charles s Robert, St Margaret Westminster, Mdx, esquire† to Robert Clay 11 May 1697
Squire John s John, Lnd, merchant† to Thomas Davis 15 Aug 1656
Squire John s William, Barrow on Soar, Lei, yeoman to John Church 13 Dec 1675
Squire William s Thomas, Dunstable, Bdf, baker to William Chooter 17 Jan 1701/2
Stace William s William, Edmonton, Mdx to Francis Pitman 9 Apr 1635
Stacey Thomas s Ralph, Eton, Bkm, husbandman† to Elizabeth widow of John Gould 9 Apr 1716 <18 Dec 1718 turned over to John Gould>
Stackhouse Samuel s Christopher, citizen and merchant tailor† to Ephraim Heather 7 Aug 1704 <3 Aug 1707 turned over to Christopher Stackhouse, citizen and merchant tailor>
Stackhouse Samuel s Samuel, citizen and tallow chandler† to Ann widow of Samuel Stackhouse 1 Dec 1735
Stacy Thomas s Francis, Southwark, Sry, tallow chandler to Thomas Searle 7 Nov 1751
Stafford Thomas s Thomas, Upper Brook Street, Mdx, wheelwright† to Richard Clark 6 Aug 1782
Stampe Thomas s Peter, Horncastle, Lin, felmonger to Francis Pitman 28 Jun 1638
Standish William s Richard, Manchester, Lan, yeoman to Thomas King 14 Feb 1647/8
Stanfeild Edward s Thomas, Derby, Dby, gentleman† to William Eyre 12 Jan 1707/8
Stanford Charles s Charles, St Giles Cripplegate, Mdx, butcher to Richard West 3 Apr 1727
Stanley James s John, East Haddon, Nth, yeoman to Joseph Watts 3 Jan 1678/9
Stanley Walter s William, Huntington [Cannock], Sts, husbandman to Thomas Collins 31 Mar 1671
Stanley William s Robert, Chatham, Ken, shipwright† to Thomas Woolhead 2 Mar 1682/3
Stanniford Christopher s Thomas, Castleton, Wil, clerk to Joseph Gibbons 1 Aug 1662
Stansby Giles s John, Badgeworth, Gls, yeoman to Giles Rodway 24 Apr 1635
Stanton Richard s Thomas, citizen and mason to Richard Kerby 2 May 1720
Statum John s John, Whittlebury, Nth, husbandman† to Elizabeth widow of Thomas Allen 11 Aug 1671
Staveley Daniel s Francis, Gainsborough , Lin, husbandman† to John Jackson 22 Nov 1637
Stavely Joseph s Joseph, Yateley, Ham, mariner† to Edward Stroude 3 Apr 1697
Staynes George s William, Cheshunt, Hrt, carpenter to Elizabeth widow of Ralph Gurney 26 Oct 1653
Stead James s James, citizen and grocer to Thomas Humphries 5 Aug 1700
Stead William s James, citizen and grocer to Thomas Humphries 9 Feb 1707/8
Steavens Robert s Arthur, St George Southwark, Sry, pinmaker to John Gill 9 Sep 1700
Steed Elizabeth d George, Rochford, Ess, saddler† to John Newport 29 Jan 1671/2
Steel John Goodson s John, Rotherhithe, Sry, lighterman to Richard Higgins 3 Dec 1782
Steele Edward s John, Blyth, Ntt, clerk† to James Bullimore 26 Mar 1685
Steele Thomas s Henry, citizen and feltmaker to Thomas Clarke 16 Dec 1685
Steere William s Miles, Hampton, Mdx, baker to Samuel West 22 Jul 1652
Steevens John s Richard, Steventon, Brk, yeoman to Thomas Gunson 10 Aug 1654
Steevens Thomas s William, Leatherhead, Sry, yeoman† to Valentine Smith 31 May 1677
Steevens Thomas s Thomas, Northampton, Nth, carpenter† to Samuel Savage 8 Oct 1761
Stein Nathaniel s John, Cow Cross [St Sepulchre], Mdx, tallow chandler to Joseph Story 2 Nov 1790 <1 Nov 1791 turned over to John Treacher, citizen and wheelwright>
Stent John s Humphrey, Portsmouth, Ham, ship caulker to John Fist 7 Oct 1728

Stephens Henry s Daniel, Fenny Stratford, Bkm, innholder† to William Downing 4 Oct 1731 <7 Jul 1736 turned over to Thomas Smith>
Stephens John s John, Whitechapel, Mdx, mariner to John Tilley 23 Jan 1721/2
Stephens William s William, Egremont, Cul, gentleman to Richard Makeham 27 Apr 1692
Stephens William s William, Pancras Lane, Lnd, citizen and barber surgeon† to Ann Hedges Gardiner, widow 11 Nov 1761
Stephenson Thomas s Thomas, Penrith, Cul, yeoman to John Johnson 31 Jul 1669
Stepto Daniel s William, Banbury, Oxf, victualler to Thomas Wells Greenall 10 Aug 1726 <7 Sep 1730 turned over to Edmund Popplewell, citizen and haberdasher>
Steptoe John s John, citizen and cooper to Richard Webster 4 Jun 1716
Sterry Thomas s Joseph, Tooting Bec [Streatham], Sry, cooper to William Gurney 20 Jul 1685
Stevens Aaron s Moses, citizen and haberdasher† to John Kerby 12 Jun 1704
Stevens Horatio s Francis, St James Westminster, tallow chandler to Richard Savage 27 Jun 1764
Stevens John s Francis, St Giles in the Fields, Mdx, bricklayer to Edmund Hall 8 Dec 1712
Stevens Robert s Robert, Chalfont St Peter, Bkm, husbandman to Nathaniel Lorkins 26 Jun 1745
Stevens William s Edward, Appleton, Brk, yeoman to John Mathewe 28 Nov 1638
Stevens William s John, Holborn, Mdx, cordwainer† to Thomas Givers 25 May 1664
Steward Edward s Edward, Coleshill, Brk, yeoman to Leonard Turner 19 Nov 1635
Steward Richard s Charles, Lnd, butcher† to John Jordaine 9 Oct 1759
Steward William s William, Throckmorton, Wor, yeoman to Robert Mathews 22 Jul 1669
Stiffe Jonathan s Jonathan, Wotton under Edge, Gls, butcher to Daniel Child 2 Jun 1675
Stiffe Thomas s Abraham, Wotton under Edge, Gls, yeoman to Daniel Child 22 Aug 1681
Stiles Simon s James, Langley Marish, Bkm, yeoman† to Josiah Ragdale 14 Jul 1674 <bond of £20 from Jane Stiles, Langley Marish, Bkm, widow and mother against son's theft>
Stimson Thomas s Thomas, Cheshunt, Hrt, flaxman to John Hierne 30 Jul 1691
Stinton Benjamin s Richard, Lnd, distiller† to Joseph Mynott 5 Sep 1692
Stinton John s Benjamin, citizen and tallow chandler† to Susanna widow of Benjamin Stinton 7 Mar 1719/20
Stock Samuel s John, Romford, Ess, blacksmith to John Tovey 4 May 1748
Stockdale George s Robert, Sebergham, Cul, mason to John Eden 5 Oct 1676
Stockwell George s Henry, citizen and fruiterer to Thomas Clare 13 Apr 1686
Stokes George s Jeremiah, citizen and haberdasher† to Thomas Case 15 Aug 1709
Stokes Padnall s William, St James Westminster, Mdx, gentleman to William Bly 8 May 1722
Stokes Richard s Richard, Walthamstow, Ess, linen draper† to John Bryan 7 May 1776
Stonard John s John, Uxbridge, Mdx, mercer† to Richard Kerby 2 Jul 1711 <3 Oct 1715 turned over to William Proudman>
Stonard Samuel s Richard, Stifford, Ess, yeoman† to Samuel Belchamber 28 Mar 1660
Stone Jeremiah s John, Shepperton, Mdx, yeoman† to Richard Weston 4 Apr 1717
Stone Joseph s Joseph, Alresford, Ham, gentleman to Samuel Bedwell 2 Jul 1696
Stone Richard s Richard, Stewkley, Hun, knight to Nicholas Charlton 16 Aug 1650
Stone Thomas s Oswell, 'Inston', Lei, yeoman to Thomas Lawrence 14 Aug 1650
Stonestreete Thomas s Reuben, Bethersden, Ken, yeoman to Thomas Lenton 2 Jan 1633/4
Stonier Richard s John, Shelton, Stoke, Sts, gentleman† to James Horton 17 Aug 1704
Storer James s John, Fulham, Mdx, blacksmith to Thomas Harnett 9 Feb 1680/1
Storer John s Thomas, Fulham, Mdx, blacksmith† to Richard Fullwood 5 Sep 1715
Storer Richard s John, Fulham, Mdx, blacksmith to Richard Fulwood 16 Nov 1680
Stoughton William s Richard, Send, Sry, yeoman to Francis Zouch 20 Mar 1665/6
Stow Jabez s John, Napton on the Hill, War, yeoman to Nathaniel Might 7 Dec 1719
Strafford William s James, St Giles in the Fields, tallow chandler to Herbert Homan 12 Jan 1774
Stratford Anthony s George, Temple Guiting, Gls, gentleman to Richard Ingram 26 Jul 1692
Stratford James s James, Teffont, Wil, tanner† to Edward Fitz 5 Sep 1732
Streate John s Roger, citizen and armorer to Benjamin Brownesmith 20 Jun 1698
Streaton George s George, citizen and butcher to Edward Hooker 12 May 1633
Streete Isaac s Abraham, Newington, Sry, yeoman to Francis Warner 18 Jun 1650
Streete James s James, Dorking, Sry, clothier† to Joseph Browne 19 Jun 1651
Streete John s Walter, Wonersh, Sry, husbandman† to Walter Lewer 3 Nov 1707
Streetin William s William, St George in the East, Mdx, victualler to William Hoare 3 Dec 1771
Strelley Richard s Richard, Langton, Lei, gentleman to Thomas Allen 11 Jun 1683

Stretton John s William, Tenterden, Ken, esquire† to George Stretton 12 Dec 1656
<bond from George Gibbon, Hawkhurst, Ken, clothier>
Strother John s Andrew, Kensington Gore, Mdx, gardener† to Benjamin Mattingley 7 Oct 1794
Strouts Thomas s John, Holy Cross, Ken, maltster to Samuel Dare 3 Jul 1744
Struper Daniel s Theodore, Wing, Bkm, gentleman to John Ayscough 1 May 1693
Strutton Henry s Thomas, Woodborough, Wil, yeoman to Thomas Grover 13 Nov 1651
Sturges Samuel s John, Exton, Rut, carpenter to John Marsh 4 Apr 1673
Stutzer Peter s Peter, Shoreditch, Mdx, victualler to John Litchfield 6 Aug 1711 <6 Feb 1715/6 turned over to Benjamin Anderton, citizen and blacksmith>
Style Francis s Francis, Sunbury, Mdx, yeoman to Lancelot Vibert 24 May 1714
Styles John s John, Winterbourne Monkton, Wil, yeoman to William Booth 24 Nov 1635
Subden John s Edward, Durrington, Wil, yeoman to Nicholas Haydon 24 Jun 1648
Subden Mathew s Edward, Durrington, Wil, yeoman to Nicholas Haydon 24 Jun 1648
Sudger Robert s Robert, St Luke Old Street, Mdx, turner to William Hedgeland 19 Dec 1760
Sudley John s James, Chingford, Ess, barber chirurgeon to John Adams 28 Feb 1671/2
Suffild John s John, Evesham, Wor, butcher to Samuel Withers 4 May 1702
Sugar Thomas s John, citizen and merchant tailor† to John Carter 6 Nov 1710
Sumart Thomas s Orpheus, citizen and tallow chandler† to George Partridge 6 Oct 1724
Summers William s John to his father 3 May 1708
Surman Jonathan s John, Christ Church Southwark, coal merchant to William Surman 4 Jul 1698
Surson Joseph s Nicholas, Holborn, Mdx, baker to Richard Williams 4 Jul 1709
Sussex Andrew s Giles, East Ilsley, Brk, blacksmith to John Sussex 4 Feb 1711/12
Sussex John s Thomas, Ilsley, Brk [*in Ms* 'Ssx'], blacksmith to Joseph Coggs 4 Feb 1678/9
Suter John s Robert, Salisbury, Wil, waggoner to John Tovey 5 Jul 1725
Sutton David s Robert, Lutterworth, Lei, yeoman to Francis Tunstedd 2 Jan 1676/7
Sutton Edmund s John, Southwark, Sry, finedrawer† to Jonathan Eade 6 Sep 1791
Sutton Edward s Bernard, Scrooby, Ntt, gentleman to William Knight 22 Feb 1648/9
<bond from Beaumont Sutton, East Retford, Ntt, gentleman>
Sutton John s Thomas, St Giles Cripplegate, Mdx, labourer† to Robert Bly 11 Mar 1696/7
Sutton John s John to his father 6 Aug 1722 <4 Jul 1726 turned over to William Tally>
Sutton Nathaniel s Stephen, Wherwell, Ham, yeoman to John Hooker 24 Jun 1634
Sutton Stephen s Stephen, Wherwell, Ham, yeoman to Nathaniel Sutton 23 Nov 1657
Sutton Thomas s John, citizen and haberdasher to Thomas Obbinson 3 Dec 1711 <turned over to Thomas Higgins, citizen and leatherseller; 2 Jul 1716 turned over to Richard Washborne, citizen and bowyer>
Swaddle Stephen s Stephen, Limehouse, Mdx, mariner† to Thomas Merriman 4 Jun 1776
Swaine Thomas s Edward, St Saviour Southwark, Sry, carpenter to William Gulliford 8 May 1716
Swallowe Philip s Ralph, Duston, Nth, tailor to Simon Dawson 1 Feb 1636/7
Swanbrough Timothy s Richard, Devizes, Wil, salesman to John Garbrand 15 Nov 1705
Swann James s John, Lewes, Ssx, maltster† to William Proudman 15 Jul 1699 <2 Mar 1702/3 turned over to Giles Hawes>
Sweeper John s Samuel, citizen and clothworker† to Richard Collier 15 Oct 1708
Sweeting John s Thomas, Runwell, Ess, yeoman to John Wood 31 Oct 1648
Swift William s William, Pontefract, Yks, grazier to William Mellor 17 May 1697
Swifte John s Isaac, Lnd, haberdasher† to Philip Peirson 25 Mar 1657
Swifte Robert s William, Meopham, Ken, gentleman to Francis Zouch 9 Mar 1681/2
Swinnock Caleb s Joseph, Lnd, clerk to Humphrey Rogers 14 Oct 1678
Syer John s Erasmus, Lnd, tobacconist to William Havens 4 Mar 1722/3
Syer Thomas s Thomas, Aylesbury Street, Clerkenwell, gentleman to Richard Wiggins 4 Jun 1782
Symmes Thomas s Thomas, Coventry, War, gentleman to John Archer 20 May 1634
Symonds Thomas s John, Bermondsey, Sry, mariner to Daniel Benge 7 Apr 1665
Syms Edmund s John, citizen and tallow chandler to Francis Houghton 14 Jul 1685

Talbot Caleb s Caleb, Leeds, Yks, maltster to Thomas Prentice 7 May 1763
Talbot Caleb s Caleb, West Smithfield, Mdx, cheesemonger to his father 6 May 1788
Talbot John s Caleb, Leeds, Yks, maltster to Caleb Talbot 9 May 1769
Talbott Joseph s Joseph, Brewham, Som, yeoman† to Thomas Kender 13 Aug 1664
Talley William s William, Evercreech, Som, yeoman to Samuel Bexhill 5 Mar 1704/5

Tanner John s William, Paddington, Mdx to Nathaniel Mathews 3 Aug 1791
Tanner Joseph s Thomas, Uxbridge, Mdx, tanner to John Burgis 5 Sep 1677
Tanner Stephen s Stephen, Lydyard, Wil, yeoman to Thomas Rust 20 Jun 1689
Tapp James s James, Ship Alley, Wellclose Square, Mdx, victualler to Thomas Uffington 4 Sep 1800 <4 Jun 1801 turned over to David Gibbs>
Tapp John s John, St James Clerkenwell, Mdx, higler† to Anthony Bunn 25 Jan 1669/70
Tapper John s Robert, Shoreditch, Mdx, ironmonger† to John Chewter 6 Feb 1720/1
Tappin John s Samuel, citizen and cook to George Wightman 8 Mar 1717/8 <3 Aug 1719 turned over to Bartholomew Wimberley>
Tarrant Nicholas s Nicholas, Great Bedwin, Wil, yeoman to John Harris 25 Aug 1647
Tasker Gillingham s John, Deptford, Ken, waterman to Dalby Feild 2 Jul 1733 <5 Mar 1735/6 turned over to Samuel Wheeler>
Tatton Thomas s Mathew, St Botolph Aldgate, Lnd, gentleman to John Tovey 3 Dec 1733
Taverner George s George, Holborn, Mdx, tailor† to Joseph Rydout 5 Sep 1680
Tavey John s Nathaniel, Church Lench, Wor, yeoman to William Freeman 12 Nov 1711
Tayler David s John, Didcot, Brk, yeoman to Thomas Obbinson 3 Aug 1713 <turned over to Edward Tomkins, citizen and cutler>
Tayler Edward s Edward, Finchley, Mdx, clerk† to John Goode 12 Jul 1661
Tayler Edward s Richard, Brailes, War, ropemaker to John Edden 16 Dec 1673
Tayler George s Nicholas, Wimborne, Dor, clerk† to William Hunt 18 Jan 1693/4
Tayler John s John, Harrow, Mdx, yeoman to Thomas Givers 16 May 1661
Tayler John s Robert, Burford, Oxf, yeoman to Thomas Cole 1 Aug 1692
Tayler John s Francis, Stanmore, Mdx, yeoman to Brian Aylife 8 Jan 1693/4
Tayler Joseph s Joseph, Spitalfields, Mdx, shoemaker to Richard Carter 10 Apr 1744
Tayler Michael s Michael, Savoy, Mdx, carpenter to William Owen 10 Jun 1693
Tayler Peter s John, 'Morting', Ssx, yeoman to Thomas Messenger 5 Oct 1713
Tayler Richard s Thomas, Higham, Ken, weaver to Thomas Cryer 19 Aug 1690
Tayler Robert s John, Lnd, gentleman† to Samuel Coleman 25 Jan 1685/6
Tayler Robert s Robert, Roxby, Lin, yeoman† to Edward Harris 6 May 1689
Tayler Thomas s John, Biggleswade, Bdf, grocer to Thomas Prentice 4 Sep 1732
Taylor Benjamin s Joseph, Spitalfields, Mdx, cordwainer to Joseph Taylor 5 Apr 1753
Taylor Charles William to William Walton 4 Dec 1798
Taylor Francis s Francis, Great Stanmore, Mdx, kidder to Benjamin Munn 12 Dec 1690
Taylor Francis s John, Watford, Hrt, tallow chandler† to John Hill 5 Jan 1736/7
Taylor George s John, Worcester, Wor, mercer† to John Castleton 26 Jan 1656/7
Taylor George s George, 'Lopera', Lan, yeoman to John Hobs 25 Aug 1662
Taylor George s Thomas, St George, Mdx, tobacconist to Valentine Winkle 6 May 1777
Taylor John s Charles, St Katherine by the Tower, victualler to William Haydon 22 Feb 1682/3
Taylor John s Richard, Bradford, Wil, farmer† to John Wilson 1 Feb 1737/8
Taylor John s Thomas, St Luke Old Street, Mdx, chocolate maker to Joseph Taylor 3 Oct 1759
Taylor John William s William, St Martin le Grand, Lnd, painter to William Easton 1 Jul 1794
Taylor Joseph s Thomas, citizen and joiner to Christopher Leake 7 Jun 1655
Taylor Richard s Thurston, 'Anslarke', Lan, yeoman to Oliver Geery 20 Nov 1656
Taylor Thomas s Thomas, Austrey, War, yeoman to Francis Dyson 1 Aug 1650
Taylor Thomas s John, Great Stanmore, Mdx, yeoman to Thomas Cole 4 Oct 1688
Taylor William s John, Fulham, Mdx, yeoman to Henry Wheeler 29 Jun 1696
Taylor William s Lawrence, St Clement Danes, Mdx, tailor to Philip Pickering 12 Nov 1722
Taylor William s William, Lambeth, Sry, shoemaker to Thomas Clarke 20 Dec 1770
Taylour Thomas s Richard, Southminster, Ess, clerk to George Clare 30 Apr 1670
Taylour William s John, Harrow, Mdx, carpenter† to Thomas Givers 6 Mar 1670/1
Tayne James s James, Stepney, Mdx, weaver to John Knowles 18 Dec 1706
Teale James s John, Yanworth, Gls, yeoman to Richard Reynolds 7 Jan 1683/4
Teale John s Dositheus, citizen and barber surgeon to Thomas Searle 4 Sep 1721
Tedder Edward s Edward, Shadwell, Mdx, barber to James Tetley 8 Dec 1712
Tegg Francis s John, Beddington, Sry, yeoman to Robert Bradley 25 Nov 1645
Temple Christopher s Christopher, Frome, Som, weaver to Andrew Godwin 16 Jun 1682
Temple Purbeck s John, Biddlesden, Bkm, knight† to William Palmer 9 May 1640
Tentor William s William, citizen and butcher† to William Haydon 26 Mar 1689

Terrell Edward s Edward, Beddington, Sry, farrier† to Francis Tegg 14 Nov 1668
Terrell Richard s William, Hagborne, Brk, yeoman to Edward Walker 5 Aug 1691
Terrell William s Richard, Trowbridge, Wil,. butcher to William Collier 9 Feb 1707/8 <7 Dec 1713 turned over to Mary Mander, widow>
Territt John s Daniel, Uley, Gls, weaver to Joseph Wedgbrough 1 Sep 1729
Tetley Henry s James to his father 2 Apr 1722
Tetley James s Henry, Ashby de la Zouch, Lei, potter† to Robert Driver 22 Aug 1691
Thacker Thomas s Joseph, St Marylebone, Mdx, vintner to George Harlow 1 Aug 1765 <7 Mar 1768 turned over to William Worthington, citizen and goldsmith>
Thatcher Charles s Robert, Wormshill, Ken, gentleman to William Thatcher 8 Jun 1681
Thatcher James s James, Limehouse, Mdx, cooper to John Palmer 29 Oct 1649
Thatcher Samuel s ?, Frome, Som, yeoman† to John Ride 27 Jan 1668/9
Thatcher Thomas s Thomas, Stepney, Mdx, mariner† to Richard Hughes 7 Mar 1697/8
Thatcher William s Thomas, Hollingbourne, Ken, gentleman† to Peter Pickering 31 Jan 1660/1
Thatcher William s Nicholas, Appledore, Ken, gentleman† to William Thatcher 27 Apr 1678
Thatcher William s Robert, Wormshill, Ken, gentleman to William Thatcher 6 Jul 1685
Thatcher William s John, Allington, Ken, gentleman† to Charles Thatcher 7 Dec 1702
Thayer James s William, Mitcham, Sry, wheelwright† to John Hills 10 Jun 1723
Thead William s Hugh, citizen and glover to Sarah widow of Thomas Chambers 5 May 1701 <22 Oct 1702 turned over to Thomas Chambers; 18 Oct 1705 to John Naseby, citizen and clothworker>
Theobald Robert s Francis, Barking, Sfk, knight to William Garfoote 7 Apr 1676
Thomas Ann d Nicholas, Wallop, Ham, gentleman to Jeremiah Broadgate 9 May 1678
Thomas Arthur s William, Whitchurch, Sal, baker to Jonathan Leigh 1 Dec 1747
Thomas Charles s Richard, Enfield, Mdx, yeoman† to Charles Thompson 10 Jan 1749/50
Thomas David s David, 'Dongay', Mgy, yeoman to Richard Ayres 12 Aug 1696
Thomas John s Daniel, St James Clerkenwell, Mdx, ciderman to John Burborrough 24 Jan 1708/9
Thomas Robert s Evan, St Vedast, Lnd, yeoman to John Caddy 2 Sep 1709
Thomas Simon s Thomas, 'Lannedon', Den, yeoman to Humphrey King 25 Sep 1668
Thomas Thomas ap William ap s William ap Thomas ap William, Monmouth, Mon† to John Pritchard 29 Sep 1641
Thomason George s Roger, Gorstella [Dodleston], Chs, yeoman to John Woods 17 Jul 1657
Thompson Charles s Thomas, Waltham Abbey, Ess, gardener to Thomas Higgins 1 Feb 1719/20
Thompson Charles s John, Holborn, Mdx, perukemaker† to William Hedgeland 31 Oct 1761
Thompson Daniel s Daniel, Marston St Lawrence, Nth, husbandman to Peter Champney 23 Nov 1652
Thompson Edward s Samuel, Barby, Nth, yeoman to Henry Lathwell 26 Oct 1678
Thompson Isaac s John, Sulgrave, Nth, gentleman to Ann widow of Thomas Saul 16 Mar 1636/7
Thompson James s James, Waltham Cross, Hrt to John Bryan 4 Sep 1800
Thompson John s Robert, Thornton, Yks, yeoman to John Burton 26 Dec 1634
Thompson John s John, citizen and weaver to James Wood 19 Oct 1658
Thompson John s John, St Clement Danes, Mdx, tailor to Charles Thatcher 4 Nov 1695
Thompson John s Robert, Barnet, Hrt, yeoman to Lancelot Kerby 5 Aug 1723 <2 Dec 1728 turned over to John Sibley
Thompson Mathew s Mathew, Reigate, Sry, yeoman† to Thomas Tully 6 Jul 1742
Thompson Miles s John, Cambridge, Cam, yeoman to Thomas Kelk 5 Feb 1634/5
Thompson Richard s Thomas, Limehouse, Mdx, shipwright to Francis Marshall 7 Dec 1671
Thompson Robert s William, citizen and haberdasher to Thomas Stevenson 21 Jun 1680
Thompson Samuel s John, Waltham Abbey, Ess, grocer to John Bryan 6 Sep 1796
Thompson William s Robert, Spitalfields, barber and perukemaker† to James Collyer 8 Apr 1727
Thompson William s Thomas, Black Notley, Ess, farmer to Benjamin Crackanthorp 5 Mar 1746/7
Thomson Brian s Brian, 'Farneham', Con, merchant to Richard Joyce 12 Apr 1686
Thorley Benjamin s William, St Margaret Westminster, labourer† to Richard Ladbrooke 4 Oct 1743
Thorly John s John, Chipping Norton, Oxf, gentleman to Thomas Obbinson 5 Mar 1710/11 <turned over to Robert Shelley, citizen and skinner>
Thornbury John s William, Dagenham, Ess, husbandman to Ralph Humfreys 11 Jan 1646/7
Thorne George s John, Winchcombe, Gls, yeoman to Thomas Dowdeswell 7 May 1694
Thorne Richard s John, Crowcombe, Som, yeoman to Thomas Stone 6 Nov 1668

Thorneborough Thomas s Thomas, Worcester, Wor, gentleman† to John Skeate 10 Jan 1639/40

Thornell Robert s Joseph, citizen and blacksmith to Samuel Osborne 9 Sep 1706 <5 Feb 1710/11 turned over to Daniel Collier, citizen and fishmonger>

Thornton Benjamin s Benjamin, Langley Marish, Bkm, yeoman to William Collier 2 Oct 1710

Thornton Richard s Giles, citizen and butcher to Thomas Styles 3 Aug 1650

Thoroughgood Thomas s Augustine, Owersby [? *in Ms* 'Hersby'], Lin, yeoman† to James Clark 13 Jan 1633/4

Thorowgood Andrew s Martin, citizen and plumber† to John Rowland 4 Apr 1667

Thorp Humphrey s William, Tatenhill, Sts† to Henry Cox 16 Nov 1641

Thorp James s James, Isleworth, Mdx, miller† to James Vaughan 3 Dec 1793

Thorp Robert s Robert, Gaddesby, Lei† to Edward Copeland 3 Feb 1706/7

Thorpe Robert s John, Lnd, grocer† to Robert Udall 30 Apr 1650

Threader William s Samuel, Hemel Hempstead, Hrt, yeoman† to John Hooker 12 Nov 1663

Thumwood John s William, Basingstoke, Ham, butcher† to Thomas Allen 17 Aug 1654

Thurgood William s John, Limehouse, wheeler and trunnel maker to Joseph Easton 6 Mar 1800

Thurketle Charles s John, St James Westminster, Mdx, gentleman to Lancelot Vibart 15 Feb 1703/4

Thurkittle Benjamin s William, Lnd, tailor to Stephen Champion 13 Nov 1696

Thurlby Sharp to William Thurlby 3 Oct 1799

Thurlby William s William, Wapping, Mdx, tallow chandler to Charles Dare 6 Jan 1789

Thurly James s John, St Olave Southwark, Sry, yeoman† to Edward Radcliffe 14 Feb 1663/4

Thurston Richard s Richard, Cheshunt, Hrt to Thomas Young 1633

Thurston Richard s Richard, Cheshunt, Hrt, gentleman to Thomas Younge 20 Nov 1643

Thurstone William s Richard, 'Egerton', Hun, yeoman† to Mary widow of Thomas Rencher 17 Sep 1706

Tibbetts Joel s John, Cheddar, Som, tallow chandler to Andrew Godwin 7 Apr 1682

Tickford Henry s John, South Mimms, Mdx, yeoman† to William White 2 Oct 1711

Tickner John s William, Weybridge, Sry, tanner to John Syms 25 Mar 1679

Tidd Samuel s Samuel, Sundon, Bdf, yeoman to William Prentice 26 Apr 1655

Tillar Richard s John to his father 2 Oct 1693

Tilley Edward s Robert, Chesham, Bkm to John Hunt 9 Apr 1635

Tilly John s Christopher, Grandborough, War, clerk to Philip Goodwin 13 Aug 1686

Tilston John s John, citizen and clothworker to Joseph Addams 11 May 1657

Timberlake Ralph s Robert, Bushey, Hrt, yeoman to Richard Wilkinson 30 Oct 1652

Timbrell Robert s Robert, Poole, Wil, glover to Henry Simond 20 Dec 1634

Timson Thomas s Thomas, citizen and haberdasher† to William Peele 2 Aug 1694

Tipping John s Robert, Oxford, Oxf, shoemaker to Samuel Brooker 1 Oct 1650

Tirrell Francis s Francis, Harrold, Bdf [? *in Ms* 'Brk'], farmer to Francis Leech 28 Sep 1761

Titley Thomas s James to his father 7 Sep 1742

Tockfield John s William, Chartridge [Chesham], Bkm, yeoman to Joseph Tockfield 5 Mar 1673/4

Todd Thomas s Henry, Windsor Court, Strand, Mdx, gentleman to John Close 7 Sep 1779

Todd William s William, ..., Dev, clerk to John Mathews 15 Jun 1647 <cancelled>

Tokefeild Richard s Richard, Chesham, Bkm, innholder to Richard Butterfeild 9 Aug 1658

Tokefield Joseph s John, Chesham, Bkm, husbandman to Francis Tunsteed 14 Feb 1666/7

Toldervey Thomas s Thomas, Leominster, Hef, clothier to Samuel Pitts 23 Jul 1747

Toldeway James s Thomas, Leominster, Hef, clothier to Samuel Pitts 17 Feb 1752

Tolson Gregory s Richard, Bridekirk, Cul, gentleman to Thomas Lawrence 13 Jul 1675

Tombs Jacob s Bartholomew, citizen and upholder† to Richard Warren 9 Jun 1707

Tomkins Benjamin s John, Abingdon, Brk, butcher to John Tomkins 3 Jun 1734 <6 Jul 1737 turned over to John Chapman, citizen and merchant tailor>

Tomkins Edward s Joseph, citizen and salter to William Harrison 6 Jul 1713

Tomkins Edward s Benjamin, citizen and butcher to Henry Hawkins 4 Mar 1716/7

Tomkins Edward s John to his father 16 Jan 1749/50

Tomkins William s Edward, citizen and joiner to Robert Dove 7 Jul 1712

Tomlins Edward s Edward, citizen and merchant tailor to Bartholomew Peele 2 Jul 1662

Tomlins Joseph s Joseph, West Ham, Ess, miller to Samuel Cox 3 Dec 1716 <4 May 1719 master† turned over by John Meyer, citizen and mercer, administrator to Thomas Marlar, citizen and haberdasher>

Tomlinson Benjamin s John, Barlby [? *in Ms* 'Barley'], Yks, gentleman to Francis Molineux 2 Nov 1683

Tomlinson William s Joseph, Lambeth, Sry, waterman to George Searle 6 Dec 1774

Tomlinson William s William, Denmark Street, Mdx, joiner to Thomas Jarvis 3 Jul 1781

Tomlison John s William, Howden, Yks, brickmaker to Samuel Fitch 4 Oct 1714

Tompkins John s John, Abingdon, Brk, butcher to Isaac Price 1 Jul 1723

Tompson William s John, 'Maddwellay', Lan, carpenter to Peter Duff 28 Sep 1669

Tong Thomas s German, citizen and merchant tailor† to Philip Peirson 12 May 1654

Tonge Edward s James, Tunstall [*no county given*], gentleman to Joseph Wicks 24? Oct 1672

Tonge William s John?, citizen and merchant tailor to John Caldwell 25 Apr 1663

Toogood John s George, citizen and joiner to John Radburne 2 May 1709

Tooth Edward s John, Sundridge, Ken, yeoman to William Massey 4 Dec 1691

Toovey William s John, Nettlebed, Oxf, yeoman to Daniel Scott 28 Jun 1710

Toovey William s Robert, Brightwell, Oxf, yeoman to Elizabeth widow of Robert Gresswell 13 May 1708

Topott John s Thomas, Leicester, Lei, gentleman† to Francis Coare 15 Aug 1701 <12 Dec 1704 turned over to Nicholas Greene, citizen and bowyer>

Tourll Samuel s Thomas, Lewes, Ssx, butcher to Thomas Stonestreete 6 Nov 1663

Tovey Daniel s William, Henley, Oxf, maltster to Daniel Dale 8 Sep 1685

Tovey Jephthah s Benjamin, citizen and carpenter† to John Harrison 4 Jul 1698

Tovey John s Thomas, Salisbury, Wil, coachman to John Tomes 9 Jun 1668

Tovey Timothy s Charles, Cropthorne, Wor, farmer to Abraham Farren 31 Jul 1758

Tovy Andrew s Henry, Corton [Portesham], Dor, yeoman to William Gibson 24 Jan 1633/4

Tovy Joseph s Charles, Tewkesbury, Gls, maltster to Walter Hore 16 Jan 1684/5

Towler Thomas s Josias, Malham Waterhouses, Yks, yeoman† to Francis Molyneux 4 Oct 1688

Towne John s William, Thame, Oxf, yeoman to Richard Towne 3 May 1697

Towne Richard s William, Thame, Oxf, yeoman to John Back 22 Apr 1686

Townesend Edward s Edward, Lambeth, Sry, yeoman to Mathew Peirce 3 Nov 1686

Townesend Henry s Richard, Soho, Mdx, blacksmith to Edward Mortimer 10 Oct 1710

Townesend John s John, 'Kainton', Gls, yeoman to Richard Parrott 1 Jul 1674

Townsend George s John to his father 3 Feb 1695/6

Townsend Horatio s William, Badsey, Wor, gentleman to Richard Parrott 25 Jul 1676

Townsend James s George, St Sepulchre, Lnd, leatherseller to Thomas Jervis 2 Nov 1769

Townsend John s John to his father 11 Nov 1700

Townsend John s John, Clerkenwell, Mdx, cheesemonger† to John Townsend 3 Jul 1732 <7 Aug 1732 turned over to Rebecca widow of Edward Bentley, citizen and cordwainer>

Townsend William s Joseph, Whitechapel, Mdx, chandler† to John Greene 1 May 1675

Townsend William s William to his father 1 Feb 1713/4

Toy Richard s Richard, Richmond, Sry, grocer to Thomas Bord 8 Jan 1766

Toye John s Thomas, Enville, Sts, bricklayer to Ann Hamon, widow 15 May 1642

Traharne William s Samuel, St James Clerkenwell, Mdx, tailor to Dorothy widow of William Symons 30 May 1650

Tratt Henry s Warner, Redbourne, Hrt, pastor† to Paul Meadowes 27 Oct 1668

Traunter Samuel s Thomas, citizen and founder to Randolph Watson 16 May 1689

Traveis Edmund s James, Whitechapel, Mdx, gentleman to Nicholas Beckitt 1 Sep 1670

Travis Joseph s William, 'Harblin', Lei, yeoman to Gilbert Cornelius 14 Dec 1650

Trawton William s John, Oxney [Peterborough], Nth, yeoman to Thomas Stiells 25 Mar 1643

Trenchard George s George, Dorchester, Dor, esquire to Nicholas Gould 24 Feb 1675/6

Tresham Clever s Maurice, citizen and poulterer to Thomas Hopkins 7 Jan 1716/7

Trewell William s Thomas, citizen and woodmonger to Benjamin Rawlins 25 Mar 1635

Trigg Henry s Henry, Dorking, Sry, tallow chandler to Joseph Gibbons 30 May 1668

Trinder John s Francis, Faringdon, Brk, maltster to Jeremiah Ridge 7 Oct 1700

Tripp Samuel s Samuel, Beaconsfield, Bkm, gentleman to Peter Rolts 16 Jun 1730

Tripp William s Samuel, Chipping Wycombe, Bkm, scrivener to Joseph Loadman 6 Sep 1703 <4 Mar 1705/6 turned over to William Andrews>

Trippett John s Richard, Awre, Gls, gentleman to Thomas Bennett 5 Aug 1695

Trobridge Joseph s George, Kenton, Dev, esquire† to Charles Doiley 18 Jan 1646/7 <bond from George Trobridge, Inner Temple, Lnd, gentleman>

Trotman John s Nicholas, Cam, Gls, gentleman to Mathew Walker 23 Jan 1676/7
Trott Edward s Richard, Saffron Walden, Ess, farrier to Ezekiel Trott 19 Dec 1664
Trott Ezekiel s Ezekiel, Saffron Walden, Ess, farrier to Joseph Sibley 9 Jul 1650
Trott John s Robert, South Mimms, Mdx, victualler to Anthony Bun 2 Jul 1660
Trowell Francis s Edward, Ratcliffe on Soar, Ntt, yeoman to Nicholas Beckitt 29 Dec 1653
Truelock Thomas s Arthur, Marsh Gibbon, Bkm, tanner† to William Dickins 1 Sep 1664
Trueman Samuel s Thomas, Nottingham, Ntt, gentleman to John Child 6 May 1695
Trumplin Arthur s Thomas, Christian Malford, Wil, gentleman to Thomas Young 2 Feb 1641/2
Tucker James s James, Poplar, Mdx, mariner† to John Eyre 7 Apr 1707
Tucker Joseph s William, Limehouse, Mdx to James Wignall 20 Dec 1775
Tucker William s John, St Clement Danes, Mdx, gardener to John Noble 15 Jun 1640
Tuder John s Henry, citizen and draper† to John Pratt 18 Jun 1680
Tue Thomas s Thomas, Sawston, Cam, yeoman to John Pricke 28 Aug 1643
Tulley Benjamin s John, Ardingley, Ssx, yeoman to William Smith 30 Oct 1678
Tully Thomas s John, Bermondsey, Sry, carpenter† to George Carpenter 3 Oct 1726
Tunsted Francis s James, Beeley, Dby, gentleman to Thomas Styles 5 May 1653
Tunsted Robert s James, Beeley, Dby, gentleman to Thomas Styles 24 Mar 1655/6
Turbervill Samuel s Samuel, Twyning, Gls, tanner to Roger Rymmer 20 Feb 1640/1
Turbutt Benjamin s Benjamin, citizen and vintner to Richard Kerby 7 May 1722
Turner Addington s Charles, Stepney, Mdx, mariner† to John Eyre 6 Feb 1715/6 <18 Dec 1718 turned over to Benjamin Clark>
Turner Edward s Edward, Grafton, Nth, husbandman† to Anthony Bun 6 Sep 1647
Turner Henry s Samuel, citizen and vintner to Thomas Obinson 27 Oct 1668
Turner James s William, St Luke Old Street, Mdx, wiredrawer† to Alexander Weedon 23 Nov 1749
Turner John s John to his father 29 Mar 1677
Turner John s Edward, Hartfield, Ssx, yeoman to William Cranwell 16 Jul 1678
Turner John s John, Leicester, Lei, dyer to Radclifff Baddily 13 Aug 1753
Turner John s Edward, Dorking, Sry, carrier to James Jenner 5 Jul 1764
Turner Joseph s Thomas, Westminster, Mdx, tailor† to William Miller 26 Nov 1668
Turner Mary d William, Walberton, Ssx, clerk† to Randolph Morgan 15 Sep 1702
Turner Richard s Richard, St Marylebone, Mdx, locksmith to Isaac Price 4 Oct 1743 <25 Oct 1743 turned over to Thomas Hales, citizen and blacksmith>
Turner Samuel s William, Fawsley, Nth, husbandman to Samuel Brooker 4 Sep 1646
Turner Samuel s John, Walthamstow, Ess, plumber to Benjamin Brecknell 6 Nov 1800
Turner Thomas s Francis, Westminster, Mdx, gentleman† to Thomas Hatton 7 Oct 1650
Turner Thomas s Thomas, Holt, Chs, husbandman† to Richard Worrall 4 May 1688
Turner William s William, All Hallows London Wall, Lnd, yeoman to Edward Knott 13 Aug 1657
Turnerley William s Francis, Leominster, Hef, maltster to William Collier 24 Sep 1677
Turnish Henry s John, White Notley, Ess, yeoman to William Hulls 3 Jul 1702 <10 Nov 1708 turned over by Mary Hulls, exec. to John Osgood>
Turpin Edward s Edward, Bassingbourn, Cam, gentleman to Peter Pickering 22 Nov 1660
Turpin James s William, citizen and haberdasher to Richard Wright 22 Jan 1667/8
Turvey Charles s John, St Katherine by the Tower, Mdx, butcher to Thomas Gilson 6 Apr 1748
Turvey Henry s John, St Katherine by the Tower, Mdx, butcher to Thomas Gibson 3 May 1738
Turvey Thomas s Thomas, St Botolph Aldgate, Mdx, cooper† to Joseph Lucas 7 Nov 1750
Turvine John s George, Hammersmith, Mdx, yeoman to Robert Moss 21 Mar 1655/6
Tustian Richard s Richard, South Newington, Oxf, yeoman† to Richard Burnby 26 Nov 1657
Tuther Joseph John s Thomas, New Road, Mdx, gentleman† to Thomas Jarvis 3 Aug 1784
Tuting Samuel s Samuel, Greenwich, Ken, gentleman to Richard Walker 15 Jun 1719
Twell John s Christopher, Great Hale, Lin, husbandman to Isaac Thompson 24 Jan 1648/9
Twiford Robert s Henry, Barton, Gls, esquire to Marmaduke Doleman 15 Aug 1634
Twining John s John, Graseley, Brk, yeoman to Edward Leman 29 Sep 1690
Twisdell Thomas s Thomas, coachman† to Edward Tomlin 12 Oct 1675
Twisleton Anthony s Brian, Maidwell, Nth, gentleman to Thomas Kelke 30 Jul 1635
Twittey William s John, Claines, Wor, yeoman† to John Child 19 Feb 1668/9
Twyford Henry s Henry, Willesden, Mdx, yeoman† to John Franck 13 Nov 1639
Tye Anthony s Richard, citizen and pinmaker to Michael Maisters 7 Jun 1666
Tyer John s Nicholas, Winchester, Ham, linen draper to Humphrey Hill 7 Jul 1640

Tyler Richard s Thomas, Barking, Ess, fisherman to Robert Lloyd 7 Nov 1775 <6 Jul 1779 turned over to Alan Parsons>
Tyler, Merat alias Robert s Robert, Ushant, Wil, yeoman† to Edward Skinner 5 Feb 1693/4
Tyler Thomas s Thomas, Nutfield, Sry, yeoman to Richard Bull 6 Jul 1648
Tyler William s Richard, Two Waters [Hemel], Hrt, papermaker to Joseph Sherwin 4 Apr 1786
Tyndell Horatio s William, citizen and cordwainer to Joseph Huntman 7 Apr 1680
Tyrer Godwin s Thomas, Sellack, Hef, doctor in divinity to Samuel Jaines 30 Apr 1678
Tyrrell William s Timothy, Oakley, Bkm, knight† to Richard Miller 5 Mar 1635/6
Tyson Thomas s Nicholas, Ipswich, Sfk, butcher to John Tyson 4 Mar 1657/8

Udall Edmund s Robert to his father 6 Jul 1670
Udall Henry s Thomas, St Margaret Westminster, Mdx, corn chandler to Henry Wine 4 Mar 1694/5
Uffington John s John, Homerton, Mdx, coal merchant to William Proudman 3 Feb 1778
Uffington Thomas s John, Hackney, Mdx, stationer† to James Wilkie 5 Jun 1792
Underwood Joseph s Thomas, citizen and cooper to Elizabeth widow of John Rutt 19 Jul 1709 <3 Aug 1713 turned over to William Townsend>
Underwood Thomas s Joseph† to John Compton 25 Jun 1750
Upington Robert s George, Puddington, Dev, yeoman to John Sampson 13 Sep 1669
Upston Richard s Richard, Bugbrooke, Nth, blacksmith† to Jegon Mandivell 5 Dec 1698
Upton John s George, Saxondale, Ntt, labourer to Joseph Barlow 6 Dec 1764
Urmston William s Roger, Cliffords Inn, Lnd, gentleman to Thomas Turner 21 Dec 1633
Urree Isaac s Ralph, Whitechapel, Mdx, yeoman to James Harding 19 Jul 1655
Usher George s George, Boars Head Court, Gracechurch Street, poulterer to Joseph Phelps 7 Aug 1798
Usher Thomas s Thomas, Great Ilford, Ess, victualler to Richard Hodgskin 28 Jan 1666/7

Vandesten Daniel s Paul, Mortlake, Sry, weaver to Richard Sparrow 25 Nov 1657
Varin Benjamin s Benjamin, Bristol, Gls, goldsmith† to John Johnson 9 Dec 1714
Varney John s Simon, Battersea, Sry, farrier† to Henry Cox 6 Dec 1649
Varnon Francis s Francis, Lnd, cook to John Turner 8 Nov 1697
Vassall Francis s Francis, citizen and draper to William Miller 20 Aug 1674
Vaughan Francis s Francis, Chelsea, Mdx, waterman to Thomas Kendar 22 Oct 1655
Vaughan Thomas s Francis, Chelsea, Mdx, waterman to Ralph Butterfeild 17 Mar 1646/7
Vaughan William s William, Lambeth Marsh, Sry, carpenter† to Joseph Sherwin 4 Nov 1788
Vaux Joseph s Thomas, Pirton, Hrt, yeoman to John Veyland 22 Mar 1679/80
Vaux Richard s Richard, St Sepulchre, Lnd, coachman to William Cranwell 22 Aug 1674
Veale George s Charles, Wollaston, Nth, mercer to Richard Weston 4 Apr 1717
Venner Samuel s Richard, citizen and haberdasher to Richard Ingram 19 Oct 1686
Ventrice Henry s Henry, East Clandon, Sry, tailor to Richard Fullwood 8 Aug 1709
Ventrys Thomas s Edward, Great Shelford, Cam, esquire† to Roger Price 29 Jan 1646/7
Verdon William s William, Nottingham, Ntt, butcher to William Wood 6 Aug 1650
Vere William s William, Littledean, Gls, yeoman† to Thomas Baynard 5 Dec 1683
Vernon George s ..., Lutterworth, Lei, yeoman to William Simcock 19 Nov 1633
Vesey James s Jonathan, citizen and grocer to John Sole 24 Jan 1664/5
Vibart Lancelot s Lancelot, citizen and feltmaker to Jeremiah Ridge 5 Sep 1692
Vibart Uriah s George, citizen and feltmaker to William Wright 5 Sep 1698
Vibert James s James, St Margaret Westminster, Mdx, wine cooper† to Lancelot Vibart 5 Jul 1743
Vicary Mary d Thomas, Westminster, Mdx, linen draper to Jeremiah Bradgate 18 Sep 1700
Vie Henry s Thomas, Drayton, Lei, tailor† to Mathew Barwell 4 Aug 1707 <22 Jan 1710/11 turned over to William Barwell, citizen and armorer>
Vincent William s John, Midhurst, Ssx, mercer to John Collington 1 Apr 1658
Vokins Avery s Robert, Sutton Wick [Drayton], Brk, yeoman† to William Gurney 30 Sep 1684
Vokins Avery s Thomas, St Margaret Westminster, tallow chandler to Avery Vokins 29 Sep 1743
Vokins Joseph s Robert, citizen and plumber to Robert Bly 3 Mar 1717/8
Vuatin James Theodore s Claudius, Piccadilly, Mdx, cook† to James Osborn 15 Apr 1790

Wace William s Francis, Stanton Harcourt, Oxf, cordwainer† to Samuel Withers 3 Feb 1679/80

Wackett William s Thomas, Hatfield, Hrt, husbandman† to William Cave 6 Jul 1737 <2 Mar 1742/3 master† turned over with consent of John Cookson, exec. to Solomon Sammons, citizen and wheelwright>
Waddington William s John, Wortley, Yks, wheelwright to William Fox 23 Jan 1638/9
Waddington William s William, Blaston, Lei, yeoman to Ann Hedges wife of William Gardiner otherwise Ann Hedges Warner 15 Apr 1754
Wade Humphrey s Thomas, St George the Martyr, Mdx, gentleman to Edward Fitz 18 Jul 1766
Wade Samuel s George, Mickleover, Dby, yeoman to John Greening 18 Jul 1698
Wadely Ellen d John, Westminster, Mdx, husbandman to Robert More 13 Jul 1647
Waight Richard s Richard, Lnd, tailor to Robert Rodway 2 Feb 1660/1
Waine John s Thomas, St James Clerkenwell, Mdx, labourer to James Coates 4 Jul 1749
Waite John s John, Orby, Lin, yeoman† to Anthony Mosely 30 Jun 1669
Waite William s Thomas, Abingdon, Brk, sacking weaver to John Stent 23 Jun 1759 <14 Jan 1762 master† turned over with consent of his widow Ann Stent to John Jones, citizen and goldsmith>
Waites John Frisbee s John, Ratcliffe, Mdx, lathmaker to John Frisbee 1 Jun 1779
Wake Thomas s John, Stratford on Avon, War, maltster to Thomas Higgins 13 Oct 1696
Wakelin Samuel s William, citizen and butcher† to Jonathan Hicks 7 May 1705
Waklyn John s John, Market Harborough, Lei, gentleman to Mary widow of William Minchin 29 Jan 1672/3
Walcott Thomas s John, Stockerston, Lei, gentleman to Gervase Beckett 16 Mar 1675/6
Walderne Thomas s Mathew, Romsey, Ham, shoemaker to Silvester Cordy 6 Apr 1654
Wale Benjamin s ..., 'Combe Lordship', War, grazier to George Wightman 2 Nov 1702
Wale Isaac s Richard, Romsey, Ham, clothier to Thomas Stone 13 Jul 1674 <bond of £400 against what his son might steal>
Wale Isaac s Richard, Romsey, Ham, clothier to John Jenkins 19 May 1676
Wale Michael s Miles, Lambeth, Sry, waterman to Cornelius Woolley 6 Aug 1722
Walke John s John, Barbados, gentleman to Richard Alexander 1 Apr 1760
Walker Charles s Richard to his father 13 Apr 1702
Walker Christopher s John, St Margaret Westminster, shoemaker† to Thomas Searle 4 Oct 1743
Walker Edward s Thomas, Thurvaston, Dby, gentleman to James Horton 8 Jan 1671/2
Walker Edward s Richard to his father 20 Jul 1705
Walker Francis s Peter, Tenbury, Wor, blacksmith to Peter Duff 8 Nov 1671
Walker John s John, Whitefriars, Lnd, yeoman to Mathew Bagg 28 Apr 1640
Walker John s William, citizen and clothworker to William Owen 24 Jul 1689
Walker John s Richard to his father 1 Jun 1702
Walker Lewin s Richard to his father 20 Jul 1705
Walker Mathew s John, Greenwich, Ken, husbandman to Samuel King 18 Jan 1663/4
Walker Nicholas s Thomas, St Martin in the Fields, Mdx, tallow chandler† to Thomas Obbinson 12 Apr 1708 <turned over to Edward Raworth, citizen and haberdasher>
Walker Richard s Edward, Greenwich, Ken, butcher to Thomas Watts 1 Sep 1675
Walker Richard s Richard to his father 11 Oct 1700
Walker Robert s Francis, Whitegate, Chs, yeoman to Andrew Partridge 26 Dec 1632
Walker Robert s Geoffrey, Sundridge, Ken, bricklayer to Henry Maundy 30 Jun 1636
Walker Robert s Robert, Rochdale, Lan, yeoman† to Robert Rodway 17 Jun 1652
Walker Vincent s John, citizen and fishmonger to Francis Rakestraw 20 Dec 1694
Walker William s Henry, Spoondon, Dby, blacksmith† to Peter Delight 23 Oct 1704
Walker Wingfield s Joseph, citizen and distiller to Jeremiah Ridge 3 Nov 1712
Wall John s John, Weymouth, Dor, mariner to Thomas Greene 3 Apr 1654
Wall William s John, Bromsberrow, Gls, saddler to John Pritchard 13 Jan 1651/2
Wallace William s James, Aston, Brk, clerk to William Cave 6 Feb 1720/1
Waller Henry s William, Tooting, Sry, butcher to James Jenner 6 Jul 1779
Waller James s William, Andover, Ham, grocer† to Thomas Dowdswell 13 Oct 1686
Waller John s Michael, Eton, Bkm, gentleman to Samuel King 18 Feb 1646/7
Wallis John s Elisha, citizen and stationer† to William Gurney 3 May 1676
Wallis Thomas s Thomas, Caldecote, Hun, yeoman to Thomas Addison 26 Jan 1664/5
Walrond Thomas s William, Brewham, Som, esquire to Roger Price .. May 1634
Walsall John s John, Barking, Ess, innholder† to Thomas Watts 2 May 1671
Walter Arthur s Richard, citizen and fishmonger to John Thompson 16 Sep 1703

Walter Richard s Richard, Adlestrop, Gls, yeoman to Walter Hoare 20 Feb 1676/7
Walters John s John, citizen and baker to Thomas Barker 1 Apr 1658
Walters Richard s Simon, Oswestry, Sal, yeoman to Margaret widow of William Smith 22 Oct 1661
Walters Thomas s Thomas, Newbury, Brk, weaver to William Minchin 16 Jul 1647
Walters Thomas s Thomas, Berkhamstead, Hrt, baker to Henry Sibley 15 Nov 1680
Walton George s John, citizen and feltmaker to Mathew Walker 18 Feb 1686/7
Walton Jeremiah s Robert, Wirksworth, Dby [*in Ms* 'Nth'], clothworker to Thomas Claro 29 Apr 1692
Walton John s John, New Parks, Lei, gentleman† to Benjamin Steevens 18 Dec 1680
Walton John s Uriah, York, Yks, yeoman to Joseph Blandford 1 Feb 1753
Walton Philip s Thomas, citizen and grocer† to Edward Leman 4 Jun 1683
Walwin John s John, Petersfield, Ham, clerk to John Sampson 23 Dec 1664
Wane Daniel s William, Arlington, Gls, yeoman to William Gaunt 2 Jun 1671
Wane John s Richard, ?dford, Ntt, husbandman to John Pratt 29 May 1682
Wansill Richard s Michael, Ducklington, Oxf, yeoman to John Bedwell 4 Dec 1721
Waple Osmond s Thomas, Shoreditch, Mdx, oilman† to Thomas Hill 2 Jun 1701 <2 Dec 1706 turned over to John Tims, citizen and draper>
Ward Abel s Thomas, Newchurch, Ham, gentleman to William Ingram 3 Feb 1672/3
Ward Abel s Thomas, High Holborn, Mdx, yeoman to William Allen 25 Nov 1700
Ward Bolstrode s John, citizen and clothworker to Edward Leman 8 Jun 1696
Ward John s Richard, Stoke, Gls, yeoman to John Skeale 21 Aug 1633
Ward John s John, Bidford, War, husbandman to William Clarke 23 Jul 1652
Ward John s John, Shoreditch, Mdx, millwright to Morgan Jones 6 Dec 1725 <6 Dec 1731 turned over to Thomas Newcomb, citizen and cooper>
Ward Jonathan s Robert, Whittington, Sal, clerk† to Richard Makepeece 13 Oct 1692
Ward Joseph s Joseph, Hinton, Nth, yeoman to Henry Pullen 3 Oct 1720
Ward Mathew s Mathew, St Giles in the Fields, Mdx, victualler to William Jeanes 25 Feb 1696/7
Ward Richard s Richard, Husbands Bosworth, Lei, yeoman to William Woodhouse 1 Aug 1656
Ward Richard s John, Sleap [Wem], Sal, yeoman to Ralph Humfreys 11 Oct 1659
Ward Robert s John, Sleap [Wem], Sal, yeoman to Ralph Humfries 19 Nov 1652
Ward [*in margin* 'Wall'] Thomas s William, Shoreham, Ken, clerk to Philip Constable 9 Sep 1700
Ward Thomas s William, citizen and cooper to Robert Wyrill 8 Aug 1715 <4 Apr 1720 turned over to William Kirk, citizen and haberdasher>
Ward William s William, citizen and clothworker to Edward Worgan 2 Apr 1705
Warde William s Edward, St Pancras, Mdx, tilemaker to William Pond 15 Oct 1672
Warden William s Charles, Edgware, Mdx, yeoman to Thomas Bennett 3 Apr 1710
Ware Edward s James, citizen and dyer to Richard Potter 8 Aug 1645
Ware William s Joseph, Hull, Yks, mariner to Caleb Talbot 5 Feb 1793
Waring John s Henry, Warwick, War, farrier to Samuel Wheeler 27 Mar 1683
Waring Robert s Brian, Waltham Abbey, Ess, yeoman† to Edmund Cutt 4 Nov 1684
Warman John s John to his father 2 Jul 1698
Warman John s Thomas, Liddington, Wil, yeoman† to Samuel Denny 3 Nov 1699
Warner Daniel s John, St James Westminster, Mdx, tallow chandler† to Thomas Bord 23 Mar 1773
Warner Edward s John, Frimley, Sry, waggoner to James Titley 29 Jul 1746
Warner Isaac s Thomas, Hammersmith, Mdx, baker† to Richard Fullwood 12 Aug 1689
Warner John s James, St Giles in the Fields, Mdx, tailor to Edmund Hemings 5 Oct 1719
Warner John s William, Hawkley, Ham, farmer to William Yalden 1 Jan 1752
Warner John s Edward, St Giles Cripplegate, Lnd, gingerbread baker to Thomas Witton 1 Aug 1771 <17 Nov 1773 turned over to Joseph Knight, citizen and skinner; 3 Oct 1775 to John Harris, citizen and haberdasher>
Warner Marmaduke s Bartholomew, Ninfield, Ssx, clerk to Edward Marshall 21 Sep 1650
Warren John s Philip, Chelsea?, Mdx, tailor to James Miller 5 Nov 1666
Warren John s Arthur, Stapleford, Ntt, esquire† to Francis Molyneux 8 Aug 1706
Warren Joseph s John, St Stephen St Albans, Hrt, yeoman† to Thomas Young 28 Apr 1640
Warren Lionel s John, Copt Hall, Ess, gentleman to John Gibbons 26 Aug 1668
Warren Michael s Michael, Bushey, Hrt, yeoman to Richard Wilkinson 9 Sep 1650
Warren Richard s Brian, 'Warren nuper Suson', Ess, yeoman† to Robert Warren 5 Mar 1693/4

Warren Robert s Michael, Bushey, Hrt, yeoman to John Kerby 8 Jan 1710/11 <3 Dec 1711 turned over to Edward Rose, citizen and haberdasher>
Warren Thomas s ?, Romsey, Ham, clerk to Benjamin Solley 6 May 1664
Warren William s William, St Margaret Westminster, gardener to Thomas Hatton 17 Jan 1665/6
Warrinor alias Cox Richard s Richard, Clatford, Ham, yeoman to William Minchin 16 Feb 1646/7
Warwick Abraham s Abraham, Wandsworth, Sry, gentleman to William Newman 8 Dec 1712
Warwick William s Robert, Bampton, Oxf, butcher to Robert Kirke 2 Aug 1697
Washborne Benjamin s Thomas, citizen and mercer to Nicholas Ortis? 2 Feb 1637/8
Wastall Samuel s Samuel, St Dunstan in the West, Lnd, gentleman to William Jeanes 29 Apr 1710
Waston Francis s William, Fladbury, Wor, tanner† to Francis Style 5 Jun 1727
Watchorn James s John, Leicester, Lei, wool stapler to John Lambert 6 Apr 1774
Waterhouse Fareconquest s Thomas, Little Hollingbury, Ess, clerk to Edmund Barcock 16 Feb 1659/60
Wateridge John s William to his father 2 Mar 1723/4
Waters Daniel s Thomas, Berkhamstead, Hrt, baker to John Hawes 30 Jun 1690
Waters Matthias s John, Bermondsey, Sry, tanner to Thomas Searle 18 May 1757
Waters Nicholas s Andrew, Hurstmonceaux, Ssx, yeoman to Daniel Moris 22 Feb 1641/2
Waterson William s Richard, Newmarket, Cam, labourer† to Richard Kirby 19 Dec 1749
Waterworth Stephen s Stephen, Gosfield, Ess, weaver to Edward Terry 26 Jun 1676
Watkins John s John, Kentchurch, Hef, gentleman to William Miller 10 Nov 1673
Watkins Thomas s Thomas, High Wycombe, Bkm, cook to William May 1 Jul 1695
Watkins Thomas s Thomas, Whitechapel, Mdx, weaver to Nathaniel Burchard 1 Mar 1735/6
Watkinson William s John, Halifax, Yks, yeoman to William Smith 10 Jan 1708/9
Watridge William s William, Wantage, Brk, mercer† to John Harrison 6 Dec 1697 <turned over to Reynolds Niccolls; 26 Feb 1702/3 to Josiah Ragdale>
Watson Benjamin s Tobias, Garthorpe, Lei, joiner to John Ascough 7 Nov 1678
Watson Benjamin s Thomas, Wandsworth, Sry, carpenter to Isaac Cox 6 Aug 1716
Watson John s William, Lincoln, Lin, alderman† to Charles Doilie 13 Dec 1647 <bond from Elizabeth Watson, Lincoln, Lin, wid>
Watson John s John, Staverton, Nth, blacksmith† to Thomas Clarke 22 Jul 1667
Watson Margaret d John, Amersham, Bkm, minister to Samuel Withers 27 Feb 1655/6
Watson Mary d John, Amersham, Bkm, gentleman to William Minchin 1 Nov 1655
Watson Robert s Edward, 'Calton', Nth, yeoman† to William Massey 21 Feb 1654/5
Watts Charles s Charles, St Katherine by the Tower, Mdx, yeoman to John Tayler 16 Jun 1691
Watts Edward s John, Tewkesbury, Gls, blacksmith† to William Hewett 10 Jun 1646
Watts John s William, Syresham, Nth, yeoman to William Gurney 19 Dec 1676 <bond of Thomas Falkner, Sherington, Bkm, yeoman as turned over to Richard Harbert, citizen and bowyer>
Watts John s Herbert, citizen and leatherseller to John Woodward 5 Dec 1709
Watts John to George Wyld 3 Oct 1799
Watts Jonas s John, Crick, Nth, yeoman† to Thomas Watts 17 Nov 1682
Watts Jonas s Thomas to his father 6 Feb 1690/1
Watts Joseph s William, Banbury, Oxf, grazier to Peter Prince 18 Apr 1646
Watts Robert s Robert, Henley, Oxf, harnessmaker to Thomas Rencher 17 Jun 1692
Watts Robert s Thomas to his father 27 Sep 1698
Watts Samuel s Samuel, St James Westminster, Mdx, gentleman to William Lucas 2 Nov 1742
Watts Thomas s Jonas, Crick, Nth, yeoman to John Archer 20 Jun 1650
Watts Thomas s Robert, Sevenoaks, Ken, glover to Thomas Cryer 5 Jul 1669
Watts Thomas s Thomas to his father 28 Nov 1687
Way Samuel s Samuel, Lambeth, Sry, smith to Thomas Searle 5 Jan 1735/6
Wayte Thomas s Richard, Swindon, Wil, grazier to William Alexander 7 Jun 1736
Weale George s Thomas, Napton on the Hill, War, yeoman to Jacob Diston 15 Jun 1665
Weall John Page s Benjamin, Harrow Weald, Mdx, yeoman to Francis Barrell Searle 4 Sep 1744
Wearge Fanshaw s John, Oxford, Oxf, gardener to John Cannell 16 Mar 1681/2
Weatherstone George s George, Kirby Street, Hatton Garden, victualler to Richard Clark 4 Aug 1789
Weaver Richard s William?, Holborn, Mdx, victualler to Richard More 17 May 1682
Weaver Richard s Simon, citizen and cutler to Henry Arundell 13 Jan 1701/2

Webb Alexander s John, Abingdon, Brk, brewer† to Richard Ayres 3 May 1697
Webb Andrew s Andrew, Wantage, Brk, yeoman to John Pidgeon 25 Feb 1660/1
Webb Daniel s Joseph, Lnd, grocer† to Joseph Lane 2 Jan 1739/40
Webb Gabriel s Richard, Ruthin, Den, gentleman to Stephen Kersinhall 24 Apr 1634
Webb John s John, citizen and vintner† to John Sussex 7 Nov 1709 <8 Sep 1710 discharged with consent of master and his mother Isabella Webb>
Webb John s John, Greenwich, Ken, gentleman† to Lancelot Vibart 17 Nov 1747 <1 Jun 1752 master† turned over to William Biggs>
Webb Nathaniel s Abraham, Kingston, Sry, tanner to Humphrey Rogers 11 Jun 1689
Webb Richard s Richard, Ruislip, Mdx, husbandman to Ralph Timberlake 4 Jun 1661
Webb Samuel s William, Paulerspury, Nth, shoemaker to James Harding 24 May 1658
Webb Thomas s Edward, Brownsover, War, yeoman to John Archer 4 Sep 1642
Webb Thomas s Thomas, citizen and weaver† to Griffith Griffiths 1 Dec 1690
Webb William s Henry, Painswick, Gls, clothier to Thomas Lawrence 13 Oct 1645
Webb William s Richard, Lnd, b? to John Kettle 23 Feb 1668/9
Webb William s William, citizen and tallow chandler† to Peter Pickering 19 May 1683
Webbe William s William, citizen and clothworker† to Clement Styles 13 Feb 1637/8
Webster Henry s William, Diss, Nfk, collarmaker† to Roger Thorpe 6 Nov 1673
Webster James s James, Dewsbury, Yks, clothier to John Webster 24 Apr 1634
Webster Richard s John, Sturton, Ntt, yeoman† to Robert Grosswell 18 Feb 1700/1
Webster Robert s William, Bitteswell, Lei, yeoman to Thomas Broadbank 7 Apr 1718
Webster Stephen Robert s George, Deptford, Ken, smith to Barnaby Kelly 1 Mar 1796
Webster Thomas s Thomas, Wyresdale, Lan, husbandman to Charles Dickinson 12 Apr 1636
Wedgbrough John s Edmund, Westminster, Mdx, gardener† to Joseph Wedgbrough 23 Dec 1747
Wedgbrough Joseph s Joseph, Kensington, Mdx, butcher† to William Pannott 1 Mar 1702/3
Wedgbrough Joseph s Joseph to his father 5 Jul 1736
Wedgbrough Richard s John, Hammersmith, Mdx, butcher to William Pannett 7 Feb 1697/8 <1 Mar 1702/3 turned over to Ralph Wenlock, citizen and butcher>
Weeden Alexander s John, Lnd, gentleman to John Chatfeild 7 Dec 1730
Weeks Richard s Richard, St Margaret Westminster, Mdx, perukemaker to John Lamplee 1 Jul 1740
Weight Isaac s Isaac, Salisbury, Wil, haberdasher to Richard Weight 5 Oct 1671
Weightman George s ?, Coventry, War, clothier to William Mayne 1 Oct 1679
Welch Roger s William, Stratton, Wil, yeoman to William Trinder 13 Sep 1633
Weld John s Thomas, Keele, Sts [? *in Ms* 'Sal'], yeoman to John Harrison 14 Sep 1660
Weld John s ?, Little Waltham, Ess, ? to William Gaunte 21 Jun 1669
Weld John s John, citizen and cook to George Wightman 3 Dec 1705 <6 Oct 1707 turned over to Benjamin Stinton>
Wele Daniel s Thomas, Pinnock, Gls, yeoman to Thomas Rakestraw 24 Aug 1698
Weller Andrew s William, Hampton, Mdx, yeoman to John Hickman 7 Oct 1633
Weller Henry s George, Fenchurch Street, Lnd, coachmaker to James Pateshall 6 Aug 1782
Wells Daniel s Thomas, Waltham St Lawrence, Brk, yeoman to John Harrison 20 May 1669
Wells Joseph s John, West Ham, Ess, waterman to Richard Morris 27 May 1703
Wells Richard s Richard, Greenwich, Ken, mariner† to Thomas Watts 3 Oct 1709 <5 Jul 1714 master† turned over by John Sherwill, exec. to Harwood Wilton, citizen and bowyer>
Wells Robert s Robert, Ratcliffe, Mdx, yeoman† to Vincent Fletcher 23 May 1671
Wells Walter s Walter, Lomans Pond, St Saviour Southwark, Sry, carpenter† to William Hedgeland 5 Dec 1768
Wells William s Thomas, Great Gaddesden, Hrt, yeoman to William Gibson 12 Feb 1635/6
Welsh John s John, West Smithfield, Lnd, mariner† to Robert Fewtrell 5 Sep 1672
Weslake Nicholas s John, St Katherine, Lnd, worsted comber to Benjamin Kendall 1 Apr 1717
West Aholiab s John, Banbury, Oxf, glazier† to Richard Weight 12 Oct 1671
West Francis s Richard, Barnsley, Yks, innholder to Ralph Barlowe 28 Aug 1637
West Jacob s William, St Thomas Southwark, Sry, bottle coverer to Henry Symons 22 Jan 1646/7
West James s John, Reading, Brk, butcher† to Edward Walker 15 Jun 1693
West James s John, Stepney, Mdx, watchmaker† to Hugh Lake 7 Aug 1745
West John s John, Soho, Mdx, gentleman† to John Ayscough 3 Jun 1695
West John s Jasper, St Giles Cripplegate, Mdx, labourer† to Richard West 7 Jun 1714
West Nathaniel s Samuel, Chipping Norton, Oxf, baker to John Burbrough 4 Jan 1713/4

West Richard s James, Basingstoke, Ham, butcher† to Elizabeth widow of Charles Godwin 6 May 1700 <25 May 1703 turned over to Edmund Browne>
West Robert s Thomas, St Olave Southwark, Sry, butcher to Richard West 5 Jul 1708
West Thomas s John, St Giles Cripplegate, Mdx, chirurgeon† to John Twell 26 Jul 1683
West Thomas s Thomas, citizen and clockmaker to Robert Southwood 29 Jan 1716/7 <turned over to his father>
West William s Samuel, citizen and tallow chandler† to James Church 22 Apr 1667 <bond from Edward West, citizen and b...>
Westal James s William, Hungerford, Wil, tanner to William Andrews 21 May 1717
Westall James s John, Wallingford, Brk, baker to Simon Westell 18 Nov 1723 <4 Oct 1725 turned over to George Bellows>
Westbrook John s Humphrey, Steep, Ham, yeoman to Thomas Husted 20 Oct 1642
Westell Simon s John, Wallingford, Brk, baker to William Hutchins 6 Jul 1713
Westfahl Henry s Henry, Stratford, Ess, gingerbread baker to Richard Tyler 5 Jun 1798 <2 Jul 1801 turned over to James Nicholls>
Weston Andrew s Andrew, St George Southwark, Sry, clerk† to William Smith 4 May 1687
Weston John s James, Thurlaston, Lei, yeoman to Elizabeth widow of Oliver Hill 9 May 1648
Weston Richard s John, Poplar, Mdx, cook† to Bartholomew Cadell 2 Apr 1661
Weston William s William, Kinnersley, Sal, husbandman to Valentine Jacob 14 Mar 1667/8
Weston William s Anthony, Abingdon, Brk, waterman† to John Sussex 6 Jan 1706/7
Westwood Gilbert s Jonathan, Croydon, Sry, clerk to Francis Pitman 30 Aug 1658
Wethered Francis s John, Hackney, Mdx, gardener to Robert Apsley 7 Feb 1648/9
Wetherell John s George, Smeaton, Yks, gentleman to John Yarling 10 Jun 1667
Weyburne John s Eli, Enfield, Mdx, maltster to William Cock 21 Jul 1663
Wharton Thomas s Thomas, Watford, Hrt, leatherdresser to Jeremiah Owen 6 Jun 1739
Wheate Peter s Samuel, Reading, Brk, tanner† to Nathaniel Perkins 5 Sep 1734
Wheately John s Robert, Whitechapel, Mdx, labourer to William Massey 2 Mar 1664/5
Wheatly Martin s Nathaniel, Banbury, Oxf, mercer to James Horton 12 May 1702
Wheeler Caesar s Arthur, Clerkenwell, Mdx, gentleman to Francis Nash 22 Aug 1660
Wheeler Caleb s Caleb, Old Street, Mdx, coal merchant to Alan Parsons 1 May 1781
Wheeler Henry s Henry, Henley, Oxf, currier to William Gurney 15 Jul 1680
Wheeler Jacob nephew Jacob Adams, Chandos Street, St George, Mdx to Henry Case 6 Nov 1800
Wheeler John s Henry, Henley, Oxf, currier to Thomas Doweswell 12 Jan 1686/7
Wheeler John s John, Shoreditch, Mdx, cutler† to Richard Janaway 11 Nov 1691
Wheeler John s John, Bermondsey, Sry, mariner to Robert Driver 9 Feb 1707/8
Wheeler Jonas s Richard, Salford, War, husbandman† to William Minchin 7 Oct 1645
Wheeler Samuel s Samuel to his father 27 Mar 1683
Whelpdale Charles s Thomas, Greenwich, Ken, vintner to Thomas Obbinson 2 Nov 1713 <turned over to Nicholas Greene, citizen and bowyer>
Whelply William s John, Berkhamstead, Hrt, glazier to William Newman 7 Dec 1705
Whetcher Richard s Richard, Clatford, Ham, cook to Simon Dowson 23 May 1637
Whinnick Ann d Robert, St Clement Danes, Mdx, victualler† to William Hulls 20 Jan 1696/7
Whisler ... s Ralph to Ralph Whisler .. May 1663
Whistler Ralph s Ralph, Southwark, Sry, baker† to Charles Fisher 25 Nov 1651
Whitbey John s John, citizen and joiner to Thomas Hopkins 3 Feb 1685/6
Whitcher Jacob s William, Frogmore, Hrt, yeoman to William Knight 2 Feb 1668/9
Whitcher Joseph s Richard, citizen and tallow chandler† to Robert Southwood 10 Nov 1668
Whitchurch Joseph to Francis Warden 1661/2
White Anthony s Anthony, citizen and haberdasher to Jacob Woollson 25 Jan 1686/7
White John s John, Piddington, Oxf, yeoman† to Thomas Higgins 6 Mar 1687/8
White John s John, Fingest, Bkm, maltster to Richard Burrabee 9 Apr 1761
White John s Henry, Hackney, Mdx, gardener to Thomas Underwood 13 Jun 1763
White Ralph s George, Haselbury Bryan, Dor, yeoman to William Gulliford 3 Feb 1700/1
White Richard s John, Great Marlow, Bkm, maltster to Richard Barrabee 15 Oct 1756
White Robert s Samuel, St Sepulchre, Lnd, gentleman to John Tyson 27 Apr 1637
White Robert s George, citizen and barber surgeon† to Robert Tibball 26 Mar 1640
White Robert s Robert, St Giles in the Fields, Mdx, gentleman to Thomas Stephenson 18 Nov 1686
White Samuel s Thomas, citizen and goldsmith to Joseph Lane 6 Apr 1719

White Thomas s Francis, Langley, Kington St Michael, Wil, gentleman to William Miller 28 Sep 1686
White Thomas s Edward, Tottenham, Mdx, wheelwright† to John Withers 6 Feb 1776 <3 Nov 1779 turned over to John Chapman, citizen and weaver>
White William s Thomas, Tur Langton, Lei, cordwainer to Benjamin Munn 30 Mar 1700
White William to John Chambers 2 May 1799
Whitehead Walter s William, Islington, Mdx, butcher† to John Jemmitt 12 Nov 1716
Whiteing Charles s William, St Giles in the Fields, brushmaker† to Edward Christopher 7 Aug 1710
Whiteing John s William, Thistleton, Rut, yeoman† to Noel Whiteing 4 Oct 1697
Whiteing Noel s William, Thistleton, Rut, yeoman† to Noel Whiteing 4 Feb 1694/5
Whiteing Richard s Clement, Edington, Wil, tailor to Valentine Jacob 27 Jan 1674/5
Whitelock Thomas s William, Ware, Hrt, gentleman to Thomas Sawtell 24 Jul 1754
Whiteover Robert s William, Winslow, Bkm, labourer to George Harlow 14 Apr 1772
Whithead George s George, Biggleswade, Bdf, carpenter to Richard Fullwood 2 Aug 1708
Whitlee Matthias s Charles, St Saviour Southwark, Sry, lighterman to Samuel Denny 19 Mar 1704/5 <12 Jan 1709/10 turned over to Robert Ayliff>
Whitley Charles s Robert, citizen and farrier† to Thomas Huatson 22 Mar 1697/8
Whitney John s John, Edmonton, Mdx, husbandman to Nathaniel Billings 17 Mar 1645/6
Whittaker John s John, Bradley, Wil, yeoman to William Andrews 4 Oct 1714
Whittle John s John, Bethnal Green, Mdx, gardener to Samuel Brown 23 May 1744
Whittle Thomas s Angel, Delpht, Holland, watchmaker to Thomas Hunt 1 Jun 1713
Whitton Thomas s William, Christ Church, Lnd, tailor† to Isaac Price 2 Oct 1739
Whitworth William s John, Queniborough, Lei, chirurgeon† to Daniel Wane 4 Aug 1712 <21 May 1718 turned over to William Wateridge>
Wiborow John s Thomas, Enville, Sts, clerk to Robert Jackson 9 Jun 1655
Wiburd John s John to his father 1 May 1688
Wiburd John s John, Shoreditch, Mdx, mealman to John Wiburd 1 Feb 1713/4
Wiburd Samuel s Eleazar, citizen and tallow chandler† to John Chewter 9 Jun 1718
Wickens William s Bennett, Bicester, Oxf, yeoman to William Wickens 20 Aug 1634
Wickes John s John, citizen and salter to Thomas Ashburner 17 Jan 1664/5
Wickes John s ?, 'Aldenham', Ham [? Hrt], ? to Thomas Harris ? Aug 1667
Wickes Paul s Paul, Lnd, clothworker† to John Brian 2 Mar 1641/2
Wickham James s ?, Shoreditch, Mdx, ? to Thomas Dubber 1 Jun 1663
Wickham John s Samuel, Pirbright, Sry, clerk to John Marsh 15 Apr 1662 <turned over to John Maxfeild>
Wickins Richard s William, Rotherhithe, Sry, tanner† to Andrew Godwin 9 Jul 1689
Wicks Edward s Edward, Harwell, Brk to Robert Hopkins 4 Feb 1794
Wicks Thomas s Edward, Harwell, Brk, gentleman to Robert Hopkins 6 Oct 1795
Wigfall Richard s William, Medbourne, Lei, yeoman to Jane widow of Robert More 14 Dec 1654
Wigg Thomas s Thomas, Brickhill, Bkm, gentleman† to William Gurney 11 Sep 1678
Wiggins David s David, St Martin in the Fields, Mdx, blacksmith† to Thomas West 1 Mar 1707/8
Wiggins John s Thomas, Chelsea, Mdx, coachman to George Wyld 7 Apr 1778
Wiggins Richard s William, St James Clerkenwell, tallow chandler† to Ann Hedges Warner 30 Oct 1744
Wiggins Thomas s Thomas, St Botolph Aldgate, Lnd, builder† to William Burnley 6 Nov 1745
Wigglesworth Richard s Thomas, Lnd, blacksmith to Thomas Pitman 6 Mar 1637/8
Wight James s Randolph, Kinnersley, Hef, clerk to William Badham 19 Mar 1693/4
Wight James s Samuel, Didcot, Brk, gentleman to William Watridge 1 Aug 1715
Wightwick Robert s George, Tenterden, Ken, grazier† to Samuel Savage 12 Oct 1737
Wigley John s Richard, Warwick, War, innholder to Thomas Day 26 May 1685
Wigly Richard s John to his father 3 Dec 1711
Wignall Geoffrey s James, Brentford, Mdx, scrivener† to Avery Vokins 4 Jun 1722
Wignall James s James, Southwark, Sry, butcher† to George Carpenter 1 Jun 1752
Wilce John s Giles, Brockworth, Gls, yeoman to Giles Rodway 26 Nov 1642
Wilcocks Robert s Basil, Westminster, Mdx, tallow chandler to John Wilcocks 29 Mar 1655
Wilcockson Thomas s George, Wolvey, War, clerk to John Wilcockson 24 Oct 1639
Wild George s George, Lambeth, Sry, boat builder to his father 7 Aug 1781
Wild Philip s Richard, Charney, Brk, yeoman to Richard Reynolds 3 Jul 1693

Wild William s James, Aldenham, Hrt, husbandman to Robert Apsley 30 May 1654
Wildbore John s John, Holborn, Mdx, labourer to William Leach 14 Jun 1675
Wilde Henry s Henry, Ramsbury, Wil, yeoman to Jeremiah Eightshillings 31 Jan 1670/1
Wildgoose John s John, citizen and weaver† to Robert Butcher 5 Jul 1659
Wilding Job s Benjamin, Sherborne, Dor, clerk to John Cooke 7 Nov 1739 <18 Jul 1740 turned over to Gilbert Dench, citizen and joiner>
Wilford Walter s Thomas, Grindle, Sal, gentleman to William Latham 9 Jun 1659
Wilford William s Francis, Holywell, Hun, clerk to Robert Marchant 24 Oct 1658
Wilkes John s John, Elstree, Hrt, husbandman to William Minchin 20 Jul 1649
Wilkie James s Andrew, Wentworth Street, Mdx, tallow chandler to Thomas Bord 3 Dec 1782
Wilkin Richard s Richard, Hanwell, Mdx, yeoman† to Samuel Wilkin 1 May 1650
Wilkins Edmund, s Edmund, St Botolph Bishopsgate, cordwainer to William Ballard 27 Apr 1674
Wilkins James s James, St Giles Cripplegate, Mdx, charcoalman to Thomas Rawlinson 7 Sep 1730
Wilkins Richard s John, Chertsey, Sry, bargeman to Philip Goodwin 28 Aug 1678
Wilkins Robert s Robert, Northampton, Nth, wheelwright to John Clarke 1 Oct 1711
Wilkins Valentine s Thomas, Prestbury, Gls, cordwainer† to Edmund Hunt 2 Feb 1669/70
Wilkinson Edward s Robert, Newcastle under Lyne, Sts, yeoman to Bartholomew Heyward 21 Mar 1634/5
Wilkinson George s Thomas, Field Lane, Holborn, Lnd, gentleman to William Gregory 2 May 1786
Wilkinson Hugh s John, St Andrew Wardrobe, Lnd, labourer to Nathaniel Messinger 10 Oct 1689
Wilkinson Mercy d William, Newcastle on Tyne, Nbl, salter to John Coates 31 Oct 1681
Wilkinson Richard s Gabriel, Wooburn, Bkm, clerk to John French 25 Jul 1637
Wilkinson Thomas s Thomas, Geddington, Nth, yeoman† to John Harrison 7 Jan 1696/7
Wilkinson Thomas s Thomas, citizen and upholder† to Philadelphia widow of Edward Osborn 19 Dec 1715
Wilkinson Thomas s George, Sunbury, Mdx, coachman to Richard Davies 1 Mar 1796 <6 Nov 1798 turned over to John Slaymaker>
Willford John s Edward, Enfield, Mdx [? *in Ms* 'Ess'], gentleman to John Appleyard 7 Oct 1690
William *see* Thomas ap William Thomas
Williams Ambrose s Ambrose, St Martin in the Fields, coachman to Francis Bannester 5 Oct 1686
Williams Benjamin s John, Sevenhampton, Gls, clerk to Robert Williams 16 Dec 1642
Williams Edward s David, Lnd, carman to Morgan Jones 3 Jun 1734
Williams James s John, Jamaica, carpenter† to Thomas Tully 27 Nov 1751
Williams John s Thomas, Ashton Keynes, Wil, husbandman to George Laman 27 May 1648
Williams John s John, Llangarron, Hef, yeoman to Thomas Farrant 1 Jun 1648
Williams John s William, citizen and tallow chandler to Martha Herbert 4 Nov 1728
Williams Josiah s John, St Giles in the Fields, Mdx, gunsmith† to Edward Fitz 9 Jul 1756
Williams Lewis s David, Llangadock, Cmn, yeoman to Samuel Shakemaple 27 Feb 1646/7
Williams Maurice s Maurice, Holborn Bridge, Lnd, victualler to Henry Soames 6 Apr 1784
Williams Owen *see* Owen Williams
Williams Richard s William, Brecknock, Bre, gentleman to Anthony Palmer 29 Dec 1656
Williams Richard s Robert, Llandyrnog, Den, labourer to William Bateman 13 Apr 1663
Williams Richard s Richard, Newington, Sry, labourer† to Henry Myles 25 Jul 1671
Williams Richard s Richard, St Clement Danes, Mdx, perukemaker to Charles Holden 1 Oct 1722 <16 Apr 1724 turned over to Thomas Jeffs, citizen and vintner; 2 Aug 1726 to Francis Style>
Williams Robert s John, Sevenhampton, Gls, clerk to Thomas Yonge 29 Sep 1634
Williams Thomas s Thomas, citizen and skinner to John Caddi 5 Mar 1704/5
Williams Thomas s Thomas, citizen and gunsmith† to Nathaniel Burchard 5 Aug 1752
Williams Thomas s Roger, Reading, Brk, wheelwright to Thomas Jarvis 7 Jan 1794
Williams William s John, Church Honeybourne, Wor, clerk to Mathew Bey 11 Jul 1641
Williams William s John, Westminster, Mdx, yeoman to Henry Bornley 13 Apr 1652
Williams William s Arthur, 'Lansis', Cae, gentleman to Francis Drinkewater 10 Sep 1663
Williams William s William, Whitechapel, Mdx, weaver† to Abraham Clarke 18 Jan 1675/6
Williams William s John, Bangor, Fln, yeoman† to John Harbert 7 Nov 1692
Williams William s William, Leominster, Hef, miller to Mary Bellis 14 Apr 1770
Williamson Thomas s Thomas, Bishop Auckland, Dur, gentleman to John Poston 26 Mar 1672
Williamson William s ... to Edward Hooker 22 Mar 1638/9
Williamson William s Daniel, St George in the East, Mdx, gentleman to Samuel Reeves 18 Jul 1759

Willie George s John, Ilminster, Som, clothier to John Willis 22 Apr 1656
Willis James s James, Christ Church Southwark, Sry, soapmaker to his father 7 Dec 1790
Willis John s John, Much Marcle, Hef, weaver to William Massey 19 Oct 1648
Willis John s John, Newbury, Brk, weaver to Benjamin Merriman 15 Sep 1756
Willis Thomas s William, Peopleton, Wor, yeoman to John Warren 5 Jul 1655
Willis William s William, Christ Church Southwark, Sry, carpenter to James Willis 5 Jul 1796
Willmott Thomas s Stephen, citizen and clockmaker to Thomas Obbinson 6 Oct 1707 <turned over to Joseph Lathwell, citizen and currier>
Willmott Thomas s Daniel, St Martin in the Fields, Mdx, innholder to Nathaniel Might 4 May 1742
Willoughby John s John, Lnd, gentleman to John Jemmett 6 Mar 1731/2 <5 Jul 1736 turned over to John Sherman, citizen and armorer>
Willy John s John, Ilminster, Som, clothier to John Tyson 14 Nov 1646
Wilmott John s John, Newnham, Gls, shipwright† to Kenelm Savill 21 Jun 1636
Wilmott John s John, citizen and merchant tailor† to Benjamin Clark 2 Aug 1714
Wilsford John s John, Sleaford, Lin, yeoman to Robert Cooper 17 Oct 1637
Wilsheire Walter s John, Batcombe, Som, clothworker† to Richard Whitcher 29 May 1650
Wilson George to John Johnson 7 Mar 1799
Wilson John s Richard, St Giles, Mdx, tallow chandler to Peter Leigh 3 Dec 1716
Wilson John s John, Bow, Mdx, butcher to Isaac Phillips 4 Apr 1780
Wilson Joseph s Thomas, Old Street, Mdx, grocer to Joseph Joslin 5 Jul 1785
Wilson Richard s Henry, citizen and mason to Thomas Browne 18 Feb 1646/7
Wilson Rudolph s Thomas, Willian, Hrt, gentleman† to Humphrey Rogers 9 Sep 1674
Wilson Thomas s Thomas, Royston, Cam, yeoman to Thomas Harrison 18 Jun 1656
Wilson Thomas s Thomas, Willian, Hrt, gentleman to Henry Hawkes 9 May 1668
Wilson William s Edward, Wapping, Mdx, mariner to Thomas Searl 1 Apr 1723
Wilton Samuel s William, Bruton, Som, maltster† to William Gurney 15 Sep 1676
Wily James s James, citizen and fruiterer to Daniel Dickins 5 May 1701 <6 Jul 1703 turned over to John Bridge, citizen and tinplateworker>
Wimberley Bartholomew s William, South Witham, Lin, yeoman† to Noel Whiteing 7 Feb 1687/8
Wimfheimer Michael s Michael, St Ann Blackfriars, Lnd, sugar baker to Evan Phillips 5 Feb 1768
Winch John s John, St Margaret Westminster, Mdx, gentleman† to Henry Lathwell 31 Aug 1680
Winchester Daniel s John, Ruislip, Mdx, yeoman to William Greenehill 29 Sep 1634
Winchester Nathaniel s Thomas, Great Parndon, Ess, butcher to Bartholomew Peele ? Apr 1668
Winders John s John, citizen and weaver† to Samuel Saywell 25 Feb 1657/8
Windle Valentine s John, Holborn, Mdx, shoemaker to Henry Soames 2 Apr 1760
Wine Henry s Henry, Westminster, Mdx, farrier to Robert Udall 3 Dec 1647
Wingfeild Abraham s Robert, citizen and shipwright to Thomas Searle 4 Nov 1728 <7 Dec 1730 turned over to Joseph Hammond, citizen and shipwright; 3 Apr 1732 to John Cotten, citizen and shipwright; 6 Oct 1735 to Robert Wingfeild, citizen and shipwright>
Wingfield Joseph s Joseph, Harefield, Mdx, gentleman to Nicholas Charlton 14 Jul 1683
Wingfield Joseph s ..., Southwark, Sry, vintner to Caleb Johnson 29 Apr 1748 <5 Sep 1749 turned over to John Reynolds, citizen and cooper>
Wingfield Robert s Robert, Rotherhithe, Sry, mariner† to James Tetley 5 Aug 1717
Winks James s William, St James Westminster, Mdx, shoemaker to John Lindsey 7 Oct 1777
Winnick Deborah d Robert, St Clement Danes, Mdx, vintner† to William Hulls 4 Jul 1698
Winter Augustine s John, Stickland, Dor, husbandman to Thomas Northover 21 Apr 1681
Winter Edward s William, citizen and merchant tailor to Granado Chester 3 Apr 1710
Winter John s William, Windsor, Brk, butcher† to Joseph Casbert 20 Oct 1669
Winter John s John, Wallingford, Brk, yeoman† to John Edden 9 May 1672
Winter William s William, All Saints Oxford, Oxf, cordwainer to Valentine Warner 10 Aug 1708 <1 Jun 1713 turned over to Robert Ayliff>
Wintle Henry s Henry, Gls, yeoman† to Daniel Weale 7 Jun 1725
Wise John s Thomas, Eynsham [? *in Ms* 'Ansum'], Oxf, husbandman to Robert Fewterell 5 May [? *in Ms* 'Mar'] 1669
Wise Jonathan s John, Romsey, Ham, millwright to Thomas Wilson 16 Oct 1676
Wise Richard s Richard, Warminster, Wil, carpenter to John Wood 14 Mar 1670/1
Wise Richard s Richard, Warminster, Wil, carpenter to Mathew Woodward 23 Feb 1671/2

Wiseman Richard s Richard, Hadleigh, Sfk, gentleman† to Richard Smith 1 Aug 1676

Withers Fulk s Nathaniel, citizen and tallow chandler to Samuel Withers 23 Oct 1684

Withers John s Thomas, Norwich, Nfk, mercer† to Richard Ireland 16 Apr 1729

Withers John s William, Bishopstone, Wil, gentleman to Jonathan Leigh 21 Aug 1760 <5 Sep 1765 turned over to John Skinner>

Withers Joseph s Samuel to his father 31 May 1698

Withers Thomas s Thomas, Newport Pagnell, Bkm, tallow chandler† to Joseph Calcott 6 Sep 1714

Withers William s Thomas, Norton, Sfk, to William Foy 10 Jan 1632/3

Witton Thomas s Thomas to his father 2 Apr 1776

Wolfe Christopher s William, Charing, Ken, gentleman to William Smith 4 Dec 1676

Wolfe Ernest s Ernest, Blackfriars, Mdx, tailor† to Gervase Beckett 13 Mar 1662/3

Wolfe Thomas s Thomas, citizen and leatherseller to John Syms 27 Sep 1684

Wonacott Samuel s John, Rotherhithe, Sry, gentleman† to Ralph White 10 Jan 1708/9

Wood Benjamin s Joseph, citizen and brewer to Francis Houghton 5 Apr 1700

Wood Henry s Cornelius, Lilbourne, Nth, yeoman to John Wood 3 Dec 1679

Wood Humphrey s Nicholas, Brixton, Sry, victualler to John Bryan 6 Sep 1785 <2 Mar 1790 turned over to Mary widow of Andrew McEwen, citizen and wheelwright>

Wood James s Robert, Great Baddow, Ess, yeoman to William Wood 18 Jan 1643/4

Wood James s Henry, Chelsea, Mdx, statuary to John Stevens 4 Dec 1800

Wood John s Lambert, Whitechapel, Mdx, labourer to Abraham Brocke 2 May 1638

Wood John s William, Runwell, Ess, yeoman to Edward Grigg 26 Aug 1640

Wood John s Richard, Tottenham, Mdx, yeoman to Samuel Browker 10 May 1655

Wood John s John, citizen and pewterer to Ezekiel Trott 12 Jul 1660

Wood John s John to his father 15 Dec 1681

Wood John s Francis, Lnd, yeoman to William Smith 17 Oct 1689

Wood John s Thomas, St Martin in the Fields, Mdx, cabinet maker to John Davinport 6 Mar 1703/4

Wood John s John to his father 1 Nov 1714

Wood Nicholas s William, Battersea, Sry, yeoman to Daniel Browne 6 Mar 1670/1

Wood Peter to William Davis 1661/2

Wood Richard s Richard, Westerham, Ken, yeoman to Thomas Cryer 17 Nov 1671

Wood Samuel s Walter, St Giles Cripplegate, Mdx, labourer† to Thomas Hopkins 4 Sep 1693

Wood Thomas s Benjamin, Stanstead Abbots, Hrt, clerk† to Samuel Hamond 24 Dec 1690

Wood William s John, citizen and merchant tailor to Henry Hawkes 29 May 1637

Wood William s William, Woolstone, Gls, weaver to Edmund Milton 10 Apr 1673

Woodcock Henry s Henry, Theobalds [Cheshunt], Hrt, farrier to Thomas Kindar 1 Oct 1652

Wooden Daniel s Stephen, East Garston, Brk, tailor to William Johnson 3 Jul 1744

Woodfeild John s Elias to his father 6 Dec 1731

Woodfeild Samuel s Francis, Priors Marston, War, butcher† to Thomas Watts 26 Aug 1689

Woodfield Elias s Francis, Rayleigh, Ess, yeoman† to William Mellor 1 Mar 1702/3

Woodfield Samuel s Samuel, Ratcliffe, Mdx, mariner† to Jonas Watts 5 Feb 1704/5

Woodford William s William, St Giles Cripplegate, Lnd, mariner to William Alden 20 Jul 1683

Woodhouse William s Richard, citizen and carpenter to James Waggoner 23 Jul 1645

Woodin William s Robert, Turvey, Bdf, yeoman to Roger Mustian 2 Jun 1647

Wooding Richard s Thomas, Bosbury, Hef, yeoman to Thomas Hodges 24 Nov 1671

Woodman George s William, St Giles in the Fields, Mdx, tailor to Thomas Ford 27 Mar 1655

Woodman Prudence d ?, Fareham, Ham to James Manning 14 Feb 1664/5

Woodward Jeremiah s Mathew, Hexton, Hrt, yeoman to Mathew Woodward 23 Oct 1672

Woodward Jeremiah s Jeremiah, Lnd, corn chandler† to Thomas Woollhead 23 Feb 1707/8

Woodward John s John, Shutlanger, Nth, gentleman† to Roger Price 30 Nov 1637

Woodward John s William, 'Grixload', Wil, yeoman to William Gulliford 5 Jan 1701/2

Woodward John s John to his father 5 Jun 1727

Woodward Jonathan s Jonathan, St Margaret Westminster, Mdx, grocer to Elizabeth widow of Francis Rackstraw 1 Oct 1722

Woodward Joseph s Mathew to his father 2 Dec 1706

Woodward Mathew to Joseph Sibley 1661/2

Woodward Mathew s Mathew to his father 21 Jan 1696/7

Woodward Mathew s Mathew to his father 22 Jul 1725

Woodward Revel s Anthony, Chesterfield, Dby, tallow chandler to Robert Thomson 7 Nov 1698

Woodward Samuel s William, Sutton, Dby, yeoman to James Church 13 Jan 1669/70
Woodward William s Henry, Faringdon, Brk, yeoman to Ann widow of John Richards 20 Aug 1634
Woodward William s Thomas, citizen and distiller to William Haydon 25 Sep 1690
Woolhead Henry s Henry, Redbourne, Hrt, victualler to Samuel Randolph 1 Nov 1680
Woolhead John s Thomas, citizen and tallow chandler to Catherine widow of Thomas Woolhead 7 Jul 1729
Woolhead Thomas s Thomas to his father 11 May 1697
Woollams Thomas s Thomas, St Giles Cripplegate, Mdx, cheesemonger to John Halsey 4 Oct 1697
Woollerton William s John, Kinoulton, Ntt, yeoman to John Jemmitt 3 Apr 1710
Woolley Cornelius s Zachary, St Botolph Aldgate, Mdx, yeoman† to James Horton 3 Jan 1688/9
Woolley Jeremiah s William, Watford, Hrt, gentleman to John Tyson ? Oct 1662
Woolley William s Joseph, Covent Garden, Mdx, chairman to Charles Breed 14 Dec 1739 <7 Sep 1744 turned over to Thomas Smith>
Woollgar Richard s William, Havant, Ham, lorimer to John Jones 16 Oct 1690
Woollhead William s Thomas, citizen and tallow chandler† to Catherine widow of Thomas Woollhead 26 May 1727
Woollson John s John, Northampton, Nth, tallow chandler to James Woollson 14 Jan 1685/6
Worgan Edward s Richard to his father 29 Oct 1684
Worgan Richard s William, Newland, Gls, yeoman to Andrew Partridge 12 Aug 1661
Workman Abraham s Abraham, Putney, Sry, gardener to Henry Dunkin 5 Aug 1783
Worledge William s William, Alresford, Ham, gentleman to John Hooker 6 Feb 1655/6
Worley George s Nathaniel, Henley, Oxf, innholder† to Robert Belson 18 Aug 1680
Worley Richard s Nathaniel, Henley, Oxf, innkeeper† to George Worley 28 Aug 1688
Worlidge John s William, Alresford, Ham, distiller† to William Hulls 7 Sep 1687
Worman John s Edward, 'Caute', Wil, husbandman† to Thomas Cole 3 May 1669
Worrall Charles s Thomas, citizen and barber chirurgeon to Benjamin Browsmith 7 Sep 1696
Worrall Valentine s Guy, citizen and dyer† to Mathew Bagge 15 Aug 1637
Worrell Richard s Richard, Mitcheldean, Gls, blacksmith to William Massey 1 Jul 1674
Worsham Andrew s Robert, Lasham, Ham, yeoman† to Thomas Reader 6 May 1653
Worster William s William, Towcester, Nth, yeoman to Thomas Dawson 22 Jan 1632/3
Worster William s Thomas, Draycote, War, gentleman to Andrew Walker 3 Nov 1649
Wortham Hale s Hale, Royston, Hrt, grocer to Peter Langthorn 7 Sep 1724
Worthington Isaac s John, Lnd, salter† to Nicholas Collins 6 Dec 1738
Wortley Joseph s Joseph, Whitechapel, Mdx, weaver to John Tovey 4 Apr 1739
Wotton John s William, Southwark, Sry, tanner to Edward Clarke 13 Apr 1759
Wray George s Henry?, Lnd, tailor† to Mathew Snablin 6 Dec 1681
Wriggleswood John s John, North Ockenden, Ess, yeoman† to Richard Parrott 28 Jan 1656/7
Wright Edward s Edward, Winchester, Ham, victualler to William Greene 8 Sep 1686
Wright Henry s Thomas, St Dunstan in the West, Lnd, barber† to John King 2 Apr 1684
Wright Humphrey s Thomas, Nether Whitacre, War, gentleman to Samuel Wright 15 Jun 1720
Wright John s George, Gorton, Lan, yeoman to John Pricheard 16 Jan 1636/7
Wright John s John, Whitechapel, Mdx, tailor to Robert Butcher 19 Aug 1656
Wright John s John, Harrow, Mdx, smith to Thomas Grover 17 Dec 1657
Wright John s Nathaniel, Lnd, gentleman† to William Garfoote 4 Sep 1667
Wright John s Richard, St Andrew Holborn, Lnd, tailor† to William Nicholson 29 Jun 1668
Wright John s Thomas, Cranford, Mdx, yeoman to John Merrick 14 Sep 1668
Wright John s Richard, Bampton, Oxf to Thomas Cole 21 Jun 1677
Wright John s Edmund, St Andrew Holborn, Lnd, gentleman to Ralph Peirson 17 May 1683
Wright Richard s Lawrence, citizen and innholder† to Thomas Nicholls 23 Jun 1643
Wright Robert s Robert, Lichfield, Sts, cordwainer to Samuel Wheeler 4 Aug 1684
Wright Samuel s Thomas, Nether Whitacre, War, gentleman to John Townsend 8 Jan 1710/11
Wright Thomas s Richard, Waltham Abbey, Ess, farmer to Francis Barber 10 Dec 1764
Wright Timothy s Timothy, Bewdley, Wor, grocer to William Webb 23 May 1673
Wright William s Robert, Bampton, Oxf, yeoman to Henry Loder 31 Mar 1633
Wright William s Roger, Weldon, Nth, labourer to William Massey 14 Dec 1657
Wright William s John, 'Ockly', Yks, yeoman to ... Weight 6 Mar 1673/4
Wright William s William, St Saviour Southwark, Sry, gunsmith to William Burgis 5 Oct 1702

Wright William s William to his father 2 Apr 1705 <7 Nov 1706 turned over by Elizabeth Farwell widow and administrator to William Proudman>
Wright William s William, citizen and tallow chandler to William Proudman 6 Sep 1725
Wright William Mallorie s William, St James Westminster, carpenter to Thomas Crowther 8 Oct 1761
Wroth Nathaniel s George, Farnham, Sry, draper† to John Wiburd 1 May 1693
Wyatt Benjamin s John, English Batch, Som, husbandman to William Collier 30 Jul 1679
Wyatt Robert s Benjamin, citizen and weaver to Benjamin Stinton 8 Apr 1700
Wyatt Thomas s John, King's Sutton, Nth, yeoman to John Lowe 7 Feb 1725/6
Wyborne Diocletian s William, Ickham, Ken, gentleman to Ann widow of Petley Wyborne 16 Feb 1675/6
Wyerell Robert s Robert, Whitechapel, Mdx, stuffmelter to Jacob Packitt 13 Oct 1692
Wyld George s George, Acton, Mdx, farmer† to Thomas Searle 12 May 1758
Wyment Thomas s Thomas, Daventry, Nth, ironmonger to William Maynard 14 Jul 1702 <14 Jul 1702 turned over to Robert Freeman, citizen and upholder>
Wynn John s Mark, St Saviour Southwark, Sry, soap boiler to Henry Miles 20 Oct 1668
Wynny William s John, Southwark, Sry, victualler to Davy Morris 11 Mar 1632/3
Wyrill Robert s Robert to his father 4 Feb 1722/3

Yalden William s Edmund, Newton Valence, Ham, clerk to William Alexander 5 Mar 1740/1
Yarborough Richard s Thomas, Snaith, Yks, baronet to Francis Molyneux 9 Jan 1696/7
Yarling John s John, Stanstead, Hrt, yeoman to Thomas Givers 19 Aug 1647
Yates Joseph s Edmund, Finmere, Oxf, yeoman to Richard Yates 28 Apr 1681
Yates Richard s Edmund, Finmere, Oxf, yeoman to William Gurney 7 Jan 1669/70
Yates Roger s Henry, Wadesmill [Thundridge], Hrt, clerk to William Hodson 13 Dec 1647
Yeal William s John, New Town, Maryland, watchmaker† to Caleb Johnson 13 May 1755 <28 Jun 1758 turned over to John Cowling>
Yearsley Thomas s William, Hertford, Hrt, pavior to John Flock Roberts 5 Aug 1777
Yeates James s Tobias, citizen and dyer† to John Greeneing 9 Aug 1688
Yeates Robert s John, Bolton, Lan, yeoman to Thomas Hodges 14 Feb 1647/8
Yefford Thomas s John, Ware, Hrt, feltmaker to John Prichard 5 Apr 1641
Yelond John s John, Exeter, Dev, pack saddler to William Dutton 11 May 1671
Yeo John s John, St Clement Danes, Mdx, tailor† to Thomas Higgins 26 Nov 1689
Yeomans James s John, Hallingbury, Ess, gentleman† to Alice widow of Edmund Barcock 16 Feb 1675/6
Yeomans John s John, Little Hollingbury, Ess, gentleman to Edmund Barcock 26 Apr 1666
Young Charles s John, West Hall, Methley, Yks, gentleman to John Hooker 9 Jun 1657
Young Giles s Christopher, Charlton Abbots, Gls, husbandman to Thomas Young 20 Nov 1637
Young John s John, Little Comberton, Wor, yeoman to John Wood 8 Jul 1641
Young Joseph s Edward, citizen and carpenter† to Thomas Hails 10 May 1659
Young Walter s Walter, Wotton under Edge, Gls, physician to Robert Butcher 14? Jul 1673
Young William s George, citizen and poulterer to John Harbert 5 Feb 1699/1700 <10 Oct 1702 cancelled>
Young William s John, St John Horsleydown, Sry, tallow chandler to Joseph Carroll 9 Jul 1761
Younge Thomas s Richard, Tewkesbury, Gls, gentleman to John Helan 28 Sep 1663 <his sister Prudence Younge promises to give her brother a new suit of clothes>
Younge Thomas s William, 'Chapwell', Bdf, husbandman† to John Sole 10 May 1664
Younger James s John, Hereford, Hef, innkeeper to George Stretton 21 Jan 1652/3

Zouch Charles s Francis to his father 4 Sep 1690

INDEX OF MASTERS

Abbott William 27
Ace Charles 39
Acton John 1
Adams (Addams) George 55; Jacob 110; John 1, 94, 99; Joseph 64, 102; Michael 84; William 38
Addison Thomas 61, 83, 106
Adie Ann 83
Agate Thomas 37
Ailiffe *see* Ayliffe
Alden William 15, 40, 65, 74, 88, 93, 114
Aldersea William 63
Alexander (Allexander) Richard 36, 106; William 2, 5, 9, 24, 25, 27, 32, 38, 45, 48, 55, 60, 71, 78, 82, 87, 92, 95, 108, 116
Allam William 73
Allen (Allin) Elizabeth 97; Mary 4, 15, 22, 51; Richard 2; Thomas 19, 29, 44, 47, 49, 82, 83, 86, 93, 95, 97, 98, 102; William 2, 4, 15, 22, 24, 25, 48, 51, 56, 83, 107
Allett Magdalen 72; William 23, 34, 71, 72, 80
Allexander *see* Alexander
Allin *see* Allen
Almey Mathew 29
Alyff *see* Ayliffe
Ambrose Ebenezer 71
Ancketill *see* Ancktell
Anckle John 6; Thomas 15, 64
Ancktell (Ancketill) Thomas 1, 3
Anderton Benjamin 13, 99
Andrews (Andrew, Andrewes) Daniel 22; Henry 50; Mary 46, 92; Thomas 61, 68; William 74, 88, 103, 110, 111
Ansell Leonard 85; Mary 78; Thomas 33, 38, 78; William 23
Anslow Henry Julius 75
Appleyard John 112
Apsley Robert 12, 75, 80, 87, 110, 112
Archer Ann 47; Edward 81; Isabel 2; John 72, 99, 108, 109; 2, Joseph 89; Peter 47
Ardinton Francis 92
Arewater Thomas 66; Thomas Charles 92, 94
Argins John 13
Arnold Latham 49; Ralph 26
Arris Henry 87
Arundell Henry 108
Ascough *see* Ayscough
Ashburner Thomas 4, 111
Ashman William 46
Asplin (Asple) Robert 11, 19, 38
Atherton Humphrey 14
Atkins John 37
Axe John 28, 30
Ayers *see* Ayres
Ayliffe (Ailiffe, Alyff, Aylife, Ayliffe) Brian 3, 5, 16, 22, 33, 42, 59, 70, 84, 86, 90, 92, 100; John 47, 55, 85, 86, 88; Mary 48; Robert 10, 38, 48, 50, 90, 111, 113
Ayres (Ayers, Ayre) Esther 76; John 39, 49, 76; Richard 5, 8, 20, 25, 101, 109; William 15 *see also* Eyres
Ayscough (Ascough) John 9, 14, 16, 20, 23, 25, 34, 39, 41, 46, 89, 95, 99, 108, 109

Babbin John 91
Bach Richard 81
Back John 3, 36, 66, 103
Backhouse Richard 8, 28, 36, 51, 55
Baddily (Badily) Radcliff 69, 104
Badham William 4, 11, 26, 55, 56, 62, 96, 111

INDEX OF MASTERS

Badily *see* Baddily
Badwell Richard 31
Bagg (Bagge) Mathew 5, 106, 115
Bagley William 20
Bague James 11, 40, 86
Bailey John 25, 58
Baker Joseph 71; Richard 44; William 23
Baldwin Jasper 19; John 4; Joshua 69
Ball Thomas 91
Ballard John 30, 38; William 112
Banckworth John 40, 71, 82
Banister *see* Bannester
Banks (Bankes) Thomas 26, 74
Bannester (Banister) Francis 36, 112
Barber Francis 11, 40, 79, 115; Thomas 11, 76
Barcock (Barcocke) Alice 116; Edmund 1, 9, 31, 41, 51, 54, 92, 96, 108, 116
Barker Arthur 10; Charles 76; Edward 5, 16, 36, 40, 59; Thomas 6, 107
Barksdale Sarah 73; Thomas 73
Barlow (Barlowe) Joseph 7, 18, 31, 63, 84, 88, 105, 109
Barnard Rebecca 5, 72; Richard 5, 16, 38, 72
Barrabee (Burrabee) Richard 110
Barrett Eleanor 7; Thomas 4, 7; William 7, 64, 84
Barton (Bartan) Henry 71; Samuel 7, 75
Barwell Elizabeth 93; Mathew 7, 11, 21, 28, 31, 32, 73, 105; Thomas 75, 93; William 105
Bateman Elizabeth 1; William 1, 5, 11, 15, 24, 45, 77, 78, 112
Bates Edward 73
Batten (Battin) Henry 7, 8, 25, 50, 63, 75
Baugh John 8, 78
Baughurst Robert 94
Bavin John 17, 42; William 80
Baynard Thomas 7, 61, 105
Baynes Mary 43; Thomas 43
Bayzand (Bayrand, Beyzand, Bezand) John 55, 63, 86
Beadle (Beadell, Bedall, Bedell) Robert 10, 29, 33; Thomas 26, 46, 88
Beardoe *see* Berdoe
Beasly Samuel 38
Beatew (Beaten, Beten, Bettew, Butewe, Buttew) Isaac 8, 24, 26, 30, 50, 58, 73, 74
Beaumont John 36
Beckett (Beckitt) Gervase 34, 84, 106, 114; Nicholas 1, 9, 15, 18, 23, 35, 39, 82, 85, 96, 103, 104
Bedall, Bedell *see* Beadle
Bedwell John 47, 79, 107; Richard 9, 27, 32, 35, 37, 44; Samuel 9, 17, 32, 40, 53, 55, 57, 60, 73, 89, 98
Bee Edward 14
Belchamber (Belchambers, Bellchambers) Samuel 5, 9, 16, 22, 30, 32, 58, 71, 98
Bellis (Belliss, Bellows) George 9, 17, 25, 44, 79, 110; Mary 9, 17, 25, 30, 44, 35, 112; Nathaniel 10, 40; Sarah 10
Belson Edmund 11, 32, 44; Mary 49; Robert 46, 49, 115; Thomas 90
Benge, Benion *see* Benyon
Bennett Mary 9, 86; Thomas 9, 12, 29, 43, 60, 77, 86, 87, 103, 107
Benson Joseph 47
Bentham Jeremy 7
Bentley (Bently) Edward 103; Rebecca 103; Samuel 57
Benyon (Benge, Benion, Binion) Daniel 40, 48, 60, 99; Gabriel 21, 38, 81, 83
Berdoe (Beardoe) Charles 54, 70, 96
Bernard Henry 89
Berridge John 10, 70
Berry John 10, 56, 69; Richard 57; Samuel 5, 58
Berryman Isaac 78

INDEX OF MASTERS

Beten, Bettew *see* Beatew
Bexhill Samuel 10, 11, 57, 99
Bey Mathew 112
Beyzand, Bezand *see* Bayzand
Biggs (Bigg) John 7, 31; Thomas 6; William 109
Bigland Ralph 96
Bignold Isaac 78
Billing (Billings) Elizabeth 40; Francis 33, 83; Nathaniel 31, 40, 73, 82, 86, 111
Binion *see* Benyon
Bird (Byrd) George 11, 90, 92; George Martin 87; John 85; William 11, 28
Blackbourne John 87; Philadelphia 87
Blackmore John 7, 14
Bland David 56
Blandford Joseph 58, 76, 107
Bliss Ann 11; John 11; Richard 11
Blizard John 29, 87
Block Bernard 46, 85, 92
Blomefeild William 7
Blower Samuel 12, 66, 79
Bly Robert 7, 46, 48, 79, 91, 99, 105; William 74, 98
Bodle John 9, 43
Bonner Bartholomew 19, 64
Boord *see* Bord
Booth Joseph 19, 62, 74, 79, 83; William 99
Bord (Boord) George 63; Joseph 4; Thomas 28, 66, 67, 88, 103, 107, 112
Bornley *see* Burnley
Botton John 49
Boucher Robert 17, 50, 60, 70, 95
see also Butcher
Bourne John 13; Thomas 65
Bowden John 2, 6, 13, 22, 41, 51, 93, 94
Bowder Francis 55
Bowers Thomas 26
Bowley John 81
Bowtell Mary 32
Bowyer George 25, 35, 41, 43, 68; William 5, 11, 24, 27, 32, 47, 53, 55, 60, 67, 68, 76, 78
Boyce Edward 18
Bradgate *see* Broadgate
Bradley Elizabeth 42; Robert 13, 42, 88, 95, 100
Bradshawe Edward 13
Bradstreete (Broadstreete) John 15, 34
Brandon Gilbert 25, 46, 70, 71, 81
Brandreth Edward 94
Brecknell Benjamin 104
Breed (Brood) Charles 20, 26, 83, 96, 115
Brent James 8, 72
Brewer Lancelot 30, 63
Brewis William 46
Brian John 26, 29, 70, 111
Brice Richard 21, 40
Bridge John 113
Bright John 54
Bringhurst Robert 9, 14, 38, 48, 78, 95
Brisco (Briscoe, Bristo, Bristoe, Bruscop) Francis 42, 64, 94; John 8, 20; Robert 1, 15, 34, 63, 73, 88, 92
Bristur Edward 79
Broadbank (Broadbanck) Thomas 18, 19, 48, 65, 66, 109
Broadgate (Bradgate, Brodgate) Jeremiah 7, 14, 17, 56, 60, 61, 101, 105; Jeremy 61

Broadstreete *see* Bradstreete
Brock (Brocke) Abraham 42, 114
Brodgate *see* Broadgate
Bromfeild John 32; Richard 34
Bromsall (Bromsell, Broomsill) Edward 41, 53; Thomas 38, 64, 74
Bromwich William 88
Brood *see* Breed
Brooke (Brookes) Abraham 34; Anthony 15; John 6; Thomas 3
Brooker (Browker) Samuel 25, 51, 66, 102, 104, 114
Brookes *see* Brooke
Broomsill *see* Bromsall
Browker *see* Brooker
Browne (Brown) Benjamin 96; Daniel 68, 114; Edmund 110; John 6, 51, 55, 68, 75, 92; Joseph 98; Samuel 111; Thomas 19, 113
Brownesmith (Brownsmith, Browsmith) Benjamin 20, 34, 36, 43, 44, 53, 54, 61, 71, 98, 115
Browning Edward 15
Brownsmith, Browsmith *see* Brownesmith
Bruscop *see* Brisco
Brushfield Thomas 16
Bryan (Brian) John 5, 11, 16, 23, 24, 26, 29, 32, 38, 44, 45, 48, 57, 70, 79, 80, 98, 101, 111, 114
Buckler William 10, 89
Buckley William 70
Bugby (Buggbie) Thomas 29, 91
Buggey (Buggy) Francis 5, 54, 87
Bull Nicholas 53; Richard 41, 46, 53, 65, 71, 81, 87, 95, 105
Bullimore James 97
Bullock Henry 10, 15, 86; Mathew 1
Bulter Gabriel 41
Bunn (Bun) Anthony 51, 52, 94, 100, 104
Burbrough (Burborrough) John 2, 56, 57, 84, 101, 109
Burby John 26
Burchard (Burchett) Nathaniel 94, 108, 112
Burdett Thomas 76, 85
Burge (Burg) John 82; Thomas 29, 42, 71
Burgis (Burges, Burgess) Edward 21, 37, 41; John 14, 16, 18, 23, 27, 28, 35, 57, 61, 79, 88, 100; Richard 44, 85; Thomas 82; William 115
Burkett Charles 27, 33
Burnby Richard 104
Burnley (Bornley) Henry 6, 58, 112; William 111
Burrabee *see* Barrabee
Burrowes (Burrow) Charles 69; Lydia 69; Thomas 17, 45, 86
Burton Francis 16; Henry 6, 9, 22, 37, 38, 46, 53, 85; John 49, 101; Joseph 6; Thomas 83
Bury John 67; Samuel 25, 30, 75
Bush John 29
Butcher Edward 13, 23, 48, 81; Humphrey 40; Robert 6, 8, 17, 20, 21, 22, 53, 61, 94, 112, 115, 116
see also Boucher
Butewe *see* Beatew
Butler Daniel 37; William 12, 16, 33, 42, 50, 71
Butterfeild Ralph 105; Richard 31, 102; Thomas 83
Butterton Nathaniel 92; Simon 52
Butterworth Jacob 17, 21
Buttew *see* Beatew
Butts John 95
Bwye James 9
Byard Elizabeth 50, 88, 93; James 8, 28, 50, 88, 93
Byrd *see* Bird

INDEX OF MASTERS

Caddy (Cadday, Caddi) John 2, 18, 51, 59, 60, 101, 112
Cadle (Cadell) Bartholomew 22, 110
Calcott *see* Callcott
Caldwell (Caldwall) John 40, 103
Callcott (Calcott) Joseph 10, 35, 36, 43, 58, 80, 114; William 31
Calloway Richard 59, 63, 88
Cannell John 18, 108
Capet Thomas 55
Carde (Card, Cardy) Silvester 16, 72, 78, 92, 97
Carpenter (Carpinter) Charles 56; Edmund 42, 53, 74; George 25, 41, 42, 47, 49, 66, 75, 104, 111; Thomas 61
Carr George 38; Thomas 86; William 50
Carroll Joseph 32, 58, 81, 84, 87, 116
Carter Eleanor 19; John 8, 11, 19, 32, 42, 62, 99; Lawrence 12, 18, 35, 86; Richard 9, 45, 56, 57, 68, 93, 100
Cartwright Charles 95
Casbert Joseph 84, 113
Case Henry 32, 84, 110; Thomas 98
Castleton John 100
Catkill *see* Cattkitt
Catterns Thomas 89
Cattkitt (Catkill, Katkitt) Nicholas 46, 58, 90
Cave Thomas 18, 22, 55, 81, 82; William 24, 27, 34, 58, 106
Chadsey John 95
Chamberlayne (Chamberlin) Edward 68; Joseph 62
Chambers John 93, 111; Sarah 27, 31, 39, 101; Thomas 18, 19, 27, 31, 39, 42, 43, 44, 58, 75, 101
Champion Stephen 33, 102
Champney Peter 51, 65, 101
Chandler Edward 67; Giles 33; Nathaniel 9, 35, 36, 44, 57, 58, 61, 85, 88, 90, 93
Chapman John 25, 102, 111
Charlton (Charleton) Nicholas 4, 18, 26, 57, 65, 66, 72, 92, 98, 113
Chater William 4, 20, 76, 81
Chatfield (Chatfeild) John 36, 48, 93, 109; Mary 20
Cheaney (Cheany, Chenney) John 8, 39, 80, 95
Cheshire (Chesshire, Chesshyre, Chysshire) Peter 14, 17, 20, 36, 40, 86; William 19, 57
Chester (Chestroe, Chestroo) Anthony 7, 23, 24, 35; Granado 3, 113
Chewter (Chooter) John 21, 94, 100, 111; Thomas 9, 21, 63, 66, 94; William 97
Child (Childe) Daniel 23, 41, 44, 98; John 6, 16, 18, 20, 41, 45, 53, 63, 65, 75, 93, 104
Chitty *see* Citty
Cholmley Hugh 63, 65
Chooter *see* Chewter
Christian John 73
Christie Alexander 22
Christopher Edward 111
Church James 9, 27, 40, 46, 59, 69, 73, 110, 115; John 3, 21, 46, 84, 93, 97
Churcher George 26
Chysshire *see* Cheshire
Citty Peter 86, 90, 94
Clant John 92
Clare (Claro) Frances 4, 21; George 21, 91, 100; Grace 15, 22, 49; Samuel 64; Thomas 4, 21, 57, 97, 98, 107
Clarebutt Daniel 4, 16, 21, 23, 53, 57, 66
Clarke (Clark, Clerke) Abraham 112; Benjamin 92, 104, 113; Edward 4, 5, 16, 17, 22, 51, 59, 69, 76, 77, 85, 96, 115; Henry 24, 41, 89; Jacob 63; James 77, 92, 102; John 18, 34, 44, 70, 77, 112; Richard 97, 108; Ruth 22; Thomas 22, 48, 90, 97, 100, 108; Walter 30; William 7, 24, 77, 78, 95, 107
Clarkson Robert 91
Claro *see* Clare

Clay Robert 13, 97
Cleave John 51, 52, 55, 60, 67, 75; Sarah 51, 67, 75
Cleaver Thomas 1
Clement (Clements) Richard 13, 58, 73; William 39, 65, 75
Clerke *see* Clarke
Clifton Joseph 12, 23, 51
Close Hannah 30, 50; John 30, 50, 80, 102
Closs Samuel 23
Coare Francis 32, 103
Coates (Cotes) James 16, 48, 106; John 14, 48, 54, 81, 88, 94, 112; Mary 48
Cock (Cocke) Henry 23; John 49, 77; Joseph 71; Sarah 66; William 7, 50, 56, 59, 64, 110
Cogan William 13, 23, 47, 56, 72, 78, 96
Cogdell John 25; William 81
Coggs Joseph 7, 49, 62, 84, 87, 99
Coker John 22
Colcraft John 26, 70
Cole Thomas 3, 43, 47, 50, 65, 67, 90, 100, 115
see also Coles
Coleman Samuel 54, 100
Coles Edward 2, 24, 40; William 30, 36, 60, 85, 93
see also Cole
Collett Henry 12, 91; Richard 86
Collier (Collyer) Daniel 13, 24, 34, 102; James 56, 67, 85, 101; John 65; Joseph 78, 81, 96, 97; Richard 1, 24, 26, 47, 50, 76, 99; William 2, 3, 8, 16, 24, 34, 48, 54, 65, 70, 93, 101, 102, 104, 116
Collington John 39, 54, 92, 95, 105
Collins Nicholas 115; Richard 18, 44, 59, 94; Robert 14, 30, 89; Thomas 73, 97
Collyer *see* Collier
Coltstock *see* Coulstoke
Comber Cleophas 13, 35
Combes Robert 14
Commins Thomas 69
Compton John 11, 25, 31, 39, 67, 71, 105
Conaway Richard 41
Constable Philip 27, 39, 42, 45, 68, 91, 107
Cooke (Cook) Carter 31; Edmund 25; George 21; Giles 4; Henry 25; John 73, 86, 112; Richard 35, 50, 87, 96; Robert 17
Cookson John 25, 106
Cooper (Cowper) Henry 10, 12, 14, 35; John 62; Joseph 30, 44, 48, 66; Richard 18, 43, 57, 67, 82; Robert 113; Susanna 10; Thomas 7, 42, 63
Copeland Edward 4, 23, 63, 67, 93, 102; James 72; Mary 78, 87
Cordy (Cordey) Silvester 5, 13, 18, 57, 106
Cornelius Gilbert 26, 46, 67, 84, 85, 95, 103
Cornley William 26
Cose Thomas 16
Cosins *see* Couzens
Cotching Joseph 63
Cotes *see* Coates
Cotten John 113
Cottrill William 22
Coulstoke (Coltstock) William 40, 66
Couppe Jacob 2; James 63
Couzens (Cosins) John 26, 78; William 7, 11
Cowley William 28
Cowling John 31, 82, 116
Cowper *see* Cooper
Cox Henry 3, 20, 49, 70, 74, 75, 95, 102, 105; Isaac 90, 108; Samuel 94, 102; Thomas 10, 11, 32
Crackanthorp, Crackinthorpe *see* Crakenthorpe

INDEX OF MASTERS

Cragg William 16
Crakenthorpe (Crackanthorp, Crackinthorpe) Benjamin 10, 90, 101
Cranwell William 9, 12, 13, 20, 36, 42, 58, 61, 62, 66, 69, 73, 104, 105
Crook John 47
Crosier Charles 15, 62, 72
Crouch John 71
Croudson Silcox 94
Crowther Thomas 43, 69, 82, 116; William 2
Cryer Thomas 36, 43, 56, 100, 108, 114
Culcheth Benjamin 45
Cutlet (Cutlett, Cuttlett) Thomas 35, 84, 96
Cutt (Cuttes) Edmund 107; James 80
Cuttlett *see* Cutlet
Cutts *see* Cutt

Dabber *see* Dubber
Daken *see* Deakin
Dale Daniel 9, 17, 24, 50, 66, 103; Richard 16, 18
Dallock (Dalock) ... 47; Thomas 72
Dane Thomas 28, 29
Daniel (Daniell) Hugh 33, 42; Jeremiah 28, 59, 85, 92
Darby James 69
Darcy (Darcey) John 8, 49, 73, 95
Dare Charles 12, 16, 20, 31, 32, 47, 50, 52, 54, 56, 70, 82, 96, 102; Rebecca 50; Samuel 3, 26, 50, 90, 99
Darker Richard 2, 14, 86
Darrant Simon 44
Dauson *see* Dawson
Davenport (Davinport) John 1, 2, 17, 19, 27, 42, 44, 52, 64, 114
Davey John 30, 95
Davidson James 70
Davies Mathew Peter 82; Richard 7, 93, 112; Robert 82; Thomas 17, 57
see also Davis
Davinport *see* Davenport
Davis Henry 81; John 78, 87; Richard 58; Thomas 91, 97; William 28, 44, 74, 85, 90, 114
see also Davies
Dawson (Dauson, Dowson) Francis 4; John 80; Simon 3, 11, 24, 35, 47, 76, 78, 99, 110; Thomas 67, 115
Day Robert 1, 14, 52, 55, 66, 69; Thomas 9, 48, 77, 111
Deacon John 89; Margaret 89
Deakin (Daken) Ann 35; William 74
Dean (Deane) Henry 25; Mathew 39
Deely Samuel 96
Delafeild Joseph 97
Delan John 26
Delight Peter 46, 106
Dell Benjamin 34; John 44, 46
Denby John 49
Dench Gilbert 112
Denny (Denney) Samuel 11, 72, 107, 111
Dent John 82
Dickens *see* Dickins
Dickenson *see* Dickinson
Dickins (Dickens) Ann 23; Daniel 113; John 23, 28, 38, 40, 57, 79; William 104
Dickinson (Dickenson) Charles 109; Robert 82
Diston Jacob 108
Dixon Zachariah 54, 86
Dodswell Thomas 14

Doiley (Doilie, Doyley) Charles 75, 76, 91, 96, 103, 108; Giles 23
Doleman Marmaduke 13, 104
Dolphin John 50
Dorrant *see* Durrant
Dorrell Joseph 19, 70
Dorrington Elizabeth 31; William 31, 65
Dove Richard 59; Robert 8, 54, 58, 59, 74, 87, 102
Dowdswell (Dowdeswell, Doweswell) Thomas 5, 23, 40, 56, 89, 95, 101, 106, 110
Downes James 73; Sarah 12, 73, 96
Downing Elizabeth 60; William 60, 98
Dowson *see* Dawson
Doyley *see* Doiley
Dranton Jeremiah 93
Draydge Richard 97
Drinkewater Francis 58, 77, 112
Driver Lewis 14; Robert 2, 16, 42, 52, 85, 101, 110
Dubber (Dabber) Eleanor 34; Ellen 10; Thomas 34, 39, 80, 82, 111
Ducroq Lewis 54
Duff Peter 103, 106
Dunbabin, Dunbarton (Dunbabin) Richard 81, 94
Dunkin Henry 52, 60, 115
Durant *see* Durrant
Durban Henry 18, 66
Durdant Thomas 32
Durnford Benjamin 41
Durrant (Darrant, Dorrant, Durant) Simon 2, 41, 44, 73
Dutton Thomas 1; William 34, 47, 59, 116
Dwight William 15, 32
Dyer John 24
Dyson Francis 26, 100

Eade Jonathan 99; William Jonathan 56
Eames Daniel 62
Eastland Henry 26, 72
Easton Joseph 102; Thomas 51; William 33, 100
Eborall (Ebrall) Agnes 59; Elizabeth 33; Richard 33, 59, 89
Edden (Eden) John 22, 43, 47, 54, 90, 98, 100, 113
Edgerley (Edgerly) Herbert 76, 89; Richard 33
Edmonds (Edmunds) Thomas 33; William 51, 52
Edrop Thomas 8
Edwards Nathaniel 10
Eeles Nathaniel 14
Egerton William 15, 79
Eightshillings Jeremiah 112
Ekins Robert 28, 39
Ellcock Samuel 29
Elliott Richard 86; William 78
Ellis James 64; John 28
Elmer James 56
Elsmere Richard 32
Ennis James 41, 42, 55, 58
Etheridge William 34
Eustis Richard 37
Evans George 13, 14, 83; Hugh 12
Eve Thomas 26, 73
Everard Thomas 35
Ewer John 28, 35, 76, 80
Ewster John 74

Eyans Rollinson 27, 53
Eyre (Eyres) John 11, 38, 42, 44, 104; Thomas 35, 53, 64; William 7, 32, 97
see also Ayres

Falkner Thomas 108
Farmer Ann 51; Christopher 65, 67, 75; William 51
Farrant (Farraine, Farren, Ferrant) Abraham 35, 66, 103; Nicholas 8, 36, 55, 93; Samuel 66; Thomas 62, 78, 112
Farwell Elizabeth 116
Fary Benjamin 28
Favell Methusaleh 66
Fawcett Robert 24, 29
Fearon *see* Ferne
Feild *see* Field
Fenny *see* Finney
Ferne (Fearon) John 15, 17, 32
Ferrall Russell 59; Thomas 36, 42
Ferrant *see* Farrant
Fewtrell (Fewterell) Robert 43, 49, 75, 91, 109, 113
Field (Feild, Fidd) Dalby 100; Mary 36; Nathaniel 36, 37, 72, 83, 86, 88; Ralph 27, 36, 80, 94; Richard 94
Figgins Thomas 58
Filewood James 40
Finney (Fenny) William 8, 32, 57, 64, 78
Fish Thomas 77
Fisher Charles 110; John 4, 7, 23, 50; Joseph 53, 72, 76; William 49
Fist John 31, 46, 59, 75, 79, 90, 93, 97
Fitch Samuel 3, 17, 37, 61, 62, 71, 85, 93, 94, 103
Fitz Edward 12, 26, 37, 43, 70, 98, 106, 112; Robert 5, 34; Samuel 71
Flaxmore (Flamnore) Thomas 51, 91
Fletcher Alice 61; Edward 61; Vincent 27, 109
Flewellin (Flewellyn, Fluellin) Robert 7, 78; William 90
Flight John 32, 64, 84; Joseph 47, 49, 72, 82, 96; Mary 64, 73
Flindall Samuel 37; Stephen 21, 41, 64, 96
Flood Edward 22
Flower Francis 68; Mary 31; William 31, 37, 47
Floyd Edward 61
Fluellin *see* Flewellin
Folkingham Theophilus 29
Ford John 8, 32, 35, 92; Thomas 4, 15, 57, 60, 65, 114
Forth Thomas 53
Forty John 38
Fossey (Foss) Edward 38, 51; Thomas 51, 65
Foster Timothy 38, 48, 60, 63, 80, 85, 95
Fowler William 17, 30, 39
Fox William 106
Foy William 114
Franck John 104
Francklin Edward 29
Free Benjamin 14, 32, 39, 45, 89, 93; Eliza 39; Elizabeth 32, 89
Freeman John 10, 39, 65, 81; Robert 116; William 100
Freer William 32
French John 61, 112; Robert 29, 32, 36, 39, 42, 48, 55, 57, 58, 62, 65, 74, 95
Frisbee John 106
Fuller Thomas 90
Fullwood (Fulwood) Richard 22, 28, 62, 65, 66, 73, 78, 81, 82, 92, 98, 105, 107, 111
Furness (Furnis) Edward 16; John 34, 39, 44, 59, 76

INDEX OF MASTERS

Gadsby (Gaddsbe) Francis 60, 66
Gainsford John 15
Gale Roger 28, 68, 76, 84; Thomas 60
Garbrand John 99
Gardner (Gardener, Gardiner) Ann Hedges 32, 33, 98, 106; John 45, 97; Martin 9, 33; Thomas 23, 62; William 106
Garfoote William 38, 101, 115
Garland John 19, 41
Garment Edward 78
Garmeson (Garnson) John 4, 51
Gason William 14
Gast John 18
Gates Richard 79
Gaunt (Gaunte) William 2, 7, 10, 25, 35, 37, 40, 45, 49, 55, 67, 69, 76, 107, 109
Gazeley (Gazelie) John 30, 41
Geery (Gery) Jasper 9, 31; Oliver 26, 100
George Andrew 18
Gerrard (Gerard) George 13, 26, 46, 60; Samuel 39, 80; Thomas 13, 80
Gery *see* Geery
Gibbons (Gibbon) George 99; John 52, 107; Joseph 35, 51, 56, 94, 97, 103
Gibbs David 100
Gibson Jeremiah 91; Thomas 104; William 37, 38, 67, 68, 75, 91, 103, 109
Gigner Francis 13, 70
Gilderson John 81
Giles Daniel 19, 36, 38, 90
Gilgrest John 18, 44, 49
Gill John 8, 35, 38, 97
Gilson Thomas 61, 91, 104
Givers (Giver) Thomas 6, 69, 71, 98, 100, 116
Glyd Richard 13, 31, 61
Goade *see* Goode
Goble William 25, 61
Goddard Robert 33, 39, 53, 79
Godwin (Godwinn) Andrew 19, 25, 39, 42, 73, 100, 102, 111; Charles 9, 50, 81, 83, 110; Elizabeth 110; John 76
Gold *see* Gould
Goode (Goade) John 11, 21, 43, 65, 68, 84, 100
Goodfellow Matthias 33
Goodier Charles 61
Goodman ... 21; Charles 9, 15; William 3, 43, 54, 57, 67, 74, 76, 81
Goodwin Andrew 48, 71; George 14, 23, 88, 90; Philip 102, 112; Starling 87
Gould (Gold) Elizabeth 97; John 45, 68, 85, 88, 97; Nicholas 12, 21, 43, 103
Gourd John 29
Gown William 95
Gray John 28, 43, 60
Greatrix James 28; Mary 28
Green *see* Greene
Greenall Thomas Wells 98
Greene (Green) James 4; John 44, 54, 90, 95, 103; Nicholas 57, 103, 110; Robert 44; Thomas 28, 35, 69, 70, 106; William 115
Greenehead William 40
Greenehill *see* Greenhill
Greeneing *see* Greening
Greenhill (Greenehill) Simon 9, 44, 84; William 113
Greening (Greeneing) John 1, 42, 58, 63, 80, 106, 116; Peter 19, 85
Greenupp William 16, 24, 31
Greenwood Charles 63; John 11
Gregory Harris 44; James 52; Joseph 38, 58; Thomas 9; William 96, 112

Gresswell (Greswell, Grosswell) Eliza 78; Elizabeth 23, 41, 42, 71, 80, 82, 83, 96, 103; Robert 23, 41, 42, 47, 61, 71, 78, 80, 82, 83, 96, 103, 109
Griffiths Griffith 68, 109; John 92; Samuel 74
Grigg Edward 114
Grinaway Peter 29
Grosswell *see* Gresswell
Grove George 57; William 13, 33, 63, 80
Grover Thomas 37, 70, 99, 115
Gudgeon Jacob 79
Gulliford Mary 45; Samuel 27; William 45, 99, 110, 114
Gunston (Gunson, Gunstone, Gunsun) Robert 13; Thomas 2, 78, 97; William 12, 68
Gurney Christopher 94; Daniel 50, 64; Elizabeth 97; Ralph 97; William 3, 5, 10, 12, 14, 16, 17, 22, 23, 24, 27, 35, 36, 43, 44, 45, 48, 50, 53, 54, 55, 57, 58, 60, 61, 62, 63, 64, 65, 66, 67, 70, 73, 74, 79, 80, 81, 82, 85, 87, 88, 90, 92, 96, 98, 105, 106, 108, 110, 111, 113, 116
Guy Edward 89; Mary 57; Nathaniel 57

Haddon, Haden *see* Haydon
Haies *see* Hayes
Haile, Hails *see* Hale
Haines (Hain, Hains, Haynes) David 41; Elizabeth 88; George 61; John 88; Richard 55; Thomas 6, 63, 67, 81, 85, 88, 94
Haits Thomas 77
see also Hasted
Hake Ann 9; Stephen 9
Hale (Haile, Hails, Hales, Hayle) Anthony 46; Michael 9, 50, 72, 75; Thomas 104, 116
Halford (Holford) Andrew 31; Samuel 37, 65
Hall Edmund 18, 34, 46, 62, 98; Edward 72; Henry 69; John 26; Mary 26; Nathan 56, 78, 80, 92; Philip 21
Halsey (Holsey) Edward 87, 90; John 23, 36, 68, 74, 76, 78, 83, 115; Miles 53
Ham John 33, 43, 46, 56, 72
Hamett (Hamnett, Harnett) John 45; Thomas 46, 63, 92, 98
Hammond *see* Hamond
Hamnett *see* Hamett
Hamond (Hammond, Hamon) Ann 103; John 54, 77; Joseph 113; Samuel 15, 32, 37, 66, 91, 114
Hancock James 66; Robert 2, 35, 73, 77
Handford (Handforth) Adrian 57, 96
Hankins John 3
Hankinson John 12, 75
Hansford (Harford) Adrian 57, 94
Hanslopp Henry 53
Hanson Francis 47; Robert 47; Samuel 95; Thomas 47
Hanwell John Maynard 79
Harbert John 10, 55, 95, 112, 116; Martha 11; Richard 108
see also Herbert
Harding James 18, 31, 46, 51, 66, 105, 109; John 11, 13, 50; Richard 30
Harford *see* Hansford
Harling George 41, 50
Harlow George 15, 17, 47, 70, 78, 83, 101, 111
Harnett *see* Hamett
Harris Edmund 27, 51; Edward 10, 35, 48, 51, 84, 85, 90, 100; Elizabeth 50, 68, 82; Giles 27, 28, 29, 42, 54, 61, 82, 94, 95; John 8, 48, 49, 76, 100, 107; Joseph 42; Mathew 82; Samuel 50, 68, 96; Stephen 47, 57, 73; Thomas 2, 4, 20, 45, 51, 77, 86, 94, 111
Harrison John 6, 8, 13, 15, 22, 24, 26, 41, 53, 54, 64, 76, 103, 108, 109, 112; Thomas 3, 4, 8, 15, 17, 113; William 102
Harton John 48; Rebecca 48
Harvy Robert 30, 62
Hasted (Hasteed, Husted) Thomas 20, 23, 30, 63, 66, 74, 91, 110
see also Haits

Hastings Elizabeth 1, 14, 28, 40, 45, 49, 59, 67, 90; John 1, 14, 28, 40, 45, 49, 67, 77, 82, 85, 88, 90
Hatton Thomas 5, 15, 16, 19, 25, 42, 45, 48, 67, 69, 76, 86, 88, 104, 108
Haughton *see* Houghton
Havell Henry 76
Havens William 68, 88, 99
Hawatt *see* Hewett
Hawes Giles 99; John 108; Thomas 20, 31, 49, 65, 79, 94
Hawett *see* Hewett
Hawkes Henry 9, 21, 28, 30, 39, 63, 113, 114
Hawkins Dinah 49; Henry 49, 63, 102
Haydon (Haddon, Haden, Hayden, Heydon) Nicholas 99; Philip 42, 46, 75, 79; Richard 16, 53; Robert 14, 50; Thomas 30, 59; William 1, 13, 14, 22, 23, 23, 34, 38, 48, 49, 67, 92, 94, 100, 115
Hayes (Haies) Thomas 20, 25, 27, 30, 39, 50, 38, 72, 91, 95, 97
Hayle *see* Hale
Haynes *see* Haines
Hayward (Heyward, Heywood) Bartholomew 112; David 18, 54; John 5; Joseph 55
Hearn (Hierne) John 51, 58, 98
Heather Ephraim 97; Richard 40; William 5, 17, 20, 24
Hedgeland William 17, 99, 101, 109
Hedges Thomas 17
Helan John 116
Hell Richard 21
Heming (Hemings) Edmund 107; Edward 66, 94
Henshaw Egerton 25, 36, 50, 52, 62, 64, 87; Elizabeth 64
Herbert John 42; Martha 42, 112
see also Harbert
Hewer John 21, 66, 67
Hewett (Hawatt, Hawett, Howett) Nicholas 10, 49, 58, 89; William 16, 108
Hewettson *see* Huatson
Heydon *see* Haydon
Heyward, Heywood *see* Hayward
Hibens Thomas 18
Hiccock Catherine 69; Thomas 69
Hickman John 109
Hicks Jonathan 47, 83, 87, 106; Robert 5, 40, 49, 53
Hide John 35, 44
Hierne *see* Hearn
Higby Richard 51
Higgins Mary 49, 52; Richard 24, 56, 97; Thomas 5, 8, 11, 12, 13, 14, 37, 43, 49, 63, 81, 85, 90, 99, 101, 106, 110, 116
Higgs John 21, 66, 74; Robert 66; Samuel 19; William 66
Hildyard *see* Hilliard
Hill Elizabeth 110; Esther 39; Hannah 23; Henry 10, 15, 52; Humphrey 4, 7, 10, 52, 68, 92, 104; James 47; John 1, 27, 42, 50, 70, 88, 100; Oliver 7, 110; Richard 20, 31, 86; Thomas 1, 26, 33, 39, 42, 44, 52, 53, 88, 107; William 23, 39, 52
see also Hills
Hilliard (Hildyard, Hillier) Henry 38; John 24; John Doble 49, 68; Thomas 20
Hills John 18, 55, 63, 91, 101
see also Hill
Hines George 20
Hippen David 22
Hitchcock Edward 1, 89
Hoare (Hore) Hopewell 64; John 53, 82; Philip 54; Walter 31, 53, 68, 103, 107; William 8, 20, 38, 72, 77, 78, 91, 98
Hobbes (Hobbs, Hobs) John 100; Josias 19; Mathew 53
Hoddilow Hannah 53; John 53

Hodges Thomas 31, 33, 48, 53, 114, 116; William 68
Hodgkin (Hodgskin) Richard 1, 44, 67, 78, 105
Hodgson Richard 13; William 76, 81
Hodman William 20
Hodson Aurelius 14, 23, 49, 66, 87, 96; William 116
Hoggins Samuel 53, 91
Holbert Richard 1, 94
Holden (Holding) Charles 112; Richard 53
Holdsworth Richard 10
Hole William 77
Holford *see* Halford
Holiday William 68
Holland Stephen 49
Holmden John 72
Holsey *see* Halsey
Holsman John 23
Holworthy (Holworthie) Edward 54, 60; James 6, 34, 52
Homan Herbert 3, 4, 19, 31, 34, 54, 64, 79, 92, 93, 98; William 16
Hooke John 70, 93; Robert 59; Timothy 6
Hooker Edward 2, 54, 95, 98, 112; John 6, 16, 31, 33, 35, 37, 44, 47, 51, 54, 75, 89, 99, 102, 115, 116
Hopkins John 82; Robert 40, 65, 93, 111; Thomas 12, 13, 19, 20, 33, 34, 54, 62, 63, 75, 103, 110, 114
Hoppe Charles 40
Hore *see* Hoare
Horlock *see* Hurlock
Hornblow William 36
Horne Edward 44
Horton Jacob 10; James 19, 20, 22, 46, 52, 55, 70, 98, 106, 110, 115
Hoskins Thomas 3
Houghton (Haughton) Francis 5, 21, 54, 63, 67, 91, 99, 114
Howell Robert 65
Howes (Howse) Mary 50; Richard 50; William 5
Howett *see* Hewett
Howse *see* Howes
Huatson Thomas 111
Hudson Aurelius 27, 72; Daniel 2
Hughes Richard 26, 54, 56, 101
Hulcup (Hulcupp) John 24, 74, 96
Hulls (Hull) Mary 80, 104; William 15, 23, 33, 39, 68, 74, 77, 80, 104, 110, 113, 115
Hulme John 1, 51, 56, 69
Humphries (Humferson, Humfrey, Humfreys, Humfries, Humphery, Humpherye) John 82; Ralph 19, 25, 31, 43, 55, 56, 62, 101, 107; Thomas 47, 56, 97
Hunt Edmund 18, 46, 56, 58, 82, 87, 112; John 11, 22, 26, 46, 62, 68, 88, 102; Joseph 18, 71; Mary 20, 56; Robert 41, 56; Thomas 111; Walter 32, 56, 70, 73, 77; William 20, 28, 43, 52, 56, 85, 96, 100
Hunterton Ralph 28
Huntman Joseph 43, 46, 78, 83, 105
Hurlock (Horlock) John 54; Joseph 87
Hurst Daniel 29, 84
Hussey Samuel 58
Husted *see* Hasted
Hutchins William 12, 28, 110; William Charles 51
Hyde *see* Hide

Ibbotson Ebenezer 19
Ingram Richard 22, 25, 30, 36, 40, 63, 73, 85, 97, 98, 105; Robert 40; William 5, 53, 79, 85, 107
Ireland Richard 2, 5, 23, 114

Isted Samuel 20, 40

Jackson Ann 59; Isaac 57, 89, 96; John 11, 56, 57, 97; Mary 28, 57; Robert 29, 61, 65, 68, 88, 111; Samuel 57, 59, 81, 86; William 57, 69
Jacob Valentine 76, 77, 110, 111
James (Jaines) Christopher 16, 87; Samuel 40, 45, 58, 105; William 18
Jannaway (Janaway, Janeway) Richard 28, 38, 40, 77, 110; William 33, 61
Jarvis (Jervis) Maurice 42; Thomas 2, 46, 57, 67, 68, 75, 89, 103, 104, 112
Jeanes Edward 82; John 6, 11, 23, 61; William 19, 35, 50, 107, 108
Jefferie, Jefferies *see* Jefferys
Jeffers Sarah 2
Jefferys (Jefferie, Jefferies, Jeffrey) John 73, 85, 92; William 2, 53
Jeffs Daniel 48, 58; Thomas 112
Jekell Thomas 8
Jellings John 46, 58, 94
Jemmett (Jemmitt) John 33, 89, 90, 111, 113, 115
Jenkins Benjamin 90; John 106; William 21, 71, 91
Jenner James 15, 35, 75, 76, 104, 106
Jervis *see* Jarvis
Johnson Caleb 113, 116; George 88; Humphrey 88; John 9, 10, 25, 33, 51, 55, 83, 86, 88, 93, 98, 105, 113; Richard 70, 79; Thomas 9, 31, 91, 93, 95; William 29, 30, 60, 91, 114
Jones John 9, 106, 115; Morgan 78, 107, 112
Jordan (Jordaine) Andrew 12, 60; John 54, 57, 63, 77, 98; William 41, 55, 89
Joslin Joseph 113
Joyce Joshua 35; Richard 10, 21, 23, 31, 37, 40, 51, 61, 83, 101

Kattkitt *see* Catkitt
Kayman George 25
Kearne Thomas 14
Kelke (Kelk) Thomas 3, 5, 24, 29, 38, 54, 59, 70, 83, 89, 93, 95, 101, 104
Kell Robert 60
Kellner Thomas 3
Kelly Barnaby 109; Jane 52; William 25, 52, 74, 79
Kendall Benjamin 8, 11, 60, 85, 109; George 79
Kender (Kendar, Kindar) Thomas 4, 19, 36, 49, 66, 69, 80, 84, 99, 105, 114
Kentish William 26
Kerby John 35, 73, 98, 108; Lancelot 101; Richard 70, 97, 98, 104; Robert 10, 48, 58, 70
see also Kirby
Kersinhall Stephen 35, 89, 109
Kerton *see* Kirton
Kettle John 8, 109
Keyte Ann 61
Keywood Ellen 15; John 15, 24, 93
Kidd John 57
Killingworth William 27, 55, 82
Kindar *see* Kender
King Charles 79, 96; Edward 7; Emma 66; Henry 77; Humphrey 19, 26, 38, 43, 46, 52, 74, 83, 85, 93, 101; John 115; Samuel 1, 4, 39, 55, 70, 72, 75, 93, 106; Thomas 67, 75, 91, 92, 97; William 4, 21, 61, 62, 66, 80
Kinglebey Thomas 96
Kingsley Edward 46
Kingston John 46
Kinns Edward 62
Kinser Roger 19
Kipping (Kippin, Kippinge) Andrew 22, 62, 87; Francis 1; Nicholas 84
Kirby Richard 9, 20, 90, 108; Robert 33
see also Kerby
Kirk (Kirke) Robert 27, 74, 108; William 62, 69, 93, 107

Kirton (Kerton) Daniel 12, 23, 32, 74, 89; Thomas 90
Kitchinman (Kitchingman) George 3, 11, 28, 38, 52, 58, 62, 70, 71, 86; Samuel 56
Knight Edward 86; Joseph 107; Joshua 1, 3, 62; Thomas 54; William 3, 15, 27, 34, 53, 61, 62, 76, 77, 80, 99, 110
Knott Edward 104
Knowles Henry 38; John 6, 27, 100
Knyveton Henry 84

Ladbrooke (Ladbrook) Ferdinand 13, 20, 33, 62, 79, 90, 96; Richard 101
Lake Hugh 17, 22, 31, 64, 109
Laman (Leaman) George 5, 18, 38, 112
Lamb Eliza 63; Elizabeth 68; Robert 37, 53, 63, 68, 82
Lambert John 9, 35, 37, 38, 39, 45, 60, 74, 108
Lamplee John 29, 109
Lance Benjamin 63, 67
Lane Joseph 5, 24, 26, 29, 41, 45, 48, 68, 71, 90, 109, 110; Luke 36; William 64
Langley Henry 4; Richard 63
Langrish John 10
Langthorn Peter 115
Langton William 63, 73, 92
Larkum Samuel 75
Lasinby (Lazinby, Leasinby) Benjamin 34, 40, 43; Joseph 19
Latham William 112
Lathwell Henry 48, 49, 51, 64, 82, 101, 113; Joseph 50, 113; Mary 64, 82
Lawrence Abraham 34, 80; Jonas 15, 34, 37, 53, 67, 80, 87; Thomas 8, 16, 42, 80, 82, 92, 95, 98, 102, 109
Lazinby *see* Lasinby
Leach (Leech) Elizabeth 16; Francis 10, 16, 18, 40, 102; William 6, 14, 58, 112
Leake Christopher 3, 29, 54, 76, 78, 80, 95, 100; Robert 36, 69
Leaman *see* Laman
Leasinby *see* Lasinby
Leaver Edward 26, 72
Lee William 3
Leech *see* Leach
Leggatt William 96
Leigh Jonathan 31, 50, 72, 76, 93, 101, 114; Mary 50; Peter 7, 31, 33, 81, 113
Lem Joseph 74
Leman Edward 19, 32, 34, 75, 77, 104, 107
Lenton Jeremy 15; Thomas 25, 29, 55, 61, 98
Leveings *see* Living
Lewer Walter 47, 98
Lewis George 77
Lille Henry 45
Limbery Marianne 2; William 2
Lindsey John 41, 46, 56, 65, 113; Thomas 66
Linnell Robert 85
Litchfield (Litchfeild) John 76, 99
Littell William 1, 77, 84, 96
Living (Leveings) Charles 93; Richard 72, 74
Lloyd Robert 17, 105
Loadman Joseph 103
Loder Henry 115
London Thomas 37
Long William 13, 17
Lord Robert 75
Lorkins Nathaniel 98
Loveage William 51
Loveioy Charles 28

Lowe John 116
Lowen William 22, 29
Lowke John 20
Lucas Elizabeth 91; Joseph 104; Michael 91; William 7, 15, 24, 29, 30, 33, 48, 53, 55, 56, 64, 68, 74, 79, 108
Ludlow Benjamin 37
Luff (Luffe) William 67, 88
Luger John 27
Lunn James 45, 60
Lyell Henry 44
Lyfe Geoffrey 67
Lyford Nathaniel 55
Lyme Peter 59

Mace John 67
McEwen Andrew 114; Mary 114
Mackerness (Makernis) Samuel 24, 47, 69, 71, 87, 96
Magener James 61
Mahew John 85
Maine *see* Mayne
Maisters *see* Masters
Makeham James 60, 96; Richard 1, 60, 67, 73, 98
Makepeace (Makepeece) Andrew 49; Arden 10; Richard 57, 67, 107
Makernis *see* Mackerness
Makin John 27, 57
Malebarr William 91
Man *see* Mann
Mander *see* Maunder
Mandevill (Mandivell) Jegon 31, 37, 82, 105
Mann (Man) Benjamin 60; Daniel 6, 12, 13, 25, 30, 68; Edward 37
Manning James 114
Mansell John 17, 32, 74; Tabitha 32, 74
March Thomas 49, 73, 79, 83
Marchant Robert 16, 42, 57, 87, 112
Markhall (Markwell) Richard 21, 92, 97
Marlar Thomas 102
Marlin John 55
Marner John 57
Marple Henry 22
Marsh John 99, 111; Robert 65; Thomas 59, 61; William 89
Marshall Edward 5, 107; Francis 22, 29, 42, 68, 83, 88, 94, 101; Robert 16
Marter James 10
Martin George 86; William 41, 69
Mascall William 70
Mason Daniel 34, 39, 66, 69; Edward 69; John 4; Thomas 68
Massey Joseph 12, 39; William 3, 6, 15, 26, 34, 55, 56, 59, 70, 79, 92, 103, 108, 110, 113, 115
Masters (Maisters) Edward 8, 39; Michael 104; William 54
Mathews (Mathew, Mathewe, Mathewes, Matthewes, Matthews) Edward 23, 45, 77, 82; John 8, 16, 27, 98, 102; Nathaniel 14, 87, 96, 100; Robert 3, 6, 14, 17, 18, 31, 37, 69, 89, 98
Mattingley (Mattingly) Benjamin 26, 99
Maunder (Mander) John 36; Mary 101
Maundy Henry 106
Maxfeild John 4, 13, 37, 111
May Mary 24; William 17, 24, 57, 75, 83, 108
Maybanke (Maybanck, Maybancke) Robert 53, 62, 70, 80, 86, 95
Maycock William 76
Maynard William 116
Mayne (Maine) William 2, 6, 7, 13, 14, 18, 23, 54, 62, 81, 83, 93, 109

Mayo William 93
Meadowes (Meddowes) Hannah 7; John 7, 19, 20, 29, 38, 72; Paul 103
Meller *see* Mellor
Mellin Peter 4, 15
Mellor (Meller) William 1, 4, 30, 69, 73, 81, 99, 114
Merchant Hippsley 46
Merick *see* Merrick
Meridale *see* Merrydale
Merrick (Merick) John 8, 41, 115
Merriman (Mirriman) Benjamin 34, 43, 113; Benjamin Howard 24; Martha 70; Thomas 4, 29, 30, 46, 70, 73, 80, 99
Merrydale (Meridale, Merydale) John 4, 7, 23, 35, 48, 81
Messenger (Messinger) Ann 37, 64; Nathaniel 9, 19, 25, 37, 59, 112; Thomas 100
Meyer (Meyers, Myers) Andrew 12; Edward 43, 53; John 102; Joseph 10
Michell *see* Mitchell
Mickins William 23, 78
Middlemore William 34, 72
Might Nathaniel 22, 26, 38, 44, 56, 98, 113
Miles (Myles) Henry 26, 28, 40, 52, 60, 72, 75, 112, 116; John 78
Millard John 51
Miller Hugh 4, 22; James 15, 49, 71, 78, 107; Richard 76, 105; William 6, 13, 15, 44, 47, 55, 104, 105, 108, 111
Mills Thomas 51
Milton (Millton) Edmund 1, 30, 114; John 8
Minchin Mary 21, 29, 106; William 5, 21, 29, 33, 46, 48, 64, 95, 106, 107, 108, 110, 112
Mirriman *see* Merriman
Mister Mark Anthony 73
Mitchell (Michell) James 2, 20, 57; John 51
Mogridg John 33
Molyneux (Molineux) Francis 29, 48, 59, 61, 68, 72, 85, 92, 103, 107, 116
Moncke (Monck, Moncks, Mouncke) John 12, 27, 38, 85, 90
Moore (More, Morre) Henry 29; Jane 11, 75, 111; Richard 67, 94, 108; Robert 11, 40, 47, 50, 71, 75, 89, 106, 111
Morgan Randolph 104
Moris *see* Morris
Morland Anthony 72
Morre *see* Moore
Morrell Robert 86
Morris (Moris) Daniel 108; David 10, 27, 54, 83, 88; Davy 116; Nicholas 33; Richard 54, 56, 89, 109
Mortimer Edward 5, 27, 89, 103
Moseley (Mosely, Mosley) ... 77; Anthony 2, 12, 29, 41, 56, 60, 76, 77, 80, 82, 106
Moses Samuel 37
Mosley *see* Moseley
Moss Robert 104
Mothewell John 58
Mouncke *see* Moncke
Mozant Ann 1; Mark 1
Muggeridge *see* Mogridg
Munden Robert 4, 19, 31
Munn Anthony 26; Benjamin 12, 53, 58, 100, 111
Murden Thomas 30
Muston (Mustian) Joseph 13, 34; Rebecca 34; Roger 24, 114
Myers *see* Meyer
Myles *see* Miles
Mynott Joseph 98

Naseby John 101

Nash Francis 40, 110; Nicholas Thomas 82; Thomas 4, 19, 30, 31, 39, 72, 74, 89, 91
Neale Edward 74; James 2
Nellham Samuel 47
Nelson William 9, 12, 26, 71, 83, 86
Nettleton Thomas 4, 48, 49, 52, 76
Neville Samuel 40
New Robert 5, 74, 94; Thomas 79
Newbolt Aaron 52
Newcomb Thomas 107
Newington John 92
Newman John 27, 89; William 43, 53, 55, 74, 82, 108, 110
Newport (Newporte) John 34, 36, 45, 97
Nicholls (Niccolls) James 110; Reynolds 108; Robert 75; Thomas 13, 27, 115
Nicholson (Nickolson) William 26, 63, 115
Noble ... 19; Ellen 17, 31; Joan 43; John 1, 2, 10, 12, 13, 43, 79, 104; Thomas 17, 26, 51, 64, 71, 91
Norman Richard 96
Northover Thomas 41, 67, 75, 113
Norwood Francis 86; Richard 32
Noss William 7, 64, 95

Obbinson (Obbison, Obinson) John 13; Thomas 3, 5, 13, 16, 21, 34, 37, 51, 57, 59, 60, 62, 68, 77, 85, 86, 95, 99, 100, 101, 104, 106, 110, 113
Olive (Olife) Edward 10, 35; Joseph 33
Oliver Thomas 50, 81
Orley Edward 62, 71; Thomas 66
Orsby John 46
Ortis Nicholas 108
Orton Ann 19; Job 12, 19, 80
Orwell George 76
Osborn (Osborne) Edward 65, 76, 88, 93, 112; Elizabeth 10; James 105; Philadelphia 65, 76, 88, 93, 112; Samuel 4, 10, 52, 55, 64, 67, 69, 80, 95, 102; Thomas 61
Osgood John 34, 47, 88, 104
Osmond William 6, 55, 71
Otrage Samuel 54
Overlove Joseph 76
Owen Jeremiah 76, 110; Nathaniel 6, 75, 94; William 87, 100, 106

Packett (Packit, Packitt) Jacob 40, 47, 77, 116; James 9, 39, 46, 49
Packman John 39, 45, 47, 56, 63, 75
Page Ezekiel 38, 45; George 94; James 60, 77; Richard 77; Thomas 12, 27
Paine (Payne) Esther 79; Nathan 44; Nathaniel 78, 85; Thomas 10, 12, 29, 57, 85; William 11, 26, 41, 43, 59, 79
Painsfoote *see* Pauncefoote
Palmer Anthony 17, 43, 112; Edward 16, 38, 47, 89, 93; John 8, 24, 31, 33, 60, 68, 86, 95, 96, 101; Richard 68, 92; Thomas 37, 60, 72, 78; William 8, 62, 100
Pannett (Pannet, Pannott) William 3, 21, 29, 80, 109
Pantree John 89
Paris Bartholomew 9
Parker Eleanor 42; John 7, 21, 38, 39, 59, 61, 66, 86, 90, 95; Ralph 27; Richard 16, 41, 51, 85; Stephen 42; Thomas 12, 20, 49, 68, 83; William 6, 32, 55, 62, 78, 80, 82, 83, 90
Parrott (Parott, Parratt, Parret, Parrett, Parrot) Edward 27; James 93; Richard 5, 11, 30, 42, 45, 55, 78, 81, 103, 115; Robert 78; William 14
Parry William 91
Parsons Alan 38, 50, 105, 110; Edward 13, 66, 69, 85; Samuel 13; Thomas 72
Partridge (Patridge) Andrew 22, 24, 28, 32, 34, 67, 79, 90, 106, 115; George 12, 22, 86, 99; Joan 79
Pateshall (Patershall) James 40, 56, 66, 78, 79, 109; Phineas 6, 21, 25, 26, 34, 45, 49, 67, 73

Patey *see* Paty
Patridge *see* Partridge
Pattenden *see* Pattinson
Patterson Richard 21
Pattinson (Pattenden) Griffith 28; John 21, 30, 66
Paty (Patey) James 32; Thomas 89
Pauncefoote (Painsfoote) Henry 3, 31, 35, 43, 56, 73
Payne *see* Paine
Peach Mary 17; Vincent 17, 52
Peale *see* Peele
Pearce (Peirce) George 1; John 24, 71; Mathew 34, 44, 103; Samuel 20
Pearson (Peirson) Philip 5, 6, 58, 80, 88, 99, 103; Ralph 6, 11, 79, 115; Thomas 11, 59
Peele (Peale, Peell) Bartholomew 2, 79, 96, 102, 113; Thomas 77; William 50, 91, 102
Peirce *see* Pearce
Peirson *see* Pearson
Pendlebury Edward 18
Pepys Richard 33
Perkins Nathaniel 34, 50, 52, 54, 58, 93, 110; William 14, 30, 34, 51, 66, 80, 85, 89
Perrin John 31
Perry John 34, 39; William 76
Pett Joseph 6, 14, 21, 57
Petty Joseph 16
Pew John 24, 73
Pheasant (Phesant) William 21, 35, 82
Phelps John 6, 30; Joseph 77, 105
Phesant *see* Pheasant
Phillips (Phillipps) Ann 80, 81; Clifford William 14; Evan 62, 64, 89, 94, 113; Isaac 4, 25, 29, 36, 43, 80, 113; John 25, 29, 31, 36, 43, 81; Samuel 17; William 56
Philp (Philpe) Anthony 11, 15, 33
Philpott Francis 73
Pickering Peter 2, 4, 5, 14, 17, 20, 30, 35, 36, 45, 58, 59, 66, 72, 85, 91, 101, 104, 109; Philip 10, 12, 24, 30, 31, 70, 71, 100
Pickett Thomas 46, 79, 81
Pidgeon *see* Pigeon
Piers Thomas 34
Pigeon (Pidgeon) John 42, 109
Pike John 33
Pilcorne Noah 23, 81
Pitman (Pittman) Francis 2, 47, 86, 97, 110; John 84; Richard 36; Thomas 19, 31, 72, 111
Pitts Samuel 102
Plant William 78
Plomber William 44, 84
Pluckwell George 82
Polden Benjamin 56
Pond William 107
Pope William 4, 39, 59, 70
Popplewell Edmund 88, 98
Pordage Joshua 96
Porter Nathaniel 4, 26, 75
Poston John 65, 112
Potengar (Potenger) James 10; Mary 82; Richard 82
Potter Richard 47, 107; Thomas 72
Poulter Gabriel 42
Pountney Richard 17, 28, 74
Powell James 6, 20, 22; William 5, 37, 91
Pratt Augustine 22; John 35, 36, 43, 57, 68, 104, 107; Lydia 13; Robert 13; Thomas 1, 9, 28, 45, 81, 85, 86
Preist (Preaist) Robert 65, 73

Prentice Joan 69; John 76; Ralph 76; Thomas 36, 83, 99, 100; William 102
Price Isaac 56, 103, 104, 111; John 48; Roger 8, 20, 22, 35, 40, 76, 82, 92, 105, 106, 114; Thomas 30, 62
Prichard, Pricheard *see* Pritchard
Prick (Pricke) John 21, 22, 62, 63, 83, 84, 104
Priest *see* Preist
Prime William 6
Prince James 20, 31, 93; Peter 17, 36, 55, 61, 69, 83, 89, 90, 108; William 2, 19, 39, 41, 55
Prior William 35
Pritchard (Prichard, Pricheard) John 36, 38, 47, 77, 93, 94, 101, 106, 115, 116
Proudlove Christopher 20
Proudman William 48, 56, 65, 70, 83, 84, 85, 98, 99, 105, 116
Prudom David 83
Pullen Henry 12, 14, 22, 29, 82, 87, 107
Putnan William 54
Pye James Hull 17

Quatermayne John 83; Thomas 83

Rackstraw *see* Rakestraw
Radburne John 16, 33, 49, 56, 89, 103
Radcliff (Radcliffe, Radliffe, Ratcliffe) Edward 21, 36, 85, 102
Radley John 28, 41, 57, 63, 69; Samuel 22; Thomas 22, 37, 47, 94
Radliffe *see* Radcliff
Ragdale (Ragsdale) John 7, 95; Josiah 8, 28, 41, 44, 46, 47, 48, 55, 69, 75, 79, 81, 84, 98, 108; Nathaniel 7, 11, 32, 46, 88; William 68
Rainser Peter 82
Rainsford Margaret 12
Rakestraw (Rackstraw, Rawkestraw) Elizabeth 4, 11, 94, 114; Francis 4, 11, 30, 81, 84, 94, 106, 114; Thomas 52, 83, 109
Randall John 8, 91; Jonathan 93; Samuel 65; Thomas 84
Randolph Samuel 27, 115
Ratcliffe *see* Radcliff
Rawkestraw *see* Rakestraw
Rawlins Benjamin 103; Henry 67
Rawlinson Thomas 28, 68, 79, 112
Raworth Edward 106
Ray Joseph 63
Rayne William 58
Rayner Roger 56
Rayton Robert 73
Reader Thomas 115
Reading (Redding Richard 6, 85, 92; Robert 87; William 8
Reaynolds *see* Reynolds
Redding, Reding *see* Reading
Redmire Samuel 19, 92
Reeves Samuel 40, 48, 52, 88, 112
Relews Thomas 91
Rencher Mary 14, 32, 102; Thomas 3, 14, 37, 64, 77, 102, 108
Reynolds (Reaynolds, Renolds) John 113; Priscilla 86; Richard 6, 30, 40, 58, 59, 86, 100, 111; Sarah 51; William 3, 28, 34, 51, 60, 79
Rice William 28
see also Wrice
Rich William Nathaniel 86
Richards (Richard, Rickard) Ann 84, 115; Charles 86; Felix 50, 79; John 84, 115
Richbell John 5, 8, 29, 53, 74, 85, 87
Rickard *see* Richards
Ricketts John 15

INDEX OF MASTERS

Rickwood Richard 1
Ride John 101
Rideout (Rydout) Joseph 17, 41, 83, 86, 100
Ridge Jeremiah 1, 8, 23, 29, 33, 60, 66, 67, 84, 86, 88, 96, 103, 105, 106; Jeremy 1, 47, 50; Thomas 1
Rigby Thomas 41, 47, 54, 70, 86
Ring James 66
Rippen Thomas 34, 66, 67, 72, 86
Ritte William 6
see also Wright
Roberts Adrian 7; John Flock 66, 78, 116; Thomas 34, 72, 75; William 93
Robince Henry 33
Robins Francis 6, 8, 17, 21, 23, 34, 82, 84, 87
Robinson John 87; William 15
Robotham Christopher 7, 65; Francis 29
Rodway Giles 51, 52, 87, 97, 111; Robert 26, 39, 54, 58, 60, 76, 87, 106
Roe Robert 41, 81
Roffe Thomas 22
Roffey Anthony 87
Rogers Humphrey 26, 99, 109, 113
Roll (Rolles, Rowles) Christiana 82; Elizabeth 37; Thomas 8, 36, 53, 82; William 24, 37
Rolts Peter 103
Rondeau James 28, 38
Rood William 2
Rose Edward 16, 108; Thomas 22, 69
Rosse (Ross) Thomas 9, 16, 56, 58, 68, 74, 88
Rotheram Richard 28, 88
Rowe Robert 81
Rowland John 15, 102
Rowles *see* Roll
Rudson John 10, 65, 91
Rumball Edmund 39; John 5, 14, 31, 48, 52, 69, 91
Runt Jonathan 59
Russell (Russel) Benjamin 38, 64, 89; John 15, 31; William 4, 23, 81
Rust Thomas 45, 100
Rutland Henry 85
Rutt Elizabeth 105; John 24, 91, 105
Rydout *see* Rideout
Rymmer Roger 104

Saffell (Saffin) Isaac 3, 34, 52, 65, 89; Margaret 89
Salter David 49
Sammons Solomon 106
Sampson John 22, 89, 105, 107
Sargent (Sargeant) Edward 94; George 90
Saul Ann 101; Thomas 101
Savage Richard 10, 15, 17, 73, 78, 93, 94, 98; Samuel 3, 12, 13, 81, 97, 111
Savill Kenelm 67, 113
Sawtell Thomas 41, 72, 73, 111
Saywell John 1, 70, 90; Samuel 113
Science Thomas 59
Scollough ... 15; John 30, 75, 95
Scott (Scutt) Daniel 2, 8, 13, 30, 36, 57, 72, 89, 90, 103; George 12, 49; James 7, 58, 60, 62, 68; Margaret 7; Robert Mitchell 96
Scotton Moses 6
Scutt *see* Scott
Seagood Thomas 73
Seakins Elizabeth 91; Mathew 91

Searle (Searl, Searles) Ann 55; Francis Barrell 11, 14, 62, 71, 87, 97, 108; George 5, 35, 40, 52, 78, 84, 85, 103; Thomas 11, 14, 15, 21, 22, 30, 42, 45, 46, 48, 63, 69, 70, 73, 75, 77, 86, 88, 91, 97, 100, 106, 108, 113, 116
Selan John 50
see also Velan
Sequens Thomas 26
Sessions Richard 1
Settle Jeremiah 23
Shakemaple John 20; Samuel 35, 39, 63, 88, 112
Sharpe John 91
Sheffeild William 68
Sheldon (Shildon) Gilbert 92; Joseph 34, 47, 82, 83, 92
Shelley (Shelly) George 12, 37, 41, 59, 63, 81, 85; Robert 101; Thomas 62, 92
Shenston John 64
Shepherd (Shepard, Shepward) James 86; Nicholas 1; Samuel 70; William 19, 36, 50, 60, 69, 72, 84, 92, 94
Sheriffe Samuel 69
Sherman Benjamin 60; John 113
Sherwill John 109
Sherwin Joseph 64, 105
Sherwood Thomas 71
Shildon *see* Sheldon
Shipman John 15
Shipton Thomas 80
Shrimpton Thomas 32, 89, 92
Shuter John 43, 44, 82
Sibley (Sibly) Henry 107; John 25, 42, 63, 73, 78, 91, 101; Joseph 21, 25, 80, 104, 114; Nathaniel 76
Simcock William 45, 69, 105
Simes *see* Sims
Simonds (Simond, Simons, Symons) Dorothy 103; Henry 73, 102, 109; William 2, 65, 87, 103
Sims (Simes, Symes, Syms) John 13, 24, 32, 67, 71, 79, 93, 102, 114
Skeale (Skeate) John 90, 102, 107
Skelton Benjamin 47, 65
Skepper John 47, 64, 93, 96
Skinner Edward 70, 97; John 114
Slater Francis 23; John 87
Slatford James 52
Slaughter John 60
Slaymaker John 112
Slowe Joseph 8, 94
Smalridge (Smaldridge, Smallridge, Smalredge) Thomas 34, 36, 38, 44, 49, 55, 59, 84, 89, 90, 91, 94, 95; William 8
Smarte John 19
Smeeton George 37
Smith (Smyth) Ann 59; Edward 68, 72; George 11, 26; Humphrey 78; John 2, 39, 42, 48, 53, 64; John Gould 5; Joseph 43; Margaret 64, 107; Mary 40, 42, 50; Richard 22, 56, 65, 78, 93, 114; Samuel 5, 88; Thomas 5, 12, 20, 37, 53, 57, 84, 94, 98, 115; Valentine 97; William 25, 27, 31, 43, 45, 59, 61, 64, 65, 67, 69, 80, 91, 92, 95, 97, 104, 107, 108, 110, 114
Snablin (Snabling) Mathew 45, 64, 81, 82, 94, 115
Snape Samuel 4, 29; Thomas 13
Snelling Thomas 96
Soames George 50, 81; Henry 9, 12, 16, 17, 19, 31, 32, 42, 54, 60, 66, 78, 83, 92, 93, 96, 112, 113; James 74
Sole (Soule) John 2, 28, 35, 87, 105, 116
Solley Benjamin 77, 108
Somner *see* Sumner
Soule *see* Sole

Southwood Robert 12, 18, 37, 41, 53, 75, 82, 110
Sparrow Richard 84, 105
Speering (Spering) Benjamin 27, 41, 43, 76
Spenceley Thomas 52
Spencer Thomas 7, 20, 70, 73; William 6, 54, 76, 83, 96
Spering *see* Speering
Spring James 40
Squire William 79, 83, 94
Stackhouse Ann 97; Christopher 97; Samuel 97
Staines George 7, 18, 93
Stainsby John 10
Staniford Christopher 73
Stanley William 27, 43
Stayner William 28, 49
Stedman Christopher 78
Steele Edward 82, 83, 88; Mary 82
Steere (Steeres) William 16, 64
Steevens *see* Stephens
Steevenson *see* Stephenson
Stent Ann 106; Henry 11, 15, 79, 80; John 37, 45, 106
Stephens (Steevens, Stevens) Benjamin 76, 107; John 36, 47, 49, 63, 74, 114; Robert 48; Roger 23, 97; Thomas 18, 38; William 1, 54, 68, 72, 90
Stephenson (Steevenson, Stevenson) Thomas 6, 19, 37, 45, 47, 92, 101, 110
Stevens *see* Stephens
Stevenson *see* Stephenson
Steward William 54
Stiells, Stiles *see* Styles
Stimson Thomas 39
Stinnett Thomas 41
Stinton Benjamin 98, 109, 116; Susanna 98
Stiver Thomas 35, 71
Stockdale George 69
Stone Thomas 18, 58, 60, 80, 101, 106
Stonestreete Thomas 80, 103
Stonier Richard 70
Storer James 49
Story Joseph 97
Stretton George 3, 12, 30, 99, 116
Stroud (Stroude, Strowde) Edward 5, 95, 97
Sturtevant Saunderson Turner 20, 29, 81
Style (Stiells, Stiles, Styles) Clement 109; Francis 1, 108, 112; Jane 98; Simon 75; Thomas 18, 37, 102, 103, 104
Sudger Thomas 82
Sumner (Somner) Christopher 12, 61, 74
Surman William 4, 47, 72, 99
Sussex John 31, 80, 99, 109, 110
Sutton Beaumont 99; John 60; Nathaniel 99; Thomas 2, 38, 71
Sweeton George 92
Swift Joseph 46, 59
Symes *see* Sims
Symonds, Symons *see* Simonds
Syms *see* Sims

Tailer *see* Taylor
Talbot Caleb 40, 41, 99, 107
Tally Esther 95; William 15, 95, 99
Tanner William 46
Tapp Thomas 52, 88

Tatlock Thomas 21
Taylor (Tailer, Tayler, Taylour) David 59; Edward 25; James 76; John 108; Joseph 4, 10, 23, 50, 100; Richard 51, 83; Thomas 18, 31, 44, 52
Teague George 51
Teale James 15
Tegg Francis 4, 74, 101
Tenter William 15
Terrell *see* Tirrell
Terry (Terrey) Edward 62, 108
Tetley (Tetly) James 2, 7, 78, 91, 100, 113
Tew Thomas 82
Tewer *see* Tuer
Thatcher Charles 35, 43, 68, 101; Thomas 20, 35, 71, 83; William 4, 20, 35, 38, 42, 82, 101
Thomas John 77
Thompson (Thomson, Tomson) Charles 101; Isaac 104; John 7, 29, 70, 77, 106; Martha 74; Mathew 7; Philip 15; Robert 25, 45, 59, 64, 74, 114; William 12, 43, 44, 59, 61, 71
Thornell Robert 24
Thornton (Thorneton) Richard 12, 14, 21, 38, 58, 75, 86, 89
Thorowgood Andrew 2, 36
Thorpe Roger 109
Thredder (Threader, Threadher, Treddar) Mary 36; William 2, 21, 36, 70, 79, 93
Thurlby William 102
Tibball (Tiball) Robert 3, 110
Tibbey Edward 10, 18
Tilbury Robert 32
Tilley James 27, 37; John 46, 51, 71, 98
Timberlake Ralph 109
Tims *see* Toms
Tipping John 24, 29, 38, 77
Tirrell (Terrell, Tyrrell) Richard 5, 27, 41, 52; William 81
Tisdale John 72
Titley James 14, 70, 107
Tockfield (Tokefeild) John 50; Joseph 6, 102
Tolderey Thomas 45
Tomes *see* Toms
Tomkins Ann 24; Edward 21, 22, 32, 45, 60, 100; John 46, 102; Redburn 53; William 6, 24
Tomlins (Tomlin) Edward 42, 88, 104
Tomlinson (Tomplinson) Benjamin 28, 40, 48, 51, 52, 65, 73, 78
Toms (Tims, Tomes) John 8, 25, 103, 107
Tomson *see* Thompson
Toogood Roger 73
Topott John 2
Toson *see* Tyson
Tovey John 18, 19, 26, 38, 72, 81, 98, 99, 100, 115; Joseph 11, 41
Towne (Town) Daniel 51; Richard 4, 8, 27, 49, 103
Townsend (Townesend, Townshend) John 25, 53, 54, 55, 63, 65, 66, 86, 103, 115; William 61, 89, 105
Tratt *see* Trott
Traunter Samuel 94
Treacher John 93, 97
Treavers John 61
Treddar *see* Thredder
Trevill (Trevell) Richard 83; William 85
Trinder Mark 21; William 109
Trobridge George 103
Trott (Tratt) Edward 90; Ezekiel 104, 114
Troughton William 68
Trumplin Arthur 52, 86

Tucker Joseph 3; William 21, 57, 69, 79, 84, 97
Tuer (Tewer) John 10, 16, 33, 40, 47, 71, 72, 75, 91
Tueson Thomas 12
Tully Thomas 38, 55, 101, 112
Tunsteed (Tunsted, Tunstedd) Francis 51, 52, 64, 73, 99, 102
Turner Addington 9; John 3, 22, 30, 36, 58, 69, 77, 83, 84, 89, 90, 105; Leonard 6, 45, 46, 47, 68, 76, 98; Margaret 45, 46, 68; Richard 80; Thomas 105
Turnish Henry 31
Twell John 13, 110
Twyford Henry 74, 79, 95
Tyler Richard 13, 74, 110; Thomas 34
Tyrrell *see* Tirrell
Tyson (Toson) John 5, 30, 33, 37, 46, 47, 50, 70, 71, 84, 90, 105, 110, 113, 115

Udall (Udell) Robert 2, 6, 21, 34, 44, 54, 61, 68, 80, 81, 95, 102, 113
Uffington Thomas 100
Underwood Thomas 15, 52, 110
Uppington (Upington) John 89; Robert 9, 73, 95
Urmston (Urmestone) Roger 6; William 68

Vaston William 29, 92
Vaughan Francis 73; James 102; Thomas 17, 30, 39, 71
Velan (Veland) John 10, 50, 54, 60, 61, 94
see also Selan
Ventrice Henry 9, 39
Veyland John 55, 105
Vibart (Vibert) Lancelot 10, 14, 18, 30, 46, 60, 61, 92, 99, 102, 105, 109
Vincent Arthur 87
Vokins Avery 54, 63, 72, 74, 105, 111
Voss William 76
Voucher Robert 12

Waggoner (Wagener) James 9, 20, 33, 79, 82, 93, 114
Waight *see* Weight
Waites John Frisbee 21
Wakeham James 47, 52
Walcott *see* Wallcott
Walker Andrew 3, 21, 29, 44, 115; Edward 1, 36, 62, 89, 101, 109; James 49; Mathew 23, 26, 64, 77, 104, 107; Richard 4, 5, 17, 69, 72, 79, 80, 96, 104; Robert 33, 37, 53, 55, 78; Samuel 12; Vincent 37, 52, 80
Wall Thomas 11, 25, 32, 67
Wallcott (Walcott) Edward 54; Thomas 69
Walter Richard 63; Thomas 47
Walton William 83, 86, 100
Wane (Wayne) Daniel 4, 19, 25, 111; George 3, 25
Ward (Warde) Abel 33, 64, 70; Henry 61; Richard 6, 16, 36; Robert 60
Wardel Samuel 50
Warden (Wardiner, Wardner) Francis 35, 37, 110
Warman John 14, 17, 24, 26, 27, 62, 83
Warner Ann Hedges 32, 106, 111; Francis 8, 98; Valentine 39, 89, 113
Warren Daniel 41; John 113; Michael 1, 11, 14; Richard 52, 102; Robert 107
Warter *see* Waters
Washborne (Washburn) Richard 1, 99
Wateridge *see* Watridge
Waters (Warter) John 44; Richard 53
Watridge (Wateridge) William 10, 87, 89, 111
Watson Elizabeth 108; John 11; Randolph 6, 12, 19, 23, 27, 29, 40, 59, 103; Robert 22

Watts Elizabeth 1; James 83; John 8, 10, 27, 53, 70; Jonas 1, 8, 15, 16, 17, 32, 64, 80, 114; Jonathan 45; Joseph 7, 10, 36, 44, 90, 92, 97; Nicholas 76; Thomas 3, 31, 53, 61, 67, 77, 84, 106, 108, 109, 114
Wayne *see* Wane
Weale Daniel 49, 63, 113
Weatherstone George 66
Weaver Thomas 48
Webb (Webbe) Daniel 48; Isabella 109; Joseph 30; William 8, 55, 59, 74, 115
Webster John 1, 15, 109; Mary 82; Richard 10, 72, 82, 93, 98; Thomas 58
Wedgbrough (Wedgbrough, Wedgeburrough) Joseph 18, 21, 41, 47, 53, 57, 68, 79, 101, 109
Weedon Alexander 42, 104
Weight (Waight) ... 115; Richard 29, 54, 109
Wellings Isaac 69
Wells Richard 39
Wenlock Ralph 109
West (Weste) Edward 110; James 45, 51, 86; Nathaniel 25, 41, 44, 84; Richard 41, 47, 60, 94, 97, 109, 110; Samuel 50, 97; Thomas 1, 3, 7, 15, 111
Westall James 18, 30, 56, 57
Weste *see* West
Westell Simon 110
Weston Richard 38, 78, 98, 105
Wheatley (Wheatly) Martin 28, 44, 90; Matthias 14, 48
Wheeler Benjamin 89; Henry 100; Samuel 19, 21, 24, 31, 39, 43, 45, 48, 59, 60, 62, 69, 100, 107, 115; Thomas 52
Whight *see* White
Whisler Ralph 110
Whitcher Richard 7, 62, 75, 87, 91, 95, 96, 113
White (Whight) Alexander 92; John 19; Ralph 26, 93, 114; Richard 87; Simon 43, 52, 64, 78; William 10, 102
Whiteaker Gabriel 69
Whiteing (Whiting) Abel 78; Noel 7, 26, 111, 113
Whitton (Witton) Thomas 17, 33, 107
Wibnell John 37
Wiburd *see* Wyburd
Wich *see* Wicks
Wickins (Wickens) William 12, 22, 37, 61, 63, 71, 111
Wicks (Wich) John 49, 50; Joseph 103
Wigg Frances 7, 9; Thomas 7, 22, 46
Wiggins Richard 18, 52, 74, 99; (Wickins), William 84; William 23
Wiggley John 24
Wightman George 16, 59, 93, 100, 106, 109
Wignall James 104
Wilcock (Wilcocks, Wilcox) George 46, 51, 53; John 6, 55, 74, 111; Robert 17, 34, 52
Wilcockson John 111
Wilcox *see* Wilcock
Wild (Wyld) George 3, 108, 111
Wildash John 57
Wilford (Willford) John 12, 34, 41, 48, 49, 50, 58; Walter 16
Wilkie James 32, 52, 105
Wilkin (Wilkins) Robert 2, 33; Samuel 14, 19, 48, 56, 77, 80, 112
Wilkinson Catherine 1, 61; Richard 1, 6, 17, 45, 55, 80, 96, 102, 107; Thomas 95
Willford *see* Wilford
Williams Edward 37, 58, 72; John 17, 44, 77, 88; Richard 33, 99; Robert 20, 33, 112; Thomas 7, 16, 46; Thomasine 17, 77; William 4, 13, 42, 50, 55
Williamson Richard 5
Willis James 113; John 113
Willoughby John 32, 42, 96
Willson *see* Wilson

Wilse John 6, 12, 70
Wilson (Willson) John 100; Ralph 49; Thomas 13, 49, 77, 113
Wilton Harward 83; Harwood 109; Mary 83
Wimberly (Wimberley) Bartholomew 21, 27, 32, 36, 39, 42, 43, 90, 91, 100
Winchester Mary 61; Nathaniel 3, 18, 48, 61, 81
Wine (Wyne) Henry 4, 12, 16, 19, 42, 55, 58, 60, 77, 79, 90, 93, 105
Wingfeild Robert 113
Winkle Valentine 100
Winney William 43, 45, 84
Wintle Henry 26
Withers John 63, 111; Joseph 25, 65; Samuel 19, 20, 22, 25, 35, 58, 59, 62, 65, 75, 81, 92, 99, 105, 108, 114
Witton *see* Whitton
Wood Humphrey 39, 64; James 15, 55, 101; John 42, 62, 75, 81, 99, 113, 114, 116; William 3, 41, 45, 105, 114
see also Woods
Woodfield (Woodfeild) Samuel 8, 13, 34
Woodhouse William 107
Wooding Elizabeth 80; Richard 5, 22, 30, 80; Robert 51
Woods James 67, 77; John 34, 73, 101
see also Wood
Woodward (Woollward) Jeremiah 65; John 16, 95, 108; Joseph 48, 65, 75; Mathew 9, 12, 14, 18, 20, 28, 36, 51, 53, 59, 64, 72, 75, 83, 85, 87, 89, 90, 113, 114
Woolhead (Woollhead) Catherine 4, 27, 95, 115; Henry 88, 92; Joseph 10, 11, 58, 84, 96; Thomas 4, 10, 12, 18, 25, 35, 61, 67, 78, 87, 95, 97, 114, 115
Woollerton William 29
Woolley Cornelius 43, 67, 85, 106; Elizabeth 67
Woollhead *see* Woolhead
Woollson Jacob 110; James 115
Woollward *see* Woodward
Worgan Edward 5, 25, 107; Richard 2, 22, 94
Worley George 115
Wormull Anthony Stoakes 18
Worrall (Worrell) Richard 1, 104
Worthington William 101
Wrice Matthias 64
see also Rice
Wright Edward 43; Job 23, 60, 76; Richard 61, 92, 104; Samuel 14, 64, 115; Susanna 60; William 30, 41, 56, 61, 62, 69, 72, 75, 91, 105
see also Ritte
Wyatt John 27
Wyberd *see* Wyburd
Wyborne (Wybourne) Ann 116; Petley 19, 20, 40, 116
Wyburd (Wyberd) John 38, 40, 44, 71, 74
Wyld *see* Wild
Wyment Thomas 52
Wyne *see* Wine
Wynn John 6, 8, 74
Wyrill (Wyrell) Robert 3, 46, 58, 63, 107

Yalden William 44, 107
Yarling John 8, 13, 25, 52, 70, 79, 110
Yates Richard 11, 58, 68, 77, 116
Yearsby Mary 37
Yeomans John 50
Yonge *see* Young
York (Yorke) Richard 27, 43
Young (Yonge, Younge) Prudence 116; Thomas 52, 63, 65, 102, 104, 107, 112, 116; William 36

Zouch Francis 57, 70, 81, 89, 90, 98, 99

INDEX OF PLACES

UNIDENTIFIED PLACES

Bradley 1
Cooten Magna 54
Funtill [? Fonthill, Wiltshire] 26
Hethorp [? Oxfordshire] 41
Lenfield 36
Northly 54
Stangate 24
Tallerton 66
Tunstall 103
Westbury 33

ABROAD

Barbados 106
France
  Perrardie 32
India
  East Indies 48
Jamaica 63, 112
Madeira 77
Netherlands
  Delpht 111
United States
  Maryland 75
    New Town 116

BEDFORDSHIRE

Ampthill 33, 95
Apsley 3, 58
Barton 42
Bedford 10, 17, 94
  Cauldwell 64
Biggleswade 8, 100, 111
Billington 69
Bolnhurst 29
'Chapwell' 116
Chellington 78
Clophill 65
Dunstable 83, 88, 97
Dunton 78
Eaton Socon
  Bushmead 59
Elstow 93
Felmersham 10
Flitton 8
Flitwick 35, 96
Harrold 102
Henlow 10, 56
'Holloway' 69
Kempston 52
Leighton 38
Leighton Buzzard 24, 38, 44, 55, 64, 76, 87
Luton 20, 94
Marston Moretaine 60
Pavenham 2

BEDFORDSHIRE [*continued*]

Potsgrove 22, 24
Pulloxhill 54
Riseley 41
Sandy
  Beeston 26
Shillington 78, 80
Silsoe 46, 54
Stagsden 2
'Stepbon' 76
Steppingley 34
Stevington 4, 74, 85
Sundon 88, 102
Toddington 57, 88
Totternhoe 66
Turvey 12, 114
Woburn 52, 55
Wootton 88

BERKSHIRE 79

Abingdon 2, 21, 51, 53, 57, 71, 93, 102, 103, 106, 109, 110
Aldworth 47
'Anglisham' 90
Appleton 8, 98
Arborfield 89
Ardington 28
Aston 17, 106
Barkham 46, 53
Basildon 29
Binfield 79
Blewbury 63, 72
Bradfield 67
Bucklebury 56
Burghfield 42, 82
Buscot 58, 62
Catmore 91
Chaddleworth 7, 90
Charney 111
Chilton 64
Coleshill 98
Compton 29
Cookham 19, 97
Cumnor
  Swinford Ferry 65
Didcot 11, 100, 111
Drayton
  Sutton Wick 105
East Garston 24, 114
East Hanney 87
East Ilsley 99
Easthampsted 24
Faringdon 24, 35, 44, 66, 86, 103, 115
Fyfield 46
Graseley 104
Greenham 62

BERKSHIRE [*continued*]

Hagborne 101
Hampstead Norris 79
Hanney 24
Harwell 54, 111
Hungerford 10, 46
    Leverton 4
Hurley 38, 91
Hurst 47, 74
Ilsley 80, 99
'Kembrieagle' 45
Lambourne 13, 30
Maidenhead 52, 57, 61, 78
Marcham 54
Newbury 5, 6, 29, 43, 50, 55, 70, 76, 91, 107, 113
North Heath 10
Peasemore 23
Reading 8, 9, 11, 13, 47, 55, 68, 71, 72, 79, 82, 94, 109, 110, 112
Shinfield
    Hartley 67
Shrivenham 5, 23, 80
Stanford 19
Steventon 45, 53, 97
Stratfield Saye 11
'Stratton' 79
Streatley 59
Thatcham 30, 64, 69
Tubney 61
Twyford 26
Ufton 43, 44
Wallingford 10, 19, 61, 70, 110, 113
Waltham 69
    Waltham St Lawrence 109
Wantage 22, 56, 84, 108, 109
Warfield 19
Wargrave 31, 93
'Weedon' 25
Welford 35
White Waltham 12, 49, 50
Windsor 30, 67, 74, 113
    Windsor Castle 60
Wokingham 2, 10, 45, 47, 54, 75, 93, 95

BUCKINGHAMSHIRE

Addington 91
Adstock 33, 58
Amersham 65, 108
Ashendon
    Pollicott 23
Aston Abbots 89
Aylesbury 6, 74, 91
Beaconsfield 12, 33, 74, 103
Biddlesden 100
Bierton 72

BUCKINGHAMSHIRE [*continued*]

Bledlow 4
Bletchley 69
Bow Brickhill 50
Bradwell 38
Brickhill 11, 111
Brickley 69
Brill 18
Buckingham 40, 41, 52, 62
    Gawcott 23
Burcott 20
Burnham 32, 42
Chalfont St Peter 95, 98
Chesham 17, 23, 30, 102
    Chartridge 102
    Lea Green 23
Chicheley 77
Chipping Wycombe 92, 103
'Clarlton' 39
Colnbrook 39
Cublington 25
Cuddington 45
Denham 41, 55
Denton 23
Dinton 18
Dorney 77
Dunton 1, 39
Edlesborough 84
Emberton 95
Eton 21, 42, 97, 106
Fenny Stratford 62, 98
Fingest 110
Fulmer 49, 65
Gawcott 4, 16
Great Horwood 17
Great Marlow 77, 91, 110
Great Missenden 38, 53, 62
Grove 7
Haddenham 88
Hanslope 35, 78, 85
Hardwick 85, 97
Hartwell 27
Hedgerley 56
High Wycombe 33, 39, 92, 93, 108
Hillesden 25
Horton 13, 50
Horwood 31
Iver 6, 28, 92
Langley 43, 49
Langley Marish 98, 102
Leckhampstead 56
Lillingstone Dayrell 75
'Little Bramford' 75
Little Brickhill 60
Loughton 89
Maids Moreton 34
Marlow 63

BUCKINGHAMSHIRE [*continued*]

Marsh Gibbon 6, 45, 104
Medmenham 25
Mentmore 54
Moreton 94
Mursley 51
  Saldon 18
Nettleden 86
Newport Pagnell 21, 29, 63, 89, 114
Newton 64, 75
Newton Blossomville 51
North Marston 27
Oakley 25, 105
'Old Bramford' 23
Olney 8
Penn 15, 45
Princes Risborough 77
Quainton 89
Radnage 63, 84
Risborough 49, 51
Shabbington 9, 26
Sherington 27, 108
Stewkley 17
Stoke Mandeville 65
Stone 9, 19, 81
Stony Stratford 16, 87
Stowe 19, 45
Swanbourne 42
Taplow 60
Thornborough 82
Tingewick 45, 54, 78
Turville Heath 88
Twyford 12, 13
Upton 62
'Virges' 27
Waddesdon 48
Wavendon 22, 44
Wendover 24, 62, 75
West Wycombe 64
Westbury 83
Weston Turville 43
Whitchurch 57
Wing 5, 23, 70, 99
Winslow 1, 45, 54, 111
Wooburn 3, 31, 49, 89, 112
Wotton 43

CAMBRIDGESHIRE

Balsham 82
Bassingbourn 104
Burrough Green 7
Cambridge 15, 38, 61, 101
Caxton 48
Cottenham 73
Dullingham 18

CAMBRIDGESHIRE [*continued*]

Ely 5, 11, 22, 72, 79
  'Eucheries' 86
Foulmere 27
Great Shelford 105
Haddenham 46
Impington 75
Kirtling 30
Linton 41
March 55
Newmarket 108
Royston 113
Sawston 104
Shelford 26
Waterbeach 68
Whittlesey 57
Wilburton 5, 76

CHESHIRE

Astbury 15, 36
Balterley 14
Barton 78
Budworth 64
Chester 7, 35, 65, 78
Clotton 2
'Connington' 83
Dodleston
  Gorstella 101
Dunham 6
Eccleston 35
Farndon 93
Great Neston 47
Halton 20
Hanbury 27
Holt 104
Macclesfield 59
Moreton 73
Norley 51
Norton 59
'Odford' 53
Over Peover 29
Pulford 29
Rode 9
Rostherne 20
Stockport 7
Tabley 68
Tilstone
  Alpraham 75
Trafford 40
Warford 81
Whitegate 106
Wimberry 85
'Witchwall Bank' 14
Wrenbury Wood 90
Yeardsley 59

INDEX OF PLACES

CORNWALL

'Farneham' 101
Fowey 6

CUMBERLAND

'Berwick Field' 53
Bridekirk 102
Bromfield 85
Castle Carrock 79
Dalston 63
Egremont 98
Green 37
Kirkoswald 43
Little Salkeld 80
Muncaster 60
  Rougholme 18
'Nuddleskew' 8
Penrith 98
Seascale 91
Sebergham 98
Tallantire 77
Wragmire 66

DERBYSHIRE

Alfreton 2
Allestree 73
Appleby 83
Beeley 104
Blackwell 35
Bradley 70
Brampton 71
Broughton 62
Chesterfield 53, 114
Dalbury 1, 47
Derby 38, 71, 74, 97
Duffield 50
Etwall 6, 33
Findern 92
Gresley 84
Hathersage 88
'Legginton' 6
Longstone 90
Mickleover 106
Normanton 30
Osmaston 67
Parwich 28, 65
Radbourne Hall 92
Ravenstone 44
Shirley 72
Smisby 7
Spoondon 106
Stanton by Bridge 35
Sutton 115
Thurvaston 106
Tideswell 87

DERBYSHIRE [*continued*]

'Wadley' 92
Wirksworth 107

DEVONSHIRE 102

Axminster 83
Bradninch 82
Butterleigh 89
Colyton 32
Crediton 78
Cullompton 23
Exeter 1, 42, 50, 66, 116
George Nympton 34
Haccombe 18
Kenton 103
Ottery St Mary 75
Plymouth 85
Puddington 105
St Giles 93
Stokeinteignhead 68
Tiverton 22, 63
Withycombe Raleigh 60

DORSET

Beaminster 28
Blandford 38, 90, 92
Bridport 47
Chardstock 75
Charlton 47
Dorchester 16, 47, 83, 103
Fifehead Magdalen 45
Fordington 96
Haselbury Bryan 75, 110
Marshwood 66
Okeford Fitzpaine 33
Portesham
  Corton 103
'Rockway' 75
Shaftesbury 9, 11
Sherborne 17, 45, 69, 112
Stalbridge 86
Stickland 113
Sturminster Marshall 23, 24
Upwey 43
Wareham 12
Weymouth 106
'Wilconin' 16
Wimborne 12, 100
  Wimborne Minster 41
Winterbourne Abbas 21
Yetminster 88

DURHAM

Bishop Auckland 112

DURHAM [*continued*]

Gainford 16
Old Park 68
'Watcoe' 78

ESSEX

Abridge 74
Barking 3, 11, 16, 17, 31, 46, 51, 81, 89, 96, 105, 106
Black Notley 101
Blackmore 42
Bocking 63, 76
Bradfield 24
Braintree 13, 68, 70, 82, 94
Brentwood 1, 42, 88
Bromley 96
Broomfield 64, 91
Bumpstead 7
Burnham 32
Buttsbury 62
Chadwell 23
Chelmsford 52, 67
Chigwell 26, 52, 67, 70
Chingford 1, 78, 99
Chipping Ongar 43
Chrishall 46
Coggeshall 59, 89
Colchester 23, 28, 29, 49, 59, 63, 68, 72, 86, 88
 North Hill 30
 St Mary Magdalen 81
Copt Hall 107
Cranham 24
Dagenham 56, 101
Dedham 14, 27, 92
Doddinghurst 22, 40
Dunmow 18
East Ham 89
Epping 91
Gosfield 108
Grays 32
Great Baddow 114
Great Bromley 21
Great Burstead 83
Great Chesterford 36, 76
Great Ilford 105
Great Parndon 113
Great Warley 63, 87
Hallingbury 116
Halstead 36
Ham 55
Harold Wood 10
Harwich 52
Hatfield Broad Oak 6
Havering atte Bower 37
Hawkwell 17

ESSEX [*continued*]

Heydon 73
Hornchurch 31, 79, 84
Ingatestone 13, 14, 35, 40
Lambourne 13, 16
Little Baddow 41
Little Canfield 68
Little Holland 50
Little Hollingbury 108, 116
Little Waltham 109
Low Leyton 36
Morton 80
Mundon 34
Nazeing 90, 92
Netteswell 39
North Ockenden 115
Orsett 90
Plaistow 4, 52, 73
Prittlewell 20, 68
Purleigh 50, 82
Rainham 5
Rayleigh 114
Rivenhall 9
Rochford 97
Romford 43, 59, 98
Runwell 99, 114
Saffron Walden 71, 104
Sewardstone 64
Sheering 2, 68
Shelley 79
South Benfleet 95
South Ockenden 28
South Shoebury 76
Southminster 100
Stanford le Hope 68
Stifford 98
Stondon 34
Stortford 20
Stratford 19, 39, 43, 84, 110
Stratford Langthorne 36
Terling 67
 Terling Place 29
Theydon Garnon 57
Toppesfield 12
Waltham Abbey 3, 24, 25, 44, 45, 79, 90, 101, 107, 115
Waltham Holy Cross 21, 44
Walthamstow 18, 26, 32, 45, 53, 54, 84, 85, 98, 104
Walton le Naze 69
Wanstead 84
'Warren nuper Suson' 107
West Ham 3, 21, 43, 54, 85, 102, 109
Wethersfield 37
White Notley 104
Witham 96
Woodford 45

ESSEX [*continued*]

Woodham Mortimer 86
Writtle 83

GLOUCESTERSHIRE 113

Adlestrop 107
Arlingham 46
Arlington 107
Ashchurch
    Aston upon Carrant 94
Ashleworth 52
Ashton under Hill 8
Awre 103
Badgeworth 97
    Witcome 87
Barrington 69, 70
Barton 95, 104
Beckford 83
Bishops Cleeve 19
Blakeney 10
Bledington 80
Boddington 11
Bourton on Water 46, 63, 64
Bristol 39, 105
Broadwell 46
Brockworth 60, 111
Bromsberrow 106
Cam 104
Campden 95
Charlton Abbots 116
Chedworth 11
Cheltenham 21, 58, 75
Cherington 87
Churchdown 6
Cirencester 9, 22, 45, 55, 59, 70, 76
Cow Honeybourne 5
'Crist' 1
Didbrook 44, 58
Dursley 80
Eastington 23, 62, 73
Fretherne
    Framilode 6
Gatcombe 56
Gloucester 40, 44, 55
Hampton 42
Hatherop 59
Hidcote 84
Hinton 8
Hinton on the Green 90
Honeybourne 26
'Hunnybull' 6
Iron Acton 65
'Itney' 31
'Kainton' 31, 103
Kempsford 90
Kings Stanley 11

GLOUCESTERSHIRE [*continued*]

'Laborton' 85
Lechlade 1, 76
Leonard Stanley 8
Littledean 105
Long Marston 48
Lower Slaughter 44
Lye 87
Maisemore 64
Minety 44
Minsterworth 22
Mitcheldean 115
Moreton in the Marsh 19
Nailsworth 58
Newent 87
Newland 115
Newnham 113
Nibley 47
Northleach 77
Oddington 50
Painswick 11, 15, 47, 109
    Spoonbed 8
    Wick Street 46
Pebworth 16
Pinnock 109
Prestbury 112
Pucklechurch 93
Quedgeley
    Woolstrop 34
Sandhurst 79
Sevenhampton 112
Slimbridge 72
Southrop 5
Stanton 56
Stoke 107
Stoke Orchard 66
Stonehouse 38
Stroud 40, 49
Stroudwater 45
Temple Guiting 98
Tetbury 65
Tewkesbury 20, 30, 35, 36, 37, 53, 67, 103, 108, 116
Toddington 22
Tortworth 28
Turkdean 79
Twyning 39, 104
Uley 101
Upleadon 71
Walton 44
Welford 72
Westcote 95
Whittington 57
Wick 11
Winchcombe 14, 59, 101
Winstone 15
Withington 32

INDEX OF PLACES

GLOUCESTERSHIRE [*continued*]

Wood Stanway 25
Woolstone 70, 71, 114
Wotton under Edge 98, 116
Yanworth 100

HAMPSHIRE 80

'Aldenham' 111
Alresford 42, 75, 98, 115
Alton 88
Alverstoke 3
    Godsport 16
Amport 96
Andover 10, 42, 53, 62, 65, 72, 77, 106
Basing 15, 64
Basingstoke 10, 72, 83, 102, 110
Bentley 63
Bentworth 46
Binstead 71
Bishops Sutton 16
Bishops Waltham 48
Boldre 24
Chilworth 54
Clatford 75, 78, 108, 110
Cliddesden 9
'Corby' 2
Crondall 37
East Meon 67, 95
East Worldham 73
Faccombe 85
Fareham 114
Fawley 76
Fordingbridge 41
Foxcott 12
Goodworth Clatford 82, 95, 96
Gosport 32, 77, 96
Havant 9, 10, 59, 115
Hawkley 107
Isle of Wight 24
Kingsclere 26, 41, 92
Lasham 115
Medstead 51
'Milbert' 82
Newchurch 107
Newton Valence 116
Newtown 21
'Nulton' 90
Old Alresford 33
Osborne 76
Overton 5
Petersfield 107
Portsmouth 12, 36, 40, 43, 88, 97
Redbridge 54
Romsey 60, 106, 108, 113
Sherfield 85
Southampton 35, 59

HAMPSHIRE [*continued*]

Steep 110
Stratfield Mortimer 71
Timsbury 61
Upper Clatford 18, 75
Upper Wallop 61
Vernhams 94
Wallop 101
Warblington 10
Wellow 92
Wherwell 55, 99
Winchester 7, 39, 61, 68, 72, 84, 91, 104, 115
Yateley 81, 97

HEREFORDSHIRE 54

Ashton 81
Avonbury
    Noaks 69
Bacton 26
Bosbury 34, 67, 114
Brilley 15, 89
Burghill
    Tillington 88
Dilwyn 18
Dorstone 79
Edvin Ralph 80
'Evengton' 62
'Fafield' 8
Fownhope 86
'Glasshouse' 86
Hereford 48, 49, 64, 65, 93, 116
Kentchurch 108
Kington 81
Kinnersley 111
Leominster 5, 60, 79, 102, 104, 112
Llangarron 112
Much Marcle 113
Norton Canon 80
Orleton 19
Pedwardine 88
Ross 15, 71
Sellack 105
Stanford Bishop 75
Weston 95
Wigmore 28
Wormsley 57

HERTFORDSHIRE

Abbotts Langley 55
Albury 79
Aldenham 10, 35, 45, 48, 51, 57, 112
'Alholland' 80
Ashwell 63
Baldock 23, 49
Barkway 18

HERTFORDSHIRE [*continued*]

Barley 89
Barnet 66, 85, 86, 101
Bennington 10
Berkhamstead 44, 59, 77, 107, 108, 110
Bishops Hatfield 35, 56
Bishops Stortford 27, 57, 90
Bovingdon 26
Braughing 23
Buntingford 22, 33, 60, 89
Bushey 51, 102, 107, 108
Caddington 88
Caldecote 3
'Chacehurst' 17
Cheshunt 16, 18, 38, 60, 66, 70, 90, 93, 97, 98, 102
    Theobalds 114
Chipping Barnet 74
Codicote 58
Digswell 33, 77
Elstree 68, 112
Essendon 65
Flamstead 76
Frogmore 110
Graveley 89
Great Gaddesden 83, 109
Green End 36
Hadham Hall 90
Harpenden 8, 33
Hatfield 41, 42, 66, 106
Hemel Hempstead 6, 36, 38, 76, 77, 94, 102
    Two Waters 105
Hertford 3, 14, 21, 23, 29, 40, 67, 80, 116
    St Andrew 6
Hexton 19, 114
High Barnet 31
Hitchin 5, 29, 31, 44, 53, 57, 92
Hoddesden 67
'Holmideane' 48
Kings Langley 23, 40
Kings Walden 88
Knebworth 18
Lilley 50
Little Amwell
    Jenningsbury 42
Little Hadham 90
London Colney 26
Long Marston 42
Much Hadham 28
North Mimms 15, 45
Northaw 36, 37, 65
Norton 64
Offley 36
Pirton 46, 105
Redbourne 28, 49, 61, 74, 103, 115
Rickmansworth 1, 28, 57

HERTFORDSHIRE [*continued*]

Ridge 56, 64, 83
    Coursers Farm 64
Royston 19, 115
Rye 89
St Albans 31, 35, 37, 38, 50, 66, 75, 79, 86
St John 21
St Paul's Walden 41, 83
    Hovend 83
St Stephen 3, 48, 49, 107
'Sarfield' 15
Sawbridgeworth 14
Shenley 7, 8
Standon 97
    Collier's End 14
Stanstead 29, 116
Stanstead Abbots 13, 114
Stevenage 65
Tewin 83, 84
Thundridge
    Wadesmill 116
Tring 75, 79
Waltham Cross 101
Ware 12, 36, 56, 80, 111, 116
    Blakesware 79
Watford 2, 5, 13, 14, 16, 35, 36, 61, 62, 70, 71, 74, 75, 78, 85, 86, 89, 100, 110, 115
Weston 48
Wheathampstead 28
Willian 113
Wormley 30

HUNTINGDONSHIRE

Brampton 3
Caldecote 106
Colne 27
Earith 15
'Egerton' 102
Elton 62
Farcett 3
Fenny Stratford 1
Godmanchester 4
Great Staughton 50
Hemingford Abbots 69
Hilton 58
Holywell 112
Huntingdon 3, 7
Hurst 8
Kimbolton
    Wornditch 50
Little Paxton 12, 27
Offord 35
    Offord Cluney 56
Ramsey 57
St Ives 30, 54, 57, 69, 79
St Neots 57

INDEX OF PLACES

HUNTINGDONSHIRE [*continued*]

Spaldwick 67
Stewkley 98
Weston 6
Winwick 15
Wyton 16

IRELAND

Cork 26, 34, 86
Dublin 82, 83
Galway 93
'Harby Maller', Cork 73
Wicklow 67

KENT

Allington 101
Appledore 101
Ash 96
Aylesford 67
Beckenham 41, 75
Bersted 77
Bethersden 80, 98
Boxley 67
Brasted 25
Brenchley 82
'Brockson' 15
Bromley 4, 53
Canterbury 77, 91
Charing 114
Chatham 10, 15, 27, 42, 57, 60, 91, 93, 97
Chiddingstone 81
Cobham 5
Cranbrook 56
Crayford 40
Dartford 42, 45
'Deane' 13
Deptford 3, 4, 10, 11, 22, 25, 27, 32, 46, 47, 51, 52, 69, 72, 74, 78, 79, 92, 93, 100, 109
Dover 22, 55, 58, 89
Eastry
    'Selson' 49
Edenbridge 20, 27
Eynsford 39, 68, 85
Foots Cray 26
Godmersham 78
Goudhurst 20
Gravesend 61
Greenwich 1, 11, 17, 27, 36, 39, 46, 47, 50, 58, 65, 67, 70, 71, 79, 80, 81, 86, 92, 104, 106, 109, 110
Guston 58
Halsted 25
Hawkhurst 90, 99
Hayes 50

KENT [*continued*]

Hever 80
Higham 100
Hinxhill 5
Hollingbourne 75, 101
Holy Cross 99
Hoo 76
Horton 48
Ickham 116
Leigh 17
'Leningston' 26
Lewisham 34, 61, 63
Little Peckham 7
Loose 6
Maidstone 8, 18, 29, 33, 37, 53, 90
    Grove Green 21
Margate 52, 55, 81
Meopham 99
Northfleet 16
Penshurst 42, 93
Platt
    Basted 2
Plumstead 53
Rainham 49
Rochester 5, 88
St Mary 7
St Mary Cray 27, 72
Sandwich 9, 21, 29
Sevenoaks 27, 39, 64, 77, 108
Shoreham 107
Southfleet 16
Speldhurst 64
Stalisfield 68
Staplehurst 27
Stone 34, 63
Stourmouth 64
Strood 51
Sundridge 74, 103, 106
Sutton at Hone 40
Swanscombe 20
Sydenham 63
Tenterden 99, 111
Thurnham 17
Tonbridge 20, 50, 90
Tonbridge Wells 74
Waltham 26
Waterham 94
West Malling 20, 41
Westerham 72, 90, 114
Willesborough 70
Woolwich 8, 34, 48, 91, 92
Wormshill 101

LANCASHIRE

Altcar 43
'Anslarke' 100

INDEX OF PLACES

LANCASHIRE [*continued*]

Ashton 90
Ashton under Lyne 95
Astley 58
Balderstone 91
Barrow in Furness
    Newbarns 75
Billington 21
Bolton 73, 116
Bolton le Moors
    Blackrod 69
Burnley 16
Dalton in Furness 83
Deane
    Westhoughton 18, 65
Eccleston
    'The Rowe' 30
Gleaston 4
Gorton 115
Halton 6, 30
    Halton Green 68
Hawkshead 44
Heaton Norris 1
Holland 86
Kirkham 12
Lancaster
    Caton 35
Levenshulme 56
Liverpool 22, 82
'Lopera' 100
'Maddwellay' 103
Manchester 10, 33, 97
Oldham 54
Ormskirk 49
Os…? 76
Parke Hill 6
'Poole' 61
Poulton
    'Magnus Martin' 72
Preston 55
'Rennell' 86
Rochdale 106
Sefton 48
Stockport
    Reddish 46
Stodday 47
Ulverston 31
Warrington 17, 52, 88
Whalley 6, 76
    Read 11
Wigan 68
Winwick 10, 14, 25
Wyresdale 109

LEICESTERSHIRE 79, 93

Appleby 72, 83

LEICESTERSHIRE [*continued*]

Ashby de la Zouch 52, 101
Ashby Parva 79
Barrow on Soar 97
Billesdon 90
Bitteswell 109
Blaston 106
Bosworth 30
Breedon on the Hill 22
Brentingby 69
Burbage 7
Burton Lazars 66
Croft 35, 86
Dadlington 30
Drayton 7, 105
East Langton 57
East Norton 15
Eastwell 91
Edmondthorpe 72
Gaddesby 25, 102
Galby 31
Garthorpe 108
Goadby 38
Great Bowden 72
Great Easton 7, 21, 31
Gumley 55
'Harblin' 103
Harborough 19, 46, 92
Hinckley 22, 77
Husbands Bosworth 16, 107
'Inston' 98
Kilby 37
Kirby Bellars 31
Knipton 83
Langton 98
Leicester 10, 14, 32, 52, 76, 77, 103, 104, 108
Little Dalby 39
Loughborough 40, 50, 74, 92, 93
Lowesby
    Cold Newton 53, 55
Lutterworth 99, 105
Market Harborough 21, 43, 66, 106
Markfield 12
Medbourne 7, 75, 111
Melton Mowbray 14, 55, 60, 63, 77, 94
Mowsley 18
Nailstone 15
New Parks 107
North Kilworth 1
Oadby 21
Orton 80
Osgathorpe 88
Peatling Magna 77
Queniborough 16, 111
Quorndon 20
Ratby 68
Rearsby 49, 71

LEICESTERSHIRE [*continued*]

Saltby 4
Saxelby 21
Scalford 28
'Scottsbitch' 2
Shawell 66
Sibson
    Wellsborough 9
Sileby 21
Smeeton Westerby 8, 28
Stockerston 106
Stoughton 28
Sutton Cheyney 85
Swepstone
    Newton Burgoland 21
Syston 1
Thorpe Arnold 8, 19, 58
Thurlaston 110
Tur Langton 16, 111
Welham 90
'Winston' 14
Witherby 61
Wymondham 29

LINCOLNSHIRE

Alford 13
Alvingham 77, 78
Axholme 36, 42
Barrowby 8
Bicker 43
Bloxholme 61
Bonby 95
Burton by Lincoln 9
Croft 38
Folkingham 77
Gainsborough 80, 97
Grantham 62
Great Grimsby 13
Great Hale 104
Hainton 3, 65
Holbeach 5
Horncastle 97
Hougham 24
Kirkby 14
Kirton 43
Kirton in Lindsey 40
Lincoln 23, 53, 85, 93, 108
Manthorpe Grange 22
Mavis Enderby 93
Normanton 19
Orby 106
Owersby 102
'Pryall?' 43
Roxby 100
Sleaford 113
South Kelsey 33

LINCOLNSHIRE [*continued*]

South Witham 85, 113
Stamford 63
Sutton 31
Swaton 6
Swinderby 2
Syston 24
Waddingworth 44
'Wigham' 68
Winceby 17
Winthorpe 77
Wroot 89

LONDON/MIDDLESEX

'Abberton' 77
Abchurch Lane 56
Acton 21, 66, 116
Aldermanbury 8
All Hallows Barking 12, 71, 85
All Hallows London Wall 19, 104
All Hallows the Great 45
All Hallows the Less 63
'Berds Watering' 52
Bethnal Green 16, 17, 28, 30, 68, 111
    Bacon Street 21
Blackfriars 30, 114
Bloomsbury 65, 72, 79
Bow 113
Brentford 7, 17, 19, 61, 66, 78, 93, 111
    New Brentford 31, 96
Bridewell Precinct 70
Brook Market 45
Cannon Street 42
Charterhouse 11
    Charterhouse Lane 32
Cheapside 27
Chelsea 13, 14, 18, 24, 38, 39, 47, 50, 53, 57, 61, 73, 90, 105, 107, 111, 114
Chiswick 48
Christ Church 68, 75, 111
    Christs Hospital 37
    Newgate Street 15, 24
        Crown Court 58
Clerkenwell 23, 42, 44, 48, 66, 72, 87, 103, 110
    Aylesbury Street 99
    Rosamond Street 38
    St James 11, 16, 24, 25, 34, 52, 54, 59, 62, 72, 73, 86, 100, 101, 103, 106, 111
    St John 50, 57
    St John Street 2, 25, 38, 40, 66
College Hill 13, 51, 90
Cowley 18, 75
Cranford 41, 84, 115
Denmark Street 103

LONDON/MIDDLESEX [*continued*]

Drayton 5, 44
Ealing 39, 56, 80, 83, 94
  Great Ealing 54
Eastcheap 73
Edgware 45, 92, 107
Edmonton 3, 9, 21, 23, 28, 41, 42, 46, 47, 58, 60, 73, 80, 81, 94, 95, 96, 97, 111
Enfield 1, 2, 10, 13, 29, 30, 31, 48, 52, 56, 73, 76, 101, 110, 112
Fenchurch Street 109
Finchley 90, 94, 100
Fish Street Hill 86
Fleet Street 37, 96
  Fleet Market 42, 96
Friern Barnet 93
  Barnet 21
  Whetstone 8, 77, 94
Fulham 3, 5, 10, 14, 22, 26, 31, 47, 54, 74, 82, 98, 100
  Walham Green 5
Gracechurch Street 1
  Boars Head Court 105
Hackney 5, 8, 16, 34, 36, 48, 49, 53, 57, 59, 61, 64, 69, 77, 97, 105, 110
    Homerton 105
    Stamford Hill 78
Hadley 8, 11, 55, 79, 80, 93
Hammersmith 25, 37, 43, 54, 62, 63, 78, 104, 107, 109
Hampstead 5, 8, 12, 18, 29, 36, 58, 63, 75, 86, 91
Hampton 15, 54, 58, 61, 81, 97, 109
  Hampton Wick 71
Hanwell 112
Harefield 113
Harlington 95
Harmondsworth 24, 25, 29, 45
Harrow 7, 10, 12, 33, 49, 76, 82, 100, 115
  Harrow Weald 108
Hayes 4, 84, 89
Hendon 25, 51, 75
Heston 51, 90
Highgate 11, 45, 47
Hillingdon 12, 44, 80, 85, 86
Holborn 1, 4, 6, 8, 11, 12, 15, 19, 22, 25, 28, 29, 30, 35, 37, 38, 40, 41, 48, 52, 53, 64, 66, 68, 74, 77, 78, 82, 90, 94, 96, 98, 99, 100, 101, 108, 112, 113
  Chancery Lane 58
  Cliffords Inn 105
  Fetter Lane 81
  Field Lane 112
  Grays Inn 13, 44, 81
  Grays Inn Lane 74
  Hatton Garden 40, 47
    Kirby Street 108

LONDON/MIDDLESEX [*continued*]

Holborn [*continued*]
  High Holborn 107
  Holborn Bridge 112
  Holborn Hill 96
  Leather Lane 89
  Middle Temple Lane 28
  St Andrew 6, 12, 15, 27, 30, 40, 41, 56, 83, 89, 96, 115
  Shoe Lane 32
Holy Trinity Minories 6, 12, 69
Hornsey 63
Houndsditch 32, 34, 67, 74, 84
Hounslow 40, 51, 66, 89
Isleworth 12, 46, 102
Islington 5, 10, 33, 40, 41, 48, 53, 64, 81, 91, 111
  Bagnige Marsh 46
Joy Lane 52
Kensington 14, 17, 21, 30, 53, 79, 88, 94, 109
  Kensington Gore 99
'Kicker End' 67
Kingsbury 96
Leadenhall Street 67, 86
Liberty of the Rolls 34, 37
Limehouse 36, 45, 51, 52, 53, 60, 65, 67, 74, 99, 101, 102, 104
Littleton 12
London 2, 4, 6, 8, 11, 12, 15, 17, 18, 19, 20, 25, 27, 28, 33, 34, 36, 37, 38, 39, 41, 42, 44, 45, 46, 51, 52, 54, 55, 58, 59, 60, 61, 62, 63, 65, 66, 67, 69, 70, 71, 72, 73, 74, 75, 76, 77, 79, 80, 83, 84, 85, 86, 87, 88, 89, 90, 92, 93, 94, 95, 96, 97, 98, 99, 100, 102, 105, 106, 109, 111, 112, 113, 114, 115
Long Lane 29
Minories 61
New Road 104
Nicholas Lane 44, 78
Northolt 4, 48
Norton Folgate 74
Norwood 37
  Southall 41
Old Artillery Ground 30
  Union Street 79
Paddington 6, 27, 28, 52, 100
Pancras Lane 98
Paternoster Row 60
Pinner 57, 77
Poplar 31, 80, 104, 110
Princes Square 25
Queen Street 60, 96
Red Cross Square 68
Rolls
  Liberty of the Rolls 34, 37

LONDON/MIDDLESEX [*continued*]

Ruislip 6, 23, 32, 35, 62, 70, 74, 85, 87, 109, 113
St ... in the Fields 17, 39
St Alban Wood Street 2
St Andrew Undershaft 66
St Andrew Wardrobe 2, 96, 112
St Ann Blackfriars 83, 94, 113
St Bartholomew the Great
  Cloth Fair 22, 49, 81
  Smithfield 91
  Smithfield Bars 39
  West Smithfield 99, 109
St Bartholomew the Less 75
St Benet Fink 88
St Benet Paul's Wharf 3, 96
St Botolph 80
St Botolph Aldersgate 15, 30, 31, 96
  Aldersgate Street 58, 83
  Little Britain 89
St Botolph Aldgate 23, 25, 33, 38, 43, 46, 57, 71, 76, 80, 81, 85, 95, 100, 104, 111, 115
  Church Row 70
  Rosemary Lane 11
St Botolph Billingsgate 31
St Botolph Bishopsgate 8, 16, 28, 32, 40, 65, 66, 70, 84, 87, 89, 112
  Bishopsgate Street 31
  Bishopsgate Without 39
  Old Bethlem Court 84
St Bride 50
St Dionis Backchurch 30
St Dunstan in the East 57
St Dunstan in the West 22, 39, 52, 55, 69, 108, 115
  Portugal Street 66
St Faith 15
St George 100
St George in the East 78, 98, 112
  Penington Street 25
St George the Martyr 106
St Giles 17, 19, 34, 37, 47, 73, 82, 113
St Giles Cripplegate 1, 3, 4, 7, 9, 23, 39, 44, 50, 55, 57, 60, 61, 62, 63, 69, 82, 88, 92, 93, 94, 95, 97, 99, 107, 109, 110, 112, 114, 115
    Barbican 39
    Beech Lane 92
    Fore Street 62
    Grub Street 93
    Little Queen Street 31, 79
St Giles in the Fields 1, 7, 8, 9, 10, 17, 19, 20, 23, 24, 31, 33, 35, 37, 39, 41, 43, 44, 45, 46, 54, 56, 57, 60, 61, 62, 64, 67, 68, 70, 72, 79, 80, 81, 85, 89, 94, 97, 98, 107, 110, 111, 112, 114

LONDON/MIDDLESEX [*continued*]

St Giles in the Fields [*continued*]
  Seven Dials 16
St Gregory 12, 18, 76
St James 23, 77
St James Dukes Place
  Dukes Place 89
St James Garlickhythe 26
St Katherine 109
St Katherine by the Tower 13, 25, 27, 28, 31, 41, 59, 61, 74, 82, 91, 94, 96, 100, 104, 108
St Katherine Coleman 70
St Katherine Creechurch 5
St Leonard Eastcheap 87
St Luke Old Street 18, 29, 33, 35, 36, 40, 51, 65, 99, 100, 104
  Chiswell Street 15
  City Road 35
  Goswell Street 93
  Old Street 1, 32, 110, 113
  Old Street Square 7
  White Cross Street 55
St Martin le Grand 11, 20, 29, 100
St Martin Vintry 20
St Mary Axe 97
St Mary Woolchurch Haw 10, 26
St Marylebone 10, 55, 56, 69, 96, 101, 104
  Bond Street 88
  Cavendish Square 43
  Edgware Road 87
  Grafton Street 40
  Oxford Road 30
  Oxford Street 55
St Michael Cornhill 55
St Michael Queenhithe 64
  Brooks Wharf 28
St Nicholas Cole Abbey 34
St Olave Hart Street
  Crutched Friars 49
St Pancras 2, 53, 71, 96, 107
  Kentish Town 53, 81
  Tottenham Court Road 50, 52
St Pauls Churchyard 54
St Peter Cornhill 25
St Peter Paul's Wharf 65
St Sepulchre 6, 12, 15, 20, 31, 37, 38, 64, 65, 72, 85, 89, 90, 93, 103, 105, 110
    Cow Cross 97
  Giltspur Street 17
  Snow Hill 60
St Stephen Walbrook 12
St Thomas Apostle 30
St Vedast 101
Shadwell 18, 31, 35, 38, 42, 46, 49, 55, 60, 61, 70, 86, 89, 100
Shepperton 98

LONDON/MIDDLESEX [*continued*]

Shoreditch 9, 17, 20, 22, 23, 26, 29, 30, 41, 44, 50, 57, 67, 68, 78, 85, 87, 96, 99, 100, 107, 110, 111
  Holywell Street 91
  Hoxton 3, 56, 89
  Long Alley 56
South Mimms 28, 40, 52, 87, 102, 104
  Mimms 78
Spitalfields 12, 25, 39, 45, 47, 63, 69, 71, 74, 79, 83, 85, 93, 94, 100, 101
    Brick Lane 74
    Paternoster Row 66
    Wentworth Street 112
    Wood Street 77
Staines 3, 32, 34, 36, 41, 71
Stanmore 39, 75, 100
  Great Stanmore 100
Stanwell 96
  Great Stanwell 69
Stepney 1, 4, 5, 6, 7, 8, 9, 15, 21, 22, 24, 25, 26, 27, 28, 30, 37, 38, 39, 40, 44, 48, 51, 56, 58, 65, 66, 68, 69, 73, 83, 89, 90, 94, 100, 101, 104, 109
  Mile End 96
  Mile End Road 74
  Ratcliffe 10, 14, 15, 16, 58, 59, 64, 86, 94, 106, 109, 114
  Ratcliffe Highway 46
  Stepney Green 30
  Wellclose Square 92
    Ship Alley 100
  White Horse Street 82
Stoke Newington 81
  Newington 71
  Newington Green 88
Stratford le Bow 11, 27
Sunbury 41, 99, 112
Teddington 8, 44
Temple
  Inner Temple 50, 76, 103
Thames Street 97
  Upper Thames Street 19
Threadneedle Street 74
Tottenham 25, 61, 89, 111, 114
Tower of London 9, 55
  Artillery Lane 3, 15
  Chequers, Tower Street 77
  Gun Street 2
  Liberty of the Tower 65, 82
  Tower Hill 70, 97
  Tower Street 58, 77
Twickenham 7, 24, 76
  Whitton 46, 53
Uxbridge 6, 15, 40, 42, 77, 98, 100
Wapping 11, 27, 30, 38, 56, 63, 64, 65, 67, 69, 71, 73, 76, 82, 87, 102, 113

LONDON/MIDDLESEX [*continued*]

Wapping [*continued*]
  East Smithfield 12, 18, 84
  Nightingale Lane 4, 22, 29
Westminster 2, 3, 9, 12, 15, 16, 25, 37, 39, 42, 44, 47, 48, 53, 58, 61, 63, 66, 72, 73, 74, 79, 81, 83, 86, 88, 90, 95, 104, 105, 106, 109, 111, 112, 113
  Broad Sanctuary 53
  Covent Garden 13, 31, 35, 36, 40, 60, 69, 75, 82, 115
  Old Pye Street 21
  St Clement Danes 7, 13, 16, 19, 22, 23, 37, 43, 51, 55, 60, 63, 64, 67, 69, 76, 80, 83, 84, 87, 88, 89, 90, 91, 92, 96, 100, 101, 104, 110, 112, 113, 116
    Clare Market 55, 64
    Houghton Street 37
  St George Hanover Square 18, 36, 41, 90, 91, 93
    Chandos Street 110
    Upper Brook Street 97
  St James 2, 3, 5, 9, 14, 23, 25, 26, 29, 31, 33, 34, 35, 48, 51, 53, 55, 56, 60, 63, 66, 70, 72, 73, 74, 86, 88, 90, 92, 94, 98, 102, 107, 108, 113, 116
    Bury Street 90
    Great Marlborough Street 48
    Husbands Street 2
    Jermyn Street 32
    Piccadilly 105
    Swallow Street 65
  St John 78
  St Margaret 3, 8, 9, 11, 12, 18, 25, 29, 34, 47, 50, 57, 60, 75, 78, 80, 82, 86, 87, 88, 93, 95, 97, 101, 105, 106, 108, 109, 113, 114
    Knightsbridge 6, 18, 59
  St Martin 14
  St Martin in the Fields 2, 4, 5, 7, 9, 12, 15, 17, 18, 19, 22, 23, 25, 27, 30, 37, 44, 47, 51, 52, 54, 56, 59, 61, 63, 64, 66, 69, 70, 81, 84, 85, 92, 94, 95, 106, 111, 112, 113, 114
    Charing Cross 58
    Drury Lane 80
  Savoy 34, 36, 78, 84, 100
  Soho 19, 39, 50, 52, 53, 62, 69, 86, 88, 90, 91, 103, 109
  Strand 6, 29, 87
    Windsor Court 102
  Tothill Street 75
Whitechapel 3, 5, 9, 13, 19, 25, 26, 27, 31, 34, 38, 39, 42, 44, 46, 50, 55, 56, 58, 66, 67, 72, 73, 75, 76, 78, 82, 89, 98, 103, 105, 108, 110, 112, 114, 115, 116

LONDON/MIDDLESEX [*continued*]

Whitechapel [*continued*]
Coverley Fields 21
Goodman Fields 81
Gulston Square 85
Mile End New Town 63
Whitefriars 36, 49, 81, 106
Whitefriars Wharf 32
Willesden 79, 104
Wood Street 63

NORFOLK

Aldeby 16
Attleborough 11
Burnham Norton 22
Costessy 3
Diss 92, 109
Dunham 14
Great Melton 65
Hindringham 49
Lynn 33, 45
Market Downham 32
Norwich 24, 52, 57, 62, 83, 114
Old Lynn 34
Scoulton 16
South Lopham 31
Warham 82
Yarmouth 13, 76

NORTHAMPTONSHIRE 24

'Abcott' 57
All Saints 8
Arthingworth 16, 43
'Ashcott' 84
Ashton
Elmington 1765
Aynho 23, 68
Northcote 26
Badby 65
Barby 60, 101
Barnack
Pilsgate 18
Blakesley 58
Seawell 15
Brackley 8, 18, 66, 78
Brampton 18
Brigstock 7
Brixworth 69, 97
Broughton 59
Buckby 90
Bugbrooke 81, 105
Byfield 16, 23
'Calton' 108
Chapel Brampton 61, 71
Charwelton 32

NORTHAMPTONSHIRE [*continued*]

'Chilworth' 31
Claycoton 14, 83, 95
Cogenhoe 94
Colly Weston 68
Corby 44
Cosgrave 8
Coton 59
Cottesbrooke 24
Courteenhall 76
Cransley 75
Crick 108
Culworth 55, 92
Daventry 8, 35, 55, 91, 96, 116
Denton 27
Desborough 3
'Dorrington' 28
Duston 48, 67, 99
East Haddon 97
Etton 10
Everton 11
Farndon 7
Fawsley 104
Finedon 36, 68
Geddington 4, 68, 70, 95, 112
Grafton 104
Grafton Regis 77
Gretton 20
Guilsborough 67
Hannington 73
Hardingstone 35, 41
Hardwick 30
Harpole 68
Hellidon 67
Helpston 62
Heyford 87
Higham Ferrers 14
Hinton 107
Hollowell 15, 67
Irchester 11
Chester 33
Isham 71
Islip 6, 76
Kelmarsh 12
King's Sutton 116
Astrop 17
King's Sutton 66
Purston 66
Kislingbury 91
Lilbourne 83, 114
Litchborough 65
M...? 53
Maidwell 15, 104
Marston 8
Marston St Lawrence 101
Milton 68
Moreton Pinkney 39, 95

NORTHAMPTONSHIRE [*continued*]

Moulton 80
Newton 30
Northampton 7, 27, 32, 45, 55, 57, 68, 77, 97, 112, 115
Norton 5, 88
Oundle 15
Pattishall 27
Paulerspury 16, 65, 74, 109
Peterborough 24, 68, 78
    Oxney 103
Raunds 40
Ravensthorpe 10
Rothwell 73
Rushden 55
'Shippin' 1
Shutlanger 94, 114
Silverstone 40, 84
Spratton 19, 30
Staverton 67, 108
Stoke 18
Sulgrave 101
Syresham 108
Thorpe 48
Thorpe Mandeville 48
Thrapston 66
Towcester 51, 68, 92, 115
Twywell 5
Warkworth
    Grimsbury 41
Weedon 92
Weldon 34, 115
Welford 73, 85
Wellingborough 2, 30, 49
West Haddon 46
Weston 35
    Weston by Welland 92
    Weston Favell 32, 48
Whittlebury 71, 97
Wicken 16
Wilby 83, 84
Wollaston 105
Yelvertoft 15

NORTHUMBERLAND

Bywell
    Styford 31
Haltwhistle
    Willimoteswyke 16
Newcastle on Tyne 3, 14, 27, 112
Warkworth 71

NOTTINGHAMSHIRE

...dford 107
Blyth 97

NOTTINGHAMSHIRE [*continued*]

Car Colston 87
Chilwell 20
Dunham 70
Eakring 72
East Bridgeford 84
East Leake 30
East Retford 99
Farndon 82
Gamston 11
Halam
    Gray Lane 36
Kelham 22
Kinoulton 115
Lenton 18
Mansfield 20, 30, 50, 72
Misterton 25
Newark 6, 13, 71, 94
Nottingham 57, 104, 105
Owthorpe 57
'Pomfrett' 40
Ratcliffe on Soar 104
Retford 18
Saxondale 105
Scrooby 99
Stapleford 107
Strelley 38
Sturton 109
Tollerton 66

OXFORDSHIRE 27

Adderbury 24
Baldon 14
Bampton 46, 63, 108, 115
Banbury 19, 44, 62, 95, 98, 108, 109, 110
'Barbert' 80
Barford 61
Beckley 39
Berrick 52
Bicester 29, 69, 90, 91, 95, 96, 111
Bix 24
Brightwell 103
Burford 4, 43, 50, 57, 100
Cassington 44
Chalgrove 84
Charlbury 40, 48, 49
Chesterton 51, 87
Chinnor 32
Chipping Norton 101, 109
Churchill 15
Clifton 93
Crowell 44
Cuddesdon 84
Dorchester 34, 83
Drayton 64
Ducklington 107

INDEX OF PLACES

OXFORDSHIRE [*continued*]

Dunstew 7
Enstone 35, 53
Eynsham 33, 47, 113
Fifield 51
Finmere 79, 116
Fulbrook 60
Garsington 16
Great Bourton 81
Hanwell 13, 33
Harpsden
  Bolney 20
Headington 14, 19, 85
Henley 3, 4, 10, 11, 12, 36, 37, 38, 45, 55, 77, 84, 85, 96, 103, 108, 110, 115
  Henley Green 74
Heyford Warren 73
'Heythorp' 41
Hornton 27
Ipsden 72
Kidlington 89
Kingston 37
Kirtlington 44
Launton 60
Lewknor 88
'Lidlington' 72
'Lillingstone Russell' 84
Little Milton 37
Lyneham 5
Marsh Baldon
  Little Baldon 21
Merton 28
Middle Aston 71
Milton 34
Mixbury 5
Mongewell 31
Nettlebed 75, 103
North Stoke 31
Old Woodstock 58
Over Norton 37
Oxford 10, 11, 22, 27, 33, 37, 39, 68, 78, 91, 102, 108
  All Saints 113
  St Mary 33
  University of Oxford 92
Piddington 110
'Sedburdfaris' 86
Shipton 91
Shirburn 8, 34
Shutford 29
South Leigh 38
South Newington 39, 104
Stanton Harcourt 9, 105
Stoke Talmage 6
Stonesfield 40, 50
Sydenham 12
T...? 77

OXFORDSHIRE [*continued*]

'Tancombe' 2
Tangley 50
Thame 17, 18, 26, 43, 58, 64, 70, 77, 78, 103
'Towsey' 26
Wardington 73, 92
Watlington 82
Weston on the Green 2, 58, 79
Wigginton 41
Witney 21, 25, 48, 53, 55, 79, 84, 92
Wolvercote 17
Woodstock 36, 43, 52, 75, 85
Wootton 19, 55, 61
Wroxton 73
Yarnton 38

RUTLAND

Brooke 85
Exton 99
Langham 55
Oakham 16, 21, 70
Thistleton 111
Whissendine 37, 92

SCOTLAND

Annandale 40
Ayrshire 46
Dundee 20
Elgin, Moray 67
Hoddam, Dumfriesshire 51

SHROPSHIRE

'Adbrightcley' 62
'Aldenham' 1
Ashford Carbonell 65
Atcham
  Duncot 67
Baschurch 80, 81
'Benton' 96
Bicton Township 85
Bishops Castle 76
'Clatwin' 3
Clun 82
'Elestam' 25
Ellesmere 83
'Elmore' 60
'Glytheford' 52
Grindle 112
High Ercall
  Somerheath 56
Kinnersley 110
Knockin 45
Ludlow 45
Milson 5

SHROPSHIRE [continued]

Montford 60
Oswestry 73, 88, 107
Rodington 56
Ryton 1
Selattyn
    Porkington 72
Shifnal 64
Shrewsbury 5, 14, 45
'Smithey' 60
'Trelester' 56
Waters Upton 56
Wem
    Sleap 107
Whitchurch 65, 72, 101
Whittington 107

SOMERSET

Ash Prior 46
Badgworth 81
Batcombe 12, 113
Bath 42, 59, 70, 77
Brewham 99, 106
Bridgewater 54, 72
Bristol 10
Bruton 34, 50, 113
Camel 78
Chard 45, 93
Charlcombe 39
Cheddar 102
Compton Martin 71
Crewkerne 61
Croscombe 53
Crowcombe 101
Donyat 82
Doulting 22
East Harptree 45
English Combe
    English Batch 22, 116
Evercreech 99
Frome 100, 101
'Gaspord' 41
Glastonbury 61
Huish 78
Ilminster 26, 113
Ilton 12
Keynsham 49
Kingsdon 3
Marston 51
Martock 82
Milborne Port 51
Milton Martock 58
North Curry 57
Nynehead 54
Sampford Arundell 78
Seavington St Michael 67

SOMERSET [continued]

Shapwick 21
Shepton Mallet 11
Shipwick 22
Somerton 56, 91
South Petherton 80
    Stretton 41
Stanton Drew
    Belluton 71
Taunton 1, 2
    Taunton Dale 3
Tytherington 45
Wells 49, 59
West Camel 69, 78
West Hatch 31
Weston 82
Wincanton 18
Winsham 85
Wrington 6

STAFFORDSHIRE

Abbots Bromley 16, 30, 77
Alrewas 81
Audley 1, 60
Betley 90
Biddulph
    Overton 59
Bilston 91
Burton on Trent 37
Butterton 89
Cannock
    Huntington 97
'Chailey' 75
Enville 103, 111
Horton 55
Keele 54, 109
Kingswinford 5
Kingswood 37
Knowle 19
Leigh
    Field 11
Lichfield 6, 36, 38, 85, 94, 115
Longdon 15
Newcastle under Lyne 14, 112
Norton 88
Perry Barr
    Oscot 41
Rolleston 40
Rowley 50
    Rowley Regis 50
Rugeley 82
Rushall 59
Stafford 47, 65
Stoke
    Shelton 98

STAFFORDSHIRE [*continued*]

Stonnall
  Lynn 34
Stretton 92
Tatenhill 102
'Ursiter Woodland' 94
Uttoxeter 23, 39
Wednesbury 1
Wolverhampton 79

SUFFOLK

Barking 101
'Bayton' 45
Bildeston 46
Bury St Edmunds 19, 61, 96
Cavendish 28
East Bergholt 70
Exning 78
Framlingham 6
'Franc' 69
Frostenden 37
Glemsford 40
Hadleigh 114
Haughley 88
Hoxne 17
Ipswich 4, 6, 19, 36, 42, 48, 74, 105
Little Stonham 41
Little Waldingfield 16
Mendham 52
Needham Market 74, 92
Newmarket 90
Norton 114
Raydon 85
Rumburgh 2
Stowmarket 25
Sudbury 12
Weston 65
Woodbridge 82
  Woodbridge Hasketon 89

SURREY 74

Ash 43
Ashtead 77
Banstead 87
Barnes 36
Battersea 20, 47, 71, 88, 89, 105, 114
Beddington 4, 100, 101
Bermondsey 3, 4, 5, 7, 9, 11, 14, 18, 23, 28, 30, 32, 34, 35, 38, 41, 42, 45, 49, 51, 64, 65, 70, 71, 74, 77, 81, 87, 90, 95, 99, 104, 108, 110
Blechingley 61, 82, 95
Bookham 6
  Great Bookham 92
Buckland 50

SURREY [*continued*]

Burstow 29, 96
Camberwell 1, 56, 61, 76, 80, 90
  Dulwich 5, 39
  Peckham 35, 68
Capel 1
Carshalton 25, 26
Charlwood 56
Chertsey 22, 66, 81, 86, 112
Chiddingfold 30
Chipstead 6
Clandon
  East Clandon 105
Clapham 4, 5, 43, 48, 57, 62
Cobham 25, 32, 34, 94
Croydon 29, 41, 42, 49, 54, 57, 59, 70, 83, 88, 91, 92, 110
Ditton
  Thames Ditton 6, 55, 95
Dorking 48, 50, 98, 103, 104
Effingham 4
Egham 36, 72, 93
Epsom 12, 32, 79
Ewell 14, 74
Farnham 6, 36, 38, 64, 92, 116
Fetcham 29
Frimley 8, 107
Godstone 65
Guildford 3, 37, 78, 94
  St Nicholas 32
Horley 62, 76, 87
Horne 28
Kingston 11, 13, 15, 23, 39, 48, 82, 84, 87, 94, 96, 109
Lambeth 2, 3, 7, 9, 11, 12, 15, 20, 21, 26, 27, 34, 35, 39, 40, 41, 42, 43, 48, 50, 52, 53, 56, 57, 59, 62, 66, 69, 70, 71, 72, 73, 75, 76, 77, 84, 85, 88, 91, 100, 103, 106, 108, 111
  Brixton 114
  Lambeth Marsh 105
Leatherhead 78, 97
Lingfield 59
Malden 87
Merton 23, 39
Mitcham 26, 35, 51, 72, 95, 101
Molesey
  East Molesey 48, 61
Mortlake 4, 24, 49, 53, 73, 84, 105
  East Sheen 26
Ne...? 72
Newdigate 16
Newington 4, 7, 26, 28, 29, 37, 42, 57, 94, 98, 112
  Blackman Street 1
  Walworth 46, 65, 88
Nutfield 54, 105

SURREY [*continued*]

Oxted 53, 65
Pirbright 111
Putney 31, 39, 52, 64, 68, 81, 115
Puttenham 50
Reigate 31, 32, 37, 56, 73, 76, 93, 101
Richmond 19, 32, 33, 46, 50, 73, 80, 94, 103
Rotherhithe 12, 14, 20, 21, 25, 27, 32, 36, 42, 43, 49, 55, 56, 60, 73, 85, 97, 111, 113, 114
Sanderstead 4
Send 98
    Ripley 89
Shere 40, 88
Southwark 8, 12, 17, 22, 29, 32, 38, 39, 42, 49, 50, 57, 62, 66, 68, 69, 78, 81, 86, 87, 91, 92, 97, 99, 110, 111, 113, 115, 116
    Bankside 33, 51, 67
    Borough 40, 46, 53
    Christ Church 25, 36, 63, 86, 87, 99, 113
    Horsleydown 68, 96
    Lant Street 63
    Long Lane 17
    Peter Street 24
    Queen Street 96
    St George 9, 22, 30, 39, 54, 60, 61, 63, 66, 72, 73, 75, 83, 84, 95, 97, 110
        Norfolk Street, Mint 4
    St John Horsleydown 1, 14, 18, 27, 47, 52, 56, 60, 62, 69, 84, 86, 91, 97, 116
        Charles Street 91
    St Mary Magdalen 20, 51, 86
    St Olave 9, 14, 26, 28, 32, 35, 37, 43, 44, 45, 52, 59, 68, 73, 75, 79, 81, 83, 88, 89, 93, 94, 102, 110
        Shad Thames 13, 62, 97
        Tooley Street 48, 86
    St Saviour 6, 7, 8, 9, 12, 17, 19, 21, 23, 24, 27, 29, 31, 33, 34, 39, 40, 50, 61, 64, 69, 74, 80, 82, 83, 86, 87, 93, 96, 99, 111, 115, 116
        Lomans Pond 109
    St Thomas 11, 15, 25, 42, 74, 95, 109
    Weston Street 30
'Stangate' 5
Stoke 22, 24
Streatham 4, 40, 52, 63, 72
    Tooting Bec 98
Sutton 24, 44
Tandridge 4, 31
Thorpe 72
    Thorpe Green 72
Titsey 28
Tooting 58, 106
    Tooting Graveney 3

SURREY [*continued*]

Walton on Thames 10, 38, 76, 90
Wandsworth 4, 10, 59, 61, 70, 74, 81, 108
Weybridge 40, 102
Wimbledon 33, 73
Windlesham 21
Woking 32
Wonersh 98
Worplesdon 50, 93

SUSSEX

...tle 32
Ardingley 68, 104
Arlington
    Michelham 68
Arundel 42
Buxted 76
Chailey 75
Chichester 7, 20, 23, 63, 97
Chiddingley 71
Cocking 73
Cuckfield 17, 35
Duncton 1
East Grinstead 9, 12
Fittleworth 33
Framfield 66
Greatham 71
Hamsey 68
Hartfield 104
Heathfield 21
Hellingly 92
Horsham 7, 34, 71
Horsted Keynes 79
Hurstmonceaux 47, 84, 108
Jevington 18
'Laydon' 86
Lewes 6, 31, 34, 35, 36, 40, 55, 57, 72, 83, 99, 103
Maresfield 71
Midhurst 12, 92, 105
'Morting' 100
Ninfield 107
Northiam 39
Petworth 20, 53, 65, 87
Ringmer 40
Rogate
    Fyning 10
Rudgwick 5
Rye 81
Shermanbury 40
Walberton 104
Warbleton 66
Warnham 12, 33, 81
Wartling 37
    Boreham Street 42
Willington 53

SUSSEX [*continued*]

Wilmington 20
Withyham 25
    Groombridge 5
Woodmancote 54

WALES

Abergavenny, Monmouthshire 88
Bangor, Flintshire 112
Bodffordd, Heneglwys, Anglesey 60
Boduan, Caernarvonshire 83
Brecknock, Breconshire 112
Broughton, Flintshire 28
'Castle Fryatt', Radnorshire 72
'Chayneast', Merionethshire 82
'Clandessen', Montgomeryshire 45
Clyro, Radnorshire 67
Criccieth, Caernarvonshire 87
Denbigh, Denbighshire 38
'Dongay', Montgomeryshire 101
Gladestry, Radnorshire 28
Glascwm, Radnorshire 83
Halkin, Flintshire 80
Hawarden, Flintshire 22
Henllan, Denbighshire 33
Lampeter, Cardiganshire 88
'Lannedon', Denbighshire 101
'Lansis', Caernarvonshire 112
Llandyrnog, Denbighshire 41, 71, 112
Llanelidan, Denbighshire 43
Llanelli, Glamorganshire 13
Llangadock, Carmarthenshire 112
Llanhennock, Monmouthshire 58
Llanrhos, Caernarvonshire 60
Llanrwst, Denbighshire 34
Llanvetherine, Monmouthshire 66
Llanvihangel-ystern-Llewern, Monmouthshire 54
Llanwenarth, Monmouthshire 88
Llanycil, Merionethshire 37
Monmouth, Monmouthshire 29, 62, 69, 74, 101
Nevin, Caernarvonshire 51
Northop, Flintshire 56
Overton, Flintshire 33
Pembroke, Pembrokeshire 73
Pembrokeshire 73
Rosemarket, Pembrokeshire 80
Ruthin, Denbighshire 89, 109
St Lawrence, Caernarvonshire 77
'Salsowney', Caernarvonshire 77
Swansea, Glamorganshire 9, 68
Welshpool, Montgomeryshire 56
Wrexham, Denbighshire 43, 82, 93

WARWICKSHIRE

Alcester 97
Atherstone 34, 51, 66
Austrey 100
Barston 20
Bidford 107
Birmingham 18
Brailes 33, 47, 62, 66, 100
Brownsover 109
Burton 13, 80
Burton Dassett 16
'Chester Over' 21
Church Lawford 73
Churchover 46
Coleshill
    Hawkeswell 7
'Combe Lordship' 106
Combrook 22
Coventry 11, 13, 20, 25, 35, 88, 94, 95, 99, 109
    St Michael 75
Draycote 115
Dunchurch 31, 60
    Toft 58
'Easmell' 19
Erdington 87
Farnborough 85
Flecknoe 4
Grandborough 102
Halford 46
'Hampton Corley' 33
Hillmorton 14, 51
Hunningham 22
Ipsley 12
Kineton 33
Kington 33
Kinwarton 54, 62
Ladbroke 24, 32
Merevale 94
Napton on the Hill 43, 98, 108
Nether Whitacre 115
Nuneaton 52, 92
Priors Marston 58, 114
Radway 78
Ratley 44
Rugby 11, 61, 82
Salford 110
    Salford Priors 51
Shuckburgh 2, 20
Shustoke 53
Snitterfield 43
Solihull 44
Southam 10
Sowe 81
Stratford on Avon 19, 69, 106
Sutton Coldfield 31, 55, 85
Tamworth 5, 8, 19

WARWICKSHIRE [*continued*]

Warwick 21, 33, 36, 43, 44, 49, 54, 71, 88, 107, 111
Water Orton 54
Wellesbourne 38
Whatcote 26
Willoughby 22
Wolston 54
Wolvey 111

WESTMORLAND

Ambleside 45
Burton 12
Keswick 14
Kirkby Lonsdale 13
Ravenstonedale 31, 38, 41, 81
    Crooks Beck 91
Skelsmergh 91
Windermere 15

WILTSHIRE

Aldbourne 92
Ashton Keynes 26, 32, 112
Avebury 2
Berwick St Leonard 26
Bishopstone 114
Blunsdon 22
Bradford 7, 100
Bradley 111
'Brickmaster' 71
Broad Hinton 1
Calne 90
Castleton 97
'Caute' 115
Charlton 42
Chippenham 21, 38
Chisledon 61
    Badbury 24
Christian Malford 86, 104
Corsham 56
Cricklade 1, 14, 16, 66, 90
Crudwell 75
Devizes 52, 83, 99
Durrington 50, 99
Edington 111
Enford 27
Fifield 7
Fisherton Anger 21
Fonthill 26
Froxfield 32
Great Bedwin 100
'Grixload' 114
Groundwell 52
Hankerton 90
Heddington 21

WILTSHIRE [*continued*]

Highworth 3, 36
Hungerford 110
Kempsford 72
'Kingswood' 6
Kington St Michael
    Langley 111
Latton 70
Laycock 73
Liddington 107
Little Hinton 93
Lydyard 100
Lyneham
    Clack 74
Malmesbury 55
    Milbourne 38
Marden 11
Market Lavington 75
Marlborough 18, 49, 60, 80, 84, 94, 95
Marston 56
Melksham 19, 37
'Milleham' 82
Monkton Farleigh 26
Oaksey 6
Overton 21
Poole 102
Porton 47
Potterne 25, 72
Purton 63
Ramsbury 48, 112
St Peter 2
Salisbury 5, 6, 48, 49, 60, 62, 76, 99, 103, 109
    Nicholas Hospital 43
'Shelsworth and Simpson' 71
Somerford 4
    Somerford Keynes 42
South Marston 13
Stanton St Bernard 95
Stratton 109
Swindon 108
Teffont 26, 37, 70, 98
    Teffont Magna 52
Tisbury 24
Trowbridge 24, 47, 93, 101
Upavon 65, 76, 82
Ushant 70
Wanborough 80
Warminster 113
West Lavington 37
West Wellow 18
Whiteparish 57
Wilton 17
Winterbourne Monkton 99
Woodborough 99
Wootton Bassett 50, 95
Wroughton 96

INDEX OF PLACES

WORCESTERSHIRE

Badsey 103
'Beadle' 21
Belbroughton 20
Bewdley 13, 115
Birlingham 17
Birtsmorton 95
Blockley 51
Bradford 11, 48
Bredon 74
Broadway 86, 89, 92
'Burrow' 72
Church Honeybourne 81, 112
Church Lench 100
Claines 104
Comberton 32
Cropthorne 103
Daylesford 58
Doverdale 65
Droitwich 36
Edvin Loach 60
Eldersfield 8
Elmley 40
Evesham 9, 30, 80, 88, 99
Feckenham 87
Fladbury 108
Flyford Flavell 61
Grafton 70
Hagley 66, 88
Hanley Castle 65
'Horne' 14
Inkberrow
  Edgiock 92
Kidderminster 13
King's Norton
  Hazelwell 71
Knightwick 82
Little Comberton 116
Overbury 35
Peopleton 113
Pershore 5, 19, 34, 73
Redmarley 30
Ripple 22
Shipston 56
  Shipston upon Stour 56
Stanford on Teme 17
Stourbridge 61, 79
Tenbury 10, 106
Throckmorton 98
Tibberton 8
Tredington 27
Wick 10
Worcester 2, 15, 69, 70, 83, 100, 102
  Bedwardine 71
  St Helen 75
  St Swithin 2

YORKSHIRE 52, 68, 91

Allerthorpe 48
Almondbury 39
'Anderby Steeple' 30
'Arelake' 68
Bainbridge 58
Barlby 103
Barningham 47
Barnsley 12, 77, 109
Beverley 59
Bilbrough 68
Bradford 56
Brompton 94
'Burlington' 83
Byland Abbey 26
'Corand' 74
Cottingwith 38
Craven 22
Darfield 27
Dewsbury 109
Dishforth 3
Doncaster 1, 85
Eggborough 8
Fishlake 93
Garsdale 29
'Goodland' 1
Great Smeaton 85
Guisborough 18
Halifax 108
Harrogate 9
Hatfield 14
Haworth 44
Heath 40
Heath Hall 28
Heckmondwike 15
Houghton 52
Howden 103
Hull 107
'Kiddall' 34
Kildale 80
Killinghall 6, 17
Knaresborough 37
Leeds 99
Little Horton 91
'Lower Wake' 4
Malham Waterhouses 103
Methley
  West Hall 116
'Nether Celton' 81
Northallerton 68
Nunnington 13
'Ockly' 115
Osmotherley 71
Pontefract 64, 99
Richmond 59, 65
Ripley 96
Romaldkirk 58

YORKSHIRE [*continued*]

Sawley 75
Scarborough 53
Scawton 43
Sedburgh 27
Sheffield 81, 85
Smeaton 110
Snaith 116
Stainton 43
Thoralby 89
Thornton 87, 94, 101
Tickhill 92
Wakefield 38, 44
Walton 4
Welbury 85
Westerdale 9
West Garforth 83
West Rounton 3
Whisperdales 9
Wibsey 95
Winestead 52
Wombwell 13
Woolster 91
Worsborough 34
Wortley 106
Yarm 17, 62
York 29, 38, 40, 48, 91, 107

INDEX OF SUBJECTS

alderman 83, 108
  alderman and knight 63
anchorsmith 23
apothecary 14, 23, 36, 52, 66, 78, 85
  citizen and apothecary 10, 14, 16, 20, 62
armorer 68
  citizen and armorer 11, 29, 92, 98, 105, 113

backmaker 59
baconman 15
bagmaker 28, 59
baker 1, 2, 5, 8, 12, 14, 15, 18, 25, 31, 32, 33, 34, 36, 37, 44, 45, 48, 50, 51, 53, 57, 63, 64, 66, 71, 72, 75, 76, 77, 78, 79, 81, 82, 88, 90, 92, 96, 97, 99, 101, 107, 108, 109, 110
  biscuit baker 11, 38
  citizen and baker 4, 14, 18, 19, 22, 30, 44, 50, 82, 87, 89, 107
  citizen and white baker 11
  gingerbread baker 107, 110
  sugar baker 113
  white baker 15
banker 7
barber 37, 53, 63, 90, 100, 115
  barber chirurgeon 6, 22, 86, 88, 99
  barber and perukemaker 101
  barber surgeon 77
  citizen and barber chirurgeon 20, 23, 32, 38, 59, 64, 115
  citizen and barber surgeon 23, 82, 83, 87, 98, 100, 110
  hairdresser 31, 65
  perukemaker 12, 17, 30, 55, 56, 101, 109, 112
  surgeon 3, 19, 27, 31, 42, 45, 48, 54, 66, 82
bargeman 3, 12, 51, 112
baronet 1, 28, 30, 116
  knight and baronet 30
basketmaker 18
bay fuller 89
beadmaker 93
beltmaker 25
blacksmith 3, 4, 16, 18, 20, 22, 24, 27, 37, 40, 42, 43, 46, 48, 49, 50, 52, 54, 55, 56, 60, 65, 68, 79, 81, 85, 91, 92, 98, 99, 103, 105, 106, 108, 111, 115
  citizen and blacksmith 13, 14, 18, 21, 23, 24, 32, 34, 51, 53, 57, 59, 70, 93, 95, 99, 102, 104
blockmaker 4, 16, 56
boat builder 5, 27, 86, 111
bodicemaker 18
bookbinder 71
  vellum bookbinder 57
bottle coverer 109
bowyer
  citizen and bowyer 1, 36, 57, 82, 83, 99, 103, 108, 109, 110
brandy merchant 31
brazier 19, 57, 59, 72
brewer 1, 3, 4, 9, 10, 13, 15, 19, 23, 32, 33, 35, 38, 42, 43, 45, 50, 52, 53, 57, 58, 59, 61, 65, 71, 76, 77, 79, 80, 81, 89, 109
  citizen and brewer 1, 12, 13, 14, 17, 29, 52, 63, 114
bricklayer 7, 14, 17, 20, 23, 24, 25, 36, 46, 58, 59, 63, 65, 73, 98, 103, 106
  citizen and bricklayer 7, 40, 57, 60, 66, 71, 92
brickmaker 5, 18, 43, 44, 49, 50, 87, 103
broderer
  citizen and broderer 4, 7, 22, 29, 31, 35, 37, 45, 48, 59, 73, 92
broker 81, 84
  piece broker 54
brushmaker 111
builder 111
butcher 1, 2, 7, 9, 10, 11, 16, 17, 18, 19, 20, 21, 22, 23, 24, 25, 26, 27, 28, 30, 31, 32, 34, 38, 39, 40, 41, 42, 43, 44, 45, 50, 51, 53, 55, 56, 57, 58, 59, 60, 61, 62, 63, 64, 66, 67, 68, 69, 70, 71, 73, 74, 75, 76, 77, 78, 80, 81, 82, 83, 85, 86, 87, 88, 89, 91, 93, 95, 96, 97, 98, 99, 101, 102, 103, 104, 105, 106, 108, 109, 110, 111, 113, 114
  baconman 15
  citizen and butcher 3, 10, 15, 16, 20, 25, 31, 34, 45, 47, 49, 53, 58, 65, 70, 72, 73, 78, 86, 93, 98, 100, 102, 106, 109
buttonseller 87

carman 15, 35, 73, 95, 97, 112
carpenter 3, 4, 5, 7, 11, 12, 13, 14, 15, 17, 18, 21, 24, 25, 27, 30, 32, 36, 39, 40, 42, 43, 46, 47, 48, 49, 51, 52, 53, 56, 58, 60, 66, 68, 73, 74, 75, 76, 80, 84, 86, 87, 88, 89, 93, 94, 97, 99, 100, 103, 104, 105, 108, 109, 111, 112, 113, 116
  cabinet maker 11, 27, 33, 114
  citizen and carpenter 4, 11, 22, 26, 35, 49, 53, 62, 64, 66, 68, 72, 73, 75, 85, 86, 90, 96, 103, 114, 116
carrier 4, 37, 42, 104
  water carrier 8
carver 45, 69
caulker 10, 42
  ship caulker 97
chaff cutter 20
chairman 115

chandler 19, 20, 21, 44, 55, 67, 81, 88, 89, 95, 103
citizen and tallow chandler 1, 7, 9, 13, 16, 17, 19, 20, 31, 33, 37, 39, 43, 45, 46, 48, 49, 52, 56, 57, 58, 60, 64, 67, 70, 76, 77, 79, 80, 81, 84, 86, 88, 91, 93, 94, 97, 98, 99, 109, 110, 111, 112, 114, 115, 116
corn chandler 36, 53, 62, 88, 89, 96, 105, 114
tallow chandler *passim*
wax chandler 32
chapman 57
charcoalman 112
cheesemonger 26, 36, 40, 41, 44, 46, 52, 54, 62, 75, 85, 88, 89, 93, 99, 103, 115
cheese factor 62
chinaman 26
chirurgeon 3, 5, 45, 47, 59, 72, 110, 111
barber chirurgeon 6, 22, 86, 88, 99
citizen and barber chirurgeon 20, 23, 32, 38, 59, 64, 115
chocolate maker 100
ciderman 101
clergymen
bachelor of divinity 68
clerk 1, 4, 5, 6, 7, 9, 10, 11, 12, 13, 15, 16, 17, 18, 19, 20, 21, 22, 24, 27, 28, 29, 30, 31, 33, 34, 35, 37, 38, 40, 43, 44, 45, 47, 50, 53, 54, 56, 59, 60, 62, 63, 64, 65, 68, 69, 70, 71, 72, 73, 77, 79, 80, 81, 82, 84, 85, 87, 88, 89, 90, 91, 94, 95, 96, 97, 99, 100, 102, 104, 106, 107, 108, 110, 111, 112, 114, 116
doctor in divinity 27, 40, 57, 73, 105
doctor of theology 82, 92
minister 3, 48, 108
pastor 103
cloakmaker 60
clockmaker 24, 94
citizen and clockmaker 2, 39, 41, 52, 59, 83, 110, 113
clogmaker 92
clothier 3, 4, 6, 8, 11, 14, 15, 16, 17, 25, 28, 29, 30, 38, 39, 40, 42, 45, 47, 48, 49, 51, 53, 61, 62, 64, 66, 69, 70, 71, 73, 74, 75, 78, 79, 82, 91, 92, 94, 95, 96, 98, 99, 102, 106, 109, 113
clothworker 6, 8, 15, 19, 42, 44, 45, 57, 64, 84, 90, 95, 107, 111, 113
citizen and clothworker 1, 3, 5, 6, 12, 18, 20, 21, 27, 28, 29, 30, 31, 32, 34, 36, 38, 39, 41, 51, 56, 59, 61, 63, 64, 75, 77, 96, 99, 101, 102, 106, 107, 109
clothmaker 47
clothsmith 7
coachmaker 2, 57, 109
citizen and coach harness maker 24, 60
citizen and coachmaker 9
coachman 6, 11, 16, 19, 25, 41, 45, 58, 62, 69, 94, 95, 103, 104, 105, 111, 112
coachmaster 57, 82
coal
coal merchant 2, 23, 29, 80, 95, 99, 105, 110
coal seller 81
collarmaker 18, 31, 82, 109
collier 70, 91
colourmaker 63
combcasemaker 52
confectioner 8
cook 2, 8, 30, 32, 34, 73, 81, 86, 90, 92, 93, 105, 108, 110
citizen and cook 8, 46, 51, 55, 57, 58, 66, 100, 109
cooper 5, 10, 11, 13, 21, 39, 41, 43, 46, 50, 53, 55, 61, 75, 78, 80, 82, 83, 92, 98, 101, 104
citizen and cooper 7, 9, 10, 25, 32, 34, 41, 53, 54, 55, 59, 82, 87, 91, 98, 105, 107, 113
wine cooper 26, 61, 93, 105
copper plate printer 12, 37
cordwainer 3, 4, 5, 6, 8, 9, 13, 15, 19, 21, 22, 24, 37, 38, 39, 49, 50, 51, 53, 55, 57, 60, 61, 63, 65, 71, 72, 73, 74, 78, 79, 80, 82, 83, 84, 92, 94, 95, 97, 98, 100, 105, 111, 112, 113, 115
citizen and cordwainer 2, 20, 46, 47, 49, 81, 87, 94, 96, 103, 105
corkcutter 59, 60
corn
corn chandler 36, 53, 62, 88, 89, 96, 105, 114
corn factor 96
corn merchant 72
cotton
cotton merchant 79
cotton spinner 92
cowkeeper 87, 96
currier 21, 29, 35, 38, 42, 69, 110
citizen and currier 18, 19, 39, 50, 51, 58, 113
cutler 6, 75, 76, 83, 94, 110
citizen and cutler 7, 14, 21, 24, 32, 43, 50, 60, 61, 67, 81, 84, 100, 108

dealer
dealer in wool 91
diamond cutter 18
distiller 13, 18, 23, 55, 56, 65, 98, 115
citizen and distiller 4, 28, 106, 115
doctors
doctor in divinity 27, 40, 57, 73, 105

doctors [*continued*]
doctor in physic 11, 56, 94
physician 116
doctor of medicine 88
doctor of theology 82, 92
draper 1, 5, 6, 11, 13, 26, 27, 28, 38, 56, 61, 78, 80, 92, 96, 116
citizen and draper 2, 6, 7, 9, 16, 20, 22, 23, 36, 44, 53, 55, 58, 59, 60, 61, 62, 71, 73, 74, 79, 84, 85, 90, 104, 105, 107
cloth draper 38
linen draper 35, 46, 50, 66, 86, 92, 95, 97, 98, 104, 105
woollen draper 13, 25, 29, 44, 90, 96
drawer 54
finedrawer 99
dyer 9, 15, 27, 29, 30, 33, 37, 38, 42, 51, 92, 104
citizen and dyer 3, 21, 22, 33, 34, 41, 45, 47, 53, 85, 86, 89, 91, 95, 107, 115, 116
silk dyer 92

enameller 72
engraver 24
esquire 2, 4, 5, 6, 10, 13, 14, 18, 26, 32, 34, 35, 40, 43, 46, 48, 49, 50, 52, 57, 59, 62, 65, 67, 71, 72, 73, 75, 76, 77, 81, 82, 83, 85, 89, 91, 92, 97, 99, 103, 104, 105, 106, 107

factor 28, 54, 70
cheese factor 62
corn factor 96
malt factor 28, 58
farmer 4, 7, 8, 10, 15, 16, 17, 20, 26, 28, 30, 31, 32, 36, 38, 39, 41, 42, 43, 45, 49, 52, 54, 55, 61, 65, 66, 68, 69, 70, 71, 72, 77, 78, 79, 80, 81, 83, 86, 87, 88, 90, 91, 93, 94, 95, 100, 101, 102, 103, 107, 115, 116
farrier 1, 5, 7, 19, 20, 31, 33, 34, 37, 39, 51, 54, 55, 56, 74, 87, 101, 104, 105, 107, 113, 114
citizen and farrier 19, 42, 55, 64, 111
felmonger 6, 17, 31, 60, 78, 83, 88, 90, 93, 97
feltmaker 8, 28, 29, 30, 35, 37, 48, 52, 64, 76, 83, 84, 85, 86, 87, 88, 95, 116
citizen and feltmaker 4, 8, 15, 22, 29, 46, 51, 94, 97, 105, 107
finedrawer 99
fisherman 93, 105
fishmonger 37, 63
citizen and fishmonger 1, 2, 5, 13, 17, 24, 34, 46, 47, 59, 61, 64, 65, 70, 78, 80, 91, 102, 106
flax
flaxdresser 65
flaxman 37, 43, 46, 53, 98
fletcher
citizen and fletcher 33, 65
flower dresser 19
founder 36, 64, 94
citizen and founder 2, 3, 9, 12, 14, 27, 38, 48, 63, 64, 78, 94, 95, 103
frameworkknitter
citizen and frameworkknitter 6, 10, 58
fruiterer 21, 29, 41
citizen and fruiterer 39, 41, 51, 70, 91, 98, 113
fuller 10, 56, 75, 79
bay fuller 89

gardener 4, 5, 6, 7, 17, 20, 21, 22, 25, 26, 31, 32, 34, 36, 39, 40, 42, 45, 47, 48, 50, 53, 54, 55, 57, 59, 60, 62, 63, 65, 69, 81, 86, 88, 97, 99, 101, 104, 108, 109, 110, 111, 115
gentleman *passim*
geographer 58
girdler
citizen and girdler 53
glass
citizen and glass-seller 1, 53
citizen and glazier 27, 70
glass bottlemaker 29
glass maker 5, 26, 66, 75
glass-seller 60
glazier 12, 22, 23, 24, 26, 32, 35, 43, 54, 96, 109, 110
looking glass maker 9
looking glass manufacturer 90
glover 25, 41, 44, 45, 55, 58, 66, 75, 82, 83, 93, 102, 108
citizen and glover 16, 26, 52, 59, 101
goldsmith 2, 33, 57, 87, 105
citizen and goldsmith 15, 23, 24, 26, 41, 43, 50, 61, 63, 69, 73, 96, 101, 106, 110
grazier 7, 15, 20, 22, 24, 25, 27, 31, 32, 45, 48, 53, 66, 75, 83, 90, 94, 99, 106, 108, 111
grocer 1, 13, 15, 16, 20, 24, 26, 28, 37, 39, 40, 42, 43, 46, 47, 52, 53, 55, 63, 64, 66, 70, 76, 77, 81, 86, 94, 95, 96, 100, 101, 102, 103, 106, 109, 113, 114, 115
citizen and grocer 11, 12, 19, 20, 21, 22, 26, 34, 38, 47, 60, 61, 69, 73, 76, 81, 92, 96, 97, 105, 107
gunner 91
gunsmith 34, 112, 115
citizen and gunmaker 18
citizen and gunsmith 112

haberdasher 1, 31, 32, 34, 48, 49, 51, 55, 69, 76, 79, 86, 94, 99, 109

haberdasher [*continued*]
citizen and haberdasher 2, 9, 16, 19, 20, 26, 27, 28, 33, 34, 35, 42, 43, 47, 49, 50, 56, 59, 61, 62, 66, 69, 74, 76, 80, 87, 88, 93, 95, 98, 99, 101, 102, 104, 105, 106, 107, 108, 110
haberdasher and hosier 38
haberdasher of small wares 63
hairdresser 31, 65
harnessmaker 7, 108
hats
citizen and hatbandmaker 40
hatbandmaker 42
hatmaker 35
hatter 53
higler 100
hop merchant 76
horner
citizen and horner 48
hosier 34, 39, 57, 63
haberdasher and hosier 38
hotpresser 52
husbandman *passim*

inkmaker 96
innholder 2, 4, 6, 10, 11, 13, 14, 18, 19, 20, 21, 22, 28, 30, 31, 33, 37, 38, 39, 40, 42, 43, 46, 47, 49, 50, 51, 52, 53, 54, 55, 56, 58, 60, 61, 62, 63, 66, 68, 70, 72, 74, 77, 78, 79, 82, 86, 89, 90, 95, 98, 102, 106, 109, 111, 113, 115
citizen and innholder 3, 10, 26, 35, 64, 79, 115
innkeeper 7, 19, 49, 86, 115, 116
instrument casemaker 85
ironmonger 13, 49, 75, 76, 77, 81, 83, 84, 90, 92, 95, 100, 116
citizen and ironmonger 49, 60, 62, 79, 93

jeweller 61
joiner 3, 19, 36, 39, 40, 47, 48, 56, 66, 67, 69, 70, 72, 75, 84, 87, 89, 90, 92, 96, 103, 108
citizen and joiner 1, 7, 13, 15, 21, 25, 30, 36, 37, 41, 46, 47, 49, 51, 54, 62, 63, 66, 67, 70, 72, 76, 79, 80, 86, 87, 91, 96, 100, 102, 103, 110, 112

keeper 93
kidder 100
knight 35, 55, 66, 98, 100, 101, 105
alderman and knight 63
knight and baronet 30

labourer 1, 2, 3, 4, 5, 7, 8, 9, 11, 16, 17, 22, 23, 25, 26, 27, 31, 33, 34, 35, 36, 37, 38, 39, 41, 45, 48, 50, 51, 52, 56, 57, 59, 63, 66, 67, 69, 70, 73, 74, 75, 78, 79, 82, 85, 86, 88, 89, 93, 94, 99, 101, 105, 106, 108, 109, 110, 111, 112, 114, 115
lacemaker 85
laceman 21, 62, 74
lathmaker 20, 70, 106
lath render 41
leather
citizen and leatherseller 13, 15, 24, 36, 37, 38, 59, 61, 63, 74, 76, 82, 85, 88, 93, 94, 96, 97, 99, 108, 114
leatherdresser 2, 65, 74, 110
leatherseller 9, 79, 103
lighterman 20, 39, 40, 47, 51, 71, 76, 97, 111
limner 58
linemaker 44
locksmith 4, 10, 104
longbowstringmaker
citizen and longbowstringmaker 19
lorimer
citizen and lorimer 11, 28, 91
lorimer 88, 115

maker
cabinet maker 11, 27, 33, 114
maltster 2, 5, 8, 11, 12, 14, 17, 22, 23, 24, 25, 27, 29, 30, 31, 32, 33, 35, 36, 37, 40, 44, 46, 48, 49, 50, 53, 54, 56, 57, 61, 64, 65, 67, 77, 78, 79, 80, 83, 84, 85, 88, 91, 92, 93, 96, 99, 103, 104, 106, 110, 113
malt factor 28, 58
mariner 1, 3, 5, 8, 9, 10, 11, 13, 14, 15, 20, 22, 25, 26, 27, 28, 30, 31, 32, 33, 36, 39, 40, 42, 46, 48, 53, 58, 59, 61, 63, 64, 65, 66, 67, 68, 69, 70, 71, 72, 74, 76, 77, 80, 81, 82, 83, 84, 86, 89, 90, 93, 94, 97, 98, 99, 101, 104, 106, 107, 109, 110, 113, 114
mason 2, 11, 12, 25, 26, 28, 33, 36, 45, 57, 58, 60, 61, 70, 75, 95, 98
citizen and mason 26, 94, 97, 113
stonecutter 10
mastmaker 31
mathematical instrument maker 78
mealman 3, 9, 10, 16, 22, 23, 25, 28, 39, 43, 51, 78, 94, 95, 111
mercer 6, 8, 9, 10, 11, 14, 16, 30, 33, 36, 42, 45, 50, 52, 53, 55, 58, 61, 63, 65, 68, 69, 72, 77, 82, 85, 94, 98, 100, 105, 108, 110, 114
citizen and mercer 12, 21, 26, 34, 40, 47, 52, 102, 108
merchant 3, 6, 18, 20, 26, 28, 32, 33, 38, 40, 42, 46, 65, 71, 74, 75, 81, 83, 91, 94, 95, 97, 101
brandy merchant 31

merchant [*continued*]
coal merchant 2, 23, 29, 80, 95, 99, 105, 110
corn merchant 72
cotton merchant 79
hop merchant 76
orange merchant 17
wine merchant 88
miller 3, 6, 9, 17, 24, 26, 38, 39, 41, 44, 55, 56, 59, 61, 74, 75, 80, 89, 102, 112
milliner 76
millwright 24, 40, 107, 113
monyer 53
musical instrument maker 30
musician 87
citizen and musician 54, 81, 87

nailor 65

oarmaker 84
oilman 11, 42, 66, 67, 79, 107
optician 86
spectaclemaker 34
orange merchant 17
ostler 60

pack thread spinner 14
packer 25
painter 12, 27, 47, 100
citizen and painter stainer 14, 29, 42, 43, 44, 86
papermaker 105
pattenmaker 37, 43, 84, 91
pavior 116
perfumer 51, 57
perukemaker 12, 17, 30, 55, 56, 101, 109, 112
barber and perukemaker 101
pewterer
citizen and pewterer 13, 32, 58, 64, 73, 76, 85, 114
pinmaker 7, 58, 67, 97
citizen and pinmaker 83, 104
planemaker 17, 29, 64, 66
plasterer 17
citizen and plaisterer 23, 31, 43, 46, 49, 69, 85
plumber 6, 35, 53, 55, 56, 104
citizen and plumber 10, 102, 105
porter 6, 11, 13, 19, 22, 23, 52, 58, 82
fellowship porter 39, 69
iron porter 63
wine porter 39, 86
potter 20, 32, 62, 78, 82, 90, 101
poulterer 5, 30, 46, 52, 55, 63, 75, 105
citizen and poulterer 16, 70, 81, 103, 116
printer
calico printer 22, 61, 70

refiner 93
ropemaker 6, 15, 43, 49, 65, 73, 100
roper 4

saddler 1, 13, 15, 33, 38, 53, 55, 67, 82, 91, 95, 97, 106
citizen and saddler 18, 35, 62, 89
pack saddler 116
sailmaker 60, 86
salesman 60, 73, 99
salter 19, 57, 79, 92, 112, 115
citizen and salter 7, 13, 16, 29, 38, 42, 47, 48, 49, 54, 58, 59, 62, 68, 69, 90, 102, 111
sawyer 12, 23, 25, 34, 51, 52, 62, 63, 73, 88
scalemaker 62
schoolmaster 27, 35, 39, 90
scrivener 27, 30, 62, 73, 80, 88, 103, 111
citizen and scrivener 7, 23, 92
sempster 35
serge
serge weaver 45
shearman 34
shepherd 12
shipwright 3, 10, 14, 18, 25, 31, 35, 36, 44, 52, 60, 72, 78, 79, 82, 91, 92, 97, 101, 113
boat builder 5, 27, 86, 111
citizen and shipwright 3, 19, 27, 67, 70, 71, 83, 95, 113
ship caulker 97
shoemaker 9, 12, 15, 18, 22, 27, 29, 32, 39, 40, 41, 46, 48, 54, 58, 61, 64, 69, 73, 77, 79, 81, 83, 88, 92, 94, 100, 102, 106, 109, 113
shopkeeper 5, 34, 37, 50, 52, 77, 81, 88
silk
silk dyer 92
silkman 70
silk weaver 7
throster 83
silversmith 8, 29
skinner
citizen and skinner 10, 40, 56, 59, 71, 84, 91, 95, 101, 107, 112
slater 47
slopseller 17
smith 5, 11, 14, 29, 36, 44, 51, 56, 68, 72, 79, 80, 90, 108, 109, 115
soapmaker 39, 70, 113
soap boiler 16, 116
spectaclemaker 34
optician 86
stablekeeper 50, 75
stationer 31, 47, 105
citizen and stationer 9, 14, 20, 48, 56, 59, 60, 73, 76, 78, 92, 93, 95, 106
statuary 114

staymaker and tailor 85
stockings
  stocking logger 12
  stocking maker 12
stonecutter 10
strong waterman 48
stuffmelter 116
surgeon 3, 19, 27, 31, 42, 45, 48, 54, 66, 82
  barber surgeon 77
  citizen and barber surgeon 23, 82, 83, 87, 98, 100, 110

tailor 7, 8, 9, 10, 12, 13, 14, 16, 17, 19, 20, 22, 24, 25, 26, 30, 32, 33, 34, 35, 36, 37, 39, 41, 43, 44, 45, 46, 47, 49, 50, 51, 52, 54, 58, 59, 60, 63, 65, 67, 69, 72, 73, 75, 76, 77, 78, 79, 80, 81, 82, 83, 84, 88, 91, 92, 93, 96, 99, 100, 101, 102, 103, 104, 105, 106, 107, 111, 114, 115, 116
  citizen and merchant tailor 1, 4, 5, 6, 10, 13, 14, 15, 16, 19, 23, 24, 27, 28, 29, 30, 31, 32, 38, 41, 42, 43, 44, 46, 49, 51, 57, 59, 60, 63, 64, 68, 69, 71, 78, 87, 89, 92, 95, 97, 99, 102, 103, 113, 114
  merchant tailor 65, 68
  staymaker and tailor 85
tanner 1, 6, 9, 10, 14, 18, 20, 30, 31, 34, 36, 39, 41, 45, 46, 47, 50, 56, 59, 64, 68, 70, 71, 72, 74, 75, 77, 82, 90, 92, 95, 96, 98, 100, 102, 104, 108, 109, 110, 111, 115
threadmaker 61, 88
throster 83
tilemaker 37, 107
tin
  citizen and tinplateworker 8, 29, 41, 75, 81, 113
  tinman 25
tobacconist 18, 23, 24, 37, 67, 93, 99, 100
  tobacco cutter 35, 93
toyman 74
trotterman 18
trunnel maker
  wheeler and trunnel maker 102
trussmaker 24
tucker 42
turner 4, 6, 25, 42, 68, 99
  citizen and turner 13, 86, 95
  ivory turner 77

undertaker 58, 65, 87, 96
upholder 37, 62
  citizen and upholder 39, 54, 68, 70, 78, 89, 102, 112, 116
  upholsterer 88

victualler 1, 2, 4, 5, 6, 9, 11, 14, 18, 19, 22, 24, 25, 29, 30, 31, 32, 33, 34, 39, 40, 43, 44, 46, 47, 49, 51, 52, 54, 55, 56, 57, 62, 64, 66, 70, 71, 72, 73, 74, 78, 80, 83, 85, 88, 90, 91, 93, 95, 96, 97, 98, 99, 100, 104, 105, 107, 108, 110, 112, 114, 115, 116
vintner 6, 12, 19, 23, 26, 29, 38, 48, 53, 67, 69, 78, 85, 101, 110, 113
  citizen and vintner 4, 13, 27, 32, 39, 42, 44, 46, 51, 54, 58, 63, 84, 88, 104, 109, 112

waggoner 61, 99, 107
warehousekeeper 87
  warehouseman 68
watchmaker 5, 16, 38, 89, 96, 109, 111, 116
  watch chaser 42
water carrier 8
waterman 1, 2, 8, 15, 32, 33, 35, 36, 37, 39, 43, 47, 50, 52, 56, 60, 62, 71, 74, 75, 77, 80, 85, 87, 93, 96, 100, 103, 105, 106, 109, 110
weaver 2, 4, 7, 8, 10, 12, 13, 15, 16, 17, 19, 21, 26, 27, 28, 29, 30, 38, 41, 42, 45, 49, 50, 51, 55, 57, 59, 60, 63, 65, 68, 70, 71, 73, 74, 76, 77, 79, 80, 81, 84, 85, 86, 89, 90, 91, 92, 93, 94, 96, 100, 101, 105, 107, 108, 112, 113, 114, 115
  broad weaver 6
  citizen and weaver 9, 13, 14, 15, 25, 29, 30, 44, 46, 50, 58, 62, 63, 66, 69, 78, 79, 93, 94, 96, 101, 109, 111, 112, 113, 116
  sacking weaver 106
  serge weaver 45
  silk weaver 7
wheelwright 2, 5, 11, 18, 40, 55, 65, 66, 74, 93, 96, 97, 101, 106, 111, 112
  citizen and wheelwright 34, 37, 40, 64, 78, 93, 97, 106, 114
  wheeler and trunnel maker 102
whitesmith 36
whiting maker 56
whitster 42, 56
wine
  wine cooper 26, 61, 93, 105
  wine merchant 88
  wine porter 39, 86
wiredrawer 8, 45, 55, 104
woodmonger 38
  citizen and woodmonger 6, 72, 77, 91, 103
wool
  citizen and woolman 26
  dealer in wool 91
  stapler 70
  woolcomber 1, 12, 17, 25, 59, 60, 94

wool [*continued*]
woolman 49
wool stapler 67, 94, 108
woolwinder 66
worsted comber 109

yeoman *passim*

THE LONDON APPRENTICES SERIES

Cliff Webb's series indexing the Apprenticeship Registers of the London Livery Companies continues to grow. He hopes to cover all Companies in due course. The 39 published volumes, (some of which include more than one company), deal with the records of the following:

Vol. no.	Title	Price
32	Apothecaries 1617-1669	£7.00
22	Armourers & Brasiers c.1610-1800	£8.00
10	Basketmakers 1639-1824	£3.50
3	Bowyers 1680-1806	£5.75
1	Brewers 1685-1800	£5.75
36	Brewers 1531-1685	£15.95
6	Broderers 1679-1713, 1763-1800	£4.60
31	Brown Bakers 1615-1646	£6.00
29	Carmen 1668, 1678-1800	£7.00
23	Coachmakers & coach harness makers 1677-1800	£8.00
6	Combmakers 1744-50	£4.60
26	Cooks 1654-1800	£8.00
30	Curriers 1628-1800	£7.00
35	Cutlers 1442-1448, 1565-1800	£13.00
11	Distillers 1659-1811	£3.95
25	Dyers 1706-1746	£5.00
6	Fanmakers 1775-1805	£4.60
28	Farriers 1619-1800	£10.00
37	Feltmakers 1676-1682, 1692-1800	£16.50
3	Fletchers 1739-54, 1767-1808	£5.75
21	Founders 1643-1800	£8.00
6	Frameworkknitters 1727-30	£4.60
6	Fruiterers 1750-1815	£4.60
6	Gardeners 1764-1850	£4.60
7	Glaziers 1694-1800	£4.20

Continued...

5	Glass-sellers 1664-1812	£4.20
4	Glovers 1675-79, 1735-48, 1766-1804	£6.00
15	Gold and silver wyre drawers 1693-1837	£4.00
8	Gunmakers 1656-1800	£4.60
6	Horners 1731-1800	£4.60
17	Innholders 1642-1643, 1654-1670, 1673-1800	£5.00
24	Ironmongers 1655-1800	£8.00
3	Longbowstringmakers 1604-68, 1709, 1714-17	£5.75
14	Loriners 1722-31, 1759-1800	£4.00
12	Makers of playing cards 1675-1760	£4.00
27	Masons 1663-1805	£5.00
12	Musicians 1765-1800	£4.00
9	Needlemakers 1664-1801	£5.20
38	Painter-Stainers 1655, 1666-1800	£9.00
13	Pattenmakers 1673-1805	£4.00
20	Paviors 1568-1800	£4.00
9	Pinmakers 1691-1723	£5.20
34	Plaisterers 1597-1662, 1698-1800	£10.00
33	Plumbers 1571-1800	£7.00
18	Poulters 1691-1729, 1754-1800	£5.00
12	Saddlers 1657-1666, 1800	£4.00
14	Spectaclemakers 1666-1800	£4.00
39	Tallow Chandlers 1633-1800	£5.95
16	Tinplateworkers 1666, 1668, 1676, 1681, 1683-1800	£5.00
12	Tobaccopipemakers 1800	£4.00
2	Tylers & bricklayers 1612-44, 1668-1800	£12.40
19	Upholders 1704-72	£5.00
31	Wax chandlers 1660-1800	£6.00
5	Woolmen 1665-1828	£4.20